Southeast Asia in the Twentieth Century

SOUTHEAST ASIA IN THE TWENTIETH CENTURY

A Reader

CLIVE J. CHRISTIE

I.B. Tauris Publishers

LONDON · NEW YORK

Published in 1998 by I.B.Tauris & Co Ltd,
Victoria House, Bloomsbury Square, London WC1B 4DZ
175 Fifth Avenue, New York NY 10010

In the United States of America and in Canada distributed by
St Martin's Press, 175 Fifth Avenue, New York NY 10010

A full CIP record for this book is available from the British Library
A full CIP record for this book is available from the Library of Congress

ISBN 1 86064 063 x hardback
ISBN 1 86064 075 3 paperback

Library of Congress catalog card number: available

Set in Monotype Garamond by Ewan Smith, London
Printed and bound in Great Britain by WBC Ltd, Bridgend

Contents

The situation in Southeast Asia in 1939 /82   The Japanese
intervention in Southeast Asia /84   The Japanese conquest of
Southeast Asia /85   The impact of the Japanese military take-over
of Southeast Asia /86   The course of the war, and its impact on
political developments /87

Readings

The defeat of Japan and surrender arrangements /115   The build-up
of revolutionary forces in Southeast Asia /116   The era of
revolution: 1945 /116

Readings

General features of the post-war period /151   The independence
settlement in the Philippines /153   The independence settlement
in Burma /154

Readings

7 The Independence Settlements: 2. Inter-ethnic Negotiations, Conflict and the Cold War — 181

Readings

8 The Decade of Instability, 1954–65 — 212

Readings

Preface and Acknowledgements

After years of teaching courses on modern Southeast Asian history, it seemed to me appropriate to try to put together a general reader on the subject that would not only provide a core text for university students, but would also serve as a general introduction to the modern history of the region for a wider readership.

The process of compilation and editing turned out to be a constant balancing act: between competing sources, countries of the region, the comparative importance of key events, and different historical approaches. In the end, space constraints and the demands of narrative coherence led me, on the whole, to choose 'classics' that have stood the test of time and have succeeded in getting to the root of crucial historical episodes, rather than always to give priority to more recent – but possibly in the long run more ephemeral – interpretations of historical events. I hope, above all, that readers will be able to gain a sense of the shape of events in Southeast Asia from the beginning of the century, roughly up to the end of the 1970s. I have taken the calculated risk of opting throughout the book for accessibility as the main objective.

I am very grateful to the British Academy South-East Asia Committee for awarding me a grant that gave me vital help in the final stages of producing this book. My main thanks go to my wife Jan. I can only repeat here what I wrote at the the beginning of my last book: that, without her help, it is difficult to see how this book could ever have seen the light of day.

I would like to thank the following for granting permission to use extracts from books and periodicals:

The extract from W R. Roff, *The Origins of Malay Nationalism* (1st publication, Yale University Press, New Haven and London, 1967; 2nd edition, Oxford University Press, Kuala Lumpur, 1994), is reprinted with kind permission from the author.

The extract from Hue-Tam Ho Tai, *Radicalism and the Origins of the Vietnamese Revolution* (Harvard University Press, Cambridge, MA, copyright © 1992 by the president and fellows of Harvard College), is reprinted with kind permission of the publisher.

The extract from Patricia Herbert, *The Hsaya San Rebellion (1930–1932)* (Monash Papers on Southeast Asia, Monash University, Melbourne, 1982), is reprinted with kind permission from the author.

The extract from E. Bruce Reynolds, *Thailand and Japan's Southern Advance 1940–1945* (Macmillan Ltd, Basingstoke, copyright © 1994 by Macmillan), is reprinted with kind permission of the publisher.

The extract from Field Marshal Sir William Slim, *Defeat into Victory* (Landsborough Publications Ltd, London, 1958), is reprinted with kind permission from Viscount Slim.

The extract from Huynh Kim Khanh, 'The Vietnamese August Revolution Reinterpreted', from the *Journal of Asian Studies* 30:4 (August 1971), is reprinted with kind permission of the Association of Asian Studies, Inc.

The extract from Anthony Reid, *The Indonesian National Revolution 1945–1950* (Greenwood Publishing Group, Westport, CT, 1985), is reprinted with kind permission of the author.

The extract from Hugh Tinker, 'Burma's Struggle for Independence: The Transfer of Power Thesis Re-examined', from *Modern Asian Studies* 20:3 (1986), is reprinted with kind permission of Cambridge University Press.

The extract from Henry A. Kissinger, 'The Vietnam Negotiations', in *Three Essays on Foreign Policy* (W. W. Norton and Co. Inc., New York, 1969), is reprinted with kind permission of the author.

The extract from Clark Clifford, 'A Vietnam Reappraisal', from *Foreign Affairs* 47:4 (July 1969), is reprinted with kind permission of Foreign Affairs.

The extract from Robert Taylor, *The State in Burma* (C. Hurst and Co., London, 1987), is reprinted with kind permission of the publisher.

The extract from Michael Langenburg, 'Gestapu and State Power in Indonesia', in Robert Cribb (ed), *The Indonesian Killings of 1965–1966: studies from Java and Bali* (Centre of Southeast Asian Studies, Monash University, Clayton, Vic. [Monash Papers on Southeast Asia no. 21], pp. 45–61), is reprinted with kind permission of the editor.

The extract from *Red Brotherhood at War* by Grant Evans and Kelvin Rowley is reprinted by kind permission of the publishers, Verso.

The extract from Tim Huxley, *Insecurity in the ASEAN Region* (Royal United Services Institute for Defence Studies (RUSI), London, 1993), is reprinted with kind permission of the publishers, RUSI.

CHAPTER I

Introduction

The shape of pre-colonial mainland Southeast Asia

Mainland Southeast Asia is divided into four parts, which have formed the 'cradles' for a succession of settled states and cultures. On the western boundary of the Southeast Asian portion of the continent is the Irrawaddy Valley region, bounded on the west, north and east sides by mountain ranges, which are themselves southern offshoots of the Himalayan range. On the eastern boundary of mainland Southeast Asia, on the eastern seaboard, is the Red River Valley, which is hemmed in to the north by the mountains of southern China, and to the west by a long mountain range known to the Vietnamese as the Truong Son, and to the Europeans as the Annamite Cordillera. A narrow coastal strip stretches south from the Red River Delta, bulging into the South China Sea, and eventually linking with the Mekong Delta.

Between the Irrawaddy Valley and the eastern seaboard lie two other distinct, but linked regions. One of these is defined geographically by the long sinuous course of the Mekong River, which flows down from the eastern Himalayan range through China's Yunnan plateau into Southeast Asia. In Southeast Asia, the Mekong is bounded to the east by the Truong Son/ Annamite Cordillera, and to the west by the highlands around Sayaboury, the Khorat plateau, and then the Dangrek and Cardamom mountain ranges, until it eventually reaches the wide flatlands of modern Cambodia and the Mekong Delta. The fourth region is that known today as the Bangkok Plain, separated from the Mekong by the mountains mentioned above, and from the Irrawaddy Delta by the Shan highlands and their southern extension.

Very roughly speaking, during the first millennium AD, the lower Irrawaddy Valley, the Bangkok Plain and the Mekong Delta regions were settled by groups of Mon-Khmer-speaking peoples, with the Mons dominating the western sector and the Khmers the east. The Red River Valley, at the northern end of mainland Southeast Asia's eastern seaboard, was for long periods the southernmost region of the Chinese empire proper, and was inhabited by the south Viet people, or the Vietnamese. The coastal region stretching southwards from the Red River to the Mekong Delta was settled by the

Chams, a branch of the widespread maritime Malayo-Polynesian language group.

The history of mainland Southeast Asia since the beginning of the second millennium has been very largely that of the southward migration, and subsequent conquest, settlement and establishment of new states in the region by a succession of ethnic groups with traceable origins in the eastern Himalayan and south China regions. Among these, three groups managed over time to establish a dominant position in the region: these were the Burmans, the T'ai or Thai peoples, and the Vietnamese from the Red River Delta. The Burmans pushed south from the eastern edges of the Himalayas into the Shan Hills and the Irrawaddy Valley in the first millennium AD, establishing themselves in the Kyaukse region of Upper Burma late in the first millennium, then, early in the second millennium, conquering the Mon-dominated Irrawaddy Delta region. The Thais and their relatives, during roughly the same period, spread out of southeast China in a southwesterly direction, skirting around the Red River Delta, eventually extending their settlement through the central Bangkok Plain and down the peninsula towards the Malay states. Relatives of the Thais – the Lao people – settled along the northern and middle reaches of the Mekong River. Between the fourteenth and eighteenth centuries, the Vietnamese steadily pushed the boundaries of their state southwards from the Red River Delta along the coastal strip, first dispossessing the Chams, and then taking control of the Mekong Delta from the Khmers.

By the eighteenth century the modern ethno-political map of the mainland had largely taken shape, with the Burmans dominating the Irrawaddy Valley (the core of modern Burma), the Thais in power in the Bangkok Plain (the heartland of modern Thailand), the Lao people dominating the northern and central reaches of the Mekong Valley (which form the heart of modern Laos), and the Vietnamese in control of the lowlands of the eastern seaboard (the core of modern Vietnam). This process of conquest, settlement and the establishment of relatively powerful states inevitably had the effect of either absorbing or pushing other ethnic groups to the edges of the Irrawaddy River, Red River and Mekong River regions, and to the edge of the central Bangkok Plain. It is for this reason that the unassimilated minorities are mainly to be found in the hills and the plateau regions of the mainland. Of those political entities formed before the beginning of the second millennium, only the Khmer kingdom of Cambodia has been able to survive as a coherent political entity into modern times. In the course of the eighteenth and nineteenth centuries, though, even Cambodia found its survival increasingly threatened by the Thai kingdom to the west, and the Vietnamese state to the east.

In linguistic terms the Malayo-Polynesian Cham, the Mon-Khmer, the Burman, the Thai/Lao and the Vietnamese form distinctive blocs. Cultural and religious considerations, however, cut across these ethno-linguistic divisions. Neighbouring populations had considerable influence upon each other, and the economic circumstances of groups created their own parallels and divisions. In terms of royal and state-related culture and religious practice, mainland Southeast Asia is a meeting-point between two broadly defined 'civilizations': one reflecting Indian influence, the other Chinese influence. In the Irrawaddy Valley, the Bangkok Plain and the Mekong region, the dominant external cultural–religious influence has been South Asian. This is reflected in the Indian-derived writing systems of the Burmese, the Thai, the Lao and the Khmer, and the dominance among the same peoples of the 'southern' Theravada ('path of the elders') Buddhism, whose texts are written in the Pali language, a dialect related to Sanskrit. In contrast, much of the cultural base of the Vietnamese people is Chinese-influenced, the writing system is based on Chinese models, and the main religious connections have been emphatically Chinese, both in their pre-Buddhist and Mahayana ('the great means of salvation') Buddhist manifestations. This religious and cultural gulf between Vietnam and the other states of the mainland Southeast Asia is not only a matter of religious affiliation and writing-systems. It amounts to a fundamental divide between two distinct civilizations, and can be observed in social structures, political cultures and domestic architecture.

In the later eighteenth and early nineteenth centuries, the three dominant states of mainland Southeast Asia – Burma, the Thai state of Siam and Vietnam – were consolidated and extended by three important dynasties. In Burma, the Konbaung dynasty pressed against Siam to the east and (more significantly) the Indian frontier states to the west. The Chakkri dynasty of Siam carried forward a similar process of expansion, directed against the scattered Lao principalities along the Mekong River, the western section of Cambodia and, in Siam's 'deep south', the northernmost Malay sultanates. At the very beginning of the nineteenth century, the Nguyen dynasty united Vietnam after centuries of *de facto* division and political turbulence. This process of regional consolidation by the three main kingdoms and ethnic groups took place at precisely the time that European colonial expansion was to enter its decisive phase in East and Southeast Asia.

The shape of pre-colonial maritime Southeast Asia

Whereas mainland Southeast Asia is naturally divided into four relatively large regions of settlement that have formed the bases for complex, sophis-ticated and more-or-less unified polities, geography has conspired to prevent any such development in maritime Southeast Asia, with the exception of certain parts of Java. The maritime region comprises the Malay portion of the peninsula and an extensive archipelago – now divided between Indonesia and the Philippines – of thousands of larger and smaller islands. Within this region, population has for centuries been very unevenly distributed. On the Malay peninsula, Sumatra and Borneo, which fall within the ever-wet tropical zone, and in some parts of the northern Philippines, the hinterlands were (and to some extent still are), on the whole, heavily forested and thinly populated. By contrast, most of the islands of eastern Indonesia and the southern portions of the Philippines have dry seasons that are too lengthy and/or stretches of flat terrain that are too limited to support substantial agricultural populations even today. Only the islands of Java and Bali, limited portions of such islands as Sulawesi and Sumbawa in eastern Indonesia, and parts of the Philippines have had the agricultural resources to sustain large populations over a period of time. Of these islands, only Java has provided the combination of broad lowland tracts of fertile soil and moderate monsoonal climate necessary for the production of the quantities of rice needed to underpin extensive, stable and populous states analogous to those of the mainland.

The primary focus of settlement in much of the maritime region, therefore, was the trading port, usually established at the mouth of a river, acting as an intermediary between the hinterland 'up-river' and the wider maritime trading networks of the region. Shifts of supply and demand in these loose trading networks continually affected the relative power, wealth and even survival of the port-polities of the islands that lacked substantial agricultural ballast. The power of these states was measured not by the normal criteria of a settled economy, but by a complex – and inherently unstable – web of allegiances stretching across the islands of the region.

Despite the kaleidoscopic diversity of states, however, the region was, and is, dominated by a single broad ethno-linguistic group: namely, the Malayo-Polynesians. The Malayo-Polynesian language family is a widely distributed one, stretching from Madagascar in the western Indian Ocean to Easter Island in the eastern Pacific, and from New Zealand in the south to Hawaii in the north. Interspersed and intermingled with the Malayo-Polynesians at the southern and eastern edges of maritime Southeast Asia are populations belonging to the Melanesian ethno-linguistic group. So far as maritime Southeast Asia is concerned, the main areas of Malayo-Polynesian settlement run from Aceh in the westernmost part of Sumatra to the eastern islands of modern Indonesia, and include the Cham remnants in central Vietnam, the inhabitants of the Philippine islands, and the Malays of the Malay peninsula, up to and including the southernmost part of Siam/Thailand. The eastern islands of Indonesia have a large Melanesian presence, however, and this has often been a source of inter-racial hostility.

In maritime Southeast Asia, ethno–linguistic boundaries do not always match cultural–religious boundaries. Portions of western and central maritime Southeast Asia came under Indian–Sanskritic–Hindu–Buddhist influence increasingly from the beginning of the first millennium AD, and very substantial traces of this period of influence remain, particularly in the culture of Java and Bali. By the thirteenth century, however, Islam had begun to push into maritime Southeast Asia from the Indian Ocean region. Islam spread along the trade routes to the main settled coastal areas, and from there into the interiors of some islands, though the patterns of conversion were uneven. Some of the more remote interior regions of the larger islands have remained impervious to Islam to this day, and the Hindu religion still dominates the island of Bali, which remains the main repository of an undiluted pre-Islamic, Hindu–Sanskritic-influenced culture.

It was partly European colonial expansion, particularly in the sixteenth and seventeenth centuries, that barred the further movement eastwards of Islamic conversion. In the sixteenth century, Spain began the process of annexing the Philippines as a Pacific extension of its American empire; with the exception of their southern and western fringes, the Philippine islands thereafter became a stronghold of Roman Catholicism. From the sixteenth century onwards, first Portugal and then the Netherlands gained control of the Spice Islands to the south of the Philippines; in the long years of colonial occupation, a substantial section of the population in the south converted to Christianity. A rough line can therefore be drawn on the map between zones of Islamic and, to the east, Christian predominance.

The first stages of European colonial take-over

Between the early sixteenth and the early nineteenth centuries, European maritime powers gradually gained footholds in key portions of maritime Southeast Asia along the maritime trade routes. Then, in the nineteenth century, this process both accelerated and changed in nature, as competing European powers began to carve out colonial empires. By the beginning of the twentieth century, France, Britain, the Netherlands and the United States gained a more or less complete control of the land mass and the islands of Southeast Asia. Portugal retained in East Timor a remnant of its former Southeast Asian possessions. Only the kingdom of Siam was able to remain independent.

This extraordinary phenomenon of European (and, later, American) global imperial dominance had immediate causes, but at the same time it had a more deep-rooted dynamic. In immediate terms, the first stimulus for this colonial venture was an inextricable combination of religious and commercial objectives. Islamic control of the eastern and southern Mediterranean was seen during the later Middle Ages as both a religious threat and a commercial impediment for the Christian world. It was, therefore, with the aim of winning the global battle for souls, as well as the more mundane pursuit of highly profitable trading opportunities, that the Portuguese, in the later fifteenth and early sixteenth centuries, finally circumnavigated the Islamic world via southern Africa, and established trading posts in India, Ceylon (Sri Lanka), the Southeast Asian port of Malacca and the Spice Islands. In the sixteenth century, Spain in like manner gained gradual control over the Philippine Islands. However, by the time that the Dutch and the British began in the following century to join in the competition for a trading foothold in the region, religious objectives had taken second place to commercial imperatives.

Once the Europeans *had* established their foothold in the region, a natural momentum propelled them into ever greater involvement. The acquisition of a trading base involved a combination of diplomacy and the threat or use of force. This, in turn, necessitated ever increasing military and political involvement in the affairs of the region, and the search for a wider defensible commercial network. Moreover, as colonial possessions became more and more clearly connected in European thinking to the expansion of national power and the protection of national interests, so colonial competition *between* the European maritime powers intensified. Already by the late eighteenth century, substantial territory had been seized, by Britain and France in particular, in North America, the West Indies and the Indian sub-continent. In Southeast Asia at this time, however, Britain had only begun to establish trading posts, particularly on the island of Penang, while French religious and commercial interests, which were mainly focused on Siam and Vietnam, had not by this stage graduated to the acquisition of territory. The Spanish, with their control of the Philippines, and the Dutch, with their extensive network of holdings in Java and the eastern islands, had the most substantial European presence in the region.

In the late eighteenth century, however, the pace of European intervention began to accelerate. For a short spell after 1795, the British took over, by treaty, some of the Dutch possessions in the East Indies while that power was under the domination of Napoleonic France. After the defeat of Napoleon in 1815, however, the British handed back these possessions, and the British and Dutch were subsequently able to reach an agreement in 1824, roughly delineating mutually agreed exclusive 'spheres of influence' in the maritime Southeast Asian sphere. The British area covered the Malay portion of the peninsula, including the vital trading settlements of Penang, Malacca and Singapore. The agreed Dutch 'sphere of influence' covered most of Sumatra, Java and the eastern islands beyond Java. Only the status of the northern part of Sumatra – the territory of the sultanate of Aceh – and the island of Borneo, remained undefined. Given the explosion of colonial expansion and inter-European colonial competition in the mid- to late nineteenth century, it was inevitable that these 'spheres of influence' would eventually be converted into colonial possessions by these two powers.

The *fundamental* dynamic behind this explosion of European global power in the eighteenth and nineteenth centuries was the impact of the scientific, industrial, technological and administrative revolutions in Europe and North America, and the consequent gap in power between these areas and the rest of the world. But the immediate stimulus for colonial expansion was the belief – held by all the main powers of Europe – that such expansion not only offered opportunities for expanded markets and investment, access to raw materials, and for the settlement of surplus domestic populations, but also, and crucially, was a key to the maintenance and expansion of national power. Colonial expansion, therefore, became an intrinsic part of the competition in the eighteenth and nineteenth centuries between the main nation-states of Europe. Along with the expansion of Europe's capacity to impose its will on the rest of the world, therefore, went an intensified competition for overseas territory and the imperative to fill 'vacuums' of territory that might otherwise be seized by a competing power. In the case of Southeast Asia, this in-built tendency to colonial expansion was given an added impetus by the fact that China was seen as a key potential market offering unlimited possibilities, and that China's government had become increasingly enfeebled and vulnerable during the course of the nineteenth century.

In the case of maritime Southeast Asia, however, the pace and extent of European expansion through the nineteenth century was determined by both European competition *and* co-operation. The British regarded Dutch control of the East Indies region as a useful guarantee that the area would not fall into the hands of a more formidable power. For their part, the Dutch were anxious to accelerate their direct control of the region, and thus secure it from the dangers of outside intervention. By the time of the First World War, the Dutch had managed to secure undisputed colonial authority over Sumatra, including Aceh, Java, the islands beyond Java up to parts of western New Guinea, Sulawesi and the southern sector of Borneo. In essence, this was a long process of 'in-filling' the gaps that still remained between the older Dutch possessions in the archipelago.

In the last quarter of the nineteenth century, the combination of an anxiety to stabilize the Malayan area, and pressure to pre-empt possible moves for intervention by competing colonial powers, pushed the British into establishing protectorate arrangements over the Malay states of the peninsula. In 1909, this British protectorate network was extended to four northern Malay states that had hitherto been protectorates of the kingdom of Siam. In 1841, a British subject, James Brooke, established a sultanate in Sarawak, an area that had previously been part of the Sultanate of Brunei, while in 1881 the British North Borneo Company took control of the northeastern-most section of that island. Although these two Bornean states operated more or less independently, they – along with the 'protectorate' of Brunei that was sandwiched between them – came within the general security umbrella of the British empire.

In the late nineteenth century, the United States itself began to enter the race for overseas empire. In the wake of the Spanish–American war of 1898 and the defeat of Spain, the United States took over the Philippines as a colonial possession, and thus created the basis for a Pacific-wide empire.

The same imperative of colonial competition pushed Britain and France into mainland Southeast Asia in the last half of the nineteenth century, particularly since the area was viewed at the time as a vital economic and strategic staging-post to the coast and interior of China. The fact that, as has already been noted, the area contained three powerful, expanding and well-organized indigenous states meant that European colonial expansion would involve prolonged confrontation with, and eventual subjugation of, two of these kingdoms. The Konbaung dynasty of Burma was subdued by the British in the period 1824–85, and the Nguyen dynasty of Vietnam by the French in the period 1858–85. In both cases, there was a similar determination on the part of Britain and France to secure at all costs dominant economic, strategic and political influence. Britain saw in Burma a crucial security flank for British India which could not be allowed to fall into potentially hostile hands. France viewed Vietnam as the vital hub for the creation of an exclusive French colonial sphere in eastern Asia. In 1885, Britain removed the Konbaung dynasty altogether, and Burma became a province of British India; in Vietnam, however, the Nguyen dynasty was allowed to survive in a truncated territory under a French protectorate.

The Chakkri dynasty of Siam alone succeeded in maintaining its independence. This remarkable feat was due to both internal and external factors. The dynasty itself adapted far more effectively than the neighbouring states of Vietnam and Burma to the realities of encroaching Western colonial power. It made timely trading concessions to the major Western trading powers; it modernized its administration and was thus able to ensure compliance with central government policies throughout the kingdom; and, albeit reluctantly, it made major territorial concessions, in its eastern provinces to France, and on its southern border region to Britain.

The other reason for Siam's survival was the *rapprochement* at the beginning of the twentieth century between the two competing colonial powers in mainland Southeast Asia – France and Great Britain. Through the 1880s and 1890s, these two powers remained colonial competitors deeply suspicious of each other's motives in Asia and Africa. It was partly as a means of forestalling any possibility of French intrigue in what was considered to be a vital strategic region that Britain felt impelled to occupy Upper Burma in the mid-1880s. A converse fear on the part of France that Britain might push its influence into the Mekong region and threaten Vietnam's western flank prompted the French forward movement into Laos and western Cambodia at the turn of the nineteenth and twentieth centuries. By 1904, however, Britain and France had concluded an alliance in Europe. This enabled the two powers to agree on the maintenance of the independence of Siam as a useful buffer-state between their zones of colonial influence, thus greatly reducing the dangers of territorial misunderstandings and conflict.

While, therefore, colonial *competition* acted as a dynamic forcing the pace of colonial intervention through the nineteenth century, colonial *consensus* subsequently played a vital role in consolidating and stabilizing the European presence in Southeast Asia.

General consideration of the scope and objectives of this book

This stage – the near-complete take-over of Southeast Asia by the colonial powers in the years before the outbreak of the First World War – is the point at which the period covered by the book begins. Before embarking on this historical investigation, however, it is important to outline in brief the main themes and questions that will dominate the book.

The first question underlying the narrative and the texts is: To what extent is there a demonstrable unity underlying the modern history of the region? On the face of it, Southeast Asia – unlike regions such as East Asia, West Asia, South Asia or even Central Asia – lacks a single dominant ethnic group, language, culture, religion, pre-colonial state or, indeed, colonial power. In many senses, in fact, the area could be seen as a spillover in cultural, religious and ethnic terms from other, more 'coherent', regions.

We will detect, nevertheless, a remarkable unity of historical experience in Southeast Asia, a unity that was and is determined as much by external intrusions as by internal historical dynamics. As has been seen, there existed a considerable degree of common interest between the major colonial powers – the Netherlands, Britain and France – by the beginning of the twentieth century, and this consensus persisted through the First World War and up to the defeat of France in the summer of 1940. This brought stability to the region throughout the main period of colonial rule.

The Japanese military interregnum, lasting from early 1942 to mid-1945, was certainly a unifying – even if extremely harrowing – experience for the region. Southeast Asia as a whole had to adjust to the imposition of Japanese power, but local populations were at the same time given unique opportunities to engage in large-scale political and military organization. In one way or another, all the major nationalist organizations of the region 'took off' as significant mass movements during the short interval of Japanese rule, even if their origins could be traced back to the preceding colonial era.

After the Second World War, the region as a whole underwent the experience of decolonization. Although this decolonization process occurred in widely different ways, what is significant in considering the unity of the region is the fact that it generally took place within a very short time-frame: namely, within the decade 1945–54. The exceptions to this rule are Malaya/Malaysia (1957–63), Portuguese Timor (1975) and the Sultanate of Brunei, which became fully independent in 1984.

No sooner had colonial rule begun to wither away, however, than Southeast Asia had to endure a new intrusion in the shape of the Cold War. In some senses, the Cold War divided rather than united Southeast Asia. It created rifts between the Indochina states and the rest of the region, and between communist and anti-communist factions within the newly independent states. There can be no doubt, however, that it was the anti-communist states and political forces of the region that helped to shape modern Southeast Asia's collective identity. It is a continuing sense of outside threat that has helped bind the region together, even after the collapse of communism as an ideological force in the early 1990s. It is, in fact, instructive to compare the relative regional stability since 1945 of Southeast Asia with that of more 'coherent' regions such as West and South Asia.

It is, nevertheless, true that Southeast Asia was, during the colonial period, composed of a number of colonial spheres of control of roughly equal power and status, and the same has been true of the post-1945 independent states of Southeast Asia. This raises real practical problems in this book of giving equal weight to the main states of the region, and due weight to the smaller states. To try to maintain this kind of balance in each historical phase would be impossible in terms of length, and would completely destroy any thematic coherence. On the other hand, simply to follow the thematic highlights and key events would obviously risk the complete sidelining of smaller or more 'non-mainstream' states.

In this book, an attempt has been made to maintain a thematic coherence for the whole region chapter by chapter, even if this has meant a concentration on certain issues and countries – as in the case of the Vietnam war. At the same time, 'decisive moments' in the history of the states of the region have, where possible, been examined, particularly when they link in with the main historical themes. Obvious examples of such decisive events are the inter-ethnic negotiations for an independent Malaya, the question of 'collaboration' in the Philippines immediately after the Second World War, the civil war in Laos between 1959 and 1962, and the civil war in Cambodia through the 1970s.

The question of 'balance' applies not only to the treatment of the different countries of the region, but also to the question of the use of suitable sources. An attempt has been made in the following chapters to maintain a careful balance between a historical perspective – usually the academic viewpoint – and the often very different perspectives of the actors in, or spectators of, historical events as they evolved. It is equally important to ensure that the writers looking at events from the Western viewpoint should be balanced by an indigenous perspective. In order to meet the commonplace criticism that history is written by the 'winners', an effort has at least been made to give space to those whose political agendas have not succeeded, and who are therefore in danger of having their views distorted or forgotten.

The most important objective of this book, however, is to try to give an idea of the 'shape of events' encompassing the region as a whole. This has necessitated what might be considered an overemphasis on the broad influence of ideology upon political events and arguments in the region, and a tendency to highlight such outside 'intrusions' into the region as the Japanese intervention, as well as the general impact of the Cold War and the perceived communist threat. The ideological dimension of twentieth-century

Southeast Asian history is, however, often unduly underrated. It can be an absolutely vital guide to the preconceptions and priorities of key political forces and individuals at different stages in the region's history. An understanding of the ideologies prevailing in any particular period, moreover, can help us to grasp the special 'idiom' that underlay the political debate of that period.

In Hegel's famous words, 'the owl of Minerva spreads its wings only with the falling of the dusk' – in other words, the 'meaning' and long-term shape of events can only begin to be understood after those events have, as it were, been 'transcended' by time. It would, of course, be presumptuous to assume that we have yet reached such a privileged perspective on the colonial period, the period of decolonization and its immediate aftermath. But we are now moving into an age where the rhetoric of nationalism and anti-colonialism seem almost as distant as the rhetoric that initially served to justify colonial rule. Perhaps, at the end of the twentieth century, we are at last reaching a point where we can consider these events, truly, as history.

The decade of the 1970s marks the ragged end of the historical era that is described in this book, and it is for this reason – as well as compelling considerations of space – that only a broad summary is given of the distinctly post-colonial era that began in the 1980s.

CHAPTER 2

Education, Reform and National Awareness, 1900–41

Faced with this national disaster, intellectuals are concerned over the future of our race. They have wanted to sound the alarm of national conscience and together find a path to salvation. But, alas, the most daring, in refuge abroad, content themselves with wailing out their hearts, without daring to risk returning. The others, less courageous still, entrench themselves in the countryside, close their eyes and ears, and do not dare to discuss these questions. (Phan Chau Trinh, *Letter to the Government of Indochina*, 1907)

The patterns of European rule

It should be noted at the outset that there has been a crucial difference in basic forms of colonial control. On the one hand, there were those areas – usually in temperate zones – of European settlement, where the indigenous population was either displaced or, in extreme cases, subjected to genocide. Here the indigenous peoples were an obstacle to the 'colonial project'. In tropical or sub-tropical areas, however, the primary interest was not in European settlement, but in building and defending trade networks, the exploitation of natural resources, and the expansion of market links with the European colonial metropolis. Southeast Asia fell into the latter category, although it should be noted that the Dutch in the East Indies and the French in Indochina encouraged European settlement to a far greater degree than did the British in their Southeast Asian possessions. British society in the Malay region, the Straits Settlements and Burma constituted a temporary administrative, military and commercial caste, whose sojourn in Southeast Asia was generally limited to the span of their careers. In their possessions, on the other hand, Dutch and French immigrants formed a significant *settler* population, living side by side with, rather than completely displacing, the native population.

In terms of government, the most thoroughgoing form of colonial control was one in which the indigenous pre-colonial administration was simply removed, and replaced by direct colonial administration. In Southeast Asia, the most clear-cut example of this kind of 'substitute' rule was that of the

British in Burma. After the final defeat of the Burmese state in 1885, the monarchy was dismantled, along with its government structure, and Burma thenceforth was administered as a province of British India. In effect, a wholly alien administrative structure was simply superimposed on Burma.

The British administrations in the Straits Settlements of Penang, Malacca and Singapore were not so much 'substitutions' for traditional rule as the *creation* of hybrid societies and economies ruled by Britain via the Colonial Office. In essence, these areas were Sino-British commercial enclaves within the 'Malay world' (*dunia melayu*).

British rule over the Malay states and the Malay region in general was an example of 'incorporation', in the sense that protectorate treaties were signed with individual Malay sultanates, in which a layer of British administration was placed on top of a local system, exercising varying degrees of control. The divergence here between appearance and reality should, however, be noted. In appearance, British rule involved loose control over, and protection of, local political systems and culture; in reality, the British within this framework developed a modern economy in Malaya. This was the basis for what has been described as a 'dual economy' and 'dual society' in British Malaya, in which a traditional Malay society, economy and political structure existed side by side with – but separate from – an immigrant economy and society.

The French in Indochina had, like the British in the Malay area, a mixture of colonial systems. In Cochinchina (the oldest French possession in Indochina) they created a classic version of 'Overseas France', with a direct administration and the ostensible aim of inculcating a French identity via education, language and culture. In other parts of Indochina – Annam, Tonkin, the Laotian States and Cambodia – a 'protectorate' system was established, with French *résidents* and *résidents-general* 'guiding' the native administrations of Vietnam, Cambodia and Laos. Once again, the divergence between appearance and reality should be noted. Even in these 'protectorate' areas, the French exercised a very considerable degree of direct authority via their *resident* system. The structure, however, enabled the French to argue subsequently that they had not displaced Vietnamese political authority, and that the Franco-Vietnamese relationship was a partnership in government.

The Dutch in the East Indies created a hybrid administration. Direct Dutch rule was imposed and the system of government was rationalized in the nineteenth century. While the rulers of the traditional states were on the whole removed or marginalized, *local* traditional officials and leaderships were incorporated as a vital regional layer of the Dutch administrative system. The intermediary role of this *priyayi* class, both during the colonial period and in the transition to independence, has been a particular matter of interest and debate for historians.

Education, 'Westernization', cultural challenge and change

Whatever the system of government imposed by the imperial powers in Southeast Asia, the sheer cost of maintaining an effective colonial administration required a degree of incorporation of the indigenous administrative elite. The demands of a Western-style administration made it imperative that this administrative elite should have access to a European education. This need was matched by a growing sense among most of the colonial powers in the late nineteenth century that the possession of empire could not be justified by economic and strategic factors alone, but that it must serve a moral agenda: namely, the provision of access to Western ideas, education and culture, along with increased provision for the welfare and development of indigenous societies. Administrative need, therefore, was neatly dovetailed with the new 'ethically' based imperial policy. It was hoped that this new partnership between the colonial power and the indigenous elite would help maintain a cheap administration and an acquiescent population, and thereby strengthen the bonds of empire. In the late nineteenth century and early twentieth century, there was a significant expansion in Burma, Malaya, Indochina and the Dutch East Indies of schools, teacher-training colleges, medical and engineering colleges, and even universities. These educational facilities were accessible only to a tiny fraction of the indigenous population, but they did ensure that the new generation of the native elite acquired a 'world view' entirely different from that of their parents.

It is out of this new generation that the leaders of the anti-colonial and nationalist movements of the early twentieth century were to come. Many of the previous generation of political leaders – monarchs, courtiers, provincial administrators, religious leaders – had attempted to resist the European powers as they tightened their imperial control in the nineteenth century, but the anti-colonial resistance movements that they had led had taken a strictly defensive stance; they had fought for the protection of existing political systems, cultures and religions from alien domination. Although some of these resistance movements were prolonged – in Aceh, the resistance to Dutch rule lasted at least thirty years – these various last-ditch defences of the *ancien régime* all ended in defeat.

The next generation of the indigenous elite was confronted by an entirely new environment: namely, absolute European power, and the apparently irresistible strength of Western culture and civilization. One reaction to this implacable fact was outright collaboration with the colonial power – a collaboration that was sometimes more deep-rooted than a mere willingness to deal with the European powers. Collaboration occasionally involved a wholesale acceptance of Western values and culture, and a willingness to promote the colonial 'project'. A classic but by no means unusual example of such collaboration is provided by the Vietnamese scholar Petrus Truong Vinh Ky (1837–98), who converted to Christianity, acted as an interpreter and go-between for the French in their negotiations with the Vietnamese monarchy, and wrote – among many other works – an authoritative French–Vietnamese dictionary that gave educated Vietnamese access to the French language and culture.

Although the majority of the new elite generation of Southeast Asia did not follow this road, they did accept one of its fundamental premises: that defence of the *ancien régime* was no longer a viable option. From this perception came the view that Asian society would have to adapt if it was not – *à la* Darwin and the processes of natural selection – to be entirely overwhelmed. Far from rejecting the opportunities presented by the new 'ethical' colonial strategy, this new generation seized them. For most of this elite, the motor that drove the new search for access to Western education and ideas was not, of course, the opportunity to advance the colonial project by collaboration, but rather the policy that the Chinese called 'self-strengthening'. This amounted to a search for the sources of the dynamism to which the overwhelming power of the West was attributed, in the areas of scientific, philosophical, economic and political knowledge.

In their search for an effective and deep-rooted focus of resistance to European power, the new educated elites were themselves 'Westernized'. This is the basis of the 'revolution' in cultural, political, social, economic and religious awareness that affected these elites so deeply in the early twentieth century. It was reflected in an explosion of literary clubs, study and discussion groups, periodicals, books and (within the strict restraints imposed by everwatchful colonial powers) political and social organizations.

'Pre-nationalism' and nationalism

The objectives of these groups, and what might be called the 'units of affiliation' that held them together, were varied. It is noticeable that many of them, particularly in the decade before the First World War, were 'nonnational', we might say 'pre-national', in their orientation, and sought to create a link with 'units of affiliation' that transcended the arbitrary colonial boundaries. Thus the 'pan-Islamic' reform movement (See 'Islamic Reform in Malaya', p. 16) sought ideally to create a new united Islamic world driven by a purified and energized faith capable of engaging on equal terms with Western civilization. There were similar attempts to create 'pan-Buddhist' organizations in the Indian sub-continent and Burma, and 'pan-Asian' political and educational networks linking India, Southeast Asia, China and Japan. The most notable example of the last was the attempt by the Vietnamese patriot Phan Boi Chau (1867–1940) to create organizational links between Vietnamese patriots and Chinese and Japanese reformers.

Nationalism and the idea of the nation-state eventually emerged, however, as the most potent European concept to influence and bind together these Southeast Asian movements in their search for cultural and political transformation. Of course, there had been state organizations and various forms of political and social identity in pre-colonial Southeast Asia. Nationalism as such, however, was an ideology that was formed in the Europe of the eighteenth and nineteenth centuries. The key to the nationalist idea is the dynamic linkage, or tension, between the creation from above of strong and unified state identities, and the emergence from below – within society as a whole – of mass identities which may either bind together or divide the members of that society. The implantation of the national idea depends on the working out of these sometimes coinciding, sometimes conflicting identities within the context of modern democratic ideas and mass politics.

In mainland Southeast Asia, the boundaries of colonial rule coincided to a great degree with the outlines of the pre-colonial states of Burma, Vietnam and Cambodia, in addition to consolidating the Lao kingdoms. These boundaries also confirmed the territorial integrity of the one Southeast Asian state that was not colonized, namely the kingdom of Siam. Under these circumstances, it was natural that deeply entrenched state loyalties of the stronger pre-colonial states should evolve relatively effortlessly into modern Vietnamese, Burmese or Siamese (later Thai) nationalism.

In island Southeast Asia and the Malay peninsula, however, the boundaries of British and Dutch colonial rule were more arbitrary, at the same time subsuming a number of disparate pre-colonial states and – as in the case of the Malay states of the Malay peninsula and Sumatra – dividing coherent cultural regions. In these circumstances, national identity and consciousness had literally to be invented, and it is not surprising that here the sense of national identity emerged only slowly, and that it had to co-exist or contend with such competing foci of identity as pan-Islam or local state identities. It was perhaps inevitable that in maritime Southeast Asia the framework of the colonial states should provide the framework for what became Indonesian, Malaysian or Philippine national identities. Anti-colonial resistance had to adapt itself to the ideas and the framework of power imposed by Europe, and to work within the divisions created by colonialism.

This process of transformation and empowerment involved pain and dislocation. It created new identities and threatened old certainties and power-bases. It created a divide between generations, and confrontations between ideologies and political programmes. But at the same time, this was an exciting period of intellectual emancipation and discovery. (See 'The Vietnamese response to French rule', p. 27 and 'Indonesia: the dilemmas of Western-ization', p. 37.)

READINGS

1. Islamic reform in Malaya

By the beginning of the seventeenth century, the Islamic world had begun its long retreat before a resurgent Europe. This retreat reached its culmination in the late nineteenth and the early twentieth centuries, and by the end of the First World War, North Africa, the whole Indian sub-continent, the East Indies, the Malay states, the fringes of Arabia and the former Arab regions of the Ottoman empire, along with large parts of Central Asia, had come under European control.

One response to this humiliating process was resistance, and there were indeed a number of examples of Islamic-inspired rebellions against colonial rule in Southeast Asia and elsewhere throughout the nineteenth century. In the long run, however, the most significant manifestation of a coherent Islamic response to European colonial rule in Southeast Asia was the so-called Islamic reform movement, which was inspired by a parallel movement for Islamic reform that took root during the late nineteenth century in the Middle East, particularly in Egypt.

In the first instance, however, the principal confrontation in Southeast Asia was not between the Islamic reformers and the colonial powers, but between the Islamic reformers and the entrenched Islamic hierarchies throughout the maritime Southeast Asia region. Before they could challenge *kafir* (unbeliever) colonial power, Islamic reformers (the so-called Kaum Muda or 'young faction') had to challenge the *ancien régime* (the so-called Kaum Tua, or 'old faction') represented by traditional Islamic scholars at the village level, and by the administrators of Islamic law at the level of the local states. The reaction of the Dutch and British colonial powers to the phenomenon of Islamic reform was, therefore, ambivalent. On the one hand, they welcomed the 'Westernization' and 'rationalization' of Islam which, they hoped, would reduce what they saw as Islam's 'fanatical' tendencies. On the other hand, the British in particular were anxious to maintain the traditional religious authority of the sultans in their respective states.

The following extract from William Roff's *The Origins of Malay Nationalism* clearly illustrates the tension between the *ancien régime* of the Malay States and a new, modern, outward-looking generation, and the ways in which this tension was expressed in the Malayo-Islamic context. It also shows how the Islamic reform movement gradually acquired a Malay nationalist tinge, particularly in the 1920s and 1930s, when issues of national identity and anti-colonial struggle began to supersede the previous generation's absorption in the essentially non-political issues of reforming Islam and adapting it to the modern world.

W. R. Roff, *The Origins of Malay Nationalism* (New Haven, CT, and London: Yale University Press, 1967). Excerpts taken from pages 56–90, 'Kaum Muda-Kaum Tua: Innovation and Reaction'.

Al-Imam and the reformists   In July 1906 a new periodical in Malay entitled *Al-Imam* (The Leader) made its first appearance in Singapore. Its aims as expressed in Shaykh Mohd. Salim Al-Kalali's introductory editorial were 'to remind those who are forgetful, arouse those who sleep, guide those who stray, and give a voice to those who speak with wisdom'. One of its first articles consisted of a kind of colloquy on 'The Proper Task: What is Most Needed for Our People'. Beginning by asserting that it is the job of a people's leaders to diagnose and prescribe for their ills, the writer goes on: 'Perhaps it may be said that we are most in need of skills of craftsmanship and agriculture, or knowledge of how to preserve our country from its enemies, or that we need education to rescue us from the slough of apathy and indolence, or that we must learn to unite for the common good ... All this is true. But the one thing that will strengthen and realize all our desires is knowledge of the commands of our religion. For religion is the proven cure for all the ills of our community.' These few lines embody, in essentials, the message which Al-Imam and its successors were to preach, with great persistence and at considerable length, during the next quarter of a century. An analysis of the message and of those groups in Malay society which either espoused or contested it holds the key to much of importance during the period covered by this study.

Al-Imam's first concern was with religion and not directly with social, even less with political, change. At the same time this distinction would have been in some measure foreign to the editors and writers of the journal, who shared the traditional Islamic concept of the undifferentiated *umat* or community in which spiritual, social, and political well-being and ends are subsumed under the one head – the good and profitable life lived according to Divine Law. Their attention was turned in the first place, therefore, to the state of Malay society. Almost all of the thirty-one issues of the journal contain at least one article, and often more, analyzing the ills of the community. In an orgy of self-vilification and self-condemnation, Al-Imam points to the backwardness of the Malays, their domination by alien races, their laziness, their complacency, their bickering among themselves, and their inability to co-operate for the common good. Nor are the Malays alone in this situation – it is one shared by the whole Islamic world. The root cause of the decline of the Islamic peoples from their past glory is that they have ceased, in their ignorance, to follow the commands of God as expressed through the mouth and the life of His Prophet Muhammad. As an instrument for discovering and understanding the Divine Law, Man has been gifted with intelligence (*akal*), an intelligence it is incumbent upon him to use and to develop. Islam is not, says *Al-Imam*, as its detractors allege, hostile to knowledge and progress such as is exemplified by the West. On the contrary, a proper understanding of and submission to the law and the spirit of Islam is our only means of competing successfully with those who now rule and lead us.

Following upon its diagnosis, *Al-Imam* goes on to practice, so far as it can, what it preaches – though it must be said that there is in its columns more exhortation than prescription. The Malays, and more especially the rulers and traditional leaders (*raja dan orang besar*) are urged to form associations to foster education, economic development, and self-awareness. The traditional practice of Islam in Malaya, adulterated by impurities of custom and belief derived from *adat* [traditional pre-Islamic custom] and from other religions, and inimical to progress, must be cleansed of these elements, and the *ulama* [religious scholars] who transmit the imperfections brought to a sense of their errors and obligations. In addition to providing numerous articles expounding the true Islam, *Al-Imam* proposed a reformed system of religious education in which, upon a sound basis of doctrinal instruction, Arabic and English and modern educational subjects shall be taught, and students encouraged to go overseas for further study. Long series of articles, often taken in entirety from Arabic originals, inculcate proper moral conduct, the elements of child-rearing, the duties of all members of society according to status and role, the exemplary history of Islam, and much else of this kind. A regular section of the journal is devoted to readers' questions and answers and to *fatwa* [legal opinions] on disputed matters of religious interpretation, with a strong emphasis throughout on the need to return to the Kuran and *hadith*, the basic texts of Islam, and to practise *ijtihad* [informed independent investigation] rather than *taklid buta* [blind acceptance of intermediate authority] for their understanding. Finally, there is a good deal of attention given to news from the Islamic countries of the Middle East, especially Turkey, and almost as much to Japan – the two areas which together represent Islam and Asia on the march.

Al-Imam was a radical departure in the field of Malay publications, distinguished from its predecessors both in intellectual stature and intensity of purpose and in its attempt to formulate a coherent philosophy of action for a society faced with the need for rapid social and economic change. For a parallel to the new journal one has to turn to the Egyptian periodical *Al-Manar*, first published in Cairo eight years earlier, which in many ways *Al-Imam* closely resembled. Nor is this surprising, for it was from the Egyptian modernist movement that the writers and sponsors of *Al-Imam* derived, almost in totality, their reformist ideas. One of the many names given to the reformist group in Malaya was, in fact, '*Kaum Al-Manar*', the *Al-Manar* faction. An examination of the contents of the Cairo journal, as detailed by Charles C. Adams in his *Islam and Modernism in Egypt*, makes clear the extent to which *Al-Imam* was modelled on it, and the Malay journal contains an abundance of references to and excerpts from its predecessor ...

The range and catholicity of *Al-Imam*'s ideas and interests represented incipient movement and growth within almost every facet of Malay life. Though it would be a mistake to regard its concerns for the Malayo-Muslim *umat* of the peninsula and beyond as an explicit form of political nationalism, in a Malaya where for the next thirty years few were to recognize allegiances outside their state and sultan, this concept of a wider unity based on religion and a common experience of colonial rule was to become increasingly symptomatic of Malay unease at the absence of effective forms of association for undeniably common ends. Like many another venture of this kind, *Al-Imam* preached initially to the persuaded, and though there is no clear evidence about the size and nature of its audience, there is little doubt that a majority of its readers came from the intellectually and socially more sophisticated element of the towns and from those religiously educated who had received some introduction to Muslim polemics in Mecca. It was written on the whole in good Malay but in a style much influenced by Arabic, with a high incidence of Arabic words and expressions, which presupposed some familiarity with that language ...

Though subscribers may have been few in number, *Al-Imam* came into the hands of religious teachers, particularly those in the new-style madrasah [religious schools], where its views on such diverse and controversial questions as the validity of *hadith*, payments for burial prayers, certain of the practices associated with Nakshabandi Sufism, the wearing of European clothing, and interest on savings bank loans led to much discussion and debate. It is in fact in the field of the new education that the immediate impact of the reformist group may be most clearly seen, both in its encouragement of religious schools of a more ambitious and elaborate kind than had hitherto existed and in the formulation of a system of education which, ideally, would take account of the need not only for a purified Islam but for modern secular knowledge as well ... It was the innovatory, and potentially disruptive, character of this teaching that brought the reformists, known pejoratively as 'Kaum Muda', the 'Young Faction', into conflict with other groups in Malay society – the official religious hierarchy, the traditional Malay elite, and the rural *ulama*, collectively the 'Old Faction', or '*Kaum Tua*' ...

It was through the medium of the new madrasah therefore, and indirectly by their publication of newspapers and other literature used in these schools, that the Kaum Muda made most of its impact on Malay society. Religious education of all degrees of refinement, from the old-fashioned *pondok* schools to reformist madrasah, had received a tremendous impetus as a result of foreign rule and all that followed in its train. The profound shock to the Malays, brought face to face with, or at the very least living alongside, alien and aggressive communities possessed of infinitely greater wealth and power, is evidenced in the anguished debate that took place among the more articulate about the causes and remedies for Malay backwardness. The panacea most frequently prescribed was education, but this was clearly a prescription that could be filled in many ways. For the peasantry, to whom the social and economic change going on about them brought perhaps some amelioration of material condition but also much uncertainty, it meant a reaffirmation of traditional values within a framework of Islamic conservatism, in an attempt to reassert the basis on which life was customarily lived. For the more purposive Kaum Muda it meant an attempt to re-think Islam in terms of the demands made by the contemporary situation, to participate, as it were, in induced social change, the dynamic of which would be provided by a reformed Islamic ideology. For only comparatively few, initially, did it mean an uncritical and holistic acceptance of all the West had to offer.

Government-provided vernacular education had been available to Malays in the western and southern states since the 1880s, but many parents were reluctant to entrust their sons to the government schools, fearing their assumed foreign and Christian bias, and turned instead to Islam ...

From the point of view of utility alone many Malays saw little advantage in vernacular education, for unless it led to further instruction in English (an urban amenity seldom available to the rural Malay), it was of small assistance in obtaining even subordinate government jobs. It may be noted, for example, that of the 2,900 boys who left Perak vernacular schools in 1903, only 24 became office or domestic servants, ten Malay school teachers, one a policeman, and one a clerk, the remainder following ordinary peasant pursuits. With the great increase in minor religious offices, however, as a result of the creation of the state establishments, and in the growth of the religious schools themselves, religious education acquired a practical as well as a moral value in preparing boys for a calling that carried considerable status within the Malay community itself ... By 1913 a correspondent to *Neracha* (The Scales) was able to point to *berpuloh* ('tens upon tens') of madrasah now operating in Perak alone, turning out a steady stream of potential teachers and religious officials. By no means all the new madrasah were in any sense Kaum Muda but a significant number of the teachers were, and the use of the Malay press and other publications as teaching media greatly stimulated controversial discussion on Kaum Muda principles.

The roots of the conflict between Kaum Muda and the Kaum Tua alliance of religious conservatism and traditional elite, though expressed in doctrinal and ritual controversies of varying substance, may be seen in the threat offered by the former to the very basis of customary authority. Cardinal among the principles of the reformists was the contention that man must use his reason (*akal*) to determine the truth about religion as about all else and abjure the blind acceptance of intermediary authority. 'The Kaum Tua', wrote *Al-Ikhwan* (The Brotherhood) in 1929,

> behave as though it was obligatory to believe all the law books of the *ulama*, and every word in them, as though they were the Kuran itself ... while the Kaum Muda hold that the Kuran and *hadith* alone have this authority, and that as none of the *ulama* are free from error, God has given us reason, or intelligence, with which to examine what the *ulama* say.

In the last analysis, the perfection and purification of Islam was for the Kaum Muda not simply an end in itself but a means for the acceleration and direction of social and economic change for the betterment of Malay society, a process held to be retarded by traditional Islam as practiced in the states. 'In other parts of the Islamic world', said one writer, 'the Kaum Muda become the instrument of progress, shaking the Kaum Tua out of their senility and stupidity ... [In Malaya] the *ulama* desire, like Saint Peter of the Roman Church, to hold the only key to the gates of heaven.'

In attempting to wrest the key from the grasp of the establishment, the reformists came into direct conflict with the state religious authorities on a wide range of ritual, doctrinal, and social questions. As fundamentalists and purists they attacked customary and 'superstitious' accretions to orthodox Islam; as modernists they proposed rationalized reformulations of Islamic practice which would better enable them and their coreligionists to compete in the modern world. In the first category, such questions as those concerning the propriety of reciting the *talkin* over the dead at burial, and whether or not the formulation of intention before prayer should be made aloud or inwardly, occasioned widespread and persistent debate among the religious. In the second category, the Kaum Muda fought a long-drawn-out battle for the acceptance of savings bank and cooperative society interest as non-usurious (and therefore falling outside the proscription upon *riba*); they also advocated greater freedom for women to receive education and participate in social affairs. The pattern of the disputes is clear. They represent, on the one hand, an attempt by those Muslims with a more intensive experience of metropolitan Islam to purify ritual and belief from purely local innovations and, on the other, an attempt by urban-centered Muslims to reformulate Islam in response to the economic and social pressures of contemporary life.

In addition to, or it might be said as a result of, these attacks by the Kaum Muda upon established religion, their ideas were regarded as attacks also upon the traditional elite, who stood behind and were involved with the religious hierarchy. Some weight was lent to this by the continual, if muted, criticisms of the Malay *raja dan orang besar* [rulers and traditional leaders], both for their allegedly dissolute and self-indulgent way of life and more positively for failing to provide a leadership that would enable their people to strive more effectively in an alien-dominated world. Again, Kaum Muda's criticism of *adat*, though confined to what were thought to be its ill effects upon the practice of Islam, and their insistence upon the equality of all men before God (and upon a more individualistic ethic), could be seen to have implications subversive of the existing social and political as well as religious order.

Official Islam reacted both by argument and by the direct use of authority. Periodicals such as *Pengasoh* (The Educator) (1918–37), a fortnightly magazine produced in Kelantan by the Council of Religion and Malay Custom and circulated throughout the peninsula, urged opposing points of view and condemned the Kaum Muda as irreligious. The section of the Muhammadan Laws Enactment of 1904 that forbade any person 'except in his own home, and in the presence of members of his own family only, [to] teach any religious doctrine unless he shall previously have obtained written permission to do so from His Highness the Sultan [of the respective Malay States]', enabled a certain control to be maintained over religious teaching, though it was much evaded. State Mufti and *Shaykh ul-Islam* issued *fatwa* condemning the new ideas as *kafir* (infidel), and reformist leaders were refused permission to speak in some mosques ...

Kaum Muda periodicals and other publications were denied entry into some states, and an amendment to the 1904 Enactment passed in 1925–26 provided severe penalties for anyone printing or publishing literature concerning the Islamic religion without the written permission of the Sultan in Council. It was used both to provide a prior check on publication within the states and in some cases to proscribe publication or force withdrawal. There was even an unsuccessful attempt in 1929 to have legislation passed in all State Councils wholly banning the import of newspapers and journals 'of the new style'. These measures seem certainly to have been taken and proposed in the hope of stemming the increasing flow of reformist literature from the Straits Settlements, particularly Penang, in the early 1920s ...

[In their protectorate treaties with the Malay Sultanates, the British permitted the Sultans to maintain control of Islam and *adat* within their respective states. In the Straits Settlements, on the other hand, which were under direct British colonial control, a far greater measure of religious diversity and freedom existed. The Settlements, particularly Penang and Singapore, accordingly became 'havens' for Kaum Muda activity, particularly religious publishing.]

But if the conflict between the reformists and religious officialdom was one aspect of the Kaum Muda–Kaum Tua dichotomy, the opposition to rural-centered Islam in the persons of the village *ulama* was another, of equal importance and of the same general characteristics. Indeed, one might say that it was from this class that religious officialdom was in the main drawn. Prior to the coming of the British, as we have seen, education in peninsular Malaya had been entirely in the hands of village religious teachers who, in their homes or in the *surau* and sometimes in the larger *pondok* schools, taught the Islam with which they were familiar: uncomprehending recitation of the Kuran, some elementary exegesis of the Kuran and *hadith*, and Malay-Muslim ethical and behavioral precepts. Often, particularly in more recent times, these teachers had completed the pilgrimage, which gave them additional status and authority, but very few could claim more than the most rudimentary and dogmatic knowledge of Islam, clouded in a haze of traditional Malay spiritual beliefs. For the vast majority of Malay peasants, the transmission of their religion, where it existed systematically at all, was through the village ulama, and this remained true – was indeed intensified – after the provision of government vernacular schools in the rural areas.

In addition to their role in this more or less formal didactic situation, the ulama were culturally important in other and pervasive ways. As imams of village mosques, as the chief religious functionaries at all important junctures of life concerning birth, circumcision, marriage, and death, and at the frequent *kenduri* [feasts] given to mark special occasions; and as the companion to the *bomoh*, or spirit doctor (and sometimes combining the two roles), in the physical and spiritual crises of life, the ulama were regarded as the arbiters of all questions of religion and much else besides. Their relationship with the peasant community of which they were a part was a close and complex one, not easily assailed by those who subscribed to a different system of ideas and values.

As might be expected, it was upon the rural ulama that the full wrath of the Kaum Muda descended. Describing them as 'hawkers of religion', obstacles to progress, and destroyers of the true faith, *Al-Ikhwan*, for example, could write that while for the ulama themselves 'their teaching is aimed only at worldly wealth, ease of living, large houses ... and not at the true Islam ... at the same time they say that those who are ragged, live in dilapidated hovels, have no money and take little trouble to accumulate it, are the sort of people our religion demands'. Ahmad Lutfi, then a Malay student at Al-Azhar, writing in *Seruan Azhar*, refers sarcastically to ulama who 'remain docile out of respect for the *orang besar* [traditional leaders] – and in the hope of gaining reward and office thereby. They collect Kuranic dicta [*ayat*] and *hadith* which serve only to strengthen their own position'. In short, he says, they are fit only to filch from the pockets of the rich and suck the blood of the poor. In their passion to defend Islam against the allegations of obscurantism made by the West, to promote both a more liberal system of education and a more individualistic approach to religious authority, the reformists in article after article castigated the village ulama as the chief hindrances to the attainment of a new world.

But it was not mainly or most importantly through the columns of newspapers and journals that the Kaum Muda–Kaum Tua conflict was fostered at village level. More often it arose as the result of the interests of the villagers themselves. It needed only one haji to return from the Middle East fired with reformist ideas, one religious teacher to study at a Kaum Muda madrasah in Singapore, Perak, or Penang, to divide a village temporarily into two rival factions. And while the main disputes were centered ostensibly around those religious questions already referred to, social questions related to them became easily involved, both as a result of independently arising social change (through the extension of popular, Western-oriented education, the introduction of rubber growing for cash, and a changing economy) and as a result of the wider implications of Kaum Muda ideas. Arguments about whether it was permissible for a Muslim to wear trousers and a tie, and whether taking interest from post office savings banks and rural cooperatives was lawful or not, divided people along the same lines as arguments about whether it was proper to pray at the local *keramat* [spirit shrine] or what was the correct interpretation of a verse of the Kuran. As Schrieke said of Western Sumatra at the same time, the terms 'Kaum Muda' and 'Kaum Tua' came to refer to unanalyzed social conflict of considerable complexity. To be

'Kaum Muda' was to espouse modernism in any form and go against tradition; to be 'Kaum Tua' was to be in favour of all that was familiar, unchanging, and secure.

The politicization of Kaum Muda   In a volume of essays originally published in the *Police Magazine* and collected in 1935 under the title *The Malayan Kaleidoscope*, Haji Abdul Majid b. Zainuddin wrote that there was hardly a village in Malaya where the Malays did not argue and discuss the teachings of Kaum Muda: 'The Kaum Tua or Old Party, from among whom have been recruited the religious officials of the country, try to insinuate in revenge that the Kaum Muda are undesirable Communists, which they decidedly are not.' The politicization of the image of Kaum Muda began to make itself evident only in the mid-1920s, notwithstanding the political implications inherent in reformist ideas prior to this time. Other writers have referred to the role played by Islamic reform in Indonesia as a kind of pre-nationalism. The same may be said of reformism in Malaya, but with the important qualification that, unlike the Indonesian movement, it never succeeded in elaborating, either organizationally or programmatically, a political nationalism capable of attracting mass support. That in other circumstances it might have done so, that there was a political edge to the knife, is clear from an examination of the writings of the polemical wing of the reformist movement in the 1920s. These are to be found primarily in two periodicals published, it may be noted, outside Malaya, by Malay and Indonesian students at the University of Al-Azhar in Cairo: *Seruan Azhar* (Voice of Azhar), 1925–28, and *Pilohan Timour* (Choice of the East), 1927–28.

Malay students had been sent for study to both Mecca and Cairo for some years, but it was only after the First World War, and particularly in the early 1920s with the rise in incomes resulting from the boom in rubber prices, that they travelled to the Middle East in any numbers. The cost of keeping a student in Cairo at this time was estimated at about $500 annually, often more, plus travelling expenses of some $300, so that only well-to-do or well-connected families could afford an education of this kind for their sons. The peak years, corresponding to the most intensive pilgrimage years from Malaya, were probably 1924–27. In 1925, 27 Malay students arrived in Cairo, bringing the total number there to about 80, with some 200 or so from Indonesia. Three years earlier in 1922, the first association of Indonesian and Malay students had been formed at Al-Azhar, Al-Jam'iah Al Khairiah (The Welfare Society), with an Indonesian as president. In October 1925, with the financial backing of a wealthy Malay student, Haji Othman b. Abdullah, the Society started the monthly journal *Seruan Azhar* 'to bring radiance and light to our homeland'. Two years later a second monthly, *Pilehan Timour*, was started, and both continued publication until lack of funds forced their closure in 1928. The two journals were banned by the Dutch in Indonesia but found free entry into the Straits Settlements throughout their lives.

As with earlier newspapers and journals, *Seruan Azhar* and *Pilehan Timour* were much concerned with those topics of a primarily religious kind already dealt with at some length. What now made its appearance for the first time in Malaya was a new and aggressive spirit of overt political discussion. This centered around three main concepts: Pan-Islamism, Pan-Malayanism (union between Indonesia and Malaya), and anti-colonial nationalism. The first of these was the least realistic in political terms and the shortest-lived, hinging as it did on the hopes aroused by the conquest of the Hejaz by the Wahhabi ruler Ibn Saud in 1924 and the ill-fated attempts to resurrect the Caliphate, and organize a rejuvenated Islamic world, which finally came to grief with the failure of the proposed Islamic World Congress at Mecca in 1926 ... International Islamic unity as a political ideal expressed in Pan-Islamism had little force or influence in Malaya in spite of an undoubted interest in the progress, welfare, and government of the Middle Eastern countries. But there was, nevertheless, among the reformist-oriented element, a certain amount of excitement at this time about the possibilities in the idea of a common Islamic renaissance that would command the respect of the West.

More important in the long run was the growth of the idea of a closer union between Malaya and Indonesia. Though not worked out in any detail, or indeed proceeding beyond sentiment and exhortation, some sort of political association between the two areas became a recurring theme in the columns of *Seruan Azhar*. The journal's first editorial, written by Mahmoud el Jounousij, made an appeal for the peoples of Sumatra, Java, Borneo, and Malaya to 'unite with one heart for progress and prosperity'. Much was made of the possession of a common religion and a common language, and numerous articles compared the present state of economic development, education, and political life under the separate colonial regimes. From this developed discussion of colonial rule as the major obstacle to true progress and reform, and it is in this area of discourse that the most outspoken political protests against the status quo occurred. In an article entitled 'What is the Advantage of Freedom?', the Malay writer Abdullah Ahmad wrote concerning the educational systems of Malaya and Indonesia: 'We do not deny that education is necessary for freedom, but we do not believe that education which is given in countries under colonial rule can contain the seeds of freedom. The knowledge that is given to peoples under foreign influence has no purpose other than to impoverish their intellects and teach them to lick the soles of their master's boots.'

This is a far cry from the carefully apolitical reformism advocated by *Al-Imam* twenty years earlier, with its emphasis on the real or imagined sins of the Malays themselves. 'It is not that we say that [the British] are indifferent to our welfare,' Sayyid Shaykh had written in 1906 discussing colonial rule, 'just that they don't do all that they should do, especially in the field of education.' Reformism was becoming more militant, but in doing so it was losing or shedding much of its explicitly religious basis. A new generation of

nationalists was appearing. Though they might have obtained their introduction to nationalism in the wider world by way of the Islamic renaissance,
they were to pursue their goals largely independently of any avowed religious
framework of ideas.

2. The Vietnamese response to French rule

When France began its forward movement in Vietnam after 1850, it confronted an intensely conservative regime, the Nguyen dynasty, that had since
1802 created a rigid Confucian state system and attempted to root out alien
'threats', particularly Christianity. The Nguyens lacked the flexibility to respond
effectively to French pressures, and between 1858 and 1885 the Vietnamese
court dithered between a policy of reluctant accommodation and ineffective
resistance. By the time that the court in Hué called, in 1885, for outright
resistance to the French in the name of the child-emperor Ham Nghi, France
had already gained an unassailable position of power.

As this extract from Hue-Tam Ho Tai's book *Radicalism and the Origins of
the Vietnamese Revolution* shows, the alternatives for the elite generation of
1885 appeared to be either outright resistance to the French, or collaboration
with the French protectorate. The dynasty itself was rapidly brought under
French control after the outbreak of the 1885 rebellion; those who continued
the rebellion, therefore, did so in the name of the Vietnamese people rather
than the dynasty, and were able to seize the patriotic high ground, even if
they were committed to a hopeless struggle.

It was only with the succeeding elite generation – symbolized by Phan
Boi Chau (1867–1940) and Phan Chu Trinh (1871–1926) – that a more subtle
and practical political agenda began to emerge. The keys to the new outlook
were, first, the strategy of learning from the West, not for the purposes of
collaboration, but in order to bring about a transformation of Vietnamese
society; only after such a revolution, it was believed, could Vietnam effectively
confront Western colonial power. The second strategy was that of trying to
build practical links with the two main Asian states that had managed to
retain their independence: China and Japan. Phan Chu Trinh is mainly
associated with the first strategy; Phan Boi Chau with the second.

The battleground in this 'revolution of cultural awareness' lay in the area
of education. In this respect, it is important to reiterate one vital fact about
French rule in most of Vietnam: that it was based, from 1885 to 1945, on
a protectorate arrangement with the Nguyen dynasty. Under the ultimate
authority of the French, the Nguyen continued to govern throughout
northern Vietnam (Tonkin) and central Vietnam (Annam). The reformers
therefore confronted *both* the dynasty and French colonialism. Paradoxically,
they invoked the liberating values of the French Republic to challenge an
instinctively conservative and authoritarian government – the Nguyen dynasty
– whose power was sustained by French colonial rule.

Hue-Tam Ho Tai, *Radicalism and the Origins of the Vietnamese Revolution* (Cambridge, MA: Harvard University Press, 1992). Excerpts taken from pages 13–26.

The Nguyen dynasty had come to power in 1802 after decades of civil war and nearly two centuries of national division. To bring back stability to the nepotism-ridden political system they had inherited, the dynasty's emperors made the Confucian civil service examinations the sole avenue to official appointment. Reacting also to the populist cultural policies of their Tay Son predecessors, they banned the demotic script used to transcribe the Vietnamese vernacular. The demotic script was looked upon by rulers and officials as a tool used by the devious to undermine Confucian orthodoxy, and with it, their legitimacy. Instead of the Vietnamese vernacular, scholars considered Chinese characters to be their own language. Students were taught to read and write Chinese; they learned the Confucian classics, T'ang-style poetry, and Ch'ing-style eight-legged essays. Their ideal was to approximate as closely as possible the learning and the life of their Chinese counterparts. But because of the vagaries of cultural exchanges and their own emphasis on examination-centered learning, Vietnamese literati had only a limited exposure to the range of ideas circulating in China. Furthermore, the generally small size of the academies did not allow for the lively scholarly exchanges that went on in Chinese institutions. What Vietnamese students absorbed, therefore, was often a formalistic kind of knowledge (*van hoc tu chuong*) that sacrificed originality to the goal of passing exams. Required to concentrate on Sung neo-Confucianism, they overlooked the contributions of philosophers whose ideas did not form part of the Nguyen examination curriculum ...

The avowed goal of traditional education was to turn a scholar into a 'superior man' (*quan tu*; Ch. *chun tzu*) through self-cultivation. But self-perfection was only a first step toward political office. The motto of the superior man was: 'Cultivate thyself, set thy house in order, govern thy country, pacify All-Under-Heaven.' Underlying this motto was the assumption that individual self-cultivation led naturally to family management and thence to political rule. An official was regarded as the 'father and mother of the people' (*dan chi phu mau*). It was his responsibility to look after their welfare and, like any father, he expected to be obeyed and respected by them. Teachers, therefore, were supposed to prepare their students not only for the examinations but also for their future role as 'fathers and mothers of the people'. Vietnamese officials clung to this self-image long after French administrators, having usurped the mandarins' power, assumed the rhetorical role of fathers of the immature and wayward Vietnamese population ...

Piety and patriotism Because Confucian social theory conceived of the country as a family writ large, filial piety and family harmony were the twin bases of social and political stability. The various relationships that existed within the family and society were articulated by the Three Bonds: loyalty (*trung*; Ch. *chung*), which a subject owed to his ruler; piety (*hieu*; Ch. *hsiao*), which governed the behaviour of a son toward his father; and fidelity (*nghia*; Ch. *i*), which bound husband and wife together. Ideally, each of the Bonds reinforced the other two. The relationship between ruler and ruled was patterned after the unequal but reciprocal relationship between father and son; the rapport between the emperor and his officials was likened to conjugal fidelity. A husband might repudiate his wife if she proved unsatisfactory (there were seven legitimate grounds for such a move), but a wife owed her husband total fidelity, even after his death. Similarly, the emperor could dismiss his mandarins, though not entirely without cause; but, just as 'a chaste woman may not serve two husbands, a loyal official may not serve two rulers'. Piety was the bedrock upon which the lives of ordinary peasants were built, loyalty the cornerstone of a mandarin's career.

In normal times, public service and family interest neatly dovetailed: a mandarin could at the same time show loyalty to the reigning monarch and promote his family's fortunes, while acting as the father and mother of the common people in his jurisdiction. History, however, often tested the relative strength of the Three Bonds and forced men to choose between them. Plenty of mandarins chose to collaborate with the French and were predictably likened to unchaste women by their detractors. French conquest, however, highlighted the conflict that could erupt between the demands of dynastic loyalty and filial piety.

Each principle was eloquently defended by two men who came from the same village of Dong Thai in Ha Tinh province (Annam) and were even distantly related through marriage: Phan Dinh Phung and Hoang Cao Khai. Both had risen to high positions and enjoyed the respect of their fellow officials. Hoang Cao Khai won a *cu nhon* degree at an early age, then proceeded to gamble away most of his patrimony. Phan Dinh Phung, less brilliant, did not obtain his degree until he was thirty-nine (he became a *tien si* the following year). But he was less erratic than Hoang Cao Khai and was admired for his rigorous, even rigid, adherence to Confucian principles.

This principled inflexibility led to Phan's ouster from the Regency Council in 1883, when he refused to go along with his fellow regents and depose Emperor Tu Duc's chosen heir in favor of another. Phan was too widely admired for the other regents to have him executed, so he was merely confined to his native village. Two years later, the crisis of succession was temporarily over, the regents having installed the twelve-year-old Ham Nghi on the throne and wielding power in his name. By then, the whole of the country had passed into French hands; protectorates had been created in Annam and Tonkin. Belatedly, the regents whisked the young emperor away from the capital and issued a decree ordering a general uprising in his name. In the hills of his native Ha Tinh, Phan Dinh Phung responded by launching the Aid the King Movement (Can Vuong). This was essentially a movement led by scholars and officials like himself and directed at other literati (the French called it the Scholars' Revolt). Hoping to put an end to the Aid the King Movement, the French tried to win Phan Dinh Phung over to their side by playing on his family feelings. They captured his brother and used him as a bait to draw Phan into submission. If Phan agreed to collaborate, he would be rewarded with a high office; if he did not, death awaited his brother and his many relatives in Dong Thai village. This was the message which an old friend, who had surrendered to the French, relayed to Phan in 1886: 'I have to tell you that I passed through Dong Thai recently and saw your ancestral temple and your ancestral tombs all in ruin through neglect; I was so overwhelmed that I cried. Brother Phan, the safety of your relations and your neighbors depends entirely upon you; whether your brother lives or dies also depends entirely upon you.'

In reply, Phan is said to have explained to his comrades-in-arms that he considered the whole nation his family: 'From the time I joined with you in the Aid the King movement, I determined to forget questions of family and village. Now I have but one tomb, a very large one, that must be defended: the land of Vietnam. I have only one brother, very important, who is in danger: more than twenty million countrymen. If I worried about my own tombs, who would worry about defending the tombs of the rest of the country? If I saved my own brother, who would save all the other brothers of our country? There is only one way for me to die now.'

Phan may have been unwilling to put piety before loyalty, but not everyone agreed with his interpretation of the primary duty of a Confucian official. Phan was rare, if not unique, among his contemporaries in speaking of his compatriots as his brothers, and in suggesting that love of country (*ai quoc*; Ch. *ai kuo*) rather than dynastic loyalty (*trung*; Ch. *chung*) was the wellspring of his struggle. There had always been officials who knew how to bow with the prevailing wind in order to protect their families, their tombs, their villages and who believed that Confucian ideology sanctified their priorities. Many were those who looked upon colonial conquest as merely another case of dynastic struggle which could be used to win merit for themselves (*cong*; Ch. *kung*) and safety for their kin by serving the new ruling house. They had an articulate spokesman in Phan's fellow villager, Hoang Cao Khai. In 1894, Khai, who was by then viceroy of Tonkin, wrote to Phan:

> When the capital fell and the emperor had to flee, you rose up in his support. In the context of that time, you did what was right, no one gainsays you. But the situation has changed now; can things go on as before? Even unintelligent and uneducated people have concluded that they cannot. With your superior understanding, is it possible that you do not realize this? I think I perceive your train of thought. You are determined to do whatever you deem right, to devote to it all your efforts and talents. It lies within man's power to do what must be done, though whether it succeeds or not depends on Heaven; one can only give of oneself to one's country, unto death. Therefore, it is up to you to persist in your endeavor, and no one may deter you from your goal.

And yet, when I see the misery our country is plunged in, I am filled with sorrow ... I have always been taught that mandarins should consider the care of the people as fundamental; there has never been anyone who did not love the people and yet was considered loyal to the emperor ... What you have done so far is truly loyal, but what sin have the common people committed that they should be caught in such suffering? It is fine to say that since you are working for the benefit of all, you no longer care for your own family; but how can you also abandon the hundreds of families of your region? I am not concerned only with the green grass of our village of Dong Thai; I am afraid that if you fight on, the whole region around Lam River and Mount Hong will turn into a lake.

Phan Dinh Phung died of hunger and dysentery in the hills one year after that exchange. When a collaborating mandarin discovered where his body was buried, he had it exhumed and burned. Phan's ashes were then shot into the river out of the mouth of a cannon, as was done to the ashes of common criminals. His name and his deeds were proscribed. Hoang Cao Khai, in contrast, died covered with riches and honors, held up by the colonial authorities as an example of true patriotism. Two of his sons became provincial governors; one of them married a royal princess and was a prominent figure in political and cultural circles in the 1920s. Who would not recoil at the cost to himself and his kin that Phan Dinh Phung paid for his interpretation of duty, or be tempted to emulate Hoang Cao Khai's brilliant career? Realizing that Phan was impervious to appeals to his family feelings, Hoang Cao Khai tried in vain to play on his regionalist sympathies. Other literati did not even bother to think in regional terms. Buttressed by un-impeachable Confucian logic, they found it more convenient and profitable to choose family piety over dynastic loyalty.

The exchange between Hoang Cao Khai and Phan Dinh Phung also illustrates competing interpretations of the causes of national defeat. Their differences, anchored in the same basic vision of human life, were a harbinger of future disagreements over the role of personal heroism and historical forces in revolution. According to popular wisdom, a person's life was determined by the interplay of two forces: talent (*tai*; Ch. *tsai*) and destiny (*mang*; Ch. *ming*). Women were popularly considered to be entirely at the mercy of fate, their happiness dependent on the men in their life. Men, however, had the power to exert control over their destiny by making use of whatever talents they possessed and were therefore not supposed to 'fold their arms and accept defeat' (*khoanh tay danh chiu thua*). Instead, they were expected to emulate King Hsia Yu, the mythical flood-tamer, or Yu Kung, who had moved mountains.

This belief in free will coexisted with the fatalistic orientation of much of Vietnamese culture, as evidenced in the poetry of even the most activist of Vietnamese statesmen ... Hoang Cao Khai claimed that in surrendering to the French he was bowing to the Will of Heaven, which had ordained the country's fall to alien rule. Others, however, believed that the history of the

country did not condone defeatism. They saw resistance, rather than acceptance, as Vietnam's recurring theme. It was in the crucible of unceasing
struggle against loss of national independence (*vong quoc*; Ch. *wang kua*) that
the meaning of Vietnam as a nation, a people, and a culture had been
forged. Phan Dinh Phung refused to blame Heaven for the country's woes
and hinted broadly that colonial conquest had been facilitated by the collective
failure of the ruling elite to uphold traditional principles: 'Over the millennia,
our country has only used its civilization to survive from generation to
generation. It does not have a large territory, its army is not powerful, it does
not possess great wealth; the only thing it has to support it is the bond
between ruler and subject, the bond between father and son, and the five
cardinal virtues ... This is why, though China is our neighbour and is vastly
more powerful than our country, yet, in the end, it has never been able to
swallow it up.'

Phan Dinh Phung seemed to suggest that, if only the correct principles
were upheld, then virtue would prevail, and the enemy would be driven out.
Hoang Cao Khai conceded that belief in a preordained fate did not relieve
men of the duty to uphold righteousness. But he was right in pointing out
that Phan was more concerned with acting morally than with pursuing success.

As time went on, success indeed became increasingly elusive. Phan Dinh
Phung's dogged resistance in the face of almost certain defeat was of a
piece with his earlier refusal to follow the lead of his fellow regents: it was
imbued by a very traditional concept of duty. Inspirational as they would be
to future generations, his feats of heroism were performed in the service of
a purely restorationist cause. Phan and other participants in the Aid the King
Movement did not contemplate the reform of Vietnamese society or of its
ruling ideology; they sought only to restore the old order by clinging to
traditional values. The death of Phan Dinh Phung in 1895 signalled not only
the end of his movement but also the beginning of a reappraisal of these
values.

The social Darwinian critique of culture   In the bitter aftermath of failure,
patriotic literati had to come to terms with the fact that nostalgia for a lost
independence was no longer sufficient to sustain the spirit of resistance.
They must be willing to learn from a new enemy, just as they had once
learned from the Middle Kingdom. Out of this painful process of cultural
reorientation was born the Reform Movement. Like Phan's guerrilla war, it
was led by scholars and aimed mainly at other scholars.

This reorientation came about largely as a result of the Social Darwinian
critique of Vietnamese culture. Once this critique was internalized, it was
never stated as explicitly as in early reformist writings. From the beginning,
Social Darwinism was used to discuss inequality between nations; only later
was it applied to individuals as well. But survival of the nation remained the
underlying theme of political discourse.

To the Vietnamese, Social Darwinism was a revelation. It provided an explanation of their country's downfall which was both familiar and startlingly new: Vietnam had indeed fallen prey to a mightier country, but its conqueror's might lay in its cultural superiority. Accustomed to using cultural criteria to gauge a country's health, Vietnamese literati easily accepted the thrust of this argument. At the same time, much of the suasive power of Social Darwinism lay in its unfamiliar worldview which, instead of celebrating equilibrium and harmony, exalted the notion of unceasing competition for supremacy and survival among actors endowed with unequal gifts and resources.

Vietnamese reformers were first exposed to the ideas of Herbert Spencer, the father of Social Darwinism, by (the Chinese) K'ang Yu-wei and his disciple Liang Ch'i-ch'ao. But it was K'ang's contemporary, the scholar and translator Yen Fu, who introduced Herbert Spencer to the Chinese reading public. In Vietnam, the first mention of Herbert Spencer came in an anonymous pamphlet written in 1904 to launch the Reform Movement, *The Civilization of New Learning (Van minh tan hoc sach)*. Its preamble could have been written by Yen Fu himself, so closely did it follow his logic. It argued that ideas alone were insufficient for the maintenance of civilization; competition, too, was required. In fact, the more ideas, the more competition; and the more competition, the more ideas were generated. Vietnam, however, had a passive rather than a dynamic civilization, which venerated the old and native and despised the new and foreign, thus inhibiting the generation of new ideas. It undervalued the importance of self-strengthening. The West exalted the people; the Vietnamese revered the ruler and paid no attention to rural conditions. All this, argued the anonymous author, should be changed.

Whereas for its Western and Chinese advocates, Social Darwinism seemed an essentially optimistic vision, to the Vietnamese it offered a bleaker scenario for the future. If only the fittest prevailed, would the country, whose weak state had already led to foreign conquest, be able to survive? Was the annihilation of the Vietnamese nation, people, and culture already determined or would human effort succeed in reversing course? Yen Fu had tempered the determinism inherent in Social Darwinism with a voluntarist dimension; so did the Vietnamese literati who embraced it. The proposals contained in *The Civilization of New Learning* were close kin to Chinese self-strengthening programs. But Vietnamese reformers dared not hope, as their Chinese counterparts did, that the reforms they advocated would enable their country to compete with the West on more equal terms and emerge victorious. All they dared hope for was survival. Their pleas thus had a more urgent and desperate ring than the pronouncements of the Chinese writers who inspired them.

The difference in outlook between Chinese and Vietnamese reformers is illustrated in an exchange that took place in Tokyo between the Vietnamese scholar Phan Boi Chau and the Chinese scholar-statesman Liang Ch'i-ch'ao in 1905. Liang, reports Phan, had been moved to tears by his description of

Vietnam's loss of independence and urged him to publicize it. Vietnam's loss of independence could serve as a warning to Chinese people of the danger they themselves were facing. He advised Phan to produce 'a serious literary presentation to the world of the plight of Vietnam in the face of France's policy of extermination'. Such a work would also encourage 'Vietnamese youth to study overseas as a start to awakening popular consciousness and improving the general level of education'. Heeding this advice, Phan wrote his *History of the Loss of Vietnam* (*Viet Nam vong quoc su*). Liang provided a preface and arranged to have the book published in his journal *Renovation of the People* (*Hsin-min ts'ung-pao*) in 1905.

What for Liang Ch'i-ch'ao was a cautionary tale was for Phan a national tragedy. 'For a human being, the greatest suffering comes from losing his country.' Thus began the *History of the Loss of Vietnam*. It was this sense of loss that spurred Phan and others to reform.

Reform and its advocates   Phan Boi Chau's advocacy of foreign learning formed part of a larger program of self-strengthening measures. Its center-piece was a call to jettison Chinese characters, upon which the whole edifice of classical learning reposed, in favor of the romanized script. First developed by traders and missionaries in the seventeenth century, the romanized script faithfully reproduced the sound and syntax of spoken Vietnamese; it thus had the potential for bridging the gap between elite and popular cultures, an objective whose importance to the anticolonial struggle was gaining recognition. But it was also associated with foreign rule. The colonial authorities promoted its use because it was easier to master than Chinese characters; furthermore, they hoped that abandoning Chinese characters would lead to the decline of classical learning and with it the legitimacy of the scholarly elite and the values that had nurtured resistance to French rule. It was therefore not without a great deal of agonized soul-searching that scholars in Tonkin and Annam allowed themselves to be persuaded of the need to learn the romanized script and new ways of looking at the world. In 1907 a group of scholars, inspired by Fukuzawa Yukichi's Keio University [in Japan], opened the Tonkin Free School (Dong Kinh Nghia Thuc). There they taught the rudiments of the new script, expounded the ideas of Chinese reformist scholars, and introduced names associated with the Enlightenment or with European nationalism into the political discourse.

The men who participated in the Reform Movement were a mixed group. Some wanted cultural change for its own sake, others because they saw it as a prerequisite for the success of anticolonial action. Phan Boi Chau was the foremost representative of the instrumentalist perspective on linguistic and educational reforms. Born in Nghe An in 1867, Phan was already eighteen when Annam fell to the French. After he became involved in the Aid the King Movement, he soon found out that his lack of a degree was a handicap among status-conscious literati. After his father became ill, he temporarily forsook political engagement for family affairs, all the while trying to succeed in the examination system. Finally, in 1900, Phan passed the regional exams with highest honors. Around that time, calls for cultural reform, which had fallen on stony ground in the 1860s, began circulating again among Vietnamese literati in the wake of the Chinese Reform Movement of 1898. Phan Boi Chau was introduced to the ideas of Rousseau and Montesquieu and to the names of nineteenth-century nationalists such as Mazzini and Cavour through the writings of Liang Ch'i-ch'ao, K'ang Yu-wei, and other Chinese reformers.

Despite his own inability to master it, as well as lingering misgivings, Phan became an enthusiastic advocate of using the romanized script as the vehicle for the new Western-inspired learning which he deemed necessary for a modern nation. For him, as for Yen Fu, the recovery of independence rather than the preservation of culture was paramount, for without the nation, how could the people and culture survive? The transformation of culture was thus less a matter of intrinsic value than of strategic necessity. But Yen Fu had been a true scholar, whereas Phan was more action oriented. Knowledge, for him, was not so much the key to self-discovery as part of a panoply of anticolonial devices. When Phan launched the Eastern Travel Movement in 1905, it was to enable students to go to China and Japan to accumulate the knowledge necessary to eventually overthrow foreign rule. His first commitment remained to political struggle, including armed struggle. In his *History of the Loss of Vietnam*, he interspersed veiled incitements to armed struggle with calls to study abroad. His basic lack of interest in cultural issues for their own sake resulted, however, in a lack of ideological sophistication, which was to vitiate his tireless efforts to create viable anticolonial movements.

A more truly culturalist approach was advocated by Phan Chu Trinh. Phan Chu Trinh, who also hailed from central Vietnam, received a degree in the metropolitan examinations of 1900, the year that Phan Boi Chau passed the regional exams. Unlike Phan Boi Chau, he had been too young to take part in the Aid the King Movement. His father, who had been involved, was assassinated during its dying days for reasons that remain obscure. Although his father died at the hands of fellow insurgents, Phan Chu Trinh blamed the monarchy for his death. Perhaps because of this event, which occurred when he was entering his teens, Phan Chu Trinh remained a lifelong foe of violence. Believing that a gradualist path was the way to avoid bloodshed, he was willing to defer independence until such time as the Vietnamese had undergone a thorough cultural and social transformation. While critical of colonial rule, he reserved his undiluted hatred for the Vietnamese imperial court, which he held responsible for the sorry state of the nation. He spent fourteen years in exile in France and, although he never learned French, he found much in French culture and political institutions worth adopting. Phan Chu Trinh was at heart a true reformer; Phan Boi Chau, the pioneer of the Revolution.

Though the Reform Movement was dominated by classically trained scholars such as Phan Chu Trinh and Phan Boi Chau, it also attracted a considerable number of graduates of the School of Interpreters. The School had opened in Hanoi in 1886 to train staff for the lower ranks of the colonial administration in Tonkin. In embracing Western learning and becoming part of the apparatus of foreign domination, graduates of the School, who were known as scholars of New Learning to distinguish them from Confucian literati, laid themselves open to suspicions of disloyalty. But many of them sincerely believed that they were working for the betterment of their country. They took part in the Reform Movement out of conviction that Vietnamese culture and society had reached a dead end. Their enthusiasm for linguistic and educational reform also derived in no small measure from the fact that, at one stroke, it vindicated their own training and careers and transformed them from cultural brokers of uncertain social standing and suspect loyalties into members of the intellectual and patriotic avant-garde ...

In Cochinchina, the Reform Movement took on distinct characteristics. After four decades of colonial rule, most educated southerners were already conversant with the romanized script. There was thus no need to fight a battle that had already been won. Southern patriots even succeeded in using Vietnamese-language newspapers such as *Agrarian Tribune* (*Nong Co Min Dam*) and *News from the Six Provinces* (*Luc Tinh Tan Van*) to spread reformist propaganda discreetly. Instead of emphasizing the need for new ideas and a new educational system, southern reformers concentrated on launching business ventures in competition with Chinese traders (and less overtly, with French settlers). They opened rice mills, fish sauce plants, hotels, restaurants, servicing shops, grocery stores. Revenues from such ventures went into supporting various anticolonial activities, in particular the sending of students to Japan and China ...

Getting scholars involved in the grubby world of commercial endeavor was only one component in a wide-ranging attempt to update Confucian values. Trade was made palatable by being presented as a patriotic endeavor. But it was filial piety, the bedrock of Vietnamese society, which attracted the most discussion. The redefinition of filial piety was occasioned by the recognition that the rift between filiality and loyalty must be healed so that piety could serve the cause of patriotism. The first efforts were quite modest. In the past, it had been argued that it was unfilial to cut one's hair or nails: like the rest of the body, they were gifts from one's parents. Now, reformers claimed it was more hygienic, and thus a higher form of piety, to keep them trimmed and clean. The demands of family duty remained unquestioned; what had changed was their concrete expression. In retrospect, therefore, the redefinition of filial piety was much less revolutionary than it appeared at the time, despite the anguish and controversy it provoked.

These attempts to reconcile piety and loyalty occurred as the institution of the monarchy was becoming increasingly hollow. Ever since Ham Nghi had fled the capital in 1885, the French had controlled the imperial succession.

In 1907 they deposed Thanh Thai, whom they had installed on the throne two decades earlier, and replaced him with his son, the child emperor Duy Tan. In the absence of a strong imperial presence, an imperceptible shift from dynastic loyalty to a less narrow patriotism was taking place.

3. Indonesia: The dilemmas of Westernization

In Vietnam, a strong pre-colonial state and pre-colonial Vietnamese identity meant that a modern nationalist programme could evolve within an existing framework. In maritime Southeast Asia, there was no such coherence of identity within the borders of the colonial states created by the British and the Dutch. In a sense, therefore, anti-colonialism preceded nationalism. As we have seen in the case of Malaya, so in the Netherlands Indies there was a strong sense in the new educated generation of the early twentieth century that the power of the *ancien régime* – represented by the conservative Islamic establishments and the elites of the regional states that had succumbed to colonial rule – would have to be challenged, reformed or by-passed before a rejuvenated, modern indigenous society could deal with the overriding question of how to confront European power. In the early stages of the twentieth century, however, many of these reformers thought in terms of working within a pan-Islamic rather than national unit; others planned for some kind of 'pan-Malay' unity that would straddle the Dutch and British colonial areas.

It was only gradually, therefore, that the concept of an Indonesian nation came into being. The entrenching of a dialect of Malay – generally used throughout the archipelago as the language of commerce – as the Indonesian national language (*bahasa Indonesia*) played a key role in this development. In addition, the fact that most of the prestigious educational facilities in the Netherlands Indies were concentrated in Java meant that the sons and daughters of the elites of the outer islands congregated together; this inevitably helped develop a sense of common interest, identity and purpose.

S. Takdir Alisjahbana (born 1908), one of Indonesia's most distinguished intellectuals and writers, himself played a key role in Indonesia's cultural and social revolution before the Second World War. In the following extract from his book, *Indonesia: Social and Cultural Revolution*, he bears personal witness to this vital era of transformation; to the sense of liberation from the shackles (*belenggu*) of the *ancien régime* that it gave the new generation of educated youth; but also to the divisions between generations that it created in Indonesian society.

S. Takdir Alisjahbana, *Indonesia: Social and Cultural Revolution* (Kuala Lumpur: Oxford University Press, 1966). Excerpts taken from pages 23–64.

Education in a dualistic society By the second half of the nineteenth century, when Indonesians at last began to come into closer contact with and thus under the influence of modern culture, Indonesian society and culture had in effect ceased developing. Everywhere the old intellectual energy, creative enthusiasm, and desire for wider fields of experience on the foundations of traditional society and culture had ebbed away, and the old *élan* had become exhausted. One can compare what happened to a river which cataracts down the mountainside until it reaches the plain below, where it loses all further impetus in a stagnant marsh. In the villages, life in all its aspects became fossilized under traditional law and custom dominated by the village elders. One day was like the next. In aristocratic circles men lived in the shadow of past glories. They evaded the challenging realities of life by escaping into a world of fantasy: the great moral and intellectual qualities, which should be exercised in ordinary everyday life, were dissipated in a round of futile trivial activities, such as the interpretation of old myths and legends. In the world of religious and spiritual experience, bold speculation and real depth of feeling dried up completely in the arid repetition of Koranic tropes and ancient commentaries. It was rare, indeed, for anyone to attempt to probe and explore the ultimate meaning of religious faith. Over the whole range of human experience the dead hand of the past weighed heavily; men kept their gaze fixed on the past without the confidence or the courage to look forward to the future.

It was this static world that modern culture came to destroy. The interference of the colonial government in village administration, in the law and courts, and the growing entry of Western initiative and organizational power into the fields of production and communication, confronted the world of the village communities, the aristocracy, and the religious groups, with new realities. Willy-nilly, men gradually became aware that there existed, apart from, and even above, their own way of life, another culture, far more vital, full of initiative, and particularly successful in dealing with all the more mundane, practical affairs of life. And then Indonesians came to feel, little by little, their own weakness and deficiencies *vis-à-vis* the foreign infidels, who had used their superior technical skills and equipment gradually to dominate their country. Faced with this scientific and technical superiority, and more particularly with the vastly higher standards of living enjoyed by the Europeans, it was at first very common for ordinary Indonesians to resign themselves to their inferiority as something in the natural order of things.

But luckily this situation did not last long, chiefly because the colonial government finally felt the necessity of giving a school education to various small groups in Indonesian society, to enable them to serve in the civil service or in private economic organizations. As a result of this educational drive an increasing number of Indonesians began to participate in the European way of life. Those Indonesians who were able to acquire a school education and who gradually managed to assume positions within the government bureaucracy or in private economic organizations, slowly undermined the position not merely of the religious and village authorities but even of the feudal hierarchy. To become an official of the colonial government or to hold a position in a European enterprise meant being accepted into a new *milieu* – the most advanced sector of colonial society. Naturally Indonesians began to set a value on the school education which the colonial government was now providing in some areas. Thus one can observe the slow process of changing values and social norms which accompanied the gradual transformation of Indonesian society and culture ...

The value attached to modern education was constantly rising as the century drew to a close. In the first two decades of the twentieth century particularly, the desire to go to school became so strong that 'more schools' came to be the most important popular demand ... Merely by living through this period, in which education was merely a means to a good job and a high social position, Indonesia gradually came to understand the wider significance of modern education for modern life. And once this new belief had taken root, however much modern education the colonial government provided, they could not possibly satisfy the demands of the Indonesian people. As a result, a series of schools organized by the Indonesians themselves, began to spring up like mushrooms alongside of the government schools, to an extent that seriously alarmed the colonial government ...

At this point I think it would be unfair to point only to the colonial government's selfish aims in giving some Indonesians a modern education. Social changes in Europe, particularly since the French Revolution which had popularized the idea of the Rights of Man, and the rise of organized movements demanding rights for workers, women, etc. – all of which can be summarized briefly as the demand for humaneness in a democratic society – aroused the conscience even of the colonial government. This conscience found its expression in the ethical orientation of the colonial administration. As a result, the act of establishing schools for Indonesians, aside from enabling the Dutch to recruit personnel for the government bureaucracy and the larger private enterprises, was also motivated by the humanitarian outlook which had become so influential in European society and culture in the eighteenth and nineteenth centuries.

When the Indonesians became genuinely aware of the significance of modern education and modern scientific knowledge, and started an incessant clamour for more of both, the Dutch began to realize that by providing this modern education they were gradually destroying their own position in Indonesia, that they were making themselves superfluous to Indonesian society. Those Dutch groups who were of the ethical persuasion accepted this outcome as a fulfilment of their historical task. But this did not mean that even the most progressive and ethically-minded were prepared for anything more than a slow evolutionary process of emancipation. And those Dutch groups which saw their own and their society's interests directly involved in the fate of colonialism, and thus were determined to maintain the colonial relationship for ever, could not help seeing in the expansion of education and the dissemination of knowledge, a terrible threat to the position of Dutch colonialism in Indonesia. From their own point of view, of course, they were quite right. It was undeniable that educated Indonesians were learning to respect themselves. Thanks mainly to their newly acquired under-standing of contemporary concepts and theories of freedom and justice (which they were taught in school), and their growing confidence in their ability to adjust to the atmosphere of modern culture, these Indonesians came gradually to ask both for themselves and for their fellow-Indonesians all the rights and opportunities that defenders of human rights fought for in Europe from the Renaissance onwards. And so the secondary schools and colleges in which young Indonesian men and women were getting a good modern education – very similar to that which young Dutch men and women were getting in Holland (one has to say this much for Dutch schools in Indonesia) – formed the nuclei for all the movements of national awakening in the twentieth century. These movements in turn sired all kinds of national-ist movements, and were in the last analysis the decisive factor in the struggle for Indonesian Independence and for the elimination of Dutch colonialism from Indonesian soil.

The modern education granted to the Indonesians, however, eventually became not only a tragedy for the Dutch but also for the Indonesians themselves. Especially for the old Indonesian society and culture, the so-eagerly demanded modern education resulted in innumerable conflicts and sufferings. Gradually the Indonesian people came to see the advantages of modern education. It provided them with better jobs and higher positions, raised their standard of living, improved their social standing, and provided them with a body of scientific knowledge of the utmost importance for modern living. This was all very appropriate for the children of the nobility and the local notables. By acquiring modern education they could maintain their former status within the new social order. There were also many members of the middle classes and the intelligentsia who found that they could use modern education to improve their social standing. In areas where local notables were of little importance, it was the teachers who stepped into the limelight. Because of their superior *savoir-faire* they not only became highly respected counsellors to their local communities, but also acted as the mouthpiece of these communities and as their representatives on official occasions. The common people would often come to talk over their problems with them. Many of these problems and difficulties were directly related to social and cultural changes of increasing complexity brought about either by the direct intervention of the colonial government or by the natural develop-ment of Indonesian society.

It is not therefore surprising that the group comprising local notables, teachers, and other officials, who had tasted the fruits of modern education to a greater or less extent, made enormous efforts to give their children the best possible modern education – at least as good an education as they had received themselves, and if possible better.

It is now generally recognized that in this period Indonesian parents made colossal sacrifices to educate their children. Since often there were no elementary or secondary schools where their children could be taught in their own villages or local towns, the parents would often send them away to other villages and towns. The more advanced the school, the farther the children were from their parents. And since, up to the outbreak of the Second World War, secondary and higher schools were to be found as a rule only in a few large cities in Java, many children from outside these cities, and especially from the Outer Islands, had to go to schools which were as much as one or two weeks sailing distance from their homes ... Thus the cost of sending a child to school was usually extremely high. It was not uncommon for more than half the parents' income to be spent in supporting one or two children studying far away. Every conceivable economy was practised in the home, and the other children were often neglected. And yet all these economies and sacrifices were accepted gladly. The whole family lived in the expectation that their situation would automatically improve once the child, who was now studying so far away, completed his education. If such thoughts and hopes could inspire families to undergo all these hardships and sacrifices, they also contained within them the seeds of future strife and disappointment. And the real tragedy only began when the child, of whom so much was expected, finally finished his studies, and the hopes that had been nursed for so long seemed on the verge of attainment.

Very often the first conflicts and disappointments centred around the choice of a wife. A boy who had grown up far from home naturally tended to choose a girl from 'foreign parts', whom he had got to know in the course of his studies, or who perhaps had even been a fellow-student. His parents and relatives, who had imagined from the time the boy was still a tiny child, that he would marry a girl from the local community, were bitterly disappointed. To them the girl that their son was bringing back from far away would always be a stranger. The depth of the disappointment and the bitterness of the conflicts likely to arise in such cases can only be understood if one realizes the enormous importance attached to marriage and the choice of a daughter-in-law in a small traditional community. In such communities marriage did not merely represent the union of boy and girl, but a further extension of all kinds of family relationships and social connexions, ordered according to strict rules and conventions, ceremonies and customs, handed down from generation to generation. It is thus not altogether surprising that in the literature of the younger Indonesian generation, which began to appear in this atmosphere of conflict between modern and traditional Indonesian culture, the conflict, in all its aspects, was a major theme. Moreover the theme was not a mere figment of the writer's imagination, but was born of the bitter ordeal of the struggle between two societies and cultures with totally different structures and values.

It should now be obvious that the conflicts that arose between parents and children on the subject of marriage, were not just isolated phenomena, but one kind of manifestation of differences and antagonisms with far broader and deeper ramifications.

Living for many years far from his parents and relatives, in a society with entirely different customs and ways of thinking, inevitably estranged a man not only from his parents and family, but also from the values, manners and customs of his native community. When he returned to this community he felt ill at ease; his manners and behaviour were stiff and awkward. He found the outlook and the values of even his closest blood-relatives completely alien to him. This feeling was naturally reciprocated. His parents and relatives felt and observed his awkwardness, and found it hard to recognize him as a member of their cultural community. Quite apart from the lack of opportunities for economic advance in the modern sense in such a small community, this was of course one of the reasons why few of those who got an extended modern education ever returned to work in the communities into which they had been born ...

Essentially, without realizing what it was doing in sending its children to school and thus exposing them to modern culture, the old society destroyed itself and its culture. The great barriers which, built from values, ways of thought, conceptions, standards and customs handed down from generation to generation, had lasted for centuries, began to crumble away, and there was nothing that could preserve them from the encircling floodtide of the modern age.

The impact of the new literature In literature particularly, the antagonism between traditional views which clung to a backward-looking social tradition, and the new individualistic attitude of looking to the future, was strongly felt. The acceptance of the new cultural attitude resulted in three quite distinctive patterns in Indonesian literature.

Firstly, by freeing themselves from the bonds of tradition, people found the courage to think for themselves, to search for their own identities, and to accept the consequences of their own actions. In the broadest sense this meant the rise of Individualism in Indonesian literature – an Individualism which aimed at the development of the individual, expressed in artistic creations reflecting that individuality.

Secondly, this liberation involved a revolt against old prejudices and conventions. Everything old was regarded as static conservatism, standing in the way of growth and progress. The contents of the literary productions of the period, which were generally rebellious and hostile to accepted ideas, customs and social conventions, show this quite plainly ...

Finally, the writer was forced to pay closer attention to the realities of life.

He stopped writing stories about gods and kings, and turned his attention to the circumstances and problems of real life. His language became more objective. He tried to depict what he really saw and to avoid the old clichés. (We can perhaps call this movement a trend towards Realism in the new Indonesian literary world.) He also attempted to compose his narratives more logically, and more consistently with the laws of society and the human personality ...

Though the birth of this new literature was partly stimulated by the influence of the economic, social and political changes of the period, it was also a direct result of school instruction and reading of the masterpieces of modern literature, at first mainly of Dutch literature. By studying European languages Indonesians mastered European ways of thinking. Their ideas of beauty were more or less modified and adapted to those prevailing in Europe at the time.

In relation to the direct influence of European literature on the young Indonesians who read so much of it in Dutch (because that was the language they knew best), it might be interesting to know that some of this early Indonesian literature was actually written in Dutch. The poets found the new thoughts and feeling stirring within them far easier to express in Dutch than in their own language. The magazines put out by the younger generation at that time included not only essays but even poetry written in Dutch. In fact, the most important literary work produced by an Indonesian around the turn of the century, the letters of Raden Adjeng Kartini, was written in Dutch and later published under the title of *Door Duisternis tot Licht* (Translated into English as *Letters of a Javanese Princess*). These letters describe the spiritual rebellion of a twenty-year-old girl against the aristocratic tradition that held her prisoner. Although the letters were not written with a deliberate literary purpose, but simply to pour out the ideas, hopes and aspirations of her overburdened heart, the writer's natural gifts and understanding of the Dutch language raised them to the level of real literature.

Between the letters of Raden Adjeng Kartini and the rise of a genuinely Indonesian literature, written in Indonesian, there is a gap of no less than twenty years. In this period was born the nationalist movement out of a new feeling of self-respect and personal responsibility, and cherishing a desire for progress within the modern world based on the Indonesian people's own efforts and capabilities. Spurred by its awareness that the colonial government would possibly never give the Indonesian people a chance to develop intellectually and physically, the movement felt compelled to return to Indonesia's own society and culture for support. The old interest in Dutch, which the colonial government could never afford to satisfy, because it feared that knowledge of the language would enable the Indonesians to advance too rapidly, was gradually diverted to a language native to the inhabitants of Indonesia. This new Indonesian-language literature began to flourish in the early twenties and was patronized both by the government-owned publishing house known as the *Balai Pustaka*, and by the advocates of the nationalist movement. Its predominant theme was the confrontation of the younger generation with its modern education and the traditional community, and the overwhelming importance of this encounter for Indonesians everywhere. In the previous chapter I pointed out how the conflict between the older and younger generations came to a head in the problem of marriage. There was a bitter conflict between young people's feeling of love as conceived in a modern individualistic society, and the duty to parents and family that traditional culture demanded. This common theme (the struggle against forced marriages; the struggle against polygamy; the struggle to preserve the love of two individuals in the face of the class prejudices of traditional society) ran, in one form or another, through all Indonesian literature published between the Wars. In the writings of this period one can see that disappointment and bitterness were felt on both sides − by the young people who were trying to shape their lives according to the ideas they had acquired from modern education, and by the older people who could not comprehend the destruction of all the hopes and beliefs that they had inherited from their forebears ...

Creating a new national language It was possible for Malay to become a *lingua franca* mainly because it was easy to learn. In Malay there are no levels as there are in Javanese, where different words are used to express the same idea depending on the age, rank and social position of the person to whom they are addressed. A foreigner wanting to learn Javanese would therefore have in reality to learn more than one language. In addition to this advantage Malay was easily simplified in intercourse with foreigners into a 'low' or 'bazaar' Malay ...

[If Malay was the natural 'lingua franca' in the East Indies, Dutch was the language of the colonial power, the language of Christian missionary work, and the language of social advancement. It was also the language that gave access to European ideas.]

The turn of the twentieth century saw the rise of an ethical trend in colonial policy which tried to impart to the Indonesians some understanding of European culture by teaching them something of the knowledge and the methodology of Western civilization. When Mr. J. H. Abendanon became the Director of the Department of Education in 1900, he made strenuous efforts to foster and spread the use of Dutch throughout Indonesia. He was convinced that a knowledge of Dutch would be the shortest way for the Indonesian people to absorb Western culture. He instituted courses in Dutch in the People's Schools (providing six years of education), and later made Dutch a compulsory subject in these schools from the 3rd to the 6th class. As a result Dutch became an extremely important subject of study in the Teachers' Colleges.

In 1908 Indonesians put forward their demands with regard to Dutch instruction for the first time. The First Congress of the *Budi Utomo* (High Endeavour), held in Djakarta, was the first general gathering of culturally-conscious educated Indonesians. On that occasion the Congress demanded that standards for admission into Dutch schools be relaxed, and that special schools be set up for those Indonesian children who wanted to carry their study of Dutch further than the elementary level. People were no longer satisfied that Dutch was merely one subject among a number of others; they realized that the scanty knowledge of Dutch thus acquired barred their children from continuing their education beyond a certain point. When Hazeu became Director of the Department of Education, Dutch began to be taught in the People's Schools from the 1st class upwards. But it was only in 1914 that the demands of *Budi Utomo* were recognized and carried out fully. In that year the Dutch Government established the Dutch-Native Schools, which used Dutch over a seven-year period, so that children who had completed their studies there could carry on their education to the most advanced levels ...

Meanwhile the problem of a national language for the Indonesian people gradually changed in character. Since 1908 the Indonesian intelligentsia had struggled to create organizations to stir the consciousness of the common people and encourage their development and progress. But they had slowly come to realize that they would never be able to create close ties with the body of people by using Dutch, which would never be understood by more than a tiny minority of Indonesians. On the premise that only by uniting the entire Indonesian people could they generate a force strong enough to challenge the colonial power, they began spontaneously to look for a language which could be understood by the great majority of the people. And so their attention was drawn to Malay, which as I have said before, had been the *lingua franca* throughout the Indonesian archipelago for centuries ... With the growing development of a consciousness of Indonesian nationality, and the rapid advances made by movements striving for Indonesian unity under the stimulus of this new consciousness, the use of Malay became increasingly widespread. But it was principally the youth movements which made the final decision in favour of developing Malay.

At the First Congress of Indonesian Youth, held in 1926, Muhammad Yamin was still talking in Dutch about the future possibilities of Indonesian language and literature. But two years later, on 28 October 1928, at the Second Congress, held in Djakarta, the Youth of Indonesia took an oath to the effect that they belonged to One nation, the Indonesian nation, had One mother-country, Indonesia, and One language, the Indonesian language. It was at this Congress that the word Malay was replaced by 'Indonesian' to describe the language. The decision not only settled the nomenclature of the language, but its place in Indonesian society. The competition between Dutch and Indonesian now came to an end. The decision, of course, also meant an acceptance of the obligation to develop the Indonesian language to enable it to replace Dutch as a means of entry into modern world culture. It is in this light that we should regard the appearance in 1933 of the magazine *Pudjangga Baru* (new writers), edited by Amir Hamzah, Armijn Pané and myself. *Pudjangga Baru* was a magazine designed to promote the Indonesian language and its literature. All the political and cultural leaders of Indonesia rallied to its support. It was the same group that took the initiative for holding the First Indonesian Language Congress in Surakarta in 1938. Notable among the resolutions passed by this Congress was its affirmation of the need to create an institute and a faculty for the study of Indonesian, to decide on technical terminology, create a new orthography, and codify a new grammar in accordance with the changes taking place in the structure of the language. In addition the Congress advanced a demand that Indonesian be made the language of the laws and the medium of exchange in the various 'representative bodies'. But all these resolutions remained on paper. There was no organization behind the Congress which could put them into effect. As a result, the really important development of the Indonesian language came later, during the Japanese occupation.

CHAPTER 3

Revolution and Constitutional Change, 1900–41

Oh come and witness our oath, O Bramah and all great Nats (spirits) of this world and the world above. O, deign to tarry a little and witness this our promise. Grant that I may live a hundred years and prosper if I keep this oath, and that from this day I may be delivered out of the hand of the infidel. Grant that I may help to destroy all unbelievers and that the strength of their captains and the might of their arms may be turned to water, so that they may not prevail against me. (Part of the Rebel Oath of the Saya [Hsaya] San Rebellion in Burma, 1930–31)

The question of colonial strategies

As has been seen in the previous chapter, in this era of the high tide of imperial dominance, the idea of the break-up of empires did not even appear on the horizon as an issue for the colonial powers. There *was* a growing notion of the need for change within imperial structures, but only in the limited sense that the newly created, educated, Westernized indigenous elite could become participants and possible eventual junior partners in empire.

The only clear exception was United States rule in the Philippines. Here there was always an ambiguity about the whole 'project' of empire, arising from the two opposing political visions dominating the American political debate: American pride in their 'anti-colonial' heritage, and the notion of their 'Manifest Destiny' that had crystallized during the American expansion westwards. Despite the fact that the United States had inherited imperial rule from the Spanish in the Philippines in 1898, steps were rapidly taken to co-opt the native landowning elite that had appeared in the Spanish period and to make moves in partnership towards self-government. Although this policy was slowed down just after the First World War by the question of the 'fitness to rule' of this elite, it was accelerated again during the Depression by the demands of economic interests in the United States itself. The convenience of working with the native landowning elite eventually took precedence over the notion that the colonial power had to 'prepare' elites for governing responsibilities and at the same time broaden the base of that governing elite through an ever-widening education policy (see 'The Philippines: the path to self-government', p. 53).

In the European colonies, the notion that the imperial power had a duty to prepare native political elites for greater political responsibility was considerably enhanced by the First World War. The sight of the main imperial powers fighting each other in a full-scale European war dealt a crippling blow to the 'prestige' that had underpinned imperial rule; it also indicated the potential vulnerability of the imperial powers in Southeast Asia. It is not an exaggeration to say that the decline of the whole European imperial structure can be dated from these war years. The war also popularized – particularly via President Wilson – the notion of the right of all peoples to 'self-determination'. Although this concept was in the end only applied to Europe in the peace settlement, it naturally lent credibility to anti-colonial activities. Britain was forced, both by the need for Indian support in its war effort and by moral pressure on the issue of self-determination, to make a commitment in 1917 to greater indigenous participation in government in India, and this by extension affected Burma. Accordingly, there was a considerable degree of constitutional change in Burma after the First World War, over the whole period from 1919 to 1939 (see 'Burma: the relationship between rural revolt and nationalist organization', p. 60).

It should be noted, however, that the experience of the First World War, particularly the desperate search for manpower to maintain the war economies of France and Britain, gave a boost to the notion that imperial possessions were vital for the protection and enhancement of national power. Thus the sense of the 'value' of empire was, if anything, strengthened after the war, and this helped to block the avenues to radical constitutional reform or rapid moves towards political participation and self-government. For example, while some minor political reforms were introduced in the Dutch East Indies – particularly the formation of the so-called *Volksraad* (People's Council) in 1916–18, with limited powers and severely restricted native representation – these changes were followed by a period of stagnation that lasted until the Second World War.

In the case of French rule in Indochina, the impetus for change was to a degree blocked, not only by a strong sense of the 'value' of empire for France, but also by the colonial 'logic' of the French themselves. While their strategy of 'assimilation' meant that Cochinchina was in theory destined to become an integral part of Overseas France, their protectorate policy in the rest of Indochina committed them to the preservation of native regimes that would themselves feel threatened by constitutional change.

The indigenous response to imperial rule: the framework of resistance

There *were* individuals and groups who actively co-operated with these imperial projects, for a variety of reasons. For the majority of the new educated generation living under colonial rule, however, 'learning from the West' did not imply any acquiescence in a permanently subordinate position. The sense of loss and defeat remained; strategies for regeneration, however, were expressed in a new European idiom. As the period of traditional resistance in the mid- to late nineteenth century had shown, a mere clinging to the old structures and values of the pre-colonial states – the *ancien régime* – was not enough in the era of the permeation of Western civilization.

In the search for a framework of resistance to European colonial rule in the early twentieth century, the new Westernized political elite of Southeast Asia looked abroad for models. These were provided by the Islamic reform movement in Egypt and the Middle East of the late nineteenth and early twentieth centuries which sought to modernize and regenerate Islam, and thereby resist European incursions into the region; and by the remarkable example of Japan which had not only maintained its independence through the period of imperial expansion, but had also systematically modernized its government while at the same time safeguarding its traditional cultural values. The most immediate model for Southeast Asia was that of China, where the decrepit Manchu dynasty – a dynasty that had in the nineteenth century allowed China to fall into a state of semi-colonized subjection to the imperial powers collectively – finally collapsed in 1911 and was replaced by a Republic. This apparent 'self-strengthening' was, however, followed by internal dis-integration, prolonged civil war and eventually a Japanese invasion – a condition of weakness that was to last until 1949.

Also influential – in ideological as well as practical terms – was the impact of the First World War. The concept of 'self-determination', bandied about during the war by the Allies on behalf of the Arabs and the Chinese, but only actually implemented in Europe, raised questions about the unit that was to exercise 'self-determination'. As the ideology of nationalism and the concept of the nation-state as the only legitimate unit of government tri-umphed in Europe, it became increasingly apparent that *this* was the idiom in which the aspirations of anti-colonialism had to be expressed. In mainland Southeast Asia, where strong pre-colonial states had existed – and where the contours of these pre-colonial states were roughly preserved in the colonial period – old historic identities and loyalties were given a new, and ultimately European-derived, nationalist gloss. In maritime Southeast Asia, where colonial authority had been extended over a number of disparate pre-colonial states, a national identity had to be created, and the boundaries of colonial authority in effect defined the newly created national identities that became the units of anti-colonial resistance.

Although traditional identities and states existed in Southeast Asia before colonialism – as they do in any sophisticated human society – it should be noted that 'nationalism', as such, is a specifically European concept, born out of the specific experiences of European history. The global dominance of nationalism as a political force and as a means of defining international political entities is the consequence of the era of global European domination.

It is paradoxical, but not in the end surprising, that the primary ideology of resistance to colonial rule – nationalism, that is – was fundamentally shaped by European ideas and experience.

Nationalism, therefore, was not just about asserting, or re-asserting, an existing identity. It involved redefining identity within a colonial region so as to develop a modern, all-inclusive sense of citizenship and belonging. This necessitated above all the moulding of a political programme that would be attractive to all communities, would draw together the urban elite and the rural hinterland and, ultimately, would create a mass political base for national-ist politics.

The problem faced by the embryo nationalist movements in Southeast Asia during the early decades of the twentieth century – and by their educated elite leaderships – lay in the gulf of ideas and outlook between these new leaderships and the vast rural hinterlands. Faced by the demands of an alien administration and the wholly unfamiliar challenges of an alien economic system, it was natural that these rural hinterlands should dream of restoring the pre-colonial world that had been uprooted, and – in times of particular economic distress and political turbulence – of following leaders who aspired to restore the *ancien régime* (see 'Burma: the relationship between rural revolt and nationalist organization', p. 60).

The development of the respective nationalist movements in Southeast Asia thus depended on the volatile and uneasy relationship between the urban elites and the rural hinterlands. This, in its turn, depended on the strategies of the colonial powers. If, as in the Philippines, the colonial power was prepared to make rapid moves towards self-government, the achievement of national goals was largely a matter of bargaining between the political elite and the colonial power. This gave the Filipino nationalist elite a virtual monopoly over the indigenous political agenda, and a common interest existed between this elite and the Americans to curtail – even prevent – the political mobilization of the rural hinterland (see 'The Philippines: the path to self-government', p. 53). On the other hand, in countries where the colonial power refused to initiate moves to self-government – such as the Dutch East Indies or French Indochina – the strength and the bargaining power of nationalist movements would almost entirely depend on their capacity to mobilize the support of the rural hinterland.

The case of Burma perfectly illustrates the dilemmas facing the new nationalist elites. In the period 1919–37, Burma, as a province of British India, was able to benefit from political and constitutional developments in India. The so-called 'Dyarchy' reforms initiated at the end of the First World War enlarged native political participation in provincial legislatures and in the provincial executive councils, and these reforms were – after some delay – applied to Burma. In 1937, Burma was formally separated from India, but was granted a considerable degree of self-government. Nevertheless, the 'stop–start' nature of British concessions during this period, and the fact that the concessions that the British were prepared to make always lagged behind the demands of Indian and Burmese nationalist leaders, meant that the latter were always vulnerable to pressures from more radical nationalists.

The Burmese nationalist leaders had, in effect, to strike a balance between sustaining an effective negotiating relationship with the British authorities, and at the same time ensuring that they could maintain nationalist credibility by building a mass base in the rural hinterland. In ideological terms, this meant balancing between the modern and realistic political idiom of negotiations with the British, and the more inchoate aspirations of the rural hinterland. In this respect, a key role was played by what could be called 'intermediate' local political leaders, who could speak the political language of the rural hinterland, but who at the same time had links with the nationalist leadership. The delicate nature of the relationship between the nationalist elite, these 'intermediaries' and the rural hinterland became particularly acute in a time of crisis, such as the Depression period in Burma in 1930–31 (see 'Burma: the relationship between rural revolt and nationalist organization', p. 60).

Nationalism, anti-colonialism and the battle of ideologies

During this period, nationalist leaders – with the possible exception of the Philippines – faced the difficult task of demonstrating to the respective colonial powers that they had mass support, while at the same time keeping within a political agenda that might enable them to gain concessions from the colonial governments. The two essential tasks for nationalist leaders were, first, the building of a sense of national identity: this was a relatively easy task in areas that had strong pre-colonial state identities, such as Burma and Vietnam, but it was far more difficult in the Malayan and Dutch East Indian region. It could, indeed, be argued that no 'Malayan' nationalist movement emerged in the inter-war years. The second essential task was that of creating a political ideology that fundamentally worked within the Western political idiom of nationalism, democracy and social and economic change, while at the same time appealing to the vast and uneducated hinterland. In these two areas of identity and ideology there was a considerable degree of competition and conflict within what could broadly be called the anti-colonial movement.

The relationship between Islam and nationalism in this period, for example, was always ambiguous. It is true that the Sarekat Islam (Islamic Association), founded in Java in 1912, formed the core of what was to become, by 1917, the first mass nationalist movement of Indonesia. In the early 1920s, however, the Muslim leadership of Sarekat Islam became increasingly alarmed at the growing takeover of this movement by radicals and communists, and by 1921–22 Sarekat Islam had split between leftist and Islamic sections. Thereafter, the main Islamic organizations, on the whole, kept aloof from the nationalist organizations of Indonesia. Islam, after all, was considered by Islamic purists to be a far more important unit of identity than the nation, and many Islamic scholars condemned – and have continued to condemn – nationalism as a form of Western-inspired secular idolatry. In this inter-war period, the main interest of Islamic organizations was in the improvement and modernization of Islamic education, although there was always – even if at a distance – an engagement, a dialogue with Indonesian nationalism.

Just as the relationship between nationalism and Islam was problematic during this period, so was that between nationalism and socialism, particularly the world-wide force of Marxism-Leninism or communism. Although social-ist and even anarchist ideas had already taken root in some parts of Asia – particularly China and Japan – by the time of the First World War, it was not until after the Russian Revolution of 1917 and the victory of Bolshevism that an Asia-wide revolutionary network, based on the ideas of Marxism-Leninism, came into being.

What attracted Asian revolutionaries to Marxism-Leninism was the fact that it combined a coherent world-view with an immediate and practical anti-colonial programme. Lenin's *Theses on the National and Colonial Questions* (see 'The ideological impact of Marxism-Leninism on Southeast Asian nationalism and anti-colonialism', p. 70) was the key text, arguing as it did that – since imperialism was the global extension of the capitalist system designed to create new sources of markets, raw materials, cheap labour and investment – the interests of the Western working class and those of the anti-colonial forces of the colonized world naturally coincided. In 1919 the Communist International or Comintern was set up in the Soviet Union, with the objective of orchestrating communist and anti-colonial activity throughout the world. In the course of the 1920s, a Comintern network was spread through East and Southeast Asia. So far as Southeast Asia was concerned, the main areas where communist organizations took root were French Indo-china, the Dutch East Indies or Indonesia, and among the Chinese diaspora in Singapore and Malaya.

Clearly, nationalist movements and the Comintern had a common interest in the defeat of colonialism and the establishment of an independent Asia. The primary interest of the Comintern, however, was in harnessing the dynamic force of nationalism for the wider purpose of generating fundamental world-wide social revolution. The relationship with nationalism was seen in terms of an alliance rather than an incorporation; an alliance, moreover, that would be pursued only so long as it served the interests of the working class and the poorer peasantry of Asia. The key to Comintern strategy in Asia was the alliance forged in the early 1920s between the Chinese Communist Party (CCP) and the Chinese Nationalist Party or Kuomintang (KMT), directed against the warlord-dominated Chinese government of the day. In 1927, however, the Chinese nationalists turned on and virtually decimated their erstwhile communist allies. There then followed a bitter civil war between the

CCP and the KMT that – barring a patriotic truce during the war against Japan between 1937 and 1945 – effectively lasted until the victory of the Chinese Communist Party in 1949. As a consequence of these events in 1927 and the collapse of the strategy of forging communist–nationalist alliances in the colonial world, between that date and 1935 the Comintern emphasized the priority of the revolutionary class struggle over nationalist objectives, and emphasized the primacy of the interests of the working class and the poorer peasantry in the anti-colonial struggle.

It was natural that the Comintern's ambiguity about the whole ideology of nationalism on one side, and the nationalist elites' suspicions over the long-term revolutionary objectives of the communist movements on the other, should have the effect of splitting and weakening anti-colonial activity in the inter-war years. The Partai Komunis Indonesia (PKI), formed in 1920, found itself completely isolated during the ham-fisted revolts it initiated in 1926–27; communism in Indonesia did not recover from the consequences till towards the end of the Second World War. Likewise the Indochina Communist Party (ICP), formed in 1930, was greatly weakened by its explicit emphasis on class struggle over broad patriotic objectives; this became evident in its revolutionary activities in 1930–31 (see 'Communist revolts in Indonesia and Vietnam', p. 76).

On the other hand, it was the communist leadership more than any other that was able to educate the rural hinterland – in the profound sense of changing their world-view and detaching them from the grip of the *ancien régime* – and at the same time mobilize them into an effective anti-colonial force. Paradoxically, they combined the most Westernized of doctrines with the most deep-rooted grass-roots activity, and as such they posed a new and worrying challenge to the colonial powers, particularly in light of their evident international links.

READINGS

1. The Philippines: the path to self-government

The historical experiences of the Philippines have never entirely synchronized with those of the rest of Southeast Asia in the modern era. By the mid-nineteenth century, the people of the Philippines had lived under three centuries of uninterrupted Spanish rule, and were the most thoroughly 'Europeanized' of all the main Southeast Asian societies. With the exception of the peoples of the southwestern islands, the bulk of the population of the Philippines had been converted to Christianity, and large segments of the society had been to some extent 'Hispanicized'. There was, however, a large gap between the educated, Spanish-speaking, landowning indigenous elite, and the population of the rural hinterlands. In fact, the gulf in terms of economic and social status between the so-called *ilustrado* elite and the rest of the population was wider than the gulf between the Filipino *ilustrados* and their Spanish rulers. In this respect, the Philippines under Spanish rule closely resembled the societies of Central and South America.

In the course of the nineteenth century, the Philippines were influenced by the political and social turbulence of Spain itself. Demands for liberal reform and for a reduction in the power of the Church were taken up by Filipino intellectuals, the most famous of whom was José Rizal, author of two seminal books attacking Spanish rule in the Philippines, *Noli Me Tangere* (1887) and *El Filibusterismo* (1891). Belated Spanish attempts at reform could not keep pace with the momentum of demands made by what had effectively become – following Rizal's execution in the 1890s – a Filipino nationalist movement. What might have become a long-drawn-out and bitter struggle for independence was, however, interrupted by the outbreak of the Spanish–American war in February 1898.

Although the United States was happy to align itself with the Filipino nationalists in order to defeat the Spanish, its objectives and those of the Filipino nationalists in fact sharply diverged. The United States' war against Spain was the consequence of an imperative to assert an American position in the Pacific, and its interest in the Philippines reflected the strategic need to establish a base from which American interests in China and the Far East could be protected. The Treaty of Paris that ended the Spanish–American war on 10 December 1898, far from granting independence to the Philippine nationalists, effectively transferred sovereignty over the Philippines to the United States.

There then followed a bitter guerrilla war, lasting for roughly two years, between the new colonial power and the proponents of the Philippine Republic who, in January 1899, under the leadership of Emilio Aguinaldo, drew up an independent constitution (the 'Malolos Constitution'). Although the strategic needs of the United States were generally recognized by American political opinion, there was considerable hesitation about the colonial responsibilities that would be involved. The United States therefore embarked on a policy – recommended by the Schurman Commission of 1899, and implemented by the Taft Commission of 1901 – of gradually introducing representative institutions and a Filipino administration, and at the same time implementing a massive campaign of education in the Philippines, with the objective of preparing the leadership and the people in general for self-government.

In order to expedite this policy, the American colonial authorities entered into a genuine partnership with the *ilustrado* class that had dominated Filipino society under the Spanish. The following article by Norman Owen describes the dilemmas that emerged in trying to push ahead towards self-government on the basis of this partnership, while maintaining what the Americans saw as their moral responsibility to ensure that Filipino society as a whole was 'fit' to undertake the responsibilities of self-government.

Norman Owen, 'Philippine Society and American Colonialism', in Norman G. Owen (ed.), *Compadre Colonialism: Studies on the Philippines under American Rule* (Ann Arbor, MI: Michigan Papers on South and Southeast Asia, No. 3, University of Michigan, 1971). Excerpts taken from pages 1–9.

By the time of American intervention in 1898, there was in the Philippines a wealthy, politically astute, consciously 'Filipino' elite. It is difficult, perhaps futile, to define the precise origins or boundaries of this group. It may have included direct linear descendants of pre-Spanish *datus* as well as Chinese mestizos who had risen along with the rising export economy in the nineteenth century. Clearly it included such Manila-based *ilustrados* as Rizal and Pardo de Tavera, but it shaded off into (1) *hacenderos* [large estate owners], (2) *caciques* [political bosses] and (3) *principalia* [municipal leaders] with only local followings. In the late Spanish period, this Filipino elite had increasingly begun to agitate for colonial reform, as it saw its political ambitions thwarted by Spanish civil, military, and religious bureaucracies. The *ilustrados* themselves did not lead the early revolutionary movement; while they were urging reform, the active revolt was begun by urban clerks and provincial gentry. Not until after [the American] Admiral Dewey and General Aguinaldo had effectively destroyed Spanish power did most *ilustrados* align themselves with the emerging Philippine Republic; yet by the time of the Malolos Constitution (January, 1899) they were clearly on their way to dominating it. At the same time, some *ilustrados* were already collaborating with the Americans, an arrangement which culminated in the appointment of three Filipinos to the Philippine Commission in 1901.

There were three basic interlocking components of *ilustrado* power – education, a personal clientele, and wealth. Education, in Manila or Europe, was the overt sign of *ilustrado* status; it led to the professions, to contact with other members of the elite, to political sophistication, and ultimately to ideological leadership of Philippine nationalism, based upon the ability to articulate national aspirations and to command respect. A constituency of followers and friends bound by ties of personal loyalty gave the elite a local base of power which Manila – whether Spanish, American or Filipino – has never been able to challenge effectively. The dyadic patron–client relationship was given a particularly Filipino flavor and intensity through such concepts as *utang na loob* (debt of gratitude) and such institutions as *compadrazgo* (ritual co-parenthood). Wealth, usually landed, sometimes commercial, was nearly indispensable to the elite – it provided both the funds for their education and the means to reward their followers and to play the role of patron properly.

The indigenous Philippine polity can best be understood as a pyramid of personal relationships, reinforced by economic dependence and socio-intellectual respect. In the nineteenth century this was a truncated pyramid; the *ilustrados* had risen as high as the Spanish would allow them to, and now found their upward path blocked. They were unable to obtain the high positions which could have helped them reward their clients (in the old Spanish bureaucratic tradition, which fit so well with Filipino values), protect their wealth, and enhance their prestige. The educated rhetoric of a Rizal or del Pilar led not to a senatorship but to exile. Although they had too much at stake to risk direct, violent confrontation with the Spanish, when the events of 1898 cleared the way, the *ilustrados* were ready; they stepped forward as the rightful leaders of the country, successfully claiming the right to speak for the Philippines.

If the *ilustrados* had not existed, however, it would have been necessary for the Americans to invent them. From the beginning, the colonialism of the United States was undercut by a strong current of anti-imperialism, and American policy was characterized by a 'vacillation in motives and aims ... almost to the very end of the colonial regime'. By the narrowest of margins the Senate had decided in 1899 to proceed with the annexation of the Philippines, but the nation lacked the will to pay the full cost of complete subjugation of the islands. The possibility of a long, brutal campaign to suppress insurgency, or of extensive commitment of funds and personnel for direct district-by-district American rule of a faraway land did not agree with either the democratic conscience or the budget. So the Schurman Commission was informed: 'The President earnestly desires the cessation of bloodshed, and that the people of the Philippine Islands at an early date shall have the largest measure of self-government consistent with peace and good order.' By 1899, the United States was already looking for Filipino leaders with whom a *modus vivendi* could be arranged, a means of saving not only the costs of repression and local administration, but also what was left of her ideals and self-image.

This approach is reflected in Colonel Charles Denby's articulation of the object of the Schurman Commission, 'to find out the views of all the *respectable and influential* people whom we can get to tell them to us, and when we go over them we will come to some conclusion'. The witnesses who testified before the Commission in the summer of 1899 exemplified the class Denby had in mind. Fourteen Philippine-born witnesses were identified by profession; all were (or had been) lawyers, doctors, notaries, merchants, or planters. In their testimony they repeatedly referred to the 'rich and intelligent', and to the 'most enlightened people', in contrast to 'low people, vulgar'. The Commission responded in kind by repeated references to 'eminent Filipinos', 'men of property and education', 'leading and prominent men', 'people of wealth and intelligence', or simply 'the better classes'. The witnesses were, of course, those who lived in or could get to Manila; by definition they did not include those who would have nothing to do with Americans; they were hardly representative of the whole nation. Nevertheless, the Commission was happy to draw from their testimony the conclusion that 'the masses of the Filipino people, including practically all who are educated or who possess property, have no desire for an independent and sovereign Philippine state'.

In short, the Americans and the ilustrados had discovered each other, and found in each other familiar values; by mid-1899 a symbiotic relationship had begun that was to continue throughout the American period and beyond.

The United States had a practical political motive for dealing with the *ilustrados*, that of implementing the first of the 'regulative principles' by which the Philippines was to be governed – enforcing 'the supremacy of the United States ... throughout every part of the Archipelago'. It was clearly realized that 'educated Filipinos' would play a crucial role in this, and it was anticipated that their 'support and services [would] be of incalculable value in inaugurating the new government'. Before the end of 1901, civilian municipal and provincial governments had been organized in most of the country, Aguinaldo had been captured, and the Taft Commission was praising the newly formed [*ilustrado*] *Partido Federal*, whose 'members were most active and effective in inducing insurgent leaders to surrender'.

But cooperation with the *ilustrados* was not only a matter of sound tactics for the Commission, it was also a matter of principle. One consistent theme runs through the pronouncements of McKinley, Root, Schurman, and Taft – that the United States ruled the Philippines not only for the ostensible benefit of the Filipinos, but in accordance with their autonomous desires and cultural values. This was implied in the second of the 'regulative principles' of the Schurman Commission, which promised, 'The most ample liberty of self-government will be granted to the Philippine people' reconcilable with good government and American rights. It was made more explicit in a famous passage from the instructions to the Taft Commission, which reminded the members that:

> the government which they are establishing is designed, not for our satisfaction or for the expression of our theoretical views, but for the happiness, peace, and prosperity of the people of the Philippine Islands, and the measures adopted should be made to conform to *their customs, their habits, and even their prejudices*, to the fullest extent consistent with the accomplishment of the indispensable requisite of just and effective government.

It is clear that a colonial power which proposes to respect even the 'prejudices' of the subject people is already thoroughly committed to compromise.

Yet the Americans were equally committed to 'just and effective government', and it was not long before they began to suspect that the two purposes might be in conflict. In theory there were 'certain great principles of government ... liberty and law ... [which] must be ... maintained ... however much they may conflict with the customs or laws of procedure' familiar to the Filipinos. But it was never easy to define, much less enforce, these principles in a Philippine context; it was always easier to enlist the support of the 'enlightened classes' than to attempt to institute sweeping reforms without them, or to implement rigorously the full panoply of programs the United States envisaged for the islands.

As a result, the Americans found from an early date that they were never in complete command of events; by 1902, Taft was already describing the obstacles created by 'caciqueism' and 'feudal relations of dependence'. Bonifacio S. Salamanca, in his excellent revisionist history of the Taft era, after emphasizing the 'limited role played by Filipinos in the provincial government' in this period, and the 'almost exclusive power of lawmaking exercised with patent arbitrariness by Americans' up to 1907, still concludes that 'if the Filipino elite did not in fact determine American actions, they nevertheless made it impossible for the United States to have a freer hand with any important undertaking which did not have their endorsement or, at the very least, their tacit approval'. It seems as if the United States, in the process of obtaining *ilustrado* support, may have unwittingly sacrificed the efficient implementation of certain other aspects of her policy – education, civil service reform, public health, economic development, and, above all, the genuine democratization of the Philippine polity. However mixed the motives of the Americans in annexing the Philippines, however unjust the attempt to impose on an alien culture their own institutions and values, it would at least have been logically consistent for the United States, having intervened, to retain the ability to carry through her dream of making the Philippines a 'Showcase of Democracy'. Instead, through a combination of political tactics and republican principles, the American administrators, by granting to Filipino leaders as much influence as they did, renounced the necessary means to enforce their own conception of what the Philippines should become. The result was an odd mixture of theory and expediency, a perpetual compromise, a modern variant of indirect rule.

This tension between the American conception of policy and the Filipino execution of it continued throughout the period of American rule. When Francis B. Harrison arrived in 1913 as the first Governor-General appointed by the Democrats, many Republicans objected that he would grant effective self-government too soon, and that the irretrievable Filipinization of American rule by Harrison would bring an untimely end to the laudable ambitions of the United States to prepare the Philippines for the modern world. Leonard Wood arrived as Harrison's successor in 1921 and attempted to slow down or reverse this process; the frustrations he encountered in this effort plagued his entire administration. The balance shifted slightly during the time of the later Governors-General and the Commonwealth [established in 1935], but the tension remained; Filipinos were more active in creating policy, but only within the limits established by the Congress and President of the United States. Each Filipino politician, each American administrator had to discover for himself the fine balance between what was desirable and what was possible; the process was a continuous one.

Historians have usually tended to concur with both Democratic claims and Republican accusations in calling 1913 the turning point, for better or worse, within the American period. But a closer look at the Taft era suggests

that the crucial decisions may have been made much earlier. In the fall of
1907 Taft, once President of the Philippine Commission, now Secretary of
War, visited the Philippines once more. In his report of January 23, 1908, he
states that 'Thus far the policy in the Philippines has worked' – an assertion
which is not surprising, inasmuch as Taft himself was largely the creator of
that policy. But between the lines of the report there are hints that the
American dream was not being realized with the swiftness and efficacy he
had once hoped for. Taft notes 'the desire of the upper class to maintain the
relation of the ruling class to the serving and obedient class', and imputes
to this both the 'languid sympathy' given by *ilustrados* to the education program
and the urgency of Filipino demands for independence. He finds it necessary
to warn that the purpose of the United States was not 'merely to await the
organization of a Philippine oligarchy or aristocracy competent to administer
government and then turn the island over to it'. And he concludes that 'it
will take longer than a generation to complete the ... education of the
common people. Until that is done we ought not to lift our guiding hand
from the helm of the ship of state of the Philippine Islands'. Implicit in this
report is the awareness that the United States had not really succeeded in
altering Philippine society in the short run; from this perspective, the
'Filipinization' under Harrison seems less a radical departure from the past
than a public recognition of continuing socio-political realities.

The implications of this *modus vivendi*, this early tacit agreement between
ilustrados and Commissioners, are not yet entirely clear. It is somewhat
simplistic to conclude that either party to the deal was deliberately betraying
principles in favor of expediency. The *ilustrados* were not solely collaborators
who abandoned the revolution to seek selfish ends. Once [US President]
McKinley had made the decision to annex the Philippines, resistance was
probably futile, and it is doubtful that the Philippine Republic could have
survived long in that era of hungry imperialism even if [Admiral] Dewey
had turned around and sailed away. Nor is it wholly fair to blame the *ilustrados*
for failing to carry out a radical social revolution; they were clearly sincere
(if self-centered) in their belief that what was good for them was good for
the country. Perhaps the only valid charge against the *ilustrados* is that they
assumed that they were leaders by right and acted on that assumption; this
should not qualify them as national heroes, but it hardly makes them traitors.

For that matter, neither had the American administrators betrayed any
deeply held radical principles. They were committed to protect property rights
not just by the Treaty of Paris, but by American tradition and personal
inclination. The members of the Commission had much in common with
the *ilustrados* who testified before them, and the two groups seemed to
compete with each other in proposals for limiting the franchise and prolong-
ing American 'tutelage and protection' of the Philippines, under which the
educated Filipinos would join the Commissioners in guiding and instructing

the unenlightened masses. The United States had, in the long run, only one basic proposal for reshaping Philippine society – education, over generations – and to this the *ilustrados*, themselves the product of modern education, had no objection. It may be that what occurred in the Philippines was less a 'Co-Optation' of the *ilustrados* than a genuine meeting of minds between the 'rich and intelligent' of both nations.

2. Burma: the relationship between rural revolt and nationalist organization

When Britain conquered Upper Burma in 1885, it did not choose to impose a protectorate on the Konbaung dynasty; instead it removed the indigenous Burmese government altogether and, in February 1886, incorporated the whole of Burma into British India as a province. Burma was seen as too strategically vital, and its dynasty as too unreliable, for the British to attempt to work through the *ancien régime*. Not only was Burma forced to submit to an alien European government but, with its incorporation into British India, it was dominated by an alien Anglo-Indian administrative system, economy and culture.

After an initial and short-lived stage of dynastic, religious and minority resistance, Burma was relatively politically quiescent up to the time of the First World War. The most significant organization to emerge in the first decade of the twentieth century was a movement that campaigned for the reform and adaptation of Buddhism to meet the challenges of the modern world: the Young Men's Buddhist Association, or YMBA, formed in 1906. The YMBA was yet another example of the revolution in cultural, educational and religious ideas that sprang up among the elite of Southeast Asia during this period.

An organized Burmese nationalist movement in the Western sense emerged only in the years after the First World War. In 1917, Britain undertook to initiate political reforms in British India with a view to (very) gradual moves towards eventual self-government within the empire. Britain's attempt in 1919 to exclude Burma from these reforms because of its alleged political immaturity compared to the rest of British India stimulated the creation of Burma's first mass nationalist organization, the General Council of Burmese Associations, or GCBA. In 1921, Britain relented, and in 1923, the so-called 'Dyarchy' constitution was introduced into Burma. This involved the creation of a part-elected, part-nominated Legislative Council, and the division of the governor's Executive Council between members appointed by the Governor, who dealt with 'reserved' subjects, and two members who were answerable to the Legislative Council.

This partial introduction of the parliamentary principal stimulated nationalist political activity in Burma, but completely failed to meet nationalist aspirations, since the vital areas of policy – such as defence, law and order, and finance – remained directly under the governor's control. In their search for power and influence at the centre, the GCBA elements working within the Legislative Council split into competing factions. More important, however, was the split between those GCBA members who gave priority to negotiating with the British for political concessions via the Dyarchy system, and those members who refused to work within the system, and instead concentrated on building a mass movement in the rural hinterland. The GCBA was split between elite bargaining and mass mobilization.

The climax came in the late 1920s, when the failure of the parliamentary elite to squeeze substantial tax and village administration reforms out of the British was highlighted by the results of the world depression: a depression to which Burma was particularly vulnerable because of its rice-export economy. It was in these circumstances that 'middle rank' nationalist politicians like Hsaya (often spelled 'Saya') San came into their own as leaders of grassroots protest. In the article below, Patricia Herbert challenges the notion that the Hsaya San rebellion was a last gasp of the *ancien régime*, and rather sees Hsaya San as an intermediary between modern nationalism and the traditional world of the peasant, and as a bridge between the cosy elite Burmese nationalism of the 1920s, and the radical, socialist-orientated nationalism of the 1930s and 1940s.

Patricia Herbert, *The Hsaya San Rebellion (1930–1932) Reappraised* (Melbourne: Monash University, 198?). Excerpts taken from pages 1–13.

The Hsaya San rebellion that occurred in British-ruled Burma in 1930–32 has attracted in recent years considerable scholarly attention. It has, above all, served as *the* Burmese case study or counterpoint in several comparative studies, most notably those by Harry Benda, James Scott and Michael Adas. A variety of interpretations of the rebellion has been offered. All Western studies have emphasized the traditional and millenarian aspects of the rebellion, with some also concentrating on economic factors and others treating it in terms of what has been called the peasant ethic. Yet unlike other Southeast Asian rebellions (for example in Java and the Philippines) there has been no full scale study of the rebellion and very little use made of Burmese language source materials. Moreover, what interpretations of the rebellion all lack (whatever the perspective from which they are written), is an internal dimension. Writings on the Hsaya San rebellion – a rebellion that from start to finish was essentially a rural rebellion – do not carry us far towards understanding the world of Burmese peasants in the 1920s and 30s.

Is such an understanding an impossible goal? It might seem so given how little appears to be known about even the more educated and articulate members of early 20th century Burmese society. In the standard accounts (such as those by Cady, Moscotti and Trager) members of the Burmese elite figure only as names in lists – lists of the founders of the YMBA, the

GCBA, members of the Legislative Council, etc. These studies have not been based upon an appreciation or examination of the many Burmese political and literary writings of the period and hence they have largely failed to advance our understanding of Burmese society at that time and of what its members thought, believed and wrote. The Burmese nationalist organizations and politicians of the early 20th century remain little more than a collection of names and events arranged in a progressional sequence from colonialism to independence. Viewed from such a perspective, the Hsaya San rebellion has predominantly been treated as a throwback, as the 'last gasp of traditional Burma'. The purpose of this paper is to challenge that view and to give a more internal dimension to the objectives and perceptions of the Burmese under British rule than can be provided by the essentially top-downwards focus of colonial reports and sources.

The main events of the Hsaya San rebellion – the biggest anti-colonial uprising in Burmese history – are quite well known and only need outlining. The rebellion's outbreak in December 1930 shattered the apparent surface calm of rural Burma and took the British authorities by complete surprise. Outside government circles it came as less of a surprise. Right on the eve of the rebellion, the leading Burmese language newspaper, *Thu'ri'ya* (The Sun), had published an editorial entitled 'A Warning to the British Government' which spoke of Burma as a 'keg of dynamite' which could explode at any time. The first targets for attack by the rebels were village headmen – four were killed in the first 48 hours and within a year altogether 38 headmen had been killed and another 250 attacked and wounded. (Why villagers should attack their own headmen will be discussed later.) Within five days the government had rushed 2,000 troops into Tharrawaddy District (the main centre of rebel activities), and on December 31 the rebel headquarters was located and destroyed.

But the rebellion was far from over and it was to take the government another 18 months to stamp it out. As well as in Tharrawaddy District, there was serious rebel activity and fighting in Pyapon, Henzada, Insein, Pegu, Prome and Thayetmyo Districts and as far afield as the Shan States. Plans for uprising in Bassein, Maubin, Toungoo and Yamethin Districts were for the most part thwarted by the authorities' prompt arrest of suspects. A confidential government report on the rebellion spoke of a 'reign of terror' prevailing throughout March and April 1931 and of large tracts of the country from April to August being in 'a state of anarchy'. In July 1931 the authorities considered the situation so serious that they (unsuccessfully) asked permission from the government of India to introduce martial law. In all, over 1,300 rebels were killed and an incalculable number wounded, and a further 9,000 rebels surrendered or were captured or arrested. Hsaya San and 125 other rebels were hanged and 1,389 were sentenced to terms of imprisonment or of transportation ...

To the colonial authorities at the time there was no doubt about the origins and causes of the rebellion. In May 1931 the government issued a report on the rebellion which stated baldly:

> As regards the causes it is well known: (1) that the Burman is by nature restless and excitable; (2) that in spite of a high standard of literacy the Burman peasantry are incredibly ignorant and superstitious; the belief in the efficacy of charms and tattooing as conferring invulnerability being still widespread; and (3) that such rebellions are usually started with the object of overthrowing the government, the history of Burma being a record of sudden and successful rebellions usually ending in the seizure of the throne and there being many prophecies current especially in Upper Burma that the throne of the King of Burma will be won again.

None of the points listed can really be considered a cause of rebellion. The Report's emphasis on the superstition and gullibility of the peasants reveals more of the British authorities' unchanging attitude to the peasant than it does factors motivating the peasants. The superstition of the Burmese peasantry is indubitable. It is the significance ascribed to that superstition that is in doubt. The government saw the peasants as having been manipulated and duped by a 'charlatan' and 'quack doctor' – Hsaya San. The use of such disparaging terms shows the authorities' inability to appreciate the standing and importance of a practitioner of indigenous medicine in rural society – a position partly indicated by the prefix 'hsaya' which is a term of respect meaning 'master', 'learned person', 'teacher'. Moreover, the Report's statement on the causes of the rebellion (quoted above) was not even original, but was in fact taken from a 1914 confidential report giving guidance to civil officers in the event of an outbreak of disturbances! This 1914 Report – which contained such statements as 'All that is required [to defeat the Burman] is prompt and reliable intelligence, tirelessness, ruthless pursuit, and at the end, straight shooting at close quarters' – was reissued to government officials in 1931 ...

Interpretations of the rebellion both at the time and subsequently have all emphasized the form of the rebellion. The symbolism of royalty, of the mythical Galon (garuda) bird, the drinking of oath-water, the rebels' faith in tattoos and amulets are all seen as evidence of the 'primitive' or 'traditional' nature of the rebellion. [See the quotation at beginning of this chapter, p. 47.] Several studies have in addition pointed to a linked aspect of the rebellion, its messianic and millennial Buddhist content. The conclusion drawn from this emphasis on these traditional and millenarian aspects has been that the Hsaya San rebellion was retrogressive – that it represented (to quote Benda) 'a turning away ... a cosmological attempt to exorcise the foreigner by recreating the traditional Burmese monarchy in a jungle clearing, complete with the magico-religious paraphernalia of old Burma'.

How true is this? To what extent was the Hsaya San rebellion the last gasp of traditional Burma? Only partly so. Undoubtedly traditional elements were important. But for Hsaya San not to have made use of such elements would surely have been more surprising than the fact that he did so. To look briefly at just one traditional element: the belief in invulnerability conveyed by tattoos and amulets. For many Burmans it would be foolhardy to embark upon a dangerous endeavour without the protection of tattoos or amulets – every bit as foolish as British observers of the rebellion considered the rebels' faith in such protection to be. When rebel soldiers were killed or wounded by the bullets of their enemy, faith in invulnerability was not necessarily shaken. It was believed either that the oath-taker must have broken his oath and so prevented himself from absorbing the power of the amulet, or that the incantation administered was faulty and the amulet or tattoo thereby rendered ineffective. It follows that an amulet that had been made, charmed and administered by someone with a high reputation would be especially desirable. Such a reputation Hsaya San undoubtedly had. He was a skilled practitioner of medicine, a *hsei hsaya* (it is worth noting that the Burmese word *hsei* can bear the meaning of both medicine and magic) and the author of a published book on medical diagnosis and another on alchemy. Hsaya San made full use of his skills when recruiting followers. He made by alchemic processes special charmed needles both for tattooing and for embedding under the skin of the forearm.

In Burma the practice of alchemy is especially associated with certain esoteric sects (or *gaìng* – termed by Mendelson 'messianic Buddhist associations'), whose members aim to acquire magical and religious powers, especially the power to become a superior being, a *weik-za*, who can live until the coming of the next Buddha or who can improve conditions for others. The Buddhist concept of a Universal Emperor (Pali: *Cakkavatti*) who is the precursor of the Future Buddha (or can also potentially be the Future Buddha) has merged into Burmese beliefs in a future king and formed the basis for millenarian expectations. The future king can be a *weik-za* and is often believed to be the embodiment of two famous past *weik-zas*, Bo Bo Aung and Bo Mìn Gaùng. Popular beliefs in the powers of a *weik-za* and in a future king draw on, and are expressed in, a folk literature (both oral and written) of cryptic sayings, rumours and prophecies. Undoubtedly many prophecies were associated with Hsaya San and added to his reputation. In Western accounts of the rebellion Hsaya San's appeal is seen primarily as that of a *weik-za*, a future king and, by extension, even a Universal Emperor. But the extent to which Hsaya San saw and presented himself in such terms or was so regarded by his followers is by no means clear. In 1972 I questioned twelve former rebels from three districts. None would admit to thinking of Hsaya San in such terms or as belonging to a *gaìng* ...

The tendency in interpreting the rebellion has been to assume that no values or symbols other than the traditional had made an impact at the rural level, or to think that traditional symbols can only be put to certain traditional uses and not used in other ways or in combination with other elements.

Where some note is taken of changes in the society, then peasants are seen as having their traditionalism reinforced by changes around them. The emphasis on form has obscured the context of the rebellion. Where the context has been examined, it has been seen primarily in terms of social and economic changes as in the stimulating recent studies of Adas and Scott. What both writers treat only very briefly is the nationalist political context of the rebellion.

In *The Burma Delta*, Adas modifies J. S. Furnivall's classic concept of the plural society [see Glossary] and gives it an historical dimension by tracing the stage by stage development of the rice delta economy of Lower Burma. Adas shows that the process which he calls the closing of the rice frontier (the taking up of all land, etc.) blocked off economic options and contributed to an agrarian crisis. In *Prophets of Rebellion*, Adas takes the subject further and argues that in this situation (blockage of options or absence of alternatives) a prophet becomes crucial and violent protest becomes directed into pre-existing millenarian channels. However, the Burmese peasant in the 1920s did potentially have another outlet and this was the organisation of rural nationalist associations called *wun-tha-nú athin*. The second socio-economic study of the rebellion, Scott's *The Moral Economy of the Peasant*, confronts the question of how peasants see their situation: Scott postulates a subsistence ethic. His evidence, however, is all from colonial period sources, and the suggestion of a moral economy ethic [see Glossary] among peasants in pre-colonial Burma is far from proven. In particular, it is possible that the peasants' opposition to taxes came about not so much because the taxes were fixed, but because the authority imposing them was not considered to be legitimate and the methods used in their collection were unjust. There is a moral element to the peasants' perception of changes – to loss of land, to violations of customs and rights, to their sense of resentment and deprivation, but it is grounded not in an age-old subsistence ethic but in the gathering momentum of the rural *wun-tha-nú* organization. The push into rebellion comes from the internal dynamics of the *wun-tha-nú* movement.

It is, I believe, not so much the economic factors that explain the rebellion but rather the way in which these and other consequences of British rule were confronted by Burmans in the years before the rebellion. The rebellion must be seen in the context of the development of twentieth century Burmese nationalism. What has been insufficiently explained with regard to the Burmese nationalist movement is the grass roots momentum and the early politicization of the Burmese peasantry.

Although Hsaya San's connections with the village nationalist associations (*wun-tha-nú athin*) have been noted by some writers, the links between the village and the central level associations and the whole scale of the *wun-tha-nú* movement have not been examined in detail. The activities of these organizations dominated Burmese nationalist politics in the years leading up to Hsaya San's rebellion. Through the Burmese records of annual, regional and local level conferences, and through a whole range of Burmese publications of the 1920s – most importantly in the village context, handbooks of model sermons for use by monks and lay preachers on nationalist politics – it becomes possible to get closer to that elusive internal dimension.

Hsaya San and villagers throughout Burma became involved through the *wun-tha-nú* movement in new, modern sorts of activity reaching beyond the limits of their own localities. They did not remain untouched by this process but acquired new aspirations and ways of articulating their grievances. In the early 1920s village associations under a variety of names proliferated rapidly, prompted and fostered by the central nationalist associations, the General Council of Burmese Associations (GCBA) and General Council of Sangha Samaggi (GCSS, the monks' association). By 1925 there were over 10,000 village associations throughout Burma, all linked to the central executive committee of the GCBA by an administrative structure of village, circle and district boards – a structure which, it is important to note, deliberately paralleled that introduced by the government with their Rural Self-Government Act of 1921. The village associations provided an alternative source of authority to that of the village headman and a channel through which government authority was challenged.

I said earlier that the writings and speeches of even the central level figures of early Burmese nationalism had received insufficient attention from scholars. Such sources throw light on the intellectual process whereby the political and cultural implications of the YMBA's and GCBA's declared aims – fostering of the Burmese race, language, religion and education – were worked out. But these works and speeches, though very important, naturally had less currency at village level than the flood of publications that accompanied the foundation of the village associations and were designed for use at that level. These publications presented a formulation of the Burmese past from a *wun-tha-nú* perspective, and advocated direct action and advised on boycott and non-cooperation tactics. An important work of this type was C. P. Hkin Maung's *Wun-tha-nú Ret-hki-tá* (Nationalist Principles), published in 1924 ...

C. P. Hkin Maung's *Wun-tha-nú Ret-hki-tá* comprised collected articles and speeches 'for the use of the *wun-tha-nú* endeavour and the monks' associations' endeavour'. Throughout the work, *wun-tha-nú* principles and preaching are linked to the life and teachings of the Buddha, and are said to be 'in accordance with the Buddha's wishes'. C. P. Hkin Maung lists twenty-two points for 'true Burman Buddhists' to reflect upon, beginning: 'Please consider whether or not the Buddhist religion revered by the Burmese is the purest and highest pinnacle in the present world and future state' and, building up step by step, says: 'Consider whether our forefathers have laid down that in this world and present existence we should be contented under, and obey, foreigners; consider whether in this world, if one's race is oppressed and reviled, our character and honour will be renowned or will be diminished.'

C. P. Hkin Maung makes many comparisons between the system of government in Britain and that of the Burmese kings. He points out that Burmese kings and officials had to observe certain principles and duties and swore to act for the people's good. The Burmese word for minister, *wun-gyi*, means literally 'great burden' and ministers are so called, he says, 'because they bear the king's burden and the people's burden and these are that the king should make no errors, that there should be no conflict or opposition with the people, and that the country should be populous and pleasant and the people tranquil and contented'. It is, he says, 'the Burmese custom that the king should with compassion and loving kindness heed the people's wishes' and he cites the Vessantara Jataka (where King Sañjaya is forced to banish Prince Vessantara because the people are so enraged that he has given away the kingdom's white elephant).

It should not be assumed that the book was just a simplistic proposition that things were better under the kings. It explored the question of what is meant by the concepts 'nation' and 'national' and what are the particular characteristics that make one truly Burmese. The purpose of the *wun-tha-nú* movement is specifically stated as being to awaken and develop Burmese national spirit, pride and character. *Wun-tha-nú* teachings such as C. P. Hkin Maung's were disseminated to villagers through the rural *wun-tha-nú* associations and teams of *damá kahtí-ká* (Pali: *dhammakatika*), or preachers of the law. These preachers, or lecturers on nationalist politics, were trained and licensed by the central GCSS and by the boycotting [the British administration] GCBA organizations ...

From 1920 to 1924 the *wun-tha-nú* movement focused its attention on campaigning against certain unpopular provisions in the government's 1907 Village Act – those, for instance, requiring villagers to build stockades and to do guard duty, entitling touring officials to demand services and supplies from villagers, and fining villagers communally for harbouring criminals or for having stolen property found in their village. The relationship between the local *wun-tha-nú* associations and the central GCBA and the way the *wun-tha-nú* movement came into conflict with the British administration is best demonstrated by reference to the records of the local Prome District GCBA conference held in April 1923 at which the Village Act was discussed. Two full days were occupied with reading and discussing 52 letters of complaints against headmen and government officials that had been submitted by village *wun-tha-nú* associations throughout Prome District ...

The GCBA structure provided a channel through which people like Hsaya San could rise up from village level through to township, district and national level conferences. Hsaya San, as Executive Officer of his local village association, in 1924 regularly submitted reports and wrote letters to *wun-tha-nú*. For example, he wrote an account of a prayer meeting that he had organised in his village to pray for the release from prison of the famous nationalist monk, Ù Ok tamá, pointing out that to use a prayer meeting for a political purpose was a new event. Hsaya San rose from village association representative to township, to district representative attending national GCBA conferences. He became a well-known speaker not just in his own locality (Belu-gyùn, Moulmein) but elsewhere ... His name first appears in national level GCBA conference reports in 1925. At the 1926 annual conference (held in Meik-hti-la), Hsaya San seconded resolutions stating that *wun-tha-nú* members should hold resolute to their principles and never apologise for their actions, and expressing dissatisfaction with the government's collection of taxes.

The GCBA conference records are full of resolutions on matters of concern to villagers: taxes, the Village Act, the headmen's use of stocks to punish villagers, the government's treatment of monks in prison, and the general need to improve conditions by flood prevention works, setting up land mortgage banks, and so on. Many of the GCBA resolutions were taken up by Burmese nationalist members who had opted to enter (rather than boycott) the Legislative Council. But, despite the efforts of the Legislative Council members and the central GCBA, any successes and reforms gained were very short lived. For example, in 1924 the government did modify the unpopular Village Act, but then in 1927 went back on this and reintroduced it in its original form. Similarly, in 1926 the government set up a Capitation and Thathameda Taxes Enquiry Committee. The Report of this Committee recommended the abolition of these taxes, but the government did not implement the recommendation on the grounds that no satisfactory substitute source of revenue could be found ...

The 1928 GCBA annual conference, held at Min-bu, decided to set up its own committee of inquiry into taxes, and specifically into abuses in the collection of taxes and the methods used. At this point Hsaya San advanced from his position of regional GCBA delegate to become President of the GCBA Committee on taxes. The GCBA inquiry, unlike the earlier government committee, was not concerned to find substitute taxes, but only to demon-strate that the taxes were causing hardship and that there were abuses in their collection. Hsaya San spent the next few months travelling the country collecting data for his report (which was to contain 170 case studies). In August 1928 he drew up a document proposing the formation of a Galon Association [a para-military organization] to be affiliated to the GCBA. Hsaya San's report on taxes was to have been submitted to the 1929 GCBA annual conference at Taung-ngu in March 1929, but the conference fell apart when the senior GCSS monks withdrew their support ... The monks were alarmed by several items on the agenda including a proposal to form 'national defence groups'. The conference broke up before the question of taxes could be discussed. The central ranks of the GCBA and GCSS turned upon each other and embarked upon an unedifying squabble by pamphlet propaganda between different factions.

At a critical time the village *wun-tha-nú* movement was left without effective leadership. The central GCBA after years of building up the expectations of its rural mass membership failed its followers, and backed away from any commitment to action. The most ardent boycotters of the early 1920s ... had one by one compromised and stood for election to the Legislative Council. Both the Legislative Council and the central GCBA had proved ineffective; nothing had been achieved. The government was taking ever stronger measures against the *wun-tha-nú* associations, thereby adding to their grievances and to the momentum of the *wun-tha-nú* movement. The villagers were, in fact, more radical than the central level Burmese nationalists and were steadfast in their adherence to the policies of non-cooperation and boycott. These were policies originally advocated by their leadership but abandoned by one group after another. By September 1929 Hsaya San had come to the conclusion: 'The country will not be got [back] by talking, writing and asking for it.' He set about organizing his Galon Association and began enrolling recruits.

Hsaya San was, therefore, a product not of traditional Burma but of a grass-roots political momentum built up during the 1920s. For years villagers had been actively campaigning about issues of concern to them, only to find that the central GCBA and GCSS leadership had turned upon itself and broken up into rival factions. Hsaya San expressed matters very clearly in a letter seeking refuge in the territory of a Shan States sawbwa. He wrote: 'Although *wun-tha-nú* associations were formed ... there has been no success.' While awaiting execution in Tharrawaddy jail, one of Hsaya San's last acts was to authorize two *Thu-rí-yá* newspaper journalists to use the proceeds from the sale of his book on medical diagnosis to buy works for a library in his memory. The first books bought (in March 1932) were the works of Lenin, Trotsky and Marx.

To expect that Hsaya San and his followers would have propounded a specific political programme during the rebellion would be misguided. After all, the nationalist literature of the 1920s devotes little space to outlining a programme for an independent Burma, but concentrates on how to *obtain* independence. Other Burmese leaders before and after Hsaya San – men like Ù Chit Hlaing and Dr Bá Maw – also tapped traditional roots and drew on traditional forms but, unlike Hsaya San, they have not been labelled 'traditional'. Later events testify to the fact that the Hsaya San rebellion heralded a new age rather than the last gasp of an old one. The young Thahkins movement of university students which founded the *Dó-bama Asì-ayòn* ('We Burmans Association') of the 1930s and prepared the way for the independent modern Burma state gained inspiration from Hsaya San. Their first annual conference, held at Yei-nan-gyaùng in 1935, began by passing a unanimous resolution that tribute and praise should be paid to Hsaya San and the monks and men who had fought and died 'for the nation and for the race' in the Tharrawaddy Galon rebellion. Thahkin Bá Sein observed that Burma was as if 'in a deep sleep' and only aroused from its 'slave and subdued mentality' by Hsaya San's rebellion. The lesson the Thahkins acknowledged they learnt from the Hsaya San rebellion was that the next time the Burmese people challenged the British government they must be properly prepared, trained and armed to drive the British out.

Is there anything to be learnt from this discussion of the context of Hsaya San's rebellion for the study of peasant rebellions in general? We can, of course, find in most rebellions a mixture of economic, traditional, millenarian and other factors. But rebellions can also be examined from the inside and within a culture, and peasants may be studied not primarily as belonging to some international category of peasants or in terms of peasant ethics or little traditions, but as members of a certain polity and culture. The key to an inside study is the written and reported declarations of the peasants themselves – a category of material which has received amazingly little attention in studies of rebellions. It has long been assumed that the development of the Burmese nationalist movement was shaped by the elite level of Burmese society. But, just as has been shown in recent studies of revolution in Java and the Philippines, an important impetus sometimes comes from those below and the role played and the perceptions held by those 'below' deserve careful attention.

3. The ideological impact of Marxism-Leninism on Southeast Asian nationalism and anti-colonialism

One of the great contradictions of European imperialism in the nineteenth century was the fact that the main imperial powers were also liberal democracies. Indeed, it was probably Europe's attempt at the beginning of the twentieth century to reconcile this contradiction that began the process of weakening these empires.

The argument of Marxism, however, was that the outward appearance of liberal democracy masked the inner reality of societies fundamentally divided between those – the 'capitalists' or 'bourgeois' – who privately owned the accumulated wealth of the economy, and the property-less mass – the 'proletariat' – who ultimately owned nothing but their own labour-power, which they sold for wages. The driving force behind this capitalist economy was the competitive search for private profit, and all the dramatic advances of scientific, industrial and technological transformation were harnessed to this end. The more sophisticated and advanced an economy became, therefore, the greater the divide between these two classes. This 'contradiction' between the increasing wealth of the economy as a whole and the competitive struggle to push down the costs of production and therefore had to *reduce* the living standards of the proletariat, would eventually, Marxists argued, lead to the breakdown of the capitalist system. By an unspecific process of revolution, Karl Marx asserted, the proletariat itself would seize control of the capitalist economy (not destroy it) and harness its productive forces to the needs of the whole society – thus creating a socialist economy.

V. I. Lenin (1870–1924) fitted the phenomenon of imperialism into this basic Marxist analysis of capitalist society. Imperialism was, he argued, a way of giving a new lease of life to capitalism, by providing new markets, new areas for investment, expanding access to cheap raw materials, and a new source of cheap labour. It also helped to blunt class antagonism between capitalism and the proletariat by providing access to emigration or employment in the colonies, by heightening a sense of racial superiority among the European working class, and by sharpening a sense of national identity in the competition for empire. The racial confrontation and the national confrontation implied in the competition for empire would help mask the *real* confrontation of capitalist society, which was class confrontation.

In Lenin's analysis, the First World War was the natural consequence of this competition for empire between the main European powers. However, instead of grasping the opportunity to convert the war between nations into a revolutionary class struggle in which the European proletariat would turn against the whole capitalist system, the European socialist parties – members of the so-called 'Second International' – supported the war efforts of their respective countries. Only the Bolshevik (later Communist) Party in Russia, under the leadership of Lenin, seized power in 1917 in a period of revolutionary turmoil, and declared the creation of a socialist state (the Union of Soviet Socialist Republics, or USSR).

For Lenin and the Russian communist leadership, 1917 created the basis for a new world order. The fundamental divide was no longer between nations or races, but between the global capitalist system and the oppressed of the world – embodied in the European proletariat and in *all* peoples, except the collaborating elements, within the colonial areas. The fact that – after the defeat of Germany in 1918 – Britain and France accepted the principle of 'self-determination' in Europe, but denied it to their own empires, strengthened the force of his argument. Liberal democracy, it seemed, had nothing to offer the colonial people. In 1919, the Russian leadership put substance behind their global theories by creating the 'Third', 'Communist' International, or Comintern, designed to link communist parties and revolutionary organizations throughout the world. Lenin's 'Theses on the National and Colonial Questions' was a key document of the Comintern, designed to link socialism and the anti-colonial struggle.

It is important, however, to understand the dilemmas that this world strategy faced. In the first place, colonial societies were backward societies where the process of industrialization had hardly begun. The main class confrontation there was not between capitalist and proletarian, but between landlord and peasant. There was a danger, therefore, that successful nationalist resistance to colonial rule might simply restore the *ancien régime*, which might be – in terms of economic and social development – even more 'reactionary' than the colonial regime itself, which had at least begun to unleash social and economic change in Asia and Africa. The main aim of the Comintern, therefore, was to develop in the colonial world a small revolutionary 'nucleus', composed of intellectuals, members of the embryonic working class in big cities like Singapore, and the poorer peasantry. This revolutionary nucleus could then enter into an alliance with the 'progressive' elements of the nationalist elite – Lenin describes them as the 'bourgeois-democrats'. This alliance alone could ensure that the forces of global revolution and the forces of anti-colonialism would unite behind a common purpose. Only after the 'bourgeois-democratic' nationalists had thrown out imperial rule could the real struggle – the struggle for socialism – begin. The alliance in the colonies between 'bourgeois-democracy' and communism was therefore only a temporary, tactical alliance.

Extracts from Lenin's 'Theses on the National and Colonial Questions' are followed here by a description by Ho Chi Minh (known by another pseudonym as Nguyen Ai Quoc), the father of Vietnamese communism, of the dramatic impact that these 'Theses' had on his political thinking. It had a similar impact on other Asian communists of the post-1919 period.

Extract from V. I. Lenin, 'Preliminary Draft of Theses on the National and Colonial Questions', in V. I. Lenin, *Selected Works*, Vol. 2 (Moscow: Foreign Languages Publishing House, 1947). Excerpts taken from pages 654–8.

The Communist Party, as the conscious champion of the struggle of the proletariat for the overthrow of the bourgeois yoke, must base its policy in the national question too, not on abstract and formal principles, but, firstly, on an exact estimate of the specific historical situation and, primarily, of the economic conditions; secondly, on a clear distinction between the interests of the oppressed classes, of the toilers and exploited, and the general concept of national interests as a whole, which implies the interests of the ruling class; *thirdly, on an equally clear distinction between the oppressed, dependent and subject nations and the oppressing, exploiting and sovereign nations* [emphasis added], in order to counter the bourgeois-democratic lies which obscure the colonial and financial enslavement – characteristic of the era of finance capital and imperialism – of the vast majority of the world's population by an insignificant minority of rich and advanced capitalist countries.

The imperialist war of 1914–18 very clearly revealed the falsity of the bourgeois-democratic phrasemongering to all nations and to the oppressed classes of the whole world by practically demonstrating that the Versailles Treaty of the famous 'Western democracies' is an even more brutal and despicable act of violence against weak nations than was the Brest-Litovsk Treaty [see Glossary] of the German Junkers and the Kaiser. The League of Nations and the whole post-war policy of the Entente [between Britain and France] reveal this truth more clearly and distinctly than ever; they are everywhere intensifying the revolutionary struggle both of the proletariat in the advanced countries and of the masses of the working people in the colonial and dependent countries, and are hastening the collapse of the petty-bourgeois national illusion that nations can live together in peace and equality under capitalism.

It follows from the above-enunciated fundamental premises that the cornerstone of the whole policy of the Communist International on the national and colonial question must be closer union of the proletarians and working masses generally of all nations and countries for a joint revolutionary struggle for the overthrow of the landlords and the bourgeoisie; for this alone will guarantee victory over capitalism, without which the abolition of national oppression and inequality is impossible.

The world political situation has now placed the dictatorship of the proletariat on the order of the day, and all events in world politics are inevitably revolving around one central point, *viz.*, the struggle of the world bourgeoisie against the Soviet Russian Republic, around which are inevitably grouping, on the one hand, the movement for Soviets [workers' councils] among the advanced workers of all countries, and, on the other, all the national liberation movements in the colonies and among the oppressed nationalities, whom bitter experience is teaching that there be no salvation for them except in the victory of the Soviet system over world imperialism.

Consequently, one must not confine oneself at the present time to the bare recognition or proclamation of the need for closer union between the working people of the various nations; it is necessary to pursue a policy that will achieve the closest alliance of all the national and colonial liberation movements with Soviet Russia, the form of this alliance to be determined by the degree of development of the Communist movement among the proletariat of each country, or of the bourgeois-democratic liberation movement of the workers and peasants in backward countries or among backward nationalities.

With regard to the more backward states and nations, in which feudal or patriarchal and patriarchal–peasant relations predominate, it is particularly important to bear in mind:

> First, that all Communist Parties must assist the bourgeois-democratic liberation movement in these countries, and that the duty of rendering the most active assistance rests primarily upon the workers of the country *upon which the backward nation is dependent colonially or financially* [emphasis added];
> Second, that it is necessary to wage a fight against the clergy and other influential reactionary and mediaeval elements in backward countries;
> Third, that it is necessary to combat Pan-Islamism and similar trends which strive to combine the liberation movement against European and American imperialism with the attempt to strengthen the positions of the khans, landlords, mullahs, etc.;
> Fourth, that it is necessary in the backward countries to give special support to the peasant movement against the landlords, against large landownership, and against all manifestations or survivals of feudalism, and to strive to lend the peasant movement the most revolutionary character and establish the closest possible alliance between the West-European Communist proletariat and the

revolutionary peasant movement in the East, in the colonies, and in the backward countries generally;

Fifth, that it is necessary to wage a determined struggle against the attempt to paint the bourgeois-democratic liberation trends in the backward countries in Communist colours; the Communist International must support the bourgeois-democratic national movements in colonial and backward countries only on condition that, in all backward countries, the elements of future proletarian parties which are Communist not only in name shall be grouped together and trained to appreciate their special tasks, *viz.*, to fight the bourgeois-democratic movements within their own nations; the Communist International must enter into a temporary alliance with bourgeois democracy in colonial and backward countries, but must not merge with it and must under all circumstances preserve the independence of the proletarian movement even if in its most rudimentary form ...

The age-old oppression of colonial and weak nationalities by the imperialist powers has not only filled the working masses of the oppressed countries with animosity towards the oppressing nations but also with distrust of them in general, even of the proletariat of those nations. The despicable betrayal of Socialism by the majority of the official leaders of the proletariat of the oppressing nations in 1914–19, when 'defence of the fatherland' was used as a social-chauvinist cloak to conceal the defence of the 'right' of 'their' bourgeoisie to oppress colonies and rob financially dependent countries, could not but enhance this perfectly legitimate distrust. On the other hand, the more backward a country is, the stronger is the hold within it of small agricultural production, patriarchalism and ignorance, which inevitably lends particular strength and tenacity to the deepest of petty-bourgeois prejudices, *viz.*, national egoism and national narrowness. As these prejudices can disappear only after imperialism and capitalism have disappeared in the advanced countries, and after the whole foundation of the economic life of the backward countries has radically changed, these prejudices cannot but die out very slowly. It is therefore the duty of the class-conscious Communist proletariat of all countries to treat with particular caution and attention the survivals of national sentiments among the countries and nationalities which have been longest oppressed, and it is also necessary to make certain concessions with a view to hastening the extinction of the aforementioned distrust and prejudices. Unless the proletariat, and, following it, all the toiling masses, of all countries and nations all over the world voluntarily strive for alliance and unity, the victory over capitalism cannot be successfully achieved.

Ho Chi Minh, 'The Path which Led Me to Leninism' (April 1960), in Ho Chi Minh, *Selected Works*, Volume IV (Hanoi: Foreign Languages Publishing House, 1962). Excerpts taken from pages 448–50.

After World War I, I made my living in Paris, now as a retoucher at a photographer's, now as painter of 'Chinese antiquities' (made in France!). I would distribute leaflets denouncing the crimes committed by the French colonialists in Viet-Nam.

At that time, I supported the October Revolution only instinctively, not yet grasping all its historic importance. I loved and admired Lenin because he was a great patriot who liberated his compatriots; until then, I had read none of his books.

The reason for my joining the French Socialist Party was that these 'ladies and gentlemen' – as I called my comrades at that moment – had shown their sympathy toward me, toward the struggle of the oppressed peoples. But I understood neither what was a party, a trade-union, nor what was Socialism or Communism.

Heated discussions were then taking place in the branches of the [French] Socialist Party, about the question of whether the Socialist Party should remain in the Second International, should a Second-and-a-half International be founded, or should the Socialist Party join Lenin's Third International? I attended the meetings regularly, twice or thrice a week, and attentively listened to the discussions. First, I could not understand thoroughly. Why were the discussions so heated? Either with the Second, Second-and-a-half, or Third International, the revolution could be waged. What was the use of arguing then? As for the First International, what had become of it?

What I wanted most to know – and this precisely was not debated in the meetings – was: Which International sides with the people of colonial countries?

I raised this question – the most important in my opinion – in a meeting. Some comrades answered: It is the Third, not the Second, International. And a comrade gave me Lenin's 'Thesis on the National and Colonial Questions', published by *l'Humanité*, to read.

There were political terms difficult to understand in this thesis. But by dint of reading it again and again, finally I could grasp the main part of it. What emotion, enthusiasm, clear-sightedness, and confidence it instilled into me! I was overjoyed to tears. Though sitting alone in my room, I shouted aloud as if addressing large crowds: 'Dead martyrs, compatriots! This is what we need, this is the path to our liberation!'

After then, I had entire confidence in Lenin, in the Third International.

Formerly, during the meetings of the Party branch, I only listened to the discussion; I had a vague belief that all were logical, and could not differentiate as to who were right and who were wrong. But from then on, I also plunged into the debates and discussed with fervor. Though I was still lacking French words to express all my thoughts, I smashed the allegations attacking Lenin and the Third International with no less vigor. My only argument was: 'If you do not condemn colonialism, if you do not side with the colonial people, what kind of revolution are you waging?'

Not only did I take part in the meetings of my own Party branch, but I also went to other Party branches to lay down 'my position'. Now I must tell again that Comrades Marcel Cachin, Vaillant Couturier, Monmousseau [French Communists], and many others helped me to broaden my knowledge. Finally, at the Tours Congress, I voted with them for our joining the Third International.

At first, patriotism, not yet communism, led me to have confidence in Lenin, in the Third International. Step by step, along the struggle, by studying Marxism-Leninism parallel with participation in practical activities, I gradually came upon the fact that only Socialism and Communism can liberate the oppressed nations and the working people throughout the world from slavery.

There is a legend, in our country as well as in China, on the miraculous 'Book of the Wise'. When facing great difficulties, one opens it and finds a way out. Leninism is not only a miraculous 'book of the wise', a compass for us Vietnamese revolutionaries and people; it is also the radiant sun illuminating our path to final victory, to Socialism and Communism.

4. Communist revolts in Indonesia and Vietnam

In the course of the early 1920s, the Communist International (Comintern), with its headquarters in the Soviet Union, set about creating the basis for a global revolutionary movement. So far as Asia and the colonized world in general were concerned, the guiding strategy was that of an alliance between revolutionary forces and the 'bourgeois-democratic' section of elite nationalist movements. The model for this strategy was the tactical alliance formed in Canton in 1924 between the Chinese Communist Party (CCP, formed in 1921), and the Chinese Nationalist Party (KMT), with the aim of throwing out the regional warlords, ending colonial control of parts of China and the Chinese economy, and uniting China. On the basis of this alliance, the Comintern was able to establish a revolutionary network throughout south China and Southeast Asia. Among the organizations in this network were the Partai Komunis Indonesia (PKI), formed in 1920, the Vietnamese Revolutionary Youth League (RYL), formed by Ho Chi Minh/Nguyen Ai Quoc (see Glossary) in Canton in 1925, and the Malayan Communist Party (MCP), a mainly Chinese urban organization formed in 1930.

It should be noted that the Comintern originally intended that colonial revolutionary movements should come under the tutelage of the communist parties of the colonial 'mother' country; that, for example, the French communists should 'guide' the Vietnamese revolutionary movement. However, logistic difficulties obstructed these links. More importantly, perhaps, Southeast Asian revolutionaries – particularly Ho Chi Minh – resisted this reproduction in revolutionary terms of the hated colonial relationship. There was a constant effort during this period to break loose from a European-guided global strategy, and instead develop policies that were relevant to the Asian situation.

Nevertheless, the international Comintern network gave confidence and coherence to the Southeast Asian communists; and the ideology of Marxism-

Leninism, translated into simple propaganda, enabled them to mobilize and at the same time transform the 'world-view' of the peasantry and the traditional rural hinterland in a way that no other movement could. Indeed, in the case of Indonesia, the PKI were in the early 1920s virtually destroyed by their own success in the mass mobilization of certain regions of Java and Sumatra. Their almost messianic message of anti-colonialism stirred up activity and expectations that they were in the end unable to control. In 1926 and 1927, ill-coordinated revolts broke out in west Sumatra and western and eastern Java under local PKI leadership. Their fragmented nature meant that they were easily suppressed by the Dutch. Although in reality these revolts weakened the PKI for almost a decade, the evidence that they provided of a global communist conspiracy greatly alarmed the colonial authorities and checked their willingness to make concessions to Indonesian nationalism.

The most traumatic event for Asian communism at this time, however, was the bloody breakup of the CCP/KMT alliance in China in 1927, and the subsequent civil war between the Chinese nationalists and the Chinese communists. The policy of encouraging alliances between communist parties and 'bourgeois-democratic' nationalist parties was reversed by the Comintern. Henceforth – and until just before the Second World War – communist parties were expected to remain aloof from mainstream nationalist activity. This was reflected in the founding programme of the Indochina Communist Party (ICP), which – after the collapse of the Revolutionary Youth League after 1927 – was formed under Ho Chi Minh's guidance in 1930 (see extract below). In this programme, the 'class struggle' within Vietnam was given virtually equal status with the 'patriotic struggle' against France.

No sooner had the Indochina Communist Party been formed, in 1930, than it found itself plunged into a situation of nation-wide unrest in Vietnam, unrest that had been largely stimulated by the disastrous local effects of the global depression. Between 1929 and 1931, large parts of Vietnam were convulsed by strikes, demonstrations and local incidents of violence directed against French and Vietnamese administrators. Although the ICP was able to give coherence and organization to what would otherwise have been a chaotic series of local uprisings – and, in the Nghe-An/Ha Tinh area of central Vietnam, were even able to set up a network of local village 'Soviets' under their authority – the crushing of these revolts by the French decimated the party at its moment of inception. The surviving Vietnamese communists, however, had learned some vital lessons in the course of the 1930–31 revolts; crucial among them was an awareness that emphasizing class struggle over national unity merely weakened the Vietnamese nationalist movement. The relationship between patriotic unity against the French and the fight for social justice within Vietnamese society itself was a strategic problem that Ho Chi Minh was to resolve in the course of the next decade.

It is interesting to compare the following analysis, by the newly formed Indochina Communist Party, of the situation in Vietnam and Indochina, with the rhetoric surrounding the Saya San rebellion in Burma at roughly the same time.

'Political Theses of the Indochinese Communist Party, October 1930', in *An Outline History of the Viet Nam Workers' Party, 1930–1970* (Hanoi: Foreign Languages Publishing House, 1970).

The characteristics of the situation in Indochina [A survey of the alliance of interest between French imperialism/capitalism, and Vietnamese 'feudalism'] Indochina (Viet Nam, Cambodia, Laos) is a settlement of French imperialism. So, its economy is dependent upon that of French imperialism. The following are the two outstanding features of the development of Indochina:

a) Indochina must develop independently, but it cannot do so because of its colonial status.

b) Class contradiction has grown ever fiercer between the workers, peasants and other toiling people on the one hand, and the feudal landowners, capitalists and imperialists on the other.

Economic contradictions:

a) Though the bulk of agricultural products is exported by the imperialists, the economy has remained feudal in character. Most plantations (rubber, cotton, coffee, etc.) belong to French capitalists. The greater part of the land is owned by native landlords, who exploit it in the feudal way, i.e. rent it in small plots to poor tenants for a very high rent. Rice yields are besides lower in Indochina than in other countries (per hectare paddy output in Malaya: 2,150 kilograms; in Siam, 1,870 kilograms; in Europe, 4,570 kilograms; in Indochina, only 1,210 kilograms). More rice is exported every year, but this is not due to the development of rice-growing, only to increased plundering of the people's rice by the capitalists.

b) The oppressive regime imposed by French imperialism hampers the development of the productive forces in Indochina. The imperialists have not built heavy industries (like iron works, machine-building etc.) for this would harm the monopoly of French industry. They only develop those industries which serve their administration and trade, for instance railway lines, small shipyards, etc.

The aim of French imperialism is to make Indochina an economic dependency of France, and so it promotes only those industries which it finds more profitable to develop in Indochina than in France itself. Raw material exploitation is meant not to help Indochina's economy develop independently, but to prevent French industry's dependence on other imperialisms.

c) Since exportation is in the hands of French capitalists, internal commerce and production is dependent upon the export requirements of the French imperialists. The more exports increase, the more the country is drained of its natural resources by imperialism. Another special feature:

French banks (*Banque de l'Indochine, Crédit foncier*, etc.) collect capital from native people to aid French exporters.

In short: Indochina's economy remains an agricultural one, with predominant feudal features. All this interferes with its independent development.

Class contradictions [the alliance of interest between Vietnamese peasants and workers]:

French imperialism, in alliance with native landlords, traders and usurers, ruthlessly exploits the peasants. It takes the country's farm produce for export, imports its own goods for sale within the country, imposes high taxation, drives the peasantry to misery and craftsmen to unemployment.

Land is more and more concentrated in the hands of the imperialists and landlords; the existence of numerous intermediaries causes the rent that has to be paid by poor tenants to be all the higher. The latter are also soaked so exorbitantly by usurers that they often are compelled to give them their lands or even their children in payment of their debts.

The imperialists pay no attention to keeping the dykes in good repair for protection against floods. Irrigation facilities are in the hands of the capitalists, who exact a high price for their use: no money, no water. And so more and more crop failures occur because of flood and drought. Not only are the peasants prevented from developing their economy, but they also grow increasingly dependent upon the capitalists and fare worse and worse; unemployment and starvation afflict more and more people.

The old economy is falling to pieces very fast, yet new industry is developing at a very slow rate; factories, workshops, etc. cannot hire all the poor and unemployed and many have to starve in the countryside where the situation is truly tragic.

In the factories, plantations and mines, the capitalists cruelly exploit and oppress the workers. Their wages, which are at starvation level, are subject to cuts by all kinds of fines. They work eleven, twelve hours a day on an average. Abuses and blows are rained on them. When they fall sick, far from getting any medical attention, they are thrown out into the streets. Social insurance is totally nonexistent. In plantations and mines, the owners pen their workers up in camps and forbid them to wander out. They use the system of indenture to recruit and move people away to places where they can impose their own law on the workers and even inflict penalties on them. Due to such harsh working conditions, large numbers of workers in Indochina suffer from dangerous diseases (tuberculosis, trachoma, malaria, etc.) and more and more of them die at a very young age.

The Indochinese proletariat is not yet numerous, but the number of workers, especially plantation workers, is on the increase. They fight ever more actively. The peasants have also awakened and fiercely opposed the imperialists and feudalists. Strikes in 1928, 1929 and the violent outbursts of workers and peasants this year [1930] clearly prove that class struggle in Indochina is gaining momentum. *The most outstanding and important feature in the revolutionary movement in Indochina is that the struggle of the worker-peasant masses has taken on a very clearly independent character and is no longer influenced by nationalism as it used to be* [emphasis added].

Characteristics and tasks of the Indochinese revolution [Although the anti-colonial struggle is at the 'bourgeois-democratic' stage – i.e. pre-socialist, and with the aim of creating an independent Vietnam/Indochina with a modern economy – it must be headed by a 'worker–peasant' alliance. This is because the nationalist elite is weak, dominated by the landlord class, riddled with landlord interests, and untrustworthy.]

The revolutionary movement in Indochina is growing day by day. In its initial period, the Indochinese revolution will be a bourgeois-democratic revolution, for it cannot yet directly tackle organizational problems of a socialist structure; the country is still very weak economically, many feudal vestiges still linger, the balance of class forces is not yet tipped in favour of the proletariat; besides imperialism holds oppressive sway. For these reasons, in the present period, the revolution will only have an agrarian and anti-imperialist character.

The bourgeois-democratic revolution is a preparatory period leading to socialist revolution. Once it has won victory, and a worker–peasant government has been established, industry within the country will develop, proletarian organizations will be reinforced, the leadership of the proletariat will be consolidated, and the balance of class forces will be altered to the advantage of the proletariat. *Then the struggle will develop in depth and breadth and the bourgeois-democratic revolution will advance toward the proletarian revolution* [emphasis added]. The present period is one of world proletarian revolution and socialist building in the Soviet Union; thanks to help from the working class exercising dictatorship in various countries, Indochina will bypass the capitalist stage and fight its way direct to socialism.

The essential aim of the bourgeois-democratic revolution is on the one hand to do away with the feudal vestiges and the modes of pre-capitalist exploitation and to carry out a thorough agrarian revolution; on the other hand, to overthrow French imperialism and achieve complete independence for Indochina. The two phases of the struggle are closely connected, for only by deposing imperialism can we eliminate the landlord class and carry out a successful agrarian revolution; conversely, only by abolishing the feudal regime can we knock down imperialism.

In order to reach these essential goals, we must set up worker–peasant Soviet power. Worker–peasant Soviet power alone is the very powerful instrument which will make it possible to overthrow imperialism, feudalism and landlordism, give land to the tillers, and legal protection to the interests of the proletariat.

The essential task of the bourgeois-democratic revolution are the following:

1. To overthrow French imperialism, feudalism and landlordism.
2. To set up a worker–peasant government.
3. To confiscate all lands belonging to foreign and native landlords and to religious organizations, and hand them over to middle and poor peasants, the right of ownership of the land being in the hands of the worker–peasant government.
4. To nationalize all big undertakings of the foreign capitalists.
5. To abolish all current taxes and corvées (forced labour) and institute a progressive tax.
6. To decree an 8-hour workday and improve the living standard of the workers and toiling people.
7. Indochina to be completely independent; national self-determination to be recognized.
8. To organize a worker–peasant army.
9. Equality between man and woman.
10. Support to the Soviet Union; alliance with the proletariat all over the world and with the revolutionary movement in the colonies and semi-colonies [viz. China].

CHAPTER 4

The Impact of the Japanese Intervention in Southeast Asia, 1940–45

This Singapore surrender has been a terrific blow to all of us. It is not merely the immediate dangers which threaten in the Indian Ocean and the menace to our communications with the Middle East. It is the dread that we are only half-hearted in fighting the whole-hearted. It is even more than that. We intellectuals must feel that in all these years we have derided the principles of force upon which our Empire is built. We undermined confidence in our own formula. The intellectuals of 1780 did the same. (Harold Nicolson, *Diaries and Letters 1939–1945* (London: Collins, 1967), p. 214)

The situation in Southeast Asia in 1939

During the inter-war years, constitutional change had occurred at very different rates across the Southeast Asian region. In the Philippines, following the United States–Philippines agreement of 1934, a self-governing Filipino government – the Philippine Commonwealth – and head of state had been installed, even though the Americans still retained ultimate sovereignty. It was, however, agreed that full sovereignty should be conceded to the Philippines within a decade.

In 1937, Burma was separated from British India and its new constitution created a Burmese government structure, with a Burmese prime minister and cabinet. The essentials of power, however, remained firmly in the hands of the British governor and Westminster. The 1930s, and particularly the years 1937 to 1941, also revealed a considerable degree of damaging infighting between the Burmese leaders competing for office, and between this leadership as a whole and the younger, more radical political leaders – particularly those connected with Dó-bama Asiayone (roughly, 'We Burmans Association') founded in 1930 – who refused to co-operate with the British political system in any way.

In Malaya and the Straits Settlements, political development and constitutional change had been delayed, first, by the fact of British commitment to 'protecting' the existing Malay sultanates and, second, by the ethnic–

economic divide between the Malays and the immigrants. The latter, mainly Chinese, had economic influence but no political rights as a community. However, a number of developments had occurred during the inter-war years: Malay political consciousness was growing; trade union and radical organizations had taken root among the Chinese immigrant community; and demands were surfacing among the elite Chinese business community of the Straits Settlements for a greater political role.

In Indonesia, the moves to greater political participation – triggered mainly by the creation of the Volksraad (People's Council) in 1918 – had been slowed down by the radicalism of the 1920s. In an alarmed reaction to what was seen as the threat of communism and political extremism, the Dutch sent key nationalist figures into internal exile in the late 1920s and early 1930s; among these figures were those who were to become leaders of the Indonesian nationalist movement after the Second World War: Sukarno, Mohammad Hatta and Sutan Syahrir. Despite this action, during the inter-war years there had been a huge burgeoning of political–nationalist activity and the development not only of political parties but also of a grass-roots nationalist following. Strong sentiments of anti-colonialism were increasingly pressing against a system unwilling to change.

The same situation prevailed in Vietnam, though not in Laos and Cambodia. In the two latter countries, the indigenous population – undisturbed, except for a tiny elite, by development or education – remained rooted in their traditional lives, while the French sustained an on-the-whole stable relationship with the respective elites of the two countries. Disturbances, such as they were, came largely from 'unpacified' minority regions and communist activity in the mainly Vietnamese work-forces of the rubber and coffee plantations.

In Vietnam, the avenues to peaceful political change had been blocked by French colonial policy, the pressure of the large and influential French 'colon' community, and the fears of communism and radicalism that were aroused in the French colonial government by the revolts of 1929–31. In the early 1930s, there was an attempt by the new emperor, Bao Dai, and his advisers to use the monarchy as a vehicle for redefining the French–Vietnamese relationship and initiating political reform; this initiative failed, however. With this failure of Bao Dai to transform the 'protectorate' into a more equal relationship in which the Vietnamese administration of Annam and Tonkin would be able to modernize itself and play an increasingly significant role, the French missed the last clear chance to develop a political relationship with moderate Vietnamese nationalism. As in Indonesia, a radicalized elite – in which, in the case of Vietnam, a well-organized if small communist movement played an increasingly significant role – was pushing against an intransigent colonial government.

The case of Siam/Thailand was special. In the late nineteenth century, the Chakkri dynasty of Siam was able to retain its independence, first, by a willingness to make timely trading and legal concessions to the colonial powers; second, by the initiation of an administrative revolution along Western lines that ensured that these agreements were enforced, and that central authority and political stability were maintained during a very difficult transitional period; and, finally, by timely territorial concessions to the neighbouring European colonial powers in Malaya, Indochina and Burma. There was, in addition, the crucial fact that Britain and France were, by the end of the nineteenth century – the very time that Siam's independence was most vulnerable – beginning to reach an accommodation, both in Europe and globally. Neither side, it turned out, was prepared to risk this accommodation by a contest for influence over Siam; both were therefore content to retain the kingdom's independent 'buffer' status.

However, by the early twentieth century pressures were growing in Siam that threatened political stability from *within*. These amounted to demands for a greater political say by the new bureaucratic elite that the administrative reforms had created. These demands were couched in the Westernized language of democracy and rights. From another perspective, this growing elite unrest could be seen as an expression of nationalist aspirations that were bucking not against colonial rule as such but against Siam's subordination to a European-dominated Southeast Asia. This discontent culminated in the Revolution of June 1932 – which, despite the democratic rhetoric, was essentially a coup d'état – as a result of which, power was effectively transferred from the monarchy to the bureaucracy. In the atmosphere of political instability that prevailed in Siam (renamed Thailand in 1939) in the decade of the 1930s, there was a gradual shift to military dominance of the state.

The Japanese intervention in Southeast Asia

During the course of the 1930s, global stability was gradually ripped apart by a combination of ideological forces and the determination of a number of states – particularly Germany, the USSR, Italy and Japan – to break down the international system that had been created in the wake of the First World War. In the wider historical perspective, the upheavals of the 1930s and 1940s could be seen as the very imperfect realization of a process of international adjustment designed to accommodate new and powerful states – including the United States – whose power and wealth were not matched by their global status.

It was, of course, the imperial powers of Western Europe – in particular Britain, France and the Netherlands – that were to be the main victims of this process of international adjustment. In ideological terms, liberal democracy retreated before the seemingly more energetic forces of communism, fascism and national-socialism (along with local variants). In international terms, the weakness of the foundations of empire – empire that had in the early twentieth century been given a liberal gloss by the introduction of half-hearted educational, political and social reforms – had already been exposed in the First World War. It was in fact only the timely alliance concluded between the United Kingdom and Japan in 1902 that protected the position of the Western imperial powers in Southeast Asia and the Far East during the First World War. With the expiry of that alliance in 1921, and the subsequent failure of Britain to enter into any solid security relationship with the United States in the Pacific region, it was only a matter of time before Europe's imperial bluff in Asia was finally called.

In the last decade of the nineteenth century and the first decade of the twentieth century, Japan had evolved from a local Asian power to an imperial power in the European mould. It was natural that, in the whole period from 1895 to 1945, Japan's imperial ambitions should primarily focus on China. With the crumbling of the Manchu empire, the subsequent failure of the Chinese Republic to restore unity or stability after the 1911 revolution, the breakup of the alliance between Chinese nationalism and Chinese communism in 1927 and the consequent civil war, China's weakness offered a perfect target for a power seeking a place in the imperial sun. Japan's ambitions were to a large extent restrained by the Anglo-Japanese alliance that lasted from 1902 to 1921; after 1921, however, a security vacuum existed in the Pacific region.

Japan's imperial ambitions were fully ignited in the late 1920s by a combination of circumstances: in particular, the impact of the global depression on an economy that was heavily dependent on the international market; growing military control over the political structure; and the weakness of an international system, based on the League of Nations, that was losing credibility by the day. Japanese incursions against China accelerated through the decade of the 1930s. Though the Chinese communists and nationalists formed a belated 'patriotic alliance' against Japan in 1937, by 1939 Japan had control of virtually the whole coastline of China from Manchuria to Hainan Island.

The outbreak of the Second World War in Europe in September 1939 offered Japan a golden opportunity to consolidate and expand its empire, particularly into Southeast Asia. Japan's immediate objective was that of cutting off aid from Burma and Indochina to the Chinese nationalist government in Chungking, the capital of nationalist China. The wider goal, however, eventually became that of the incorporation of Southeast Asia as the economic hub of an expanded Japanese empire. The realization of these ambitions depended on a two-fold strike against Western interests in the Pacific: the first against the European imperial powers in Southeast Asia, and the second – much more risky – against the United States' Pacific territorial possessions and its Pacific fleet.

The Japanese conquest of Southeast Asia

In September 1939 Japan, having captured Hainan Island, hovered over Southeast Asia. The two states that were the immediate focus of interest for

Japan at this stage were French Indochina, with its railway link to the interior of nationalist-controlled China, and Siam/Thailand, strategically placed as it was at the heart of mainland Southeast Asia. From late 1939 to 1941, a complex diplomatic struggle for influence in Thailand was waged between the Western powers and Japan (see 'Thailand and Japan in the Second World War', p. 89). Already, by 1938, Thailand had appeared to be moving towards Japan and away from its traditional European regional mentors, Britain and France. This was reflected in the consolidation of military rule and the adoption by Marshal Phibun Songkhram, Thailand's military leader, of a quasi-fascist authoritarian style of government, and a pro-Japanese stance on international issues. The decisive lurch to Japan came, however, after France's defeat in Europe at the hands of Germany in the summer of 1940.

Japan's open incursion into Southeast Asia was triggered by this French defeat. In the autumn of 1940, the French were compelled to grant the Japanese the right to establish military bases in northern Indochina, thereby cutting off the aid route to nationalist China. In the winter of 1940–41, the French were forced by the Japanese to concede territories in western Laos and Cambodia to Thailand; these were territories that had been gained by France at Siam/Thailand's expense in the early twentieth century. In July 1941, after the German invasion of the USSR, Japan extended its military presence from north to south Indochina; the French administration in Indochina – cut off, and controlled by the French government set up in Vichy after the German defeat of France – had no alternative but to acquiesce. The stage was now set for the Japanese take-over of Southeast Asia.

On 7 December 1941, Japan attacked the United States naval base at Pearl Harbor in the Hawaiian islands, and at the same time launched its attack on Southeast Asia. Within a mere few months the Japanese had, in a devastating series of military blows, taken Malaya, Singapore, Burma, Borneo and the whole of the Dutch East Indies, as well as the Philippines. The crushing military defeat of Britain in Southeast Asia, symbolized above all by the fall of Singapore, was to have the most far-reaching consequences of all Britain's defeats in the Second World War. It began the drama – a drama that was to be played out over the ensuing decades – of the collapse of the European imperial system (see 'The impact of the fall of Singapore', p. 97). By early 1942, Japan stood at the gates of Australia and British India.

The impact of the Japanese military takeover of Southeast Asia

The Japanese incorporated their conquests in Southeast Asia within their 'Greater East Asian Co-Prosperity Sphere'. Thailand became a hub of the Japanese position in Southeast Asia. On 25 January 1942 it joined the war on the Japanese side, and it subsequently exploited its temporary strength to reclaim territory from Burma and Malaya as well as the territory it had already gained from French Indochina. French Indochina itself remained intact under a 'Vichy'-dominated regime, but had to co-exist with an over-powering Japanese military presence. In the course of 1943, the members of the political elites of Burma and the Philippines who had remained behind after the British and American defeats accepted independence – absolute in theory, but strictly curtailed in practice – from the Japanese. The Dutch East Indies/Indonesia and Malaya, however, remained under direct Japanese military rule. In these latter military-controlled regions, Japan was careful to leave day-to-day administration in the hands of the traditional administrative class that had served the colonial powers. At the same time, however, Japan released exiled politicians, such as Sukarno and Hatta, and encouraged the formation of a plethora of anti-Western, pro-Japanese, 'pan-Asian' mass organizations. Unlike the colonial powers, therefore, the Japanese unleashed mass grass-roots political activity; but only on their terms, and on condition – so far as Indonesia was concerned – that independence not be raised as an issue.

Faced with the task of defending a huge Pacific-Asian area, the Japanese adopted a contradictory policy towards Southeast Asia. On the one hand, as has been noted above, they facilitated, by mid-1943, the creation of in-dependent governments in Burma and the Philippines that would, they hoped, consolidate Japan's position in Southeast Asia and increase support for their war effort. They also encouraged anti-Western political or religious forces, including pan-Asian, regional and Islamic organizations. On the other hand, they tended, in practical terms, to rely on exactly the same local-level adminis-trators who had worked with the colonial powers. This was to create tensions that would burst out into the open – particularly in Indonesia – after the Japanese defeat. In addition, despite all the pan-Asian rhetoric, there was considerable resentment caused in Southeast Asia during this period by arbitrary and racist Japanese behaviour, and by the increasing economic hardships faced by a region where normal trading links were cut off and key resources were dedicated to the use of the Japanese war machine.

The course of the war, and its impact on political developments

The Allies had been humiliatingly defeated by the Japanese in Southeast Asia, but from their bases in eastern India, Australia and southern China, military preparations were immediately under way for the restraint of further Japanese advances and for the gradual reconquest of Southeast Asia.

Like the Japanese in Southeast Asia, the Allies built up networks of local military support, mainly for intelligence-gathering, sabotage and guerrilla operations directed against the Japanese war machine. Key elements among those drawn into this hotch-potch military alliance were the Chinese com-munist guerrillas in Malaya, and minorities in Burma and along the Burma–India frontier.

From the military point of view, the turning-points in the war came when, in late 1944 and early 1945, the United States reconquered the Philippines and the easternmost islands of Indonesia, and when – in the Burma–India theatre – the Japanese offensive against India failed in early-mid 1944 in the Kohima and Imphal campaigns.

The effect of this progressive 'squeezing' of the Japanese position in Southeast Asia was virtually to cut Japanese-held Southeast Asia off from the Japanese mainland. This led to an intensified effort by the Japanese military command to build local support for their war effort. The key to this was the unleashing of nationalist aspirations, particularly in Vietnam and Indonesia. In March 1945, the Japanese forcibly removed the French administration in Indochina and replaced it with quasi-independent regimes, under the respective monarchies, in Vietnam, Laos and Cambodia. In early 1945, the Japanese encouraged Indonesian nationalist leaders to prepare for the creation of an independent Indonesia.

At this crucial juncture the flagging fortunes of the communist movement and the Left in general in Southeast Asia were suddenly improved. In the period of the 1930s and up to 1941, communism in Southeast Asia had been forced underground by intense colonial repression, by isolation from more moderate, non-revolutionary sections of the respective nationalist movements, and (not least) by ideological confusion in the years 1939–41 as to the 'line' that the Comintern should take towards the Western democracies on one side and the fascist threat on the other. This was resolved by the German invasion of the Soviet Union in May 1941; thereafter the priority of all orthodox communist movements was the global defeat of fascism. This put communist movements in Southeast Asia in the incongruous – but temporarily highly advantageous – position of siding with the colonial powers to bring about the defeat of Japan.

Throughout Southeast Asia, communist guerrilla movements established themselves and launched, with varying degrees of intensity and effectiveness, anti-Japanese activities. In Vietnam, the Indochina Communist Party (ICP) formed a 'patriotic front' – the so-called 'Viet Minh' – in May 1941 on the Chinese–Vietnamese border. The objective of this organization was to liberate Vietnam from the unholy alliance of the 'colonialist' French and the 'fascist' Japanese. In the Philippines, the key resistance to the Japanese was led by the communist-dominated Hukbalahap guerrilla movement (formed in 1942), and the same role was played by the communist Malayan People's Anti-Japanese Army (MPAJA) in Malaya. Communists in Burma gained an important position in the military–political organizations – the Anti-Fascist Organization (AFO) and Anti-Fascist People's Freedom League (AFPFL) – secretly established against the Japanese by Aung San, defence minister of the supposedly pro-Japanese Burmese government. Finally, the Partai Komunis Indonesia (PKI) was able to rebuild its influence and organization in Java during the dying days of the Japanese occupation. As the Japanese position crumbled in Southeast

Asia, so the prestige of the communist movements and their political influence was enhanced – not least because of their military links with the Allies.

By the late spring of 1945, Burma had been reconquered by Britain's South-East Asia Command (SEAC) and plans were being laid for the re-conquest first of Malaya, and then of the rest of mainland and maritime Southeast Asia. But the apparently commanding position of the West was an illusion. The war years and the period of Japanese occupation had funda-mentally changed the political environment of Southeast Asia. Mass political movements had taken root in Southeast Asia during these years which, whatever their diverse ideological complexions and their internal divisions, were united in their aim of preventing the return of colonial authority (see 'The British reconquest of Burma', p. 104). This determination was matched by the new international climate of anti-colonialism, and consensus behind the idea that the principle of self-determination should now be applied *globally*. Most telling of all, perhaps, was the fact that, at the end of the war, the United States not only dominated Japan and the Pacific, but also had gained a strong foothold in Southeast Asia. And, just as Japan saw Thailand as the hub of its Southeast Asian forward strategy in 1939–41, so the United States built its post-war Southeast Asian policy on Thai–American friendship. The United States' strong defence of Thailand's post-war territorial integrity, in the face of British suggestions that Thailand should be punished for its support of Japan during the war, was an early indication of the fundamentally changed power-relationships in the region in 1945 (see 'The United States' new role in Southeast Asia', p. 110).

READINGS

1. Thailand and Japan in the Second World War

When people look back on the twentieth century, it is likely that they will be less amazed by the rapid collapse of the European empires than by the fact that they were able to survive for so long. It could be argued, in fact, that after the First World War, the disintegration of these empires in Asia was only a matter of time. What sustained the European empires through the 1920s, at least, was, first, the sheer momentum of the concept of white prestige in the colonies themselves – what could be called the colonial bluff; the common interests of the main colonial powers that prohibited serious inter-colonial rivalry; the ambiguous semi-alliance, semi-rivalry between the European democracies and the new world-power, the United States; and the temporary moderation of Japan's foreign policy.

Seen in this context, the Revolution in Siam in 1932 has a significance far beyond its domestic repercussions. On the face of it, this was nothing more than a bloodless coup d'état launched against the absolute monarchy by a combination of military and civilian officials (the so-called People's Party) which used the language of democracy and even revolution, but which soon reached an accommodation with the loyalists within the elite. The consequence was the creation of a political system with a very limited structure of representation, where power was concentrated in the hands of leading factions in the bureaucracy, and where the key symbol of the *ancien régime* – the monarchy – was retained.

The wider significance of this coup lay in the fact that it represented an assertion of modern Siamese, or Thai, nationalism. The kingdom of Siam had retained its independence only by accommodating itself to European dominance in Southeast Asia, and acquiescing in the exertion of considerable European influence over the internal affairs of Siam, via diplomatic pressure and the use of European advisers in key posts. The Chakkri royal family itself sent its children to English public schools to be educated, and the ties with Britain in particular were very close.

The 1932 coup and its aftermath was a sign that the cosy world of Franco-British dominance in mainland Southeast Asia was coming to an end. Even if the democratic and socialist programmes of some of the People's Party leaders came to nothing, a new Thai nationalist ideology did take root in the 1930s. This was bolstered by the growing power of the army in Thai politics after 1932 – particularly after 1938 – and by the example of Japan where, by the late 1920s, the armed forces had begun effectively to dominate the political system and initiate a period of successful military expansion into China.

The importance of this shift in Thailand's political position rapidly became apparent in the world crisis of the late 1930s. The gradual – sometimes hesitant – movement of Thailand towards a full-scale alliance with Japan between 1938 and 1941 is chronicled in the following extract from E. Bruce Reynolds's *Thailand and Japan's Southern Advance, 1940–1945*. Given that gaining a foothold in Thailand provided the key to the conquest of maritime Southeast Asia and to the launching of attacks against the defences of India itself, the strategic significance of Thai policy at this time is obvious. As has so often been the case since, Britain was able at this time to cover its weak position only by diplomatic finesse.

E. Bruce Reynolds, *Thailand and Japan's Southern Advance, 1940–1945*
(London: Macmillan, 1994). Excerpts taken from pages 25–80.

Japanese–Thai relations moved into a new phase in December 1938 when Phibun Songkhram, the young and vigorous defense minister, assumed the leadership of Siam's government. The Japanese, who considered him favorably disposed toward them, now had reason to believe that they had gained the upper hand in the contest for influence in Bangkok. Phibun was by no means wholeheartedly 'pro-Japanese', however, and would act according to his perception of national and personal interest. His critics might add that he failed to see any distinction between the two.

In his rise to power Phibun had reinforced his position within the army and even brought a portion of the rival navy behind him by vigorously advocating increased defense expenditures. External events played into his hand, too. As British minister [equivalent of ambassador] Crosby reported, Germany's gains in Austria and at Munich, and Japan's offensive in South China 'lent weight to the argument that the road to safety, as well as to glory, was the military one'. These factors made Phibun the heir apparent when, after a budget dispute, Phraya Phahon [then Prime Minister] dissolved a recalcitrant National Assembly in September 1938 and resigned.

The British had good reason to be nervous about Phibun's ascendance. Not only had he once justified his military buildup by pointedly observing that Japan had won the respect of the Europeans through successful militarization, he also clearly was impressed by the achievements of Mussolini and Hitler. In this admiration he was joined by many other Asian nationalists of the time. As Burma's Ba Maw later recalled:

> we must never forget the tremendous spell that Hitler and the Axis cast over the East generally. It was almost hypnotic. The Axis leaders were believed irresistible. They would create a new world order, as they declared they would and were actually doing; and the East as a whole was longing for some kind of really new order.

Colonial subjects like Ba Maw and India's Subhas Chandra Bose hoped that such wholesale change would bring liberation for their homelands, while the leaders of Asia's three independent states – Japan, China, and Siam – hoped that fascist/national socialist techniques might help foster the spirit and discipline needed to unify and strengthen their nations. Of course, the Japanese already possessed such qualities in remarkable degree, yet their further enhancement was a central goal of Japan's right-wing political activists of the 1930s. While communism, the ideological opposite number to fascism/ national socialism, also seemed to offer means of rapidly developing national power, its rigidly egalitarian theme and its rejection of tradition made it unappealing to the socially conservative military men who had seized the political initiative in Asia's independent states.

Germany's considerable prestige in Asia further enhanced the appeal of national socialism. Asian military officers admired Germany's nineteenth-century success in nation building, its military and technical capabilities, and the discipline of its citizenry. A number of them had trained in Germany, including three of the four senior army officers who led the 1932 coup in Siam. Although all three independent Asian states had joined the Allied side during World War I, they had done so for pragmatic reasons, not because of any particular enmity toward the Germans. Germany's recent phoenix-like rise from the ashes of defeat had rekindled admiration for that nation's strengths.

In Siam, Phibun had referred favorably to Germany and Italy in his speeches, and the Thai had purchased naval vessels from the Italians, as well as from the Japanese. An American correspondent reported that Phibun received 'foreign callers, other than high-ranking diplomats ... under a huge, life-size, and autographed photograph' of Mussolini, and foreign observers were struck by the similarity between Phibun's military training corps, the Yuwachon, and the Hitler Youth organization ...

Moreover, in promoting Thai nationalism, the Phibun regime used two appeals that, at least superficially, paralleled key elements in the Nazi program: the scapegoating of a highly visible domestic minority group, and irredentism based on a claim of racial affinity. The Chinese, whose economic domination was quite real – they controlled 90 per cent of the nation's commerce according to a 1938 report by the Thai government's British financial advisor – provided a ready target in the first instance. The return of territory lost to the French became the objective in the second ...

The Phibun government attempted to deal with the Chinese issue by imposing immigration restrictions, arresting and deporting suspected Chinese nationalist agitators, and closing Chinese schools and newspapers. The new cabinet also sought to encourage Thai economic advance by preserving certain occupations for citizens and by establishing state-sponsored enterprises to compete with the Chinese in various fields ...

This program was in no way comparable in severity to the brutal Nazi repression of the Jews, and the concerns that inspired it were cultural and political, not racial, since most members of the Thai elite had Chinese blood themselves. Still, there always was the danger that overzealous officials might push matters too far. Already, Wichit, the regime's chief propagandist, had stirred controversy by publicly referring to the Chinese as the 'Jews of the East' and suggesting that Nazi-style measures might be appropriate.

Meanwhile, the military clique's interest in asserting territorial claims had been made apparent in 1936 when the Defense Ministry circulated maps depicting the nation's 'lost territories'. Although land also had been sacrificed to the British, the irredentists focused on the more extensive and more 'essentially Thai' areas taken by the French. In their view, France had stolen nearly one-half of the nation's territory, almost half a million square kilometers.

The Phibun regime further signalled its interest in territorial expansion in June 1939 when it changed the country's name from Siam to Thailand. Although this was explained as nothing more than replacement of a foreign appellation with the English equivalent of the Thai language name for the state (Prathet Thai), Wichit had publicly linked the change to the view that the state was the legitimate homeland for all members of the Thai (or T'ai) race. According to Wichit's dubious racial theories, these included not only the Lao and the Shan, but also the Khmer.

Although the crackdown on Chinese nationalists and Thai interest in regaining 'lost territories' seemed to create opportunities for the Japanese,

British minister Crosby adopted a hopeful stance at the beginning of Phibun's premiership, noting that he showed signs of 'moderation and a sense of statesmanship which a year or two ago nobody would have expected'. Like other foreigners, Crosby was impressed by the new premier's impeccable manners and personal charm ...

[But] when Crosby returned from vacation in May 1939 he found striking evidence of a tilt toward Japan. The head of the Council of Regents, Prince Athit – whom Crosby described as pro-British 'sometimes ... to the verge of indiscretion' – reported overhearing talk by military figures from Phibun's inner circle that Britain and France would be unable to protect their possessions in Asia against a Japanese advance. In particular, Sin, the leader of the navy, foresaw a Japanese seizure of Hong Kong and Saigon, followed by a campaign to take Singapore by land. Prince Athit thought Phibun seemed to agree with this. In fact, at meetings on 21 and 22 July 1939, the premier would tell his cabinet that Thailand must look to Japan because the British could no longer be relied on.

This policy shift can be understood only in the context of international events during the first half of 1939. In Europe, the forces of General Francisco Franco, backed by the Germans and the Italians, had captured Madrid and claimed victory in the Spanish civil war; Hitler had seized all of Czechoslovakia; and Mussolini had marched into Albania. Crosby judged the Thai 'pretty badly shaken' by the fall of the latter two states. He believed that they had begun to fear that their country was 'only too likely to be left to her fate' if the Japanese moved southward. The bold occupation of Hainan Island in February and the Spratley Islands in March by Japan's navy seemed to presage just such an advance. Concurrently, the Japanese were debating German proposals to strengthen bilateral ties, and key figures in the army were pushing hard for an alliance. When the Germans and Italians established a political and military alliance in May, the Thai surely expected an early Japanese move into the Axis camp.

Not only had Britain and France refrained from challenging the advancing Axis powers in Europe, but the British evidently lacked the will and power to stand up to the Japanese in Asia. After accusing the British of harboring native terrorists in the northern Chinese city of Tientsin, Japanese forces had blockaded the British concession there in June 1939. Faced with the Axis menace in Europe, the British were forced to negotiate with the Japanese from a position of undisguisable weakness. Given the fact that the British ambassador in Japan, Sir Robert Craigie, believed that the Japanese had plans mapped out for a general assault on British possessions in Asia, and that he had narrowly averted war by negotiating a settlement of the Tientsin affair, it is hardly surprising that the Thai anticipated an early Japanese advance.

The advisor to the Thai Foreign Ministry, the suave, sophisticated veteran diplomat Prince Wan Waithayakon, emphasized to Crosby on 10 August 1939 that these events, not an affinity for Japan's cause, had led Phibun to turn to Japan ... He pointedly warned Crosby that because Britain 'seemed to lack the power and the will to safeguard her own interests in Eastern Asia', Thailand could not rely on British protection. He emphasized that while his government had no desire to take sides, a choice might have to be made if war came. Phibun himself made similar comments to a visiting Australian businessman, suggesting that the British dispel doubts about their resolve by stationing a fleet at Singapore ...

But the pro-Japan boom of mid-1939 proved to be short-lived and the series of events that led to its collapse clearly demonstrated the impact of European events on Thai strategy. First, Germany and the Soviet Union shocked the world by announcing their nonaggression pact on 23 August 1939. In the wake of this bombshell, which for the moment eliminated the prospect of a Japanese alliance with Germany, the cabinet fell in Tokyo. Then when the Germans began their assault on Poland at the beginning of September, the British and French declared war ...

Impressed by the new resolve of Britain and France, the Thai reverted to a middle-of-the-road stance between the European powers and the Japanese. The government also noticeably slackened its anti-Chinese campaign, apparently because Chiang Kai-shek's regime had shown greater-than-expected staying power in its war with Japan. In January 1940 Crosby had a particularly cordial session with Phibun. Acknowledging his past indiscretions, the premier indicated that experience and increased responsibility had taught him patience and given him new wisdom. As late as March, Prince Athit assured the British minister that although the Japanese had the navy's Sin 'in their pocket', the situation seemed generally favorable for the British and French ...

[Then came the German attack on France in Spring 1940.]

A clear indication of the impact the German offensive had on Thai thinking is a position paper that Wichit had presented on 4 May. He described neutrality as desirable, but impractical, because Thailand could not defend it. Passivity, he argued, would only invite disaster, but aggressive action to align with the likely victor could bring profit. Wichit saw Japan (a 'tiger' that could not be trusted) as a certain benefactor from the events in Europe. He did not expect the United States to fight, so he anticipated a Japanese southward advance. In such an event, he asserted, Thailand's best chance lay in befriending the Japanese 'tiger' ...

He argued that although Thailand needed to make a decision to join Japan before the outbreak of hostilities, there would have to be at least token resistance if the Japanese violated Thailand's sovereignty first. This would permit Thailand to save face and justify an alliance with Japan as a necessary bow to superior power. He also urged an all-out effort, based on appeals in the name of the nation's honor, to prevent, or at least to limit, any Japanese troop presence in Thailand. He concluded that cooperation with Japan, the rising power in the region, would save the country and might later bring territorial reward.

In late May, Phibun had taken a tour of southern Thailand and extended his stay, a move Crosby suspected was designed to give him time to reflect on the world situation. Upon his return he held a press conference, and afterwards met privately with a few editors. Through a parable about the problems a person would face if his well-known neighbors were suddenly ousted by a newcomer, Phibun revealed his uneasiness about the prospect of a drastic change in the regional power configuration. In a similar vein, he inserted kind words about defeated France in his National Day speech of 24 June.

Crosby astutely pinpointed the reason for this unease about the prospect of Japanese domination in a 30 June cable. He pointed out that from the Thai perspective the most advantageous diplomatic situation was a balance of power between their colonial neighbors and the Japanese that enabled them to play one side off against the other. This would be lost if Japan emerged as the predominant power, and the Thai would have no choice but to swing over to the Japanese side.

Japanese strategists, meanwhile, were fretting lest their country 'miss the bus'. With the Netherlands and France defeated and their resource-rich Asian possessions ripe for the picking, Japan needed to reach an understanding with Germany about the disposition of these territories, or take control of them before the Nazis did so. This lent new momentum to the push for joining the Axis alliance. Also, the army – which now exceeded even the navy in its enthusiasm for southward advance – saw in the new circumstances a chance to end the troublesome and costly war in China. As part of maneuvers to cut off Chiang Kai-shek's supply lines, the Japanese would coerce the British into closing the Burma Road and begin pressuring the French colonial regime in Indochina to permit the stationing of Japanese troops.

The Thai immediately recognized Indochina's vulnerability – Phibun told Crosby on 6 July that he expected Japan to set up another Manchukuo [the Japanese puppet-state in Manchuria] there – and a clamor developed for Thailand to claim a share of the spoils. At the beginning of July, an official of the Thai Foreign Ministry frankly told Crosby that if the Japanese took over Indochina the Thai would attempt to reclaim their former territories ...

[Thereafter, events in the region moved rapidly. In the autumn of 1940, the Japanese forced the French Indochina administration to accept the stationing of Japanese troops and airfields in northern Indochina. In January 1941, the French, after a brief and militarily inconclusive border conflict with Thailand, were forced by the Japanese to hand territory in Laos and Cambodia back to Thailand. And in July 1941, Japanese troops were allowed by the French into southern Indochina. This was clearly the prelude to a decisive Japanese attack on Southeast Asia. By November 1941, the British, French and American failure to respond vigorously to the Japanese threat decided the Thai government to throw in their lot fully with the Japanese.]

In Tokyo, a 1 December Imperial Conference set the beginning of the war on 8 December (local time). When Hara, the head of the Privy Council, raised a question about which way Thailand would turn, Prime Minister Tojo acknowledged that he could not say. Describing Thailand as 'in a quandary', he added that Japan hoped to get Thailand's cooperation just before the beginning of operations, and that every effort would be made to avoid clashes with the Thai army ...

Aware that time was running out, Tamura [Japanese diplomatic representative in Thailand] pressed his efforts to obtain Thai military cooperation at a meeting with Phibun on 2 December. Maintaining a coy stance, Phibun attempted to bargain, using the 'national honor' ploy recommended by Wichit. The prime minister warned Tamura that while he did not wish to fight against Japan, he could not merely capitulate. He indicated, though, that a fight could be averted if Japan allowed Thailand to save face. As he had suggested previously, Phibun said that he would 'look the other way' if the Japanese invaded the Kra Isthmus south of Prachuap Khiri Khan, but he pleaded:

> Please avoid passing through the Bangkok plain. This is a matter of my own and Thailand's dignity. If, in order to attack Burma, you must pass through central Thailand, please delay the passage until I have time to carry out a plan to prepare for it. Please do not pass through Bangkok without any prior notice, because this will be a loss of face for the Thai people.

Of course, what Phibun did not say was that such a delay would also give him time to gauge the British response and decide whether or not the Japanese assault on Malaya was likely to succeed.

Tamura apparently learned that same evening that the Japanese strike would come on 8 December, less than six days hence. He sympathized with Phibun's predicament and considered delay of the Burma operation a small price to pay for maintaining friendly relations with Thailand, so the next day, 3 December, he sent Yahara to Saigon to plead again that adequate time be allowed for negotiations. Then, in the later afternoon, he returned to Phibun's office to make certain that they had a clear understanding. Phibun offered a 'firm promise' that he would not obstruct Japanese activities south of Prachuap Khiri Khan, and pledged that he would positively cooperate 'if the Japanese army saves the Thai government's "face" by controlling the invasion of central Thailand'. He also requested that the Japanese units in Thailand be kept as small as possible, and that Japan facilitate recovery of the Thai 'lost territories' [in British Malaya and Burma]. Phibun assured Tamura that he had sufficient power to carry through his end of the bargain ...

Fully cognizant that a Japanese advance was imminent, Phibun continued to lay the groundwork for a move into the Japanese camp. Between his two meetings with Tamura, he took the floor at a 3 December cabinet meeting to argue the case for cooperation with Japan in the most personal terms.

Predicting war within two weeks, he noted that if Thailand fought Japan, even in league with Great Britain, the cabinet members themselves would be certain victims. If the British finally won the war, he emphasized, 'Thailand might survive, but not us'. Conversely, cooperation with Japan would pose less risk of destruction, and Thailand might recover more 'lost territory'. According to Wanit's account, Phibun concluded a three-hour appeal by asking those in agreement with his position to stand up. Wanit told Tsubokami that Sin and four of Phibun's loyal army followers – Boriphan, Kriangsak Pichit, Seri Roengrit, and Wichit Songkhram – had done so.

Still, Phibun was reluctant to close off other options. One day after his 'let's join with Japan' speech, he had Direk once again request a clear warning from Britain and the United States that those countries would automatically declare war if the Japanese attacked Thailand. Direk told Crosby that the Japanese had aborted an invasion planned for the previous day, but that it would occur soon. He also urged that Britain avoid violating Thai sovereignty first.

This late initiative suggests that until the last minute Phibun hoped that the Japanese advance still might be deterred. Maybe, just maybe, a strong last-minute Anglo-American ultimatum – a move that Washington would ultimately rule out – combined with the well-publicized 2 December arrival of two British warships in Singapore, would have the desired effect. Phibun surely realized that it was a faint hope, but he clung to it because only Anglo-American deterrence could rescue him from facing the contradiction between his public pledges to resist any trespassers and his secret promise to permit Japanese passage.

2. The impact of the fall of Singapore

On 7 December 1941, Japanese troops landed on the eastern coast of southern Thailand and in the adjoining Malay state of Kelantan. By 15 February 1942, after sweeping through the Malay peninsula, they had forced the surrender of Singapore itself. The helplessness of the British was re-inforced by the sinking of the two battleships, HMS *Prince of Wales* and HMS *Repulse*, by Japanese aircraft off the coast of Malaya.

In a way, this defeat was not surprising. Despite the numerical superiority of British forces, the fact was that this was a confrontation between a hodge-podge colonial army of the Victorian era, and a highly motivated, cohesive army of the new era of militarized nationalism.

For Britain, this was the beginning of the long retreat from empire. As the following extract from Louis Allen's book, *Singapore 1942–1946*, indicates, members of the House of Commons in London were aware of the long-term significance of the event. Just as important as the defeat itself was the fact that Britain had given overall military priority to the European and Middle Eastern theatres at the expense of the Far East, and that a growing segment of British political opinion – increasingly influential in Parliament – believed that empire was in any case no longer justified.

In fact, British military planners had known long ago that Britain's strategic position in the Far East largely depended on bluff. The construction of the Singapore naval base in the wake of the expiry of the Anglo-Japanese alliance in 1922 had been ultimately little more than a morale-boosting operation. It was never likely that the British could hold Southeast Asia if it faced the combination of a war in Europe and a hostile Japan. Singapore's fall confirmed an existing reality: that Britain was no longer a global power. Australia took due note, and thenceforth entrusted its security to the United States.

Although Britain was forced to retreat from Burma within a few months of the fall of Singapore, India miraculously held. The main threat to Britain in India in 1942 came not from an already overstretched Japanese army but from internal unrest in India itself. The fact that Britain – against the odds – was able to hold the line in what was an extremely vulnerable position gave it crucial time to build up an armed force (the Fourteenth Army of Lieutenant-General, later Field Marshal, William Slim) that was in a position in 1943–44 to repulse Japanese attacks on the Indian border and, in early 1945, to launch a decisive counter-offensive into Burma.

Louis Allen, *Singapore 1941–1942* (London: Davis Poynter, 1977). Excerpts taken from pages 13–36.

At nine o'clock in the evening of 15 February, 1942, the telephone rang in the house of the Marquis Kido, the Japanese Emperor's closest adviser. It was the Prime Minister, Lieutenant-General Tojo, with a message for His Imperial Majesty. A telegram had just been received from Malaya. Singapore had fallen. At 19.50 hours on that day, the Japanese Army in Malaya had received the unconditional surrender of the British defenders. An hour later, General Sugiyama, the Chief of Staff, called on the Emperor in person. He was bubbling over with enthusiasm at the speed and courage of the Japanese Army, which had taken the city in such a short time. Kido had an interview with the Emperor the following morning from 10.50 to 11 am, and although they were concerned with routine diplomatic business – the correct form of dress for a proposed envoy to the Vatican – Kido could see how deeply moved the Emperor still was by the news from Malaya.

The Emperor had been bitterly sceptical at first about Japan's preparedness for a southward advance and had upbraided Sugiyama for over-confidence, and for making promises about a speedy ending to the war in China which he had not achieved; but the promises about Malaya had been more than fulfilled, and the Emperor composed a Rescript to his troops:

> Our army and navy [he wrote] working in close co-operation in Malaya, have resolutely carried out difficult maritime escort tasks, transport duties and landing

operations, and in the teeth of tropical diseases, and enduring intense heat, they have harried and hunted a strong enemy and broken through his defences at every point, capturing Singapore with the speed of the gods, and destroying Great Britain's base in East Asia.

We express our profound esteem for these deeds.

The Emperor took his white horse to the bridge over the moat from the Imperial Palace, and went out into the winter sunshine. For an hour he sat there, on horseback, the focus of the triumphant gaze of a victorious people. Back in the Palace, he made a decree about the captured city. Henceforth, he declared, it would no longer be called Singapore. It would become 'Shonan', 'the radiant South' ...

The day after the Emperor of Japan re-named Singapore Shonan, the British Prime Minister, Winston Churchill, faced an angry and disturbed House of Commons. Surprisingly enough, their anger and his concern were not for Singapore – at least not at first. His statement to the House dealt with the successful escape of the German battleships *Scharnhorst* and *Gneisenau* from Brest up the English Channel, in spite of British attempts to sink them. *Hansard* devotes three columns to this event, and only one to Singapore, which was the second item in Churchill's speech. He made a plea for no recriminations to be made and did not think a debate would be appropriate ...

Of course, his own attitude must have been ambiguous. Grievous as the loss of what he considered the 'fortress' Singapore must have been, particularly since it was defended by tens of thousands of troops; and although he had received the news of the loss of the *Prince of Wales* and the *Repulse* as the blackest news of the whole war; yet the main redeeming feature of Japan's entry into the war was never lost on him. Japan's attack had brought America into the war. From that moment, Britain was saved. Whatever happened, victory would come. His inner confidence in this was so profound that it coloured everything else ...

[The House of Commons gathered again on 24 February to hear Churchill's report on the war situation.]

For two days the British Parliament expressed itself on the recent reverses, but since no particular subject was singled out, the debate ranged first round administrative detail, from Churchill's own nostalgic evocation of the small War Cabinet days of Lloyd George in 1916, to the machinery of the Pacific War Council and Imperial Defence. It was a smoke-screen. There were more urgent matters than committee procedure and he knew it. When he finally came to the business of Malaya, he stalled and proved inept.

The defenceless state of Penang was recalled, in inexcusable terms:

I saw that some gentlemen who escaped from Penang announced to the world with much indignation that there was not a single anti-aircraft gun in the place. Where should we have been, I should like to know, if we had spread our limited anti-aircraft guns throughout the immense, innumerable regions and vulnerable points of the Far East instead of using them to preserve the vital life of our ports and factories here and of our fortresses which were under continuous attack and all our operations with the field Armies in the Middle East?

No one picked him up on this question-begging allusion, or asked why the intolerable alternative had arisen in the first place, but there was a gasp of disbelief when, without more ado, he told the House, 'I have no news whatever from Singapore' ...

Some members hauled the debate back to the Far Eastern issues. Sir Archibald Southby said openly what had been at the back of many members' minds, that a tiny fraction of the aircraft which had been sent to Russia should have been made available in Malaya: 'One month's supply of the aircraft sent to Russia would have saved Malaya.' He went on to hope that Burma would be saved, and that if Britain had to choose between Burma and the Dutch East Indies she would choose Burma. Mr J. H. Martin pressed the issue closer. Pre-war ineptitudes in policy-making were responsible for the catastrophe in Malaya. But even given these initial blunders, why was there no policy for evacuating the tens of thousands of troops in the Island in case of defeat? Why was no effort made to revictual the garrison, if it was true that lack of food and water forced the surrender? Sir Percy Harris was puzzled by the fact that 'the native population have been standing by as idle spectators of what has been happening in the Colonies' as opposed to the 'magnificent fight for their own country' which the Filipinos were putting up. Mr A. Sloan, the member for South Ayrshire, had no doubts about why the public conscience had been so shocked by the events in Malaya. His speech, more perhaps than any other, turned the attention of the House to the economic role of Malaya and to what, in his view, were the shortcomings of those who fulfilled it. It was a legend that lingered, and one that did great damage:

> Malaya and Singapore were merely names of far-off places in foreign lands. They conveyed little to the average mind. The general public do not study Stock Exchange reports. They are entirely ignorant that rubber, tin and oil are the main attractions there. They are in the main completely unconscious that this area is the greatest sink of corruption in the whole world. They are unfamiliar with the fact that these ornaments of British capitalism have done more to degrade Britain in the eyes of the East than any scoundrels since our depredations in Africa. These tin, rubber and oil companies have exploited the bodies and souls of the natives of the Far East. Those natives have lived in poverty and misery, and the only crime they have committed is to be born in the richest country in the world. Those companies have made fabulous fortunes ...
>
> How is it that the natives of Singapore were so indifferent to the fate of that island ... Is there any cause for wonder? Their land was invaded by an Imperialist-minded army, but they were already dominated by another of the same type. What material difference would it make to the Malayans? Merely changing one set of vultures for another, not the difference perhaps of a bowl of rice.

Mr Sloan quoted the despatch from the *Times* correspondent (Ian Morrison) which declared that both officials and British residents were completely out of touch with the people. British and Asiatics lived their lives apart, Morrison had said. There was never any fusion or cementing of these two groups. British rule and culture and the small British community formed no more than a thin and brittle veneer. 'Surely this is about the most complete and damning indictment of British Imperialism ever written', he went on, and he accused the British companies in Malaya of being more concerned with loss of assets than with the loss of soldiers' lives ...

His forthrightness found little response. But Mr Pethick Lawrence claimed that he and others had been saying for years that the administration of the British Colonies was a scandal. For a century before 1929 there had been no labour legislation and no social services: 'The coloured man was the bottom dog who could be exploited to an almost unlimited extent by his white master.' Britain was losing her Colonies in the war precisely because of 'Blimpery' which had remained blind to these conditions.

Leslie Hore-Belisha gave a more balanced view, in which social criticism was fairly mingled with strategic considerations. Britain had lost an important part of her Colonial Empire, and with it a crucial source of supply. Japan had forced an entry into the Indian Ocean and could interfere with communications to the Middle East, India and Australasia. The Colonial Secretary had admitted the loss of Singapore was inexplicable, and it was not anticipated. An army of considerable dimensions had been lost. The mistakes made were not entirely military. Colonial administration left much to be desired. It had not enlisted the support of local people, it lacked imagination and foresight ...

Commander Stephen King-Hall forthrightly called what happened in Singapore 'the greatest surrender in numbers of British troops in the whole history of the British Army'. He contrasted the feeling of February 1942 with the mood after Dunkirk. Then, the Prime Minister was the epitome of the nation. 'We felt very near him and he must have felt very near us.' They had been dangerous times, but great times. The times were dangerous again, but there was no more greatness. There was instead a sense of apathy and frustration in the air, 'a littleness'.

Professor A. V. Hill, who sat for Cambridge University, and voiced the mind of the scientific 'boffins', turned crisply to the Navy and accused it of being disastrously out-of-date. It had persistently clung to the conception of the large capital ship as the basis of the Fleet. These ships could not protect themselves effectively, alone, against enemy air attack. Those who had expert knowledge and had not been misled by tradition had known this all along. The sinking of the *Prince of Wales* and *Repulse* had made it manifest to all. The decisions about the future of the Navy should therefore be taken out of the hands of the admirals ...

Captain Lionel Gammans combined strategic considerations with a defence of the Malayan civilian community which had come in for a verbal beating at the hands of Mr Sloan. Captain Gammans had spent fourteen years in Malaya, and had travelled in Japan, China and Manchuria. He was sure the full impact of the loss of Singapore had not yet sunk in. It was a political as well as a military disaster. We had lost half the world's tin and rubber. The Japanese now had raw materials which would permit them to wage a prolonged war. They need no longer worry about tin, rubber, iron ore, fats or oil, and our strategy had been aimed precisely at depriving them of these things. Five million British subjects had passed under enemy rule. He poohpoohed the notion that local people had not been encouraged to resist. He himself had commanded a company of Chinese volunteers before the war, and it had always been difficult to fill the ranks. They had no desire or aptitude for military service. But as to the ultimate impact of what had happened he had no illusions:

> Perhaps the greatest tragedy of all was the scene on that Sunday morning when the Union Jack was pulled down on the flagstaff on Fort Canning in the middle of Singapore, and that great city, which Raffles founded and our own kith and kin built up, came for the first time under the Rising Sun. Do not let us underestimate the significance of that event. Our contact with Asia has been a long and on the whole an honourable one, and during all those years the Union Jack has never once been lowered. The story of that scene at Fort Canning will reverberate in the bazaars of India, on the plains of China and in the islands of the South Seas when everyone of us has long since been dead and gone.

The House of Lords undertook its own inquisition, but profited from a greater supply of information from the Colonial Secretary, Lord Cranborne, making his maiden speech as Leader of the House, than Mr Churchill had seen fit to supply to the Commons. As he saw it, the troops had orders to hold the place to the last, and did so. This valiant phrasing gave rise to sympathetic cheers, but Lord Wedgwood pronounced a gloomier verdict: 'The surrender of Singapore is the blackest page in our military history for all time.'

Nonetheless, after the fall of Singapore, the Japanese did two things which proved, in the long run, contrary to their interests.

The losses sustained by Nagumo's aircraft in the raids on Ceylon [after the fall of Singapore] meant that only two of the fleet carriers in that raid could take part in the Battle of the Coral Sea a month later. The others had to return to pick up new machines and new pilots. The replacements were said to be inferior to the original pilots of his force. If, therefore, Nagumo had not reached out for Ceylon, or if the RAF had been less successful, the carrier group might not have been short of skilled pilots and might have avoided the reverses which were to come, in the Coral Sea and at Midway.

Secondly, on the political rather than the strategic level, the Japanese Army committed a grave error of judgement after the surrender. Although it is true that General Yamashita did not allow the main body of his troops to enter Singapore City, a punitive expedition under Major-General Kawamura, the commander of 5 Division Infantry Brigade Group, was sent into the city to deal with Chinese residents who were known to be hostile to Japan, to have been connected with fund-raising activities on behalf of Chiang Kai-shek's Nationalist regime in Chungking, or to have been members of the Chinese Volunteer Force.

Kawamura's detachment consisted of Kempei (secret police) supported by two battalions of infantry. Thousands of Chinese were herded into concentration camps and questioned. Those who failed to answer in a satisfactory manner were machine-gunned, bayonetted or otherwise done away with. Massive fines were imposed on the Chinese community as a whole. The killing and the terror were such that they reached the ears of the central authorities in Tokyo. The former head of the Kyoto Kempei, Colonel Otani Keijiro, was sent out to investigate. He left Haneda Airport on 26 February and landed at Kallang on 6 March 1942. Otani spent a total of eighteen months in Singapore and Malaya, being responsible for the preservation of peace and order in the occupied territories. Even though he was a Kempei, and had experience of repressive police activities in Manchuria, it was not long before he realized how contrary to the permanent interests of Japan were the brutal methods of the first few days of occupation. Whatever the political control of the British had been, economic life was firmly in the hands of the Chinese. If the Japanese were to exploit Malaya and Singapore as sources of supply, co-operation between the Chinese community and Japanese military government was essential. As Otani points out, it was only natural that Yamashita should want to secure his base by ensuring that all British stragglers should be brought into POW camps and anti-Japanese elements neutralized. But there were sensible and more effective ways of doing this than those used.

As soon as he set up his office in Kempei headquarters, he received an endless stream of Chinese visitors reporting the disappearance of a father, a brother, a son, and in each case the story was the same. They had been arrested by the Japanese Army and nothing had been heard of them since.

So the rumours which had reached Tokyo were true. Even so, Otani recalls that such rumours were somewhat ambivalently greeted there. Some right-wing Japanese rejoiced at what had happened, since in their view it showed that the Japanese Army had gone the right way about destroying the base of Nationalist China's anti-Japanese activities in South-East Asia. Others were critical. What had begun as a *shukusei* (purge) of Chungking [i.e. pro-nationalist] Chinese ended up by being a *bogyaku* (atrocity) to be remembered along with the rape of Nanking as one of the biggest blots on the reputation of the Japanese Army. It was unfortunate for the future of military government under the Japanese that it should have started under a reign of terror, which made a mockery of Japan's claims to be acting as liberator of oppressed colonial peoples. What happened in Singapore in the three days 21, 22 and 23 February ensured that throughout South-East Asia the economically influential communities of overseas Chinese became irreconcilably confirmed in their hostility to Japan's New Order.

Afterword Resistance against the Japanese in Malaya and Singapore was subsequently headed by Chinese communist guerrillas of the Malayan Peoples' Anti-Japanese Army (MPAJA).

3. The British reconquest of Burma, 1945

When the Second World War began in September 1939, Burma had a Burmese prime minister (U Saw) and cabinet, but a British governor, Dorman-Smith, who retained authority over defence, security, the minority regions and foreign policy. Britain's and France's misfortunes in Europe in 1939 and 1940 stimulated in Burma, as in India, the demand that Britain should grant immediate independence. The key political figures engaged in the nationalist agitation of this period were Dr Ba Maw, an older-generation politician who had previously served as prime minister, and Aung San, who headed a group of younger radicals of the Dó-bama Asiayone ('We Burmans Association'). By the time of the Japanese invasion of Southeast Asia, Prime Minister U Saw had been exiled for trying to establish contact with Japan, Ba Maw was in prison, and Aung San had fled to Japanese-occupied China.

In the spring of 1942, Japan invaded Burma and quickly overran the disorganized British defences there. After a long interval of negotiations, in August 1943 the Japanese permitted the establishment of an independent Burmese government with Ba Maw as overall 'leader' and Aung San holding the key posts of defence minister and leader of the embryonic Burmese army. Burma was a front-line in the war, and hence its independence was little more than nominal; but the existence of the independent government gave Aung San the opportunity to build up, under his command, a quasi-military, quasi-political defence force, known as the Burma National Army (BNA).

Meanwhile, governor Dorman-Smith set up a government-in-exile in Simla, India, and began long-term planning for Burma's future. Within Burma itself, military liaison was established by the British with certain border minorities – the Muslim Arakanese, Chins, Nagas and Kachins – as well as the Karens of southeast Burma. These minorities gave the British invaluable support along the military front-line, and in guerrilla activities behind enemy lines.

In early 1944, the Japanese launched a series of military offensives along the Burma–India border. Lieutenant-General Slim's Fourteenth Army was able to hold the line and, in early 1945, it launched a full counter-offensive into Burma. It was during this period that Aung San stealthily began preparations to switch sides, setting up a secret Anti-Fascist Organization (AFO), later transformed into the Anti-Fascist Peoples Freedom League (AFPFL), whose mass base was provided by his Burma National Army. In March 1945, the BNA launched a rebellion against its Japanese allies.

In this extract from his book *Defeat into Victory*, Field Marshal Slim describes his first meeting with Aung San on 16 May 1945, after Britain had reoccupied most of Burma. In it we can see the first signs of differences in British policy towards Burma. While Dorman-Smith and his exiled government in India wanted to avoid any action that would give credibility to Aung San, Slim and the military were faced with the immediate reality of trying to administer a devastated country with an inadequate administrative cadre, and of having to deal with the BNA/AFPFL, a mass organization that clearly had the capacity to disrupt British plans to restore law and order in Burma. Slim quickly recognized both Aung San's political astuteness, and the potentially powerful position he occupied.

Field Marshal Sir William Slim, *Defeat into Victory* (London: Landsborough Publications, 1958). Excerpts taken from pages 419–24.

[Problems facing the British reoccupying forces in Burma in the Spring of 1945.] Another problem which, with startling suddenness, loomed upon us was that of the care and administration of the civil population. We had, almost overnight, acquired most of Burma, and with it eighty per cent of its inhabitants – some thirteen millions of them. There was no civil government for us to take over; it had completely disappeared. Insecurity and dacoity [banditry] were rife. Great acreages had gone out of cultivation, while trade had vanished with the breakdown of communications and the loss of security. The almost complete absence of consumer goods had spun the Japanese paper currency into wild inflation. The whole population was short of clothing, necessities, and above all of food. Indeed, large sections of it were on the verge of starvation. Towns had been burnt and many were deserted, their inhabitants having taken to the jungle where they lived hazardously in miserable destitution. The Japanese throughout their occupation had done little or nothing to meet the essential needs of the civil population. Even where bombs and battles had spared them, public utilities, water supplies, and roads had, through Japanese indifference, deteriorated to a shocking degree.

Almost without exception our return was welcomed. It was only in those areas on the north where the liberating troops were [Nationalist] Chinese, and memories of their behaviour in the 1942 Retreat still lingered, that there was an element of nervousness. With the vast majority of the Burmese the trouble was that they expected us to bring them an immediate return to the carefree conditions of happy Burma before the war. This, alas, we could not do at once.

The first necessity was to restore the framework of government throughout the country, but we were hampered by an acute shortage of qualified officials who could be installed in the civil districts which we rapidly, one after the other, liberated. Of the original British civil servants, some had in the past years vanished into other services or joined the armed forces. Too many, it seemed to me, were held in India under the exiled Burmese Government. Our own Civil Affairs staff [drawn from Southeast Asia Command] were all allotted to the parts of Burma already in our hands before the last advance. As they retreated, the Japanese had taken with them many of the Burmese officials, who, mostly unwillingly, had served under them, while those who supported Ba Maw's puppet government had fled, to avoid their own country-men as much as to escape us. Gradually, Burmese civil officials of all ranks began to come out of hiding and report for duty; others were located and persuaded to return; but all had to have their records checked before they could be reinstated. However, in a surprisingly short time considering all the difficulties, a civil administration, somewhat skeleton in form, was set up and, with increasing efficiency, functioning.

It was an even more difficult matter to get the economic life of the country running again. Not only were we lacking many requirements for the army, but outside Burma there was a world shortage of the articles most needed to supply the desperate necessities of the civil population – notably cotton goods. Even were imports from abroad obtainable, they would not relieve the situation until communications within Burma were restored, and the ports, especially Rangoon, operating again. Nevertheless, even before we got the army back to full rations, we diverted some of its supplies and part of our precious air-lift to succour the most distressed areas.

Parallel with this problem of the civil administration, was a smaller Burmese politico-military one. How to treat the Burmese National Army, originally Japanese sponsored, but now in arms against them? I had all along believed they could be a nuisance to the enemy but, unless their activities were closely tied in with ours, they promised to be almost as big a nuisance to us. It seemed to me that the only way satisfactorily to control them was to get hold of their Commander-in-Chief, Aung San, and to make him accept my orders. This, from what I knew of him and of the extreme Burmese nationalists, I thought might be difficult, but worth trying.

Aung San had had a chequered career. In 1930 as an undergraduate at Rangoon University, like most Asian students, he took an active, and at times a rather violent, interest in politics. By 1939, he was the secretary of the extremist Nationalist Minority Group [sic] and served a seventeen-day prison sentence for his activities. About this time he was contacted by Japanese agents, who saw in the energetic and able young nationalist a promising tool for their own ripening designs. It thus happened that, when, in 1940, Aung San's organization was proscribed, he and some thirty others of its members were able to evade the police and reach Japan. Here, they were given military training in a Japanese officers' school and were indoctrinated with the belief that Japan would shortly drive the British out of Burma and bring freedom to its people. When the invasion did occur, Aung San and his companions came with it. The Japanese used them as a nucleus round which to collect irregular Burmese forces and to organize a Fifth Column throughout the area of operations. They were undoubtedly a help to their masters in many ways and, on one or two occasions during the Retreat, fought bravely against us, though their chief combat duties were the ambushing and murdering of stragglers.

Aung San, whose intelligence and courage had brought him to the fore, showed anxiety to set up a Burmese Government, but the Japanese, although they wanted a puppet government, were not prepared to accept him as its head. Perhaps they had already sensed he would not be the pliable and submissive dupe they required, and in any case they had Ba Maw, who was much more what they wanted. Instead, they appointed Aung San Commander-in-Chief of the Burma Defence Army, later the Burma National Army, that was set up under the closest Japanese control.

It was not long before Aung San found that what he meant by independence had little relation to what the Japanese were prepared to give – that he had exchanged an old master for an infinitely more tyrannical new one. As one of his leading followers once said to me, 'If the British sucked our blood, the Japanese ground our bones!' He became more and more disillusioned with the Japanese, and early in 1943 we got news from Seagrim, a most gallant officer who had remained in the Karen Hills at the ultimate cost of his life, that Aung San's feelings were changing. On the 1st August 1944 he was bold enough to speak publicly with contempt of the Japanese brand of independence, and it was clear that, if they did not soon liquidate him, he might prove useful to us. Force 136 [a British 'behind-the-lines' commando force] through its agents already had channels of communication and, when the revolt of the Burma National Army occurred and it was clear Aung San had burnt his boats, it was time to deal directly with him. With the full approval of Admiral Mountbatten, the agents of Force 136 offered Aung San on the 21st April a safe conduct to my headquarters and my promise that, whether we came to an understanding or not, I would return him unharmed to his own people. He hesitated until the 15th May, but on that day it was reported to me that he and a staff officer had crossed the Irrawaddy at Allanmyo, and were asking to meet me. I sent an aircraft, which flew them to my headquarters at Meiktila the next day.

The arrival of Aung San, dressed in the near Japanese uniform of a Major-General, complete with sword, startled one or two of my staff who had not been warned of his coming. However, he behaved with the utmost courtesy, and so, I hope, did we. He was a short, well-built, active man in early middle age, neat and soldierly in appearance, with regular Burmese features in a face that could be an impassive mask or light up with intelligence and humour. I found he spoke good English, learnt in his school and university days, and he was accompanied by a staff officer who spoke it perfectly, as well he might, if it were true as I was told that his father had been a senior British official who had married a Burmese lady.

At our first interview, Aung San began to take rather a high hand. He was, he said, the representative of the Provisional Government of Burma, which had been set up by the people of Burma through the Anti-Fascist People's Freedom League. It was under this Provisional Government that he and his National Army served and from whom they took their orders. He was an Allied commander, who was prepared to co-operate with me, and he demanded the status of an Allied and not subordinate commander. I told him that I had no idea what his Anti-Fascist People's Freedom League was or represented. As far as I and the rest of the world were concerned, there was only one Government of Burma and that was His Majesty's, now acting through the Supreme Commander, South-East Asia. I pointed out that he was in no position to take the line he had. I did not need his forces; I was destroying the Japanese quite nicely without his help, and could continue to do so. I would accept his co-operation and that of his army only on the clear understanding that it implied no recognition of any provisional government. He would be a subordinate commander who would accept my orders and see that his officers and men also obeyed them and those of any British commander under whom I placed them. He showed disappointment at this, and repeated his demand to be treated as an Allied commander.

I admired his boldness and told him so. 'But' I said, 'apart from the fact that you, a British subject, have fought against the British Government, I have here in this headquarters people who tell me there is a well substantiated case of civil murder, complete with witnesses, against you. I have been urged to place you on trial for that. You have nothing in writing, only a verbal promise at second-hand, that I would return you to your friends. Don't you think you are taking considerable risks in coming here and adopting this attitude?'

'No', he replied, shortly.

'Why not?'

'Because you are a *British* officer', he answered. I had to confess that he scored heavily – and what was more I believe he meant it. At any rate he had come out on my word alone. I laughed and asked him if he felt like that about the British, why had he been so keen to get rid of us? He said it was not that he disliked the British, but he did not want British or Japanese or any other foreigners to rule his country. I told him I could well understand that attitude, but it was not for us soldiers to discuss the future government of Burma. The British Government had announced its intention to grant self-government to Burma within the British Commonwealth, and we had better limit our discussion to the best method of throwing the Japanese out of the country as the next step towards self-government.

We resumed in good temper, and I asked him to give me the strengths and present dispositions of his forces. This he was either unwilling or unable to do – I thought a bit of both. I pressed him in this, but could get nothing definite. I had the impression that he was not too sure what his forces were, where they were, or what exactly some of them were doing. I said I had had reports that there were many bands of armed Burmans roaming about, claiming to belong to his army, who were no better than dacoits preying on their own countrymen. Rather to my surprise, he agreed and said he hoped we would both of us deal severely with these men, who were no troops of his. He went on to say that, at first, he had hoped the Japanese would give real independence to Burma. When he found they would not, but were tightening the bonds on his people, he had, relying on our promises, turned to us as a better hope. 'Go on, Aung San', I said, 'You only come to us because you see we are winning!'

'It wouldn't be much good coming to you if you weren't, would it?' he replied, simply.

I could not question the truth of this. I felt he had scored again, and I liked his honesty. In fact, I was beginning to like Aung San.

I told him that after the war we should revive the old regular Burma Army, under British officers, on the basis of the Burma Rifles battalion which still existed, and that there would then be no place for any other army – his would have to go. He at once pressed that his forces should be incorporated in the new army as units. This was obviously not altogether the solicitude of a general for his men, but the desire of a politician to retain personal power in post-war Burma. I answered that I thought it most unlikely that the Burmese Government would accept them as units, but that I saw no reason why they should not, subject to a check of their records, be enlisted as individuals on the same terms as other recruits. He persisted in pressing for incorporation as units, but I held out no hopes of this. He then asked me if I would now supply and pay his units in the field? He was obviously finding this beyond his powers, and I knew that, if we did not accept the responsibility, his men would be reduced, as many were already, to living by exactions from the people – as dacoits in fact. I said I would not consider paying or supplying his troops unless he and they were completely under my orders. In our final talk, he had begun to take a more realistic view of his position, but he still would not definitely commit himself. Before he accepted the role of a subordinate commander, he said, he must consult with his 'government', and he asked to be returned, suggesting that he should meet me again in about a week's time. I agreed, warned him of the consequences of refusing terms which, in view of his past, were most generous, shook hands, and sent him off by air again.

I was impressed by Aung San. He was not the ambitious, unscrupulous guerrilla leader I had expected. He was certainly ambitious and meant to secure for himself a dominant position in post-war Burma, but I judged him to be a genuine patriot and a well-balanced realist – characters which are not always combined. His experience with the Japanese had put his views on the

British into a truer perspective. He was ready himself to co-operate with us in the liberation and restoration of Burma and, I thought, probably to go on co-operating after that had been accomplished. The greatest impression he made on me was one of honesty. He was not free with glib assurances and he hesitated to commit himself, but I had the idea that if he agreed to do something he would keep his word. I could do business with Aung San.

Operations against the Japanese were continuing over wide areas, and I wanted to get the role of Aung San's forces clear before clashes occurred between them and our troops. Having reported to my superiors the results of our interview and my views on his reliability, I therefore, instead of waiting for him to come in again, sent him, a few days later, definite proposals.

I would employ and ration all units of the Burma National Army then in action, provided they reported to and placed themselves unreservedly under the orders of the nearest British commander. I would recommend that suitable individual members of the B.N.A. should be allowed to volunteer for recruitment in the future Burma defence forces. Aung Sang accepted these terms without haggling, asking only that he should be consulted on major decisions on the employment of the B.N.A. and on the enlistment of its members into the regular forces. On the 30th May, my Deputy Chief Civil Affairs Officer told Aung San that I had informed the Supreme Commander of our arrangement and that it was in force. Accordingly, somewhat to their surprise, our troops began to meet parties of Burmese in Japanese uniforms, who marched in, and whose officers stated they were reporting for duty with the British. They were regarded with considerable suspicion at first but, almost without exception, obeyed orders well. They proved definitely useful in gaining information and in dealing drastically with small parties of Japanese.

4. The United States' new role in Southeast Asia

When Japan began its invasion of Southeast Asia in December 1941, Thailand, as we have seen, threw in its lot with the Japanese. On 25 January 1942, Thailand declared war on Britain and the United States. The Thai minister (more or less equivalent to ambassador) in Washington, however, refused to deliver this declaration, and the United States equally refused to accept Thailand's belligerent status, instead preferring to treat it as an 'enemy-occupied country'.

While the United States' relationship with Thailand remained close throughout the war, Britain on the other hand had no particularly friendly feelings towards a country that had facilitated the invasions of Malaya and Burma, and had taken slices of territory from northern Malaya and eastern Burma. As the net closed in on Japan in Southeast Asia in early 1945, the British were clearly determined to extract their pound of flesh from Thailand. In particular, they wanted the immediate return of territories that Thailand had taken in the war, and the conclusion of a security agreement that would protect Malaya's northern border from a repetition of the events of late 1941.

Despite the disastrous defeats that Japan had inflicted on Britain in 1941 and 1942, Churchill had been consoled by the knowledge that the American entry into the war would guarantee ultimate victory for the Allies. It rapidly became apparent, however – particularly in the Far East and Southeast Asia – that American and British objectives did not necessarily coincide. The question of the post-war settlement of Thailand gave an early example of this difference of perspective between the two Allies. For reasons made plain in the following American foreign policy memoranda, the United States was determined to protect Thailand from British revenge: the most the Americans were prepared to concede was that Thailand would have to return all territories that had been seized from Burma, Malaya, Cambodia and Laos after January 1941.

The Americans – for historical reasons – were intensely suspicious that Britain intended to exploit the alliance with the United States in order to restore its pre-war empire. It could be argued, however, that the United States' manifest effort to build a friendly relationship with Thailand was the first building block for the projection of American influence into the heart of post-war Southeast Asia.

Foreign Relations of the United States, 1945, Vol. vi (Washington, United States Government Printing Office, 1969). Excerpts taken from pages 1242–6.

Memorandum Prepared in the Division of Southwest Pacific Affairs, January 13, 1945

MEMORANDUM FOR THE PRESIDENT

Subject: Future Status of Thailand

British policies towards Thailand are divergent from ours. The British regard Thailand as an enemy and it is their view:

1. That Thailand's postwar independence should be conditioned on its acceptance of 'special arrangements for security or economic collaboration ... within an international system'.
2. That the peninsula of Thailand from Malaya to about 12° north latitude should be considered a vital strategic area and its defense under international security arrangements be undertaken by a protecting power or by an international consortium. This is reported to be the opinion of Mr. Churchill. Such action might substantially impair Thai administrative rights in the area.
3. That actual military government will not be needed, except perhaps in combat zones. However, they believe that an Allied Control Commission

should be established in Thailand, which should be continued for some time.

4. That they should not deal at the present time with any Thai Government.

In contrast, we do not regard Thailand as an enemy but as an enemy-occupied country. We recognize the Thai Minister in Washington as 'Minister of Thailand' with a status similar to that of the Danish Minister [Denmark at that time being under German occupation]. We favor a free, independent Thailand, with sovereignty unimpaired, and ruled by a government of its own choosing. Thailand is the one country in Southeast Asia which was still independent before the war. We believe that it would be prejudicial to American interests throughout the Far East if, as the outcome of the war in which we will have had the major part in defeating Japanese aggression, Thailand should be deprived of any of its prewar territory or should have its independent status impaired. The history of European pressure on Thailand and of European acquisition of territory in Southeast Asia, is vivid in Asiatic memories. This Government cannot afford to share responsibility in any way for a continuance towards Thailand of prewar imperialism in any guise ...

It is the view of the Department that an effort should be made to persuade the British to alter their plans so that they are not inconsistent with our own. It is believed that if Thailand joins in the war against Japan she should be treated as a liberated country and her government be recognized, at least provisionally. Although there are disadvantages from a political viewpoint in having American troops, except where militarily essential, participate in the recovery of European colonial areas, there would be advantages from a political viewpoint in having American troops under independent American command responsible for the liberation of Thailand, rather than in having Thailand occupied as enemy territory by British forces. Whether or not American forces should be used in Thailand, however, is a question which would presumably be decided in the light of overall strategic considerations ...

Memorandum by the Director of the Office of Far Eastern Affairs, State Department [Washington], January 25, 1945

BRITISH–AMERICAN POLICY TOWARD THAILAND

I. *The Problem*
To attempt to persuade the British Government to harmonize its policy toward Thailand with our own.

II. *Recommendations*
It is recommended:

A. That the Department inform the United States Joint Chiefs of Staff of the disparity between American and British views in regard to Thailand, request them to use their influence on the Combined Chiefs of Staff in order to prevent the adoption of measures inconsistent with American policy toward Thailand, and ask them to furnish the Department with such pertinent information as they may deem consistent with military security and which might be of value to the Department in its further discussions with the British Government on the subject of Thailand.

B. That we make a further approach to the British Government in which we suggest in general that agreements be sought between the Thai Government on the one side and the British, Chinese and United States Governments on the other, which would include at least the following basic considerations:

1. The Thai Government would agree:

a. To render military cooperation at such times and in such manner as may be requested by the appropriate military authorities.

b. To accept the territorial boundaries of Thailand as of January 1941 [i.e., before the cession of Lao and Cambodian territories to Thailand by France] without prejudice to later peaceful negotiations for possible boundary adjustments and territorial transfers.

c. To assume the responsibility of a sovereign nation in the pattern of an international security organization [i.e. the United Nations].

2. The British, Chinese and United States Governments would agree:

a. To respect the sovereignty and independence of Thailand.

b. To regard Thailand as an Ally, liberated or in process of being liberated from the enemy ...

c. To restrict military government to combat zones occupied by Allied troops and to restore such areas to the control of the Thai Government as rapidly as military operations permit.

III. *Basic Factors*
A. *The American Position*
The United States has adopted the policy of treating Thailand as an enemy-occupied state, and favors the restoration of prewar Thailand as a sovereign state under an independent government.

B. *The British Position*
Great Britain regards Thailand as an enemy and favors an extended occupation of the country after liberation from the Japanese, the establishment of an Allied Control Commission, and the imposition of economic and military conditions within an international system which might substantially impair Thai administrative control.

[Afterword: In the Anglo-Thai treaty signed in January 1946, territory that had been taken by Thailand from eastern Burma and northern Malaya was returned to the British. In November 1946 – after more bitter and prolonged wrangling – a Franco-Thai treaty provided for the return to French Indochina of Laotian and Cambodian territories taken by Thailand in 1941.

Thailand's independence and territorial integrity was, however, secured, and Britain's vague plans to impose some kind of internationalized buffer-zone in the south of Thailand was not pursued. This was an early sign of the new influence that the United States exercised in the mainland Southeast Asia region.]

CHAPTER 5

The Aftermath of War: Revolution

Everything is ablaze!
Everything is ablaze!
Comrades, comrades,
Let us awaken and arise
Stabbing, attacking until dried and hard.
Comrades, comrades,
Let us swing our swords at the Bright World.

(from the poem *Prepare! An Appeal to my Generation*, by Chairil Anwar, 1944)

The defeat of Japan and surrender arrangements

In August 1945, while the Allies were preparing and allocating responsibilities for the final assault on Southeast Asia and Japan, the Japanese suddenly surrendered. Overnight, the Allies, and particularly the largely British and Indian South East Asia Command (SEAC), were faced with the responsibility of overseeing the surrender and repatriation of an almost intact Japanese army in Southeast Asia, the release of Allied and civilian prisoners held by the Japanese, the maintenance of law and order, and the eventual transfer of power to civilian governments. The zone of responsibility for South East Asia Command covered Malaya, Singapore, Sumatra, Java, Thailand and the southern part of Indochina. As a consequence of American pressure, nationalist China assumed similar responsibilities over northern Indochina. The Philippines and Burma were, of course, already under American and British control respectively.

If things had proceeded according to plan, then it is safe to assume that there would have been an orderly process of SEAC supervision of the Japanese surrender and repatriation, followed by a transfer of power from SEAC to the former European colonial powers of the region, the legitimate pre-war authorities. That this smooth sequence of events did not occur was due, first, to the fact that South-East Asia Command was severely over-stretched after August 1945, and in no way capable of carrying out all its tasks and filling the vacuum of power left by the Japanese surrender; and, second, to the fact that nationalist governments, backed by mass movements that had taken root during the war, were able to seize power and embed themselves in the countrysides of Vietnam and Indonesia.

The build-up of revolutionary forces in Southeast Asia

In immediate terms, the 'overstretch' of South-East Asia Command meant that there was a vital interval of a few weeks before it was ready after the Japanese surrender even to begin to assume its responsibilities in Malaya, Vietnam and Indonesia. It was during this interval that the mass nationalist movements were able to seize power and establish some form of governmental legitimacy. More important still was the fact that the British military command – with their pitifully limited resources – were only ever able to establish bridgeheads of military authority in southern Indochina, and along the coasts of Sumatra and Java. These bridgeheads, however – particularly Saigon and Jakarta – were sufficient to enable scratch collections of French and Dutch soldiers and civilians to establish military–administrative foci, from which they planned the reoccupation of their colonial possessions through a combination of force and negotiations. What could be described as the 'revolutionary' period of 1945 and 1946 ensured that these efforts would ultimately not succeed.

The era of revolution: 1945

In this 'vacuum' period between the Japanese surrender and the arrival of SEAC, the communist Malayan People's Anti-Japanese Army (MPAJA) – which had, following the fall of Malaya to the Japanese, built up a series of guerrilla bases in the interior of the peninsula – moved out of their jungle camps, and immediately began to administer arbitrary justice against 'collaborators' and political enemies in general. This was directed against both Chinese and Malays who had in one way or another worked for the Japanese. But since much of the administrative and police apparatus was Malay-dominated, Malays became a particular target for MPAJA revenge attacks, and these attacks on 'collaborators' soon took on an ethnic dimension. This inevitably led to Malay retaliation and, in some areas, inter-ethnic conflict and a serious breakdown of law and order. Since the British were determined at all costs to reassert their control over all their former colonies, this period of anarchy gradually came to an end as the British established their military rule. But the behaviour at this time of the Chinese-dominated communist guerrillas, and the Malay reaction, was to sour relations between the two communities for years, and it was only in 1949 that Malaya was to see the beginnings of the creation of a united nationalist movement.

In Vietnam, the war years from 1940 to March 1945 had seen a kind of *de facto* co-existence between the French colonial administration and the

Japanese military command in Saigon. As already noted, the Indochina Communist Party in 1941 set up a patriotic front, the so-called Viet Minh, on the Vietnamese-Chinese border. Until 1945, however, this movement confined itself largely to developing a politico-military nucleus and spreading propaganda – strictly patriotic, not communist – throughout Vietnam. In March 1945, however, the situation changed dramatically. The Japanese military, anticipating an Allied offensive in Southeast Asia and fearful that the French colonial army in Indochina might turn against them, removed the French administration, put the French army and colonial administrators behind barbed wire, and established independent governments in Laos, Cambodia and Vietnam. In all three countries, they handed over authority to the very monarchies that had worked with the French, along with a motley collection of nationalist politicians. In Vietnam in particular, this new 'independent' government lacked both nationalist credibility and the ability to impose its authority over the provinces. In the period of political vacuum created by the removal of the French colonial administration, the weakness of the Viet-namese substitute government, and the concentration of Japanese minds on an increasingly desperate military situation, the Viet Minh were given the opportunity to build their political and military infrastructure and spread an administrative network throughout Vietnam. By the time the Japanese sur-rendered in mid-August 1945, the Viet Minh movement was ready to seize the opportunity, brush aside the Japanese-installed Vietnamese government and declare independence (see 'The Vietnamese Revolution', p. 118).

In Vietnam, the nationalist movement (the Viet Minh) that led the country to independence in this so-called 'August Revolution' followed a broadly based patriotic–nationalist programme, but was controlled from within by a well-organized and unified communist party, the Indochina Communist Party (ICP). In Indonesia, the situation in 1945 was far more complex.

Despite the fact that the Japanese military authorities had encouraged the creation of various regional and religious organizations, youth movements and militias throughout Sumatra and Java, they had kept a tight lid on overtly nationalist organization and rhetoric. In early 1945, however, they had at last allowed the nationalist leadership – with Sukarno and Mohammad Hatta playing a key role – to begin the process of preparing for independence. This provoked an explosion of ideological debate and political competition, both at the central and the regional level – a process that had been stifled by the immobility of Dutch rule in the inter-war years, and held in check by Japan's anxiety to maintain control over an economically vital area.

Throughout the first half of 1945 there was an intense debate over the ideological principles that should guide the independent state. This debate largely centred on the dispute between the strict Muslim leaders, who wished to see the creation of an Islamic state in Indonesia, and the secular-national-ists, whose views were embodied in the *pancasila* principles promoted by Sukarno (see 'Sukarno and the Pancasila principles', p. 131). At the same time the plethora of religious and proto-nationalist organizations created under the Japanese built up their numbers, and increasingly competed for influence in the provinces.

Events came to a head in August 1945, when the Japanese surrendered. On 17 August 1945, under intense pressure from radical *pemuda* (youth) groups in Jakarta, the Indonesian political leadership declared the independence of the Republic of Indonesia. This show of nationalist unity, however, masked profound ideological and political differences. While the leaders of the Republic in Jakarta wanted to establish a nation-wide administration as rapidly as possible, and therefore came to depend on the same administrative cadre that had worked with the Dutch and the Japanese, youth and revolutionary organizations – including the resurgent Indonesian communists – wanted to see a thoroughgoing social revolution directed against precisely this collaborating elite stratum. There was, in other words, a fundamental divergence at this time between those who wished, after independence, to maintain administrative continuity and coherence under a 'responsible' leadership, and those who saw independence as a stepping-stone to fundamental change *within* traditional indigenous society (see 'The Origins of the Indonesian Revolution', p. 139).

READINGS

1. The Vietnamese Revolution

In the colony of Cochinchina, the French authorities had pursued a so-called 'assimilation' policy designed eventually to turn the region into a part of 'overseas' France, peopled by 'brown Frenchmen'. In the rest of Indochina they had maintained the indigenous system of government within an overall protectorate administration. These two policies left no room whatsoever for alternative political developments. Nationalist activity and demands for self-government or independence were therefore treated as a threat by the French colonial administration and the Nguyen dynasty alike.

During the course of the 1920s, the Constitutionalist Party had campaigned in Cochinchina for greater Vietnamese representation in the government institutions of the colony, for such liberal reforms as greater press freedom, and for easier access to French citizenship rights. However, its increasing failure to 'deliver' reforms from the French, even on these minimal demands, led to a loss of support for this moderate party, and its eventual demise. During the whole of the inter-war period, temporary bursts of (very limited) French liberalization were invariably followed by periods of repression. Every time the French even tentatively lifted the lid of repression, accumulated political and national aspirations boiled over, and they hastily put back the lid. Even the young emperor Bao Dai's attempt to use the Vietnamese dynastic government as an avenue for very moderate reforms was immediately discouraged.

By the time of the outbreak of the Second World War, the French grip on Indochina appeared to be unbreakable. This grip was, if anything, tightened during the course of the Second World War. It was perhaps because of this political repression that Vietnamese energies were often diverted into the local religious cult organizations that mushroomed during the 1920s and 1930s. The most prominent of these were the Cao Dai movement (see Glossary), formed in 1926, with its main area of recruitment in Saigon and the area to the northwest of Saigon, and the radical Buddhist sect, the Hoa Hao, with its main area of influence along the southwestern Vietnamese–Cambodian border. The future significance of these groups was to lie in their strong regional roots. These were particularly important in periods of anarchy, such as the years 1945 and 1946.

By March 1945, it was clear to the Japanese that they could no longer trust the French colonial regime, particularly if, as seemed likely, the Allies were to attack Indochina. They accordingly removed the French colonial regime through a *coup de force*. Nominally, authority then reverted to the monarchies of Vietnam, Laos and Cambodia. In practice, however, Vietnam fell into a condition of increasing anarchy, made worse by a famine – brought about by the cumulative dislocations of war – that raged in the poorer regions of north and central Vietnam. Precisely because of previous French policy, there was no mass nationalist organization ready to fill the vacuum. As Huynh Kim Khanh shows in the following authoritative article, 'The Vietnamese August Revolution Re-interpreted', this absence of a mass nationalist organization provided the communist-created Viet Minh movement with the opportunity to occupy the empty political space in much of Vietnam. In some areas of the south, however, it was local organizations, such as the Cao Dai and the Hoa Hao, that formed what amounted to local warlord governments.

It should be noted that the status and credibility of the Viet Minh movement was greatly enhanced by the fact that its communist leaders had, since 1941, maintained a firm anti-French ('the colonial enemy') and anti-Japanese ('the fascist enemy') stance.

Huynh Kim Khanh, 'The Vietnamese August Revolution Re-interpreted', *Journal of Asian Studies*, Vol. 30 (1970–71). Excerpts taken from pages 761–82.

August 1945 was an important turning point in Vietnamese history. Within two weeks of the capitulation of Japan, a series of events followed one another in rapid succession. On August 13 the news of Japan's offer to surrender reached Vietnam. On that same day the Viet Minh's 'Provisional Committee of the Liberated Zone' issued an order for general insurrection. The Indochinese Communist Party (I.C.P.) held a special conference for three days (August 13–15) on how to deal with the immediate situation. On August 16 and 17, a People's National Congress – originally planned for the end of July – met at Tan Trao, representing 'all social classes, associations, and nationalities [ethnic groups]'. The sixty-member congress cut short its work and terminated deliberations in two days, creating a 'Committee for National Liberation' which was to act as the Provisional Government of Vietnam, headed by Ho Chi Minh. In view of the urgency of the situation, an Insurrection Committee headed by Vo Nguyen Giap was also created and was fully empowered to act in place of the Committee for National Liberation. Simultaneously, local 'People's Revolutionary Committees' in villages and counties of practically every province in North and Central Vietnam took over the political and administrative networks and began to exercise power. The transfer of power was accomplished smoothly and with practically no bloodshed. Within the next ten days, power throughout Vietnam fell into Viet Minh hands. Except for a few provinces next to the Chinese borders, all other areas of Vietnam were under the control of the People's Revolutionary Committees. Hanoi was taken over on August 19th, Hue on August 23rd, and Saigon on August 25th. On August 30th, Emperor Bao Dai, the last monarch of the Nguyen Dynasty, formally abdicated. Three days later, on September 2nd, Ho Chi Minh proclaimed the success of the revolution, pronounced the Vietnamese 'Declaration of Independence' and presented to the nation a government of the Democratic Republic of Vietnam (D.R.V.). In Vietnam's history, the events of August 1945 are subsumed under the title, 'The August Revolution' ...

Communism in Vietnam – the early periods   Communism under one form or another had been a part of Vietnamese political scenery since 1925. In that year Ho Chi Minh created in Canton the Association of Vietnamese Revolutionary Youth (*Viet Nam Thanh Nien Cach Menh Hoi*) or, in short, *Thanh Nien* (Youth). *Thanh Nien*, although endowed with a Communist core, and using Communist organizational techniques, was never officially a Communist Party. In May 1929, after severe internal dissension occurred on the question of transforming it into a Communist party, *Thanh Nien* disintegrated. Thereupon rival Communist groups appeared within Vietnam competing for membership and vying with one another in instigating revolutionary actions (workers' strikes, peasants' demonstrations, etc.). On February 3, 1930, these rival factions became united at a special conference held in Hong Kong under the chairmanship of Ho Chi Minh. Out of this conference the 'Vietnamese Communist Party' (*Viet-nam Cong-san Dang*) was born. In October, following a Comintern directive, this name was changed to 'Indo-Chinese Communist Party' (*Dong-duong Cong-san Dang*) or I.C.P.

Until the August Revolution (and the formal dissolution of the I.C.P.) in 1945, the Communist movement of Vietnam went through three periods. The first period, February 1930 to September 1931, was characterized by a nationwide, Communist-initiated, revolutionary movement typified by workers' strikes and peasants' demonstrations. No other anti-colonial movement since the *Can Vuong* (Rally to the King) Movement of the late nineteenth century had been so widespread. The Tax Protest Movement of 1908 had been confined to a few provinces of central Vietnam. The Yen Bay Mutiny and related anti-colonial activities organized by the *Viet-nam Quoc dan Dang* (Vietnamese Nationalist party, or *V.N.Q.D.D.*) [modelled upon the Chinese Kuomintang] were limited to five provinces in the North. The Communist-initiated revolutionary actions involved twenty-five provinces in all three regions of Vietnam. The movement began as an 'economic struggle', i.e. workers' strikes at plantations and factories, demanding higher wages and better working conditions, and peasants' demonstrations demanding postponement or reduction of taxes. It culminated in the establishment of 'Soviets' in Nghe-an and Ha-tinh [in north-central Vietnam]. Under the leadership of the I.C.P., peasants in several regions of these provinces destroyed the existing government administrative machinery and replaced it with their own. In the following repression by the colonial regime, practically all the Party networks were destroyed. In March 1931, the *entire* Standing Committee of the I.C.P. Central Committee, including Tran Phu, the Party's secretary-general, fell into the hands of the French police. In the same month, the Regional Committee of North Vietnam in Haiphong was destroyed, followed by the destruction of the Regional Committee of Central Vietnam. Soon afterward, Ho Chi Minh himself was arrested in Hong Kong by the British authorities. Gradually, all the leading cadres of the movement were arrested. By September 1931, little trace of Vietnamese Communism was left. Its first period had come to an end.

The second period of Vietnamese Communism was characterized by its active involvement in the open and legal movement during the Popular Front period (1936–1939). Between late 1931 and the middle of 1935, there was, in Vietnam, virtually no overt Communist activity worth noting. The I.C.P. began to regroup late in 1934 and, in March 1935, it held the first National Party Congress in Macao. Soon afterward, Communist-initiated revolutionary activities began to appear in Vietnam – in a new front, with new types of activities, and with a new ideological orientation. Between 1925 and 1931 Communist activities in Vietnam had been secret and illegal, emphasizing 'economic struggles' by organizing workers' strikes and peasants' demonstrations. From the beginning of 1935, however, a 'cultural front' was opened. A number of Vietnamese Communists, either released from French prisons or returning from abroad, published magazines and books. They started a series of lively public debates on issues such as materialism vs. spiritualism, art for the sake of art, or art for the sake of life, etc., utilizing this means to openly propagandize Communist theory. In the South, the movement began with *La Lutte* (The Struggle) and *Dong Nai* (name of a river in southern Vietnam); in the North, there was *Le Travail* (Labour), *Doi Moi* (New Life), *Hon Tre* (Soul of Youth), *Tan Xa-hoi* (New Society), etc. Taking advantage of the liberal colonial policies promulgated by the Popular Front [a left-wing coalition] government in France, the I.C.P. emerged late in 1936 and began to organize overt, legal political activities. Strikes, demonstrations, public political debates took place all over Vietnam. In the frenetic movement to demand 'democratic reforms' – abolition of the government monopoly of salt and alcohol, equal rights for women, enlargement of the educational system, etc. – the Party put aside temporarily its call for independence and land reforms. In September 1939, following the collapse of the Popular Front government, colonial repression resumed and took a heavy toll. The I.C.P. urban networks were destroyed throughout Vietnam. Two thousand Party workers were arrested, including important Party leaders. The Party rural bases were, for the moment, saved; but late in 1940, following the abortive Nam Ky insurrection in the South, they were in turn destroyed – this time drastically. Eight thousand people were sentenced, of which more than one hundred received the death penalty. Some of the most experienced Moscow-trained Party officials were executed. For the second time, the I.C.P. suffered what seemed to be a fatal blow at the hands of the colonial regime.

The Viet Minh front   With the creation of the Viet Minh Front, Vietnamese Communism entered a new stage, one which led directly to the August Revolution. In May 1941, the Executive Committee of the I.C.P. held its Eighth Conference at Pac Bo, Cao Bang Province, near the Chinese border. This Conference, the first ever held under the chairmanship of Ho Chi Minh on Vietnamese soil, arrived at and enunciated policies which were to shape the orientation, organizational structure and revolutionary activities of the I.C.P.

Ever since October 1930, the Party had considered itself as waging a 'bourgeois-democratic revolution', the first stage in the Comintern theoretical conception of the two-stage revolution. In theory, the bourgeois-democratic revolution in Vietnam had two parallel objectives; first, anti-imperialism or the liberation of Vietnam from French colonial imperialism and second, anti-feudalism, or the destruction of the landowning-mandarinate class. In practice, Communist activities in Vietnam since 1930 had emphasized the mobilization of workers and peasants in opposition to both the French colonial regime and the Vietnamese urban bourgeoisie and landowning class. The Eighth Conference in May 1941, however, set forth a radical redefinition of the nature and tasks of the Vietnamese revolution. It considered that 'the preparation for insurrection is the central responsibility of our Party in the present period'. It called for a 'national liberation revolution' and temporary postponement of the class struggle. As stated in the Resolution of the Conference,

> The Indochinese revolution at present is not a bourgeois-democratic revolution. It is no longer a revolution to solve the two problems of anti-imperialism and land [reforms], but a revolution to solve only one urgent problem – national liberation. Thus, the Indochinese revolution during this period is a revolution of national liberation.

Such a 'national liberation revolution' can succeed when there exists a unity of all

> revolutionary forces throughout Indochina; not discriminating between workers, peasants, rich peasants, landlords, or national capitalists. Whoever loves our country and race will together form a united front, gathering all the forces to do everything possible to fight for independence, destroying the French and Japanese bandits who have occupied our country.

On May 19, 1941, at the conclusion of the conference, the Alliance for Vietnamese Independence (*Viet nam Doc lap Dong minh Hoi*), or the Viet Minh Front, was created. It was the organizational expression of the united front proposed by the Resolution of the Conference.

Conceptually, the Viet Minh Front was never a 'party' in the usual sense. Rather, it was an organizational link of politicized social groups organized and promoted by the I.C.P. on functional, ethnic, and religious lines. As stated in the Viet Minh *By-laws*:

> 3. *Conditions for joining the Viet Minh.* Only organizations can be members of the Viet Minh. Any political party or organization of Vietnamese or minority people living in Vietnamese territory, regardless of their social class, religion, or political inclination – which accepts the objectives, goals and program of the Viet Minh Front and is approved by the Viet Minh General Staff (*Tong Bo*) is allowed to join the Viet Minh.

In practice, the I.C.P. created several mass or front organizations, the 'National Salvation Associations' (*Cuu Quoc Hoi*) – such as 'Peasants' National Salvation Association', 'Workingmen's National Salvation Associations', 'Women's National Salvation Association', 'Teen-Agers' National Salvation Association', etc. Together, these associations acted as an architectural front which shielded the I.C.P. Individually, each of these organizations translated esoteric Communist slogans into the everyday language and jargon of its own members. The Viet Minh Front was, in theory at least, the coalition of these National Salvation Associations.

From 1941 onward the Viet Minh Front – and not the I.C.P., which was officially played down – took several steps to prepare for the general insurrection. With regard to anti-Japanese forces outside Vietnam, the Viet Minh Front sought, with little success, to collaborate with both the Allied forces (mainly the Chungking government and also the American O.S.S. [forerunner of the C.I.A.]) and Vietnamese political groups exiled in southern China. Within the country, it sought to create several 'Liberation Committees' and 'National Liberation Associations'. In 1944, using what few weapons they could get from the people or from raiding isolated French posts, armed propaganda teams began to harass the Japanese and the French in mountainous regions of North Vietnam. Generally speaking, by March 1945, when the Japanese coup d'état occurred, Viet Minh activities had not had much effect.

Preparation for insurrection   The ease, rapidity, and smoothness of the Viet Minh seizure of power throughout Vietnam in the latter part of August 1945 has given the erroneous impression that the success of the August Revolution had been a result of fortuitous circumstances. While this view explains something about the political flux in Vietnam at the time – the favorable conditions for revolutionary actions which had been created by a vacuum of power following the Japanese surrender, a political crisis of the Tran Trong Kim Cabinet [see Glossary], and the confused socio-political conditions in general – it says little about the preparation for seizure and assumption of power undertaken by the Viet Minh. Communist preparation for insurrection had been decided upon as early as the Eighth conference of the I.C.P. Central Committee in May 1941 at which the Viet Minh Front was created, specifically to implement this resolution. By late 1942, in the remote mountainous regions of Cao Bang, near the Chinese border, secret 'Viet Minh Committees' had begun to exercise effective power through a parallel administrative structure. However, it was not until a base territory (*can-cu dia*) was established in these regions, and not until December 1944, that the Vietnamese Communists established an 'armed forces', composed of 34 'fighters' armed with 17 rifles, 14 hunting rifles, 6 time bombs and one American-made submachine gun with 150 bullets with a budget of 500 piasters (app. $50.00 U.S. at the time). Despite all the theoretical and psychological preparation, Viet Minh activities were confined mainly to these mountainous areas until after the Japanese coup de force.

Practically all the Viet Minh preparation for insurrection, in terms of organizational and propaganda activities, took place during the five-month Japanese interlude. Unlike the other political parties which were caught off guard by the Japanese coup and unsure about their political direction, the Viet Minh were able to assess the situation carefully and to carry out methodically a plan for insurrection. In the evening of March 9, 1945, the very same evening of the Japanese coup d'état, the Standing Bureau of the I.C.P. Central Committee held an enlarged conference to assess the new political situation and determine plans for actions. The conference observed in its directive – now called 'The Historical Directive' – that the Japanese coup had created an 'acute political crisis': French power had been destroyed, Japanese power was not yet consolidated, and the population 'in between' was in consternation. Yet the Central Committee considered, then, that the conditions were not yet 'ripe' for an insurrection. First, the French resistance against the Japanese was so feeble that the Japanese retained virtually their normal strength. Second, the noncommitted population must necessarily go through a period of disillusionment with the fake Japanese-granted 'independence', before they turned toward the revolutionary forces. Finally, except for a few localities where natural topographical conditions were favorable and where the Party had fighting units, the Viet Minh forces were not ready to make the uprising. In short, at the time of the Japanese coup the Viet Minh Front perceived the impossibility of waging an immediate insurrection. The Central Committee considered, however, three potential circumstances as aiding the 'ripening' of the conditions for insurrection:

a) The political crisis ... [i.e. the elimination of French colonial power in March 1945];
b) The terrible famine ... [see below];
c) The decisive stage of the war (imminent Allied landing in Indochina to attack the Japanese).

The five-month Japanese interlude saw feverish Viet Minh-initiated organizational and military activities. One of the most important resolutions of the I.C.P. Conference held during the first days of the Japanese coup was to immediately wage and expand guerrilla warfare and to establish a revolutionary base in order to prepare for a general insurrection. Implementing this decision, a two-faceted campaign was initiated. On the military front, two separate guerrilla forces of the Vietnamese highland – National Salvation Forces (*Cuu-quoc quan*) of the Bac-son-Vu-nhai base and the Vietnamese Propaganda Liberation Forces (*Viet nam tuyen-truyen giai-phong quan*) of the Cao-bang region – were united into the 'Vietnamese Liberation Forces' (*Viet nam giai-phong quan*). Within a few days after the coup d'état, they were able to recruit from the formerly French-employed Vietnamese militia to reach the number of 3,000 troops. The Liberation Forces were also able to pick up weapons and ammunition from the fleeing French, including even heavy machine guns and mortars. In general, military guerrilla actions were calculated to harass the Japanese, to protect Viet Minh bases and to help in the attacks on rice granaries, all of which was aimed at having a propaganda effect and not at competing with the powerful Japanese forces in the military field.

Far more attention, however, was paid to political tasks during this period. In numerous rural areas throughout North and Central Vietnam local 'People's Revolutionary Committees' were created as a parallel administrative structure competing with the government authorities. Wherever possible, these committees would supplant the latter. By the beginning of June, scarcely three months after the Japanese coup, a 'Liberated Zone' was created, covering the territory of nine provinces of the highland of North Vietnam and governing over one million people. This 'Liberated Zone' (*Khu Giai Phong*) was administered by a Provisional Committee headed by Ho Chi Minh himself. It became a military and political center for the Viet Minh-directed revolutionary movement ...

The I.C.P. and the Viet Minh Front paid special attention to the problems caused by the famine [1944–45]. Initially, the famine caused difficulties for revolutionary mobilization. In some northern provinces, several Viet Minh cadres, following the command of the Party to stay close to the masses, died of starvation. Among those who survived, little fighting spirit was left. Yet, the I.C.P. quickly perceived that the famine could be used as a means to stir up hatred against the French and the Japanese and at the same time to give the mass an I.C.P.-oriented 'political consciousness'. Late in 1944 and beginning 1945, following the slogan 'Destroy the granaries, solve the danger of hunger', Viet Minh cadres in North and northern Central Vietnam had already organized and led peasants in destroying hundreds of granaries. The Front coupled an appeal to well-to-do people to help out the hungry with an appeal to 'join the Viet Minh'. A Viet Minh propaganda leaflet in the days immediately before the Japanese coup said in part:

> Hunger! Hunger! Keep your paddy and rice! Destroy the granaries of the bandits. Chase out the French and the Japanese! Our land we till, we don't pay taxes. Our paddy we eat, don't let it be robbed of us!
> To accomplish this, compatriots ought to quickly join the Viet Minh.

The struggle against the famine paid rich dividends. The locations where the population was hardest hit by the famine and where were the most daring Viet Minh-led attacks on the Japanese rice-transports and granaries – such as Nam Dinh and Thai Binh – were also the areas where its influence was most extensive. Like the harassing military attacks on the Japanese, the movement to destroy the granaries was explicitly calculated to have propaganda effects, to spread the 'prestige' (*thanh-the*) of the Viet Minh Front. In August 1945, when the 'opportune moment' arrived, virtually everywhere in the rural areas throughout North and northern Central Vietnam, Viet Minh-led 'Liberation Committees' or 'People's Revolutionary Committees' emerged and smoothly took over the business of government. The revolution only came later to large cities such as Haiphong, Hanoi, Hue, and administrative seats of the provinces. Two weeks after the Japanese offered to surrender, most of Vietnamese government administration was in Viet Minh hands.

The August Revolution   The events of the August Revolution, especially the takeover of Hanoi, Hue, and Saigon, are now relatively well known. We need only concern ourselves here with the I.C.P. perception of the situation and plans for the insurrection. By July 1945, the I.C.P. perceived that the situation was becoming increasingly 'fruit ripe' (*chin mui*) for an insurrection. The enemy was now placed in an untenable position. The cadres were ready to sacrifice. The masses were willing to lend their support. In other words, both the 'objective conditions' and the 'subjective conditions' required, following Lenin's recipe for an insurrection, were present. As we have seen, the Central Committee convened a National Conference of the Party and a 'People's National Congress' to make final preparations for the insurrection. The I.C.P. National Conference had barely met, on August 13, when the news of Japan's capitulation arrived. That evening the Insurrection Committee issued its first order, launching the national insurrection. The I.C.P. National Conference, which met until August 15 decided,

1. The very favorable opportunity for the conquest of independence has arrived.
2. We are in an extremely urgent situation. All our operations must be based on the following three principles:
a. Concentration – Concentration of our forces on the essential tasks.
b. Unity – Unity of action and of command in political and military affairs.
c. Timeliness – Acting in good time and not to let slip any opportunity.

To legitimize their actions, the People's Congress, held at Tan Trao immediately after the I.C.P. National Conference, created the Provisional Government. Meanwhile, Vo Nguyen Giap, Chairman of the Insurrection Committee and head of the Liberation Army, led the insurrectionary armed forces toward Thai Nguyen, opening the *official* I.C.P.-led insurrection …

In some places insurrectional activities began as early as August 13, immediately after hearing the news that Japan had surrendered. Most places acted without instructions from the Central Committee. Throughout North and northern Central Vietnam, the rural areas were taken over first, followed by the insurrection in the cities and provincial headquarters. This pattern was reversed in southern Central Vietnam and South Vietnam, where I.C.P. cadres had been greatly decimated five years earlier and party networks destroyed. In these regions I.C.P.-manipulated coalitions with existing political groups were formed, giving their support to the Provisional Government. By the time Saigon was taken over on August 25, most of the country was already in Viet Minh hands.

The hectic insurrectionary activities throughout Vietnam during the second half of August 1945 were capped by the two events of great symbolic importance: the abdication of Emperor Bao Dai and the pronouncement of the Vietnamese Declaration of Independence. On August 30, Emperor Bao Dai, the last ruling monarch of the Nguyen Dynasty, abdicated formally in favor of the revolutionary Provisional Government. In front of 50,000 people gathered at the Ngo Mon Gate of the Imperial Palace, Tran Huy Lieu, representing the Provisional Government of the Democratic Republic, received from Emperor Bao Dai the gilt Seal and Sword (symbols of sovereignty) and formally declared the end of monarchy in Vietnam. Emperor Bao Dai became Citizen Nguyen Vinh Thuy, who was later to be elevated to the ceremonial position of 'Supreme Advisor' to the government of the Democratic Republic. It was neither the first, nor the last, time that Bao Dai assumed the role of puppet. The second event took place on September 2nd, when Ho Chi Minh, representing the new republican government, pronounced the Vietnamese Declaration of Independence in front of half a million Vietnamese gathered at Ba Dinh Square, Hanoi …

The August Revolution is seen as the climactic moment of the century-long Vietnamese struggle for independence from Western imperialism. The event at Ba Dinh Square is considered, in this light, as formally establishing the end of French colonial imperialism, the end of the Confucianist-oriented monarchical regime, the regaining of Vietnamese independence and the beginning of the Democratic Republic of Vietnam.

The August Revolution – a look backward In the discussion concerning the origins, nature, and forms of revolutionary actions in the August Revolution, several questions have been raised. We concern ourselves here with only one, the most often asked, namely, why the I.C.P., and not any other Vietnamese political parties, succeeded in winning power and popular support in August 1945. To this question, several answers have been given ...

Two explanations ... deserve special consideration. One, often put forward by I.C.P. detractors, saw the success of the Viet Minh in gaining power in August 1945 as a result of fortuitous circumstances. According to this argument, there was then a vacuum of power in Vietnam following the Japanese surrender. The Japanese had destroyed the French colonial regime in March. When they in turn capitulated to the Allies, their troops were in consternation and became dispirited. Taking advantage of this situation, the Viet Minh Front easily took over power in front of indifferent Japanese eyes, or even with Japanese connivance. The mass support for the Viet Minh Front, following this theory, had been gained by the Viet Minh's exaggeration of what little connections it had with the Allied forces.

A second explanation, often presented by D.R.V. historians, saw the Communist success in August 1945 as a result of skillful analysis of the revolutionary situation and long-term planning and preparation. The success of the August Revolution must accordingly be seen as a result of the 'correct revolutionary line' and of the 'creative application of Marxist-Leninist principles to the revolutionary conditions of Vietnam' by the I.C.P. leadership. Following this argument, the origins of the August Revolution go back to the Eighth Conference of the I.C.P. Central Committee in May 1941, when a new revolutionary line was decided upon (putting aside temporarily the question of class struggle in favor of national unity in the struggle against French colonialism), when the Viet Minh Front was created, and when plans for insurrection were first put forward. The success of the I.C.P. in August 1945, in other words, was the result of long-term revolutionary preparations involving propaganda and organizational work. As Tran van Giau, one of the best known I.C.P. leaders, would have it, the success of the August Revolution was the end result of both an art and a science of insurrection. The scientific principles of insurrection were already laid down by Lenin, it was the I.C.P. artists who mixed the ingredients and applied the paint.

While there is sufficient evidence to support either of the two explanations discussed above, by itself each is inadequate. 'Chance' alone explains little, the 'chance' which existed in the peculiar combination of historical factors in the Vietnam of August 1945 – the Japanese had just capitulated, the French were still far away, and the Allied forces had not yet arrived – offered itself not just to the Viet Minh Front but equally to all other political parties. At best, the theory of chance tells us the obvious, that is, the conditions of political flux of August 1945 were extremely favorable to an insurrectional attempt. It fails to explain how an organized political force can obtain and maintain political power. The explanation of 'revolutionary skills', often narcissistically propounded by Vietnamese Communists, is equally unsatisfactory. The I.C.P. skills in revolutionary analysis, organization, propaganda, and leadership were undoubtedly superior to *all*, save none, of Vietnamese political parties. These skills, however, would have been useless, if there had not been a favorable 'revolutionary environment'. Specifically, if the Japanese Army in Indochina had not destroyed French colonial power, it is doubtful whether all the 'revolutionary skills' already mentioned would have brought the I.C.P. close to any of its desired objectives. By the time of the Japanese coup, *several* of the most seasoned, Moscow-trained I.C.P. leaders had already 'sacrificed', and most of those who were still alive were in French prisons or 'concentration camps' (*trai tap-trung*). Every single Vietnamese insurrectional uprising, Communist-initiated or otherwise, had been swiftly and brutally suppressed by the colonial regime. It is difficult to see how, without the Japanese coup, any Vietnamese insurrectional attempt could have succeeded.

In retrospect, historical fortuity and revolutionary ability played [an] equally important role in the August Revolution. Yet both of these elements in the success of the August Revolution do not refer *exclusively to the events of August 1945*, as theorists of the August Revolution on both sides of the ideological fence have been inclined to believe. More than any one single event, the Japanese coup of March 1945 served as the catalyst and contributed decisively, though incidentally, to the success of the August Revolution. Its most obvious, and most important, contribution was the elimination of the French colonial regime, the most dangerous, most implacable, and most capable enemy of the Vietnamese revolution. The destruction of French colonialism was *conditio sine qua non* for the success of a Vietnamese revolution, any Vietnamese revolution. Unexpectedly, the coup and the subsequent Vietnamese 'independence' awakened patriotism and a sense of social concern among urban Vietnamese, who were to swell the revolutionary ranks in short order. Indeed, the Japanese coup may be considered as the turning point in the fortune of both French colonialism and Vietnamese nationalism. The resultant collapse of the old order and the Japanese preoccupation with the war created a 'vacuum of power' in the areas of Vietnam remote from administrative and military centers – a vacuum which was quickly filled by Viet Minh-created 'Liberation Committees'. The Japanese coup d'état, in other words, created favorable conditions for revolutionary actions. The possible profitable exploitation of such conditions depended upon the strategic and tactical calculations of an organized political force.

Favorable conditions were, however, only one part of the conditions for an insurrectional success. Destroying French colonialism, the Japanese coup merely provided the Vietnamese revolution with an opportunity, a chance for success. The rest was up to the Vietnamese revolutionaries themselves. Parenthetically, this was not a new discovery of the Vietnamese Communists, nor Lenin's. The old shrewd Machiavelli already told us in *The Prince* that *Fortuna* (chance) controls only half of men's actions; the other half is left to *virtù* (ability) and *necessita* (existing conditions which limit men's freedom of actions). The I.C.P.'s activities in the very same night of the Japanese coup demonstrated clearly that they correctly perceived the 'acute political crisis' and the 'favorable conditions' for revolutionary actions, both of which had just been created by the coup. The I.C.P. also wisely perceived that the conditions were not yet 'ripe' for an insurrection. The French had been destroyed, but Viet Minh forces were nowhere near an ability to challenge the Japanese Army. It was also doubtful whether or not the majority of the population knew, at this stage, who the Viet Minh were. Except for the famine, which initially caused many difficulties to the local, rural-based Viet Minh organizations – difficulties which the Viet Minh Front managed to overcome and even exploit to their own advantage – the political conditions during the five-month Japanese interlude became increasingly favorable to an insurrectional attempt. Political participation among Vietnamese of all classes became increasingly active. In urban areas, where Viet Minh influences were the weakest, Viet Minh members secretly infiltrated existing political groups and eventually either took over control or weaned away the most active and susceptible elements. In the countryside, Viet Minh-led attacks on the granaries and rice-transport became daily occurrences. Everywhere secret 'Liberation Committees' were formed. In the month immediately prior to the Japanese capitulation, large areas of North and northern Central Vietnam were either overtly or secretly under some form of Viet Minh influence. In most places throughout Vietnam, the Viet Minh capture of power was received with enthusiasm, or at worst, unopposed.

The August Revolution was the most significant turning point in the recent history of Vietnam. Whether and to what extent it was a 'success' is a matter of interpretation. In a narrow sense, the immediate events of August 1945 were only the final climax of a five-month political drama – a drama which began on March 9 and was supposed to have ended on September 2, 1945. The drama has continued. It has been transformed into a tragedy which has torn Vietnamese society asunder and involved practically the entire world. In a more general sense, the August Revolution marked the end of the period of *direct* foreign domination in internal Vietnamese affairs, formally abolished the monarchical–mandarinate political system, brought large numbers of Vietnamese into the political process, and finally, fulfilled a wish to Vietnamese at the time, namely, making Vietnam a part of the world political configurations. Events in Vietnam since 1945 demonstrate, however, that the August Revolution was less than a total success. Foreign imperialism has remained in Vietnam in different forms and under different pretexts. Vietnamese independence and unity have not yet been completed [written in 1971]. If anything, the August Revolution represented a beginning. The process of social and political changes which began with the events of August 1945 has effected a definite transformation of Vietnamese society and its politics, a process which is still ongoing, whether or not desired by foreigners.

2. Sukarno and the *pancasila* principles

Like the French in Indochina, the Dutch provided little leeway in the 1920s and 1930s for the development of an Indonesian nationalist movement that could bargain for political concessions and increased representation in the manner of Indian and Burmese nationalists. Although the consultative powers of the Volksraad (People's Council), set up in 1918, were minimally expanded in the ensuing years, in the end it could not satisfy Indonesian aspirations, either as a forum for political dialogue, or as a launching-pad for progressive constitutional change. The first mass nationalist movement, the Sarekat Islam, split in the early 1920s; then, in 1926 and 1927, the Indonesian Communist Party (PKI) was crushed as a political force following its abortive revolts. There was a short resurgence of nationalist activity in the late 1920s in which the east Javanese intellectual Sukarno and his Indonesian National Party (or PNI) played a key role, but in the course of the early 1930s the new generation of nationalist leaders that had emerged were sent into internal exile.

When the Japanese stormed through the islands in 1942, they ended the Dutch administration, but notably failed to encourage Indonesian nationalist aspirations. Indonesia was regarded as unready for independence; moreover, the Japanese were anxious to maintain direct control over the vital raw materials of the area. The regions of Sumatra, Java and the eastern islands were administered separately by the Japanese armed forces; and, although politicians like Sukarno, Mohammad Hatta and Sutan Syahrir were released from exile, and although indigenous political organizations and militias were created, the latter were only allowed to operate – openly at least – on the basis of broad pan-Asian and pro-Japanese, not nationalist, agendas.

By mid 1944, when the Japanese desperately needed to unite Indonesians behind their war effort, they finally relented on the issue of independence. It was not until late May 1945, however, that the Badan Penyelidik Usaha Persiapan Kemerdekaan Indonesia (BPKI, or 'Body to Investigate Measures for the Preparation of Indonesian Independence') was created. It was in this forum that Sukarno proposed his *pancasila*, or five principles, as the basis of the independent Indonesian state. Despite all the vicissitudes of Indonesian history since that date, these five principles have remained the pillars on which the Indonesian state is based.

Certain important general themes can be noted in Sukarno's *pancasila* principles. The key assertion was that nothing could be achieved until

Indonesia had complete control of its own destiny: total independence, therefore, was the absolute priority. However, Sukarno stressed that independence in itself was not the ultimate goal; it was the 'golden bridge' which had to be crossed before Indonesians could decide what kind of society they wanted to build. Sukarno himself expressed what was no doubt a consensus view – not only in Indonesia, but throughout the colonized world of that time – that the new society should be based on socialist rather than capitalist principles. It was not just the Asian communists who linked capitalism with imperialism; it was an outlook shared by nearly all the generation of nationalists who were to lead their countries to independence.

Sukarno's argument for the *geographic* basis of national identity should also be noted. Ever since 1945, Indonesian nationalism has asserted the 'primordial' unity of the Indonesian islands: this has, of course, foreclosed any right to exercise self-determination on the part of the regions of Indonesia. It also provided a retrospective justification for Indonesia's seizure of Portuguese Timor in 1975.

Underlying the whole of Sukarno's political philosophy, as expressed in this speech, is his emphasis on *mufakat*, or debate, discussion and consensus. We should, however, note here a specific element in Sukarno's vision that was to become increasingly apparent in the two decades after 1945: while on the one hand he had a horror of the 'winner-takes-all' version of Western party-political democracy, which he felt would contribute to the fragmentation of Indonesia, he interpreted 'consensus' as a continuing dynamic tension between ideological and religious principles and forces, *not* as some form of flaccid conflict avoidance. If these ideological confrontations were not to tear Indonesia apart, therefore, they needed to operate within the framework of an authoritarian leadership. These concepts were to form the basis of the 'Guided Democracy' structure he set up in 1959 (see Chapter 8).

President Sukarno, 'The Birth of Pancasila'. Extract from speech given on 1 June 1946 (Ministry of Information, Republic of Indonesia, 1952)

Honourable Chairman:

Three days have passed during which the members of the Investigating Committee in Preparation for Independence [BPKI] have made known their opinions, and now I have from the Chairman the honour of stating my opinion also. I will comply with the Honourable Chairman's request. What is that request of his? The Honourable Chairman asked this gathering of the Investigating Committee in Preparation for Independence to draw up a draft of the basic principles for Free Indonesia ...

What is it that is called freedom? In the year 1933 I wrote a booklet. A booklet called 'Kearah Indonesia Merdeka' [Towards a Free Indonesia]. In that booklet of 1933, I stated that freedom, political independence, was nothing more than a bridge, a golden bridge. I said in that booklet that on the far side of that bridge we would rebuild our society ... I remind you once again, Free Indonesia, political Independence, is nothing more than, and does not differ from a bridge! ...

There are two millions of youths, whose single slogan is: 'A Free Indonesia, Now': If, for instance, the Japanese Army today were to surrender affairs of state to you, would you decline it, saying: just a moment, wait a while, we ask that this and that be finished first, and only then we will dare accept the affairs of state of Free Indonesia? (Cries of No! No!)

If, for instance, at this very moment the Japanese forces were to transfer state responsibilities to us, then we would not hold back for one minute, we would at once accept these responsibilities, we would at once begin with the independent Indonesian state! (Thundering applause) ...

We are today facing an all important moment. Do we not understand, as declared by dozens of speakers, that in very truth international law simplifies our task? For the organization, the establishment, the recognition of an independent state, there need not be any condition which is complicated, which is hairsplitting. The only condition is a territory, a people, and a stable government. This is sufficient in international law ... As soon as there is a territory, a people, a government, recognized by one other free state, there is already what is termed: freedom. No matter whether the people can read or not, no matter whether the people have a good economy or not, no matter whether the people are stupid or clever, if according to international law, the nation possesses the conditions for a free state, that is, a people, a territory, and a government, it is free.

Do not let us waver or be ponderous, and wanting to finalise beforehand a thousand and one imaginary matters! Once again I ask: Do we want to be free or do we not? Do we want to be free or do we not? (Reply from audience: We want to be free!)

Gentlemen! Now that I have spoken about the matter of 'freedom', I will proceed to speak of the matter of principles ...

First principle: nationalism To begin with, I ask: Do we intend to set up Free Indonesia for one particular individual, for one particular group? To set up Free Indonesia, which in name only is free Indonesia, but in reality is only something to crown some individual, to bring power to a wealthy group, to give power to a group of nobles?

Is our objective like that? Certainly not! Our compatriots the 'nationalists', who are present here, as well as our compatriots the 'Moslems', have all agreed that no such state is our goal. We intend to establish a state 'all for all'. Neither for a single individual, nor for a group, neither for a group of nobles, nor a group of wealthy people – but 'all for all'. This is one of the principles which I will explain again. And so, what I always have at heart, not only in these days of this session of the Investigating Committee, but ever since the year 1918, for more than 25 years, is this: The first principle, best to become the foundation for the State of Indonesia, is the *principle of nationalism*.

We will establish an Indonesian *national* state ...

What is it that is termed nation? What are the requirements for a nation?

According to [Ernest] Renan [see Glossary], the requirement for a nation is 'the will to unite'. It is necessary that the people feel themselves united and wish to be united.

Let us consider a definition by another person, namely the definition by Otto Bauer in his book, 'Die Nationalitatenfrage', where the question is raised: 'Was ist eine Nation?' and the answer was: 'A nation is a unity of conduct which comes into being because of [a] unity of destiny.' This, according to Otto Bauer, is a nation ...

[But] men and place cannot be separated! Impossible to separate people from the earth under their feet. Ernest Renan and Otto Bauer only looked at men alone. They thought only about their 'Gemeinschaft' and the feeling of men, 'L'âme et le désir'. They were only thinking of character, not thinking of the earth, the earth inhabited by those people. What is that place? That place is a country. That country is one entity. God Almighty made the map of the world, created the map of the world. If we look at the map of the world, we can show where are the 'entities' there. Even a child, if he looks at the map of the world, can show that the Indonesian Archipelago forms one entity. On the map can be shown an entity of a group of islands between two big oceans, the Pacific Ocean and the Indian Ocean, and between two continents, the continent of Asia and the continent of Australia. Even a child can see that the islands of Java, Sumatra, Borneo, Celebes, Halmahera, the Lesser Sunda Islands, the Moluccas, and the other islands in their midst are one entity. Similarly any child can see on the map of the world, that the islands of Japan stretching on the eastern brink of the continent of Asia, as a breakwater of the Pacific Ocean, are one entity ...

And so, what is it that is called the Land of our Birth, our country? According to geopolitics, Indonesia is our country. Indonesia in its entirety, neither Java alone, nor Sumatra alone, nor Borneo alone, nor Celebes alone, nor Ambon alone, nor the Moluccas alone, but the whole Archipelago ordained by God Almighty to be a single entity between two continents and two oceans, that is our country ...

Briefly speaking, the people of Indonesia, the Indonesian Nation is not only a group of individuals who, having 'the will to unite', live in a small area like Minangkabau or Madura or Jogja or Pasundan or Makassar, but the Indonesian people are all the human beings who, according to geopolitics ordained by God Almighty, live throughout the entity of the entire archipelago of Indonesia from the northern tip of Sumatra to Irian [New Guinea]! All, throughout the islands! The Indonesian nation, the people of Indonesia, the Indonesian human beings numbering seventy million persons, but seventy million who have already become one, one, once again one! (Loud clapping.)

This is what we should all aim at: the establishment of one National State based on the entity of one Indonesian soil from the tip of Sumatra right to Irian. I am confident that there is not one group amongst you which does not agree, neither the Moslems nor the group called 'the Nationalist Group'. This is what all of us should aim at.

Let no one think that every independent country is a national state. Neither Prussia nor Beieren, nor Saxony, is a national state, but the whole of Germany is a national state. Not the small areas, neither Venice, nor Lombardy, but the whole of Italy, the entire peninsula in the Mediterranean bounded to the north by the Alps, is the national state. Neither Bengal, nor Punjab, nor Behar and Orissa, but the entire triangle of India must become a national state.

Similarly, neither were all the states of our homeland which were independent in the past, national states. Only twice have we experienced a national state, that was in the time of *Sriwijaja* [see Glossary] and in the time of *Modjopahit* [or *Majapahit*; see Glossary]. Apart from those we have never experienced a national state. I say with full respect for our former Rajas, I say, with a thousand respects to Sultan Agung Hanjokrokusumo, that [the seventeenth century central Javanese kingdom of Later] Mataram, although independent, was not a national state.

With a sense of respect towards Prabu Siliwangi of [the Sundanese – west Java – kingdom of] Pejajaran, I say that his kingdom was not a national state. With a sense of respect towards Prabu Sultan Agung Tirtayasa, I say that his kingdom in Banten [in northwest Sunda], although independent, was not a national state. With a sense of respect towards Sultan Hasanuddin in Celebes where he erected the Kingdom of Bugis [in southern Sulawesi], I say that the independent land of Bugis was no national state.

The National state is only Indonesia in its entirety, which was set up in the time of Sriwijaja and Modjopahit, and which now we also ought to establish together. Therefore, if you, gentlemen, are willing, let us take as the first principle of our state *Indonesian Nationalism*. Indonesian Nationalism in the fullest sense! Neither Javanese Nationalism, nor Sumatran Nationalism nor the Nationalism of Borneo, or Celebes, Bali, or any other, but the Indonesian Nationalism which at one and the same time becomes the principle of one National State ...

Second principle: internationalism But ... but ... undoubtedly there is a danger involved in this principle of nationalism. The danger is, that probably men will narrow down nationalism to chauvinism, the creed of 'Indonesia über Alles'. This is the danger. We love one homeland, we feel ourselves one nation, we possess one language. But our homeland Indonesia is only a small part of the world. Remember this.

Gandhi said 'I am a nationalist, but my nationalism is humanity'. The nationalism we advocate is not the nationalism of isolation, not chauvinism, as blazoned by people in Europe who say 'Deutschland über Alles', who say that there is none so great as Germany, whose people they say are supermen, cornhaired and blue-eyed 'Aryans', whom they consider the greatest in the world, while other nations are worthless. Do not let us abide by such formulas, gentlemen, do not let us say that the Indonesian nation is the noblest and most perfect, whilst belittling other people. We should aim at the unity and brotherhood of the whole world.

We should not only establish the state of Free Indonesia, but we should also aim at making one family of all nations. It happens that this is my second principle. This is the second principle of philosophy I propose to you, gentlemen, to which I give the name of *'internationalism'*. But when I say *internationalism*, I do not mean cosmopolitanism, which does not recognize nationalism, which says there is no Indonesia, no Japan, no Burma, no England, no America and so on. Internationalism can not flower if it is not rooted in the soil of nationalism. Nationalism can not flower if it does not grow within the garden of internationalism. Thus, these two, gentlemen, principle one and principle two, which I have first proposed to you, are dovetailed together.

Third principle: representative government Well then, what is the third principle? That principle is the principle of consent, the principle of *representative government*, the principle of consultation. The Indonesian State shall not be a state for one individual, neither a state for one group, nor for the wealthy. But we are to establish a state 'all for all', 'one for all, all for one'. I am convinced, that the necessary condition for the strength of the Indonesian state is conferring, is representative government.

For Islam, this is the best condition for the promotion of religion. We are Moslems, myself included, – a thousand pardons my Islamism is far from perfect, – but if you open up your breast, and look at my heart, you will find it none other than Islamic. And this Islamic heart of Bung Karno ['Brother Sukarno'], hopes to defend Islam by agreement, through discussion! By means of agreement, we shall improve all matters, we shall promote the interest of religion, that is, by means of talks or discussions in the House of Representatives ...

Therefore, I ask you gentlemen, both those that are not Moslem, and in particular those who are, to accept this principle number 3, that is the principle of conferring, of representative government. In the House of Representatives there will be great conflicts of opinion. There is not one state truly alive, if it is not as if the cauldron of Tjondrodimuko [a mythical volcano] burns and boils in its representative body, if there is no clash of convictions in it. Both in an Islamic state and also in a Christian state, there is always a struggle. Accept principle number 3, the principle of consent, the principle of *people's representation!* ...

Allah, God of the Universe, gave us the capacity to think, so that in our daily intercourse we might constantly burnish our thoughts, just like the pounding and husking of paddy to obtain rice, in turn to become the best Indonesian food. Accept, gentlemen, then, principle number 3, which is the principle of conferring!

Fourth principle: social justice Principle number 4, I will now propose to you. During these three days I have not yet heard of that principle, *the principle of prosperity*. The principle: there shall be no poverty in free Indonesia. Our principles should be: Do we want a free Indonesia whose capitalists do as they wish, or where the entire people prosper, where every man has enough to eat, enough to wear, lives in prosperity, feels cherished by the homeland that gives him sufficient keep? Which do we choose, gentlemen? Do not imagine, gentlemen, that as soon as the People's Representative body comes into being, we shall automatically achieve this prosperity. We have seen that in the states of Europe there are representative bodies, there is parliamentary democracy. But is it not precisely in Europe that the capitalists are the bosses? ...

I suggest: if we are seeking democracy, the need is not for the democracy of the west, but for conferring, which brings life, which is politico-economic democracy, able to bring about social prosperity! The people of Indonesia have long spoken of this matter. What is meant by 'Ratu Adil?' [see Glossary] What is meant by the conception of Ratu Adil is *social justice*. The people wish for prosperity ... Therefore if we truly understand, remember, and love the people of Indonesia, let us accept this *principle of social justice* which is not only political equality, gentlemen. In the field of economic [matters], too, we must create equality, and the best common prosperity.

The body for consultation which we will establish should not be a body for the discussion of political democracy only, but a body which, together with the community, will be able to give effect to two principles: *political justice and social justice* ...

Fifth principle: belief in God Gentlemen, what is the fifth principle? I have already expounded 4 principles:

1. *Indonesian nationalism.*
2. *Internationalism — or humanism.*
3. *Consent, or democracy.*
4. *Social prosperity.*

The fifth principle should be:
To set up Free Indonesia with faith in God the Almighty.

The principle of Belief in God! Not only should the people of Indonesia have belief in God, but every Indonesian should believe in *his own* particular God. The Christian should worship God according to the teachings of Jesus Christ, Moslems according to the teachings of the Prophet Mohammad, Buddhists should discharge their religious rites according to their own books.

But let us all have belief in God. The Indonesian state shall be a state where every person can worship God in freedom ...

Let us observe, let us practise religion, whether Islam or Christianity, in a civilised way. What is that civilised way? It is the way of mutual respect. (Clapping amongst the audience.) The Prophet Mohammad gave sufficient proofs of tolerance, and of respect for other religions. Jesus Christ also showed that tolerance. Let us within the free Indonesia which we are going to organise along those lines, let us declare: that the fifth principle of our state is belief in God, belief in God with a high code of honour, belief in God which has respect for one another. I shall be glad indeed if you agree that the state of free Indonesia shall be founded upon belief in God the Almighty ...

Gentlemen: I have already proposed to you 'The principles of the State'. There are five. Is this Pantja Darma? No. The name 'Pantja Darma' is not suitable here. Darma means duty, whereas we are speaking of principles ...

The name is not Pantja Darma, but I call it according to the advice of a linguist, a friend of ours: *Pantja Sila*. *Sila* means *basis* or *principle*, and upon those five principles we shall build free Indonesia, lasting and age-long. (Loud applause.) ...

As I said a while ago: we are establishing an Indonesian state, for which all of us should be responsible. All for all ... If I compress what was five to get three, and what was three to get one, then I have a genuine Indonesian term, the term '*gotong rojong*' (mutual cooperation). The State of Indonesia, which we are to establish, should be a state of mutual cooperation. How fine that is! A Gotong Rojong state! (Loud applause on all sides.)

The principle of Gotong Rojong between the rich and the poor, between the Moslem and the Christian, between those not originating from Indonesia and their children who become Indonesians. This, gentlemen, is what I propose to you ...

Principles such as I have proposed to you, gentlemen, are the principles for a free Indonesia which will endure. For decades has my breast burned fiercely with these principles. But do not forget that we live in a time of war, gentlemen. During this time of war we are going to establish a state of Indonesia – in the midst of war's thunder. I even render thanks to the Divine God that we are to establish an Indonesian state not under the full moon, but with the sound of the drums of war and in the fury of war. Free Indonesia shall emerge a tempered free Indonesia, free Indonesia tempered in the fury of war, and a free Indonesia of that kind is a strong Indonesian state, not an Indonesian state which would turn soft after some time. It is because of that, that I thank God Almighty ...

If the people of Indonesia desire that the Pantjasila I propose become a reality, that is, if we wish to live as one nation, one free nationality, if we wish to live as a member of a free world imbued with humanism the principle of conferring, to live in complete social Justice, to live in peace and prosperity, if we desire to live in the belief of God in the fullest and completed sense, we must not forget the conditions for its realization, and that is struggle, struggle, and once again struggle.

Do not imagine that with the existence of the state of Free Indonesia, our struggle is at an end. No! I even say: Within that free Indonesia our struggle must continue. The struggle, however, must be of a different nature from what we have been carrying on so far. Then we, as a united people, shall continue our struggle to bring realization to our ideals contained in Pantjasila. And, particularly in this time of war, have faith, cultivate in your hearts the conviction, that free Indonesia cannot come if the people of Indonesia do not dare take a risk, do not dare dive for pearls into the depths of the ocean. If the people of Indonesia are not united, and are not determined to live or die for freedom, the freedom of Indonesia will never be the possession of the Indonesian people, never, until the end of time! Freedom can only be achieved and owned by a people whose soul is aflame with the determination of 'Merdeka, – freedom or death!'

3. The origins of the Indonesian Revolution

When the Japanese surrendered to the Allies in August 1945, they still held absolute control of all except a few fringes of the Indonesian islands. Although controlled political activity had been allowed, particularly in Java, many areas had been completely quiescent during the Japanese occupation. The surrender unleashed a new unrestricted era of political activity.

The problem for the new *de facto* leaders of the new Indonesia – Sukarno and Mohammad Hatta – lay in the fact that the Japanese had, in their surrender to the Allies, accepted responsibility for the maintenance of political authority in Indonesia until the Allies could take over. Even if the Japanese had wished merely to hand over power to an independent Indonesia, they did not have the power to do so, at least openly. It was this central fact that forced the Indonesian leaders to act with extreme caution. If they had made one false move that antagonized the Japanese military authorities, the whole fragile structure of an independent state that they were in the process of developing could have been crushed.

The following extract from Anthony Reid's *The Indonesian National Revolution 1945–1950* outlines the details of the complex period of the summer and autumn of 1945 in Indonesia. In it we can clearly see the origins of one of the major confrontations of the ensuing period of revolution and war: that between the elite leadership who needed to build an effective administrative machine – and therefore needed to rely on the indigenous administrator class, the *pamong praja*, who had worked with the Dutch and the Japanese – and the various youth and Marxist organizations who did not merely want independence, but also wished to bring about full-scale revolutionary change within Indonesian society. This conflict was not simply an internal matter: the Indonesian leadership knew that a responsible, working state was required in order to deal with the Japanese military and, later, the British of South-East Asia Command (SEAC), the Dutch, and the international community.

The broad phenomenon called the 'Indonesian Revolution' contained within it, in fact, a number of tensions that were to affect Indonesian politics for the next decades. In addition to the tension between the nationalist 'establishment' and the revolutionary forces, there was the difference of opinion between strict Muslim leaders and the more secular nationalists on the very foundations of the state; between those regions – mainly in Java, Sumatra and Sulawesi – where nationalism had been strong, and those areas that, if anything, feared nationalism and Javanese domination more than they resented Dutch colonial rule; and between political and military leaders who wanted an essentially authoritarian political structure, and those Western-influenced liberals who favoured the creation of a parliamentary democracy.

Anthony Reid here shows that the institutions of the Republic were not the consequence of leisurely deliberation, but were created in the heat of the moment in order to meet immediate needs. The political framework was in a state of constant flux in these early months. More important still, though the system set up in the revolutionary period was highly centralized in conception, in reality central government power over the regions was weak, and relied ultimately on the remarkable consensus in Java and Sumatra in favour of immediate independence. Beneath that, the dislocation and hardship of the last part of the war was now compounded by *de facto* anarchy, where local tensions and confrontations burst unchecked into the open.

Anthony Reid, *The Indonesian National Revolution 1945–1950* (Hawthorn, Victoria: Longman, 1974). Excerpts taken from pages 19–39.

Proclamation of the Republic

Blueprint for a state The opportunity, long awaited by nationalists, to come together to plan a future independent state, was realized at the hands of the Japanese on 28 May 1945. The sixty-two member *Badan Penyelidik Usaha Persiapan Kemerdekaan Indonesia* (Body to investigate measures for the preparation of Indonesian Independence) or BPKI, inaugurated on that day, was given considerable freedom by the Japanese to debate constitutional and ideological questions. Fortunately for the harmony of proceedings, its composition ensured the domination of Sukarno's secular nationalist mode of thinking. On the one hand inadequate representation was afforded the outer islands (half a dozen members had been born in the outer islands though long-term residents of Java); the Muslims (seven members); Youth (none); and Western-oriented Marxists (Hatta was the nearest). On the other hand most of the *pamong praja* [civil servant] representatives were sceptical about the operation and unprepared for detailed practical debate. For Sukarno and his fellow nationalists this was the chance to prove that the humiliations endured under the Japanese had not been in vain. It was, above all, Sukarno who provided the drive which pushed the committee to a conclusion with a speed which surprised the Japanese.

After three days mainly devoted to ideological manifestos, the BPKI formed a subcommittee of seven under Sukarno to resolve the knotty religious question. The full committee met again from 10–17 July in a more determined mood, and in that short time adopted a constitution of fifteen Articles. The most difficult minority had been the Muslim representatives, who had always argued the need for a Muslim state in which religious law would be enforceable. Sukarno's position, outlined in his famous *Pancasila* (five principles) speech of 1 June, was that the State should be based on 'belief in the One, Supreme god', whether worshipped in Muslim or Christian terms. If the Muslims wanted more than this they should strive for it through the democratic process. Muslim representatives were far from satisfied, and Sukarno directed all the force of his personality to achieve a compromise. On 22 June the subcommittee produced a draft prologue to the constitution, which conceded 'the obligation for those who profess the Islamic faith to abide by Islamic Laws'. The July session of the BPKI made the further concession that the president should be a Muslim. Although well short of Muslim hopes, this was to prove the highest point in their pursuit of an Islamic State.

Other issues provided less opposition to the long held principles of the secular nationalist mainstream which was led by Sukarno and given legal precision by Professor Soepomo. By considerable margins the BPKI voted for a republic rather than a monarchy (55–6); and for a unitary rather than a federal state (17–2 in sub-committee). The authoritarian element already evident in Sukarno's pre-war thinking was reinforced by the conditions of the war against the Western democracies. All the leading members felt obliged to reject 'Western' liberalism and individualism. It was predictably the few members born outside Java, notably the Minangkabaus [west Sumatrans] Hatta and Yamin and the Ambonese [eastern Indonesian] Latuharhary, who provided what little ineffective defence there was for the rights of the region and the individual as against the centre.

The draft '1945 Constitution' which the BPKI adopted placed few restrictions on the power of the president. Elected every five years by a supreme advisory council (MPR), he had full executive power including the appointment and dismissal of ministers, while he shared legislative power with a representative assembly (DPR) and could veto all legislation. As Sukarno informed a critic of this last provision: 'What embodies the sovereignty of the people is the president, not the representative assembly'. About the composition of the MPR and DPR the constitution stated only that this would be fixed by law.

The Japanese had also allowed the BPKI the unusual privilege of debating the boundaries of the future Indonesian state. A substantial majority (45 to 19) opted for a 'Greater Indonesia', embracing Malaya, British Borneo, and Portuguese Timor as well as the former Netherlands India.

The collapse of Japanese defences and communications during the middle months of 1945 caused a drastic change of pace in independence preparations. By mid-July Tokyo was planning for independence 'at the earliest possible moment' and forcing local commanders to rush their plans accordingly. Hurried conferences during the ensuing three weeks produced a draft timetable in which independence, scheduled for 7 September, would be prepared by a *Panitia Persiapan Kemerdekaan Indonesia* (Committee for the Preparation of Indonesian Independence), or PPKI, which would meet from 18 August to complete the work of the BPKI. The 'Greater Indonesia' idea was rejected by the Japanese, presumably because the relatively few Malay radical nationalists who supported it were of limited use in mobilizing the mixed population of south and central Malaya (the overwhelmingly Malay northern Malayan states having already been consigned to Thailand). Nevertheless the whole of former Dutch territory was to be declared independent in September, including the unprepared Navy-administered area. Effective Indonesian control could come later. 'Those areas which have not completed preparations shall gradually be transferred to the jurisdiction of the new independent nation in accordance with the progress of independence preparations.' The detailed execution of these measures would be left to the military commanders in Java, Sumatra, and the Navy Area, who were expected to retain an influential 'advisory' position in their respective areas after independence. Despite the strong unitary sentiment of the Java BPKI meeting, Japanese planning as well as the collapse of communications suggested that a highly autonomous federal structure was more likely to emerge. The Sumatra command and the Navy even began to organize separate independence preparation committees in their respective areas.

The announcement that independence would be rapidly prepared by a new committee was duly made on 7 August, after it had become certain that Russia would enter the war. Two days later Sukarno, Hatta, and the elderly BPKI chairman Radjiman flew to Dalat (south Vietnam), to be told formally by Marshal Terauchi, Commander of the Japanese Southern Army, that independence was in their hands. Only while in Vietnam did the Indonesian leaders learn about the atomic bomb on Hiroshima, though they could not know how close Japan was to surrender. They returned on 14 August to a Jakarta seething with rumour and unrest.

On the last stage of the return journey Sukarno and Hatta were accompanied by the Sumatran delegates to the PPKI, now rescheduled to begin its meetings on 16 August. Twenty-two members had been appointed to this body, including eight specifically representing the islands outside Java. Despite communications difficulties the Japanese managed to fly two prominent nationalists from Makassar (Sulawesi) as well as the three Sumatrans. These were the only areas outside Java where significant independence preparation had occurred. The PPKI was to meet, however, in circumstances wholly different from those of its conception.

The revolutionary situation and youth The final year of the Japanese occupation was one of unprecedented hardship for the majority of Indonesians. The shipping of goods was impossible; such essentials as cloth were almost unobtainable; inflation was out of hand. Every district was expected to meet its own needs as well as those of the Japanese, who began stock-piling supplies against the threatened counter-attack. The 1944 rice crop was disastrous. In many districts Japanese rice requisitions made the difference between subsistence and starvation ... Starvation, beggary and disease were visible as never before in the streets of the cities, particularly in Java.

Young men gained partial diversion from these pressures through the increasing tempo of Japanese propaganda and mass mobilization. In Java and Sumatra, Japanese strategy placed coastal defence in the hands of Indonesian militia, with the main Japanese and Gyugen/PETA [Japanese-created Indonesian militia] forces holding centres further inland. Other Indonesians were hastily trained for guerrilla operations behind future Allied lines. In addition to the more long-standing youth corps in Java such as Hizbullah and Barisan Pelopor, shadowy groups emerged throughout Indonesia with names reminiscent of Japanese ultra-nationalism – 'Black Dragon', 'Back Fan', 'Death-defying Unit'. The mystique of such groups has been well described: 'Xenophobia, radicalism, strong comradely loyalty, authoritarianism, superb, if almost suicidal courage, and a belief in salvation through direct action' ...

This mixture of deprivation and high-pitched, theatrical propaganda was explosive. Despite the Japanese reputation for terrible and often arbitrary retaliation, peasant uprisings with varying degrees of religious inspiration had occurred since late 1943 on a scale unknown since the 1920s, though in traditionally volatile areas like Aceh, West Java, and Toli-Toli (north Sulawesi). In 1945 a Dayak revolt became widespread in West Borneo. Supernatural portents of disaster were seen all over Java. All these were sure signs of popular restiveness. However only the growing rebelliousness of educated youth in the last months of the war had serious potential for revolution.

Influential politicians, intellectuals, religious leaders, and *pamong praja* [civil servants] all enjoyed privileges from the Japanese which insulated them from the suffering. Elite status in a sense embracing all these groups therefore came to be perceived and resented to an unprecedented degree. 'The reputation of the leaders', said one of them, 'is ruined in the eyes of the people.' The educated *pemuda* (youth) themselves constituted an élite, especially those whose personal connections with leading politicians gave them a prominence in the whole pemuda movement. Nevertheless their youth freed them from direct responsibility to the Japanese. As a group they stood apart from the older élite, and increasingly saw themselves as representing the aspirations of 'the people' as against the compromised leaders. Last-minute Japanese attempts to court pemuda leaders as potential anti-allied activists gave them a new sense of solidarity and power as the occupation regime began to crumble ...

17 August 1945: the Proclamation The return of Sukarno and Hatta to Jakarta on 14 August brought to a head the confrontation between two generations. The older leaders, Hatta as well as Sukarno, knew that an orderly transfer of Government from Japanese to Indonesian hands was virtually certain provided that war continued as expected for at least a few more weeks. Whatever happened thereafter the Indonesian Government would be in a strong position to bargain with all comers. The rumours of surrender on the 14th, confirmed with virtual certainty the following day, came as a severe shock to their plans. The only way left open to them appeared to be to speed up the plans for independence with tacit Japanese approval. To act provocatively against the Japanese seemed to spell inevitable disaster to the structure built up thus far – a disaster in which Sukarno and Hatta themselves would be the first casualties ...

The conflict came to a head on 15 August, when the Japanese Emperor's noon broadcast made clear to Japanese officers and a few of their Indonesian confidants that the war was really over. Sjahrir was planning a strike against the Jakarta radio station for that evening in the hope that Sukarno would agree to a 'revolutionary' independence declaration. Sukarno, and after some initial hesitation also Hatta, insisted on first establishing from the Japanese command both that Japan had officially surrendered and that it would not oppose a speeding up of the already agreed progression to independence. If this assurance could be obtained they planned to put the issue of independence before a hastily summoned special session of the PPKI at 10 a.m. on the 16th. On the afternoon of the 15th the two leaders and Subardjo learned unofficially from Admiral Maeda that the surrender was a fact, but little more ...

[The radical *pemuda* groups wanted an immediate declaration of independence without reference to the Japanese military. Sukarno and Hatta were aware, however, that the Japanese surrender terms gave the latter responsibility for government until the Allies could take over. Officially, the Japanese authorities did not sanction a declaration of Independence. Unofficially, certain Japanese officers (see below) were able to guarantee that the Japanese would turn a blind eye to any such declaration, so long as it was discreetly worded.]

The final confrontation of this proclamation drama came at Maeda's [Japanese admiral in the occupation forces] residence between 3 a.m. and dawn on 17 August. The pemudas present had obviously lost their struggle to have independence proclaimed in defiance of the Japanese. Nevertheless as a final flourish they made their bid to alter the text of the independence proclamation carefully worked out by Sukarno, Hatta, and Subardjo in consultation with the Japanese Maeda, Nishijima, and Miyoshi. This read:

> We the Indonesian people hereby declare Indonesia's Independence. Matters concerning the transfer of power and other matters will be executed in an orderly manner and in the shortest possible time.

Sukarno on behalf of the pemudas objected to the caution of the second sentence, and demanded its replacement by the words:

> All existing government organs must be seized by the people from the foreigners who still occupy them.

Not surprisingly, this change was rejected by the PPKI majority. Finally the pemudas absurdly demanded that they rather than the PPKI delegates should sign the proclamation, since they represented the people and the PPKI represented only the Japanese. As a compromise Sukarno and Hatta alone signed it as 'representatives of the Indonesian people' at about 5 a.m. Later in the morning Sukarno read the proclamation formally to a few hundred people gathered outside his own house. The Republic was symbolically launched with the raising of the red-white flag.

To whom should go the credit for the proclamation of Indonesian independence – the heroic pemudas or the cautious leaders? *perjuangan* (struggle) or *diplomasi*? The issue was close to the heart of Indonesian political debate, for it represented in microcosm the conflict which endured throughout the revolutionary process ...

The weakest part of the pemuda case was the inadequacy of their revolutionary plans. The threat of violence in August was still very limited. When challenged Sukarni and Wikana talked pathetically in terms of killing Ambonese or burning Chinese homes. Without the support of the PETA and Heiho [militia] units (most of which refused to move without authorization from Sukarno and Hatta), and without any mass organization, this was about all they could do. Thus they were only too ready to retreat from their high posture given some concession to their pride. Undoubtedly the threat of violence was a factor predisposing the Japanese to treat the proclamation leniently, but this was the threat less of a pemuda revolution than of a general descent into anarchy.

On the other hand, had Sukarno and Hatta really acted speedily to declare independence on 15 August it seems probable by hindsight that the Japanese would have allowed them to get away with it. The anxiety of the older politicians to seek assurances which the Japanese could not give suggests that pemuda pressure was necessary to impress the real urgency upon them ...

Despite the fact that the PPKI included a good percentage of outer island delegates and faced a very different situation from the BPKI, very few changes were made to the constitution worked out in July. The most important change resulted from the urgings of a Japanese Navy spokesman, who impressed upon Hatta the dissatisfaction of important Christian minorities within the Navy-administered area over the concessions to Islam. Hatta was able to persuade the principal Islamic spokesmen in the PPKI to accept the elimination of all references to the special place of Islam, on the plea of not alienating any minorities at such a critical moment for the republic. The other major changes related to the transitional period before the representative bodies, allowed for in the constitution, could be elected. Until then, 'their competences shall be exercised by the President assisted by a National Committee'. In case presidential powers were not yet adequate it was added that for six months following the end of the war the President 'shall regulate and prepare everything stipulated by the constitution'. Sukarno and Hatta were elected President and Vice-President by the PPKI ...

The PPKI met formally again on 19 and 22 August. During these sessions satisfaction was given to the outer island delegates who had pressed for a high degree of regional autonomy. Indonesia was divided into seven provinces: West Java, Central Java, East Java, Sumatra, Kalimantan (Borneo), Sulawesi (Celebes), Maluku (Moluccas and New Guinea), and Sunda Kecil (Lesser Sunda Islands from Bali to Timor). Governors were named for each province, in most cases from among PPKI members themselves. Below the province level was the residency (*Shu*), the key unit of Japanese administration, under a resident. At both residency and province level there would be a national committee to advise and assist the executive. In practice the beginning of the revolution was clearly going to provide ample scope for regional autonomy, as the centre could provide little assistance in the matter of wresting power from local Japanese commanders.

The PPKI entrusted Sukarno and Hatta with the appointment of a Central Indonesian National Committee (Komite Nasional Indonesia Pusat or KNIP), as the provisional representative advisory body. Twelve ministries were decided on. The President was to establish a national armed force to replace the disbanded PETA/Gyugun and Heiho ... This section would be called *Badan Keamanan Rakyat* (People's Security Body) or BKR. Finally it was decided to establish a state party headed by the President and Vice-President, to mobilize all forces for the love and defence of the homeland. It would be known as the *Partij Nasional Indonesia* (PNI) in deliberate evocation of Sukarno's pre-war party ...

On 22 August the PPKI completed its work. The delegates from Sumatra and Sulawesi flew home in Japanese aircraft the following day. A theoretical basis had been laid for an élitist, authoritarian state, embodying the dislike of liberal democracy which was a common feature of Javanese and Japanese nationalist thinking. The hope was that the progress made in Jakarta could be repeated throughout Indonesia, with leaders trusted by the Japanese using the threat of pemuda violence to gain ever larger concessions from sympathetic or disinterested local commanders.

The extension of republican authority in Java: August–September 1945 News of the independence proclamation was transmitted throughout Java within hours by young Indonesians in Japanese news and telegraphic agencies. Bandung [west Java] pemudas succeeded in broadcasting it over the local radio. In each major centre of the island there was a nucleus of the élite and a larger group of pemudas who, through their respective connections with the capital, knew and understood the independence proclamation within a few days. Outside these small groups the proclamation was either disbelieved or regarded as just another act in the play being stage-managed by the Japanese. The public announcement of the Japanese surrender, made only on 22 August following a meeting of Japanese commanders in Singapore, made a much more profound impression on most Indonesians. An era indisputably had ended. Nobody could be sure what would come in its place.

The 'revolutionary' pemuda élite and the pragmatic older nationalists each attempted to provide direction in their own way. For the latter the primary stress was on gaining control of the administrative apparatus in Java. Most of the members of the first Republican ministry announced on 4 September were 'collaborating' nationalists who had already been appointed heads or advisers of the departments concerned by the Japanese. The major exceptions in the seventeen-member Cabinet were Foreign Minister Subardjo, who had been attached to Maeda's navy office, and the Information Minister Amir Sjarifuddin, still languishing in prison as the leader of the anti-Japanese underground of 1942–3. Although the Japanese could not officially recognize any Republican cabinet, they could continue to recognize the remaining individuals within it as Indonesian heads of their respective departments. As the Indonesian employees of government departments proved increasingly unresponsive to instructions from their Japanese superiors, the latter yielded effective control fairly readily to the Republican ministers.

A similar process occurred at the local level, with the promotion of Japanese-appointed vice-residents to Republican residents. Special efforts were made to ensure the support of the four Javanese princes for the Republic. Despite strong anti-monarchic traditions in the nationalist movement the PPKI had recommended no change in their status. On 19 August a ministerial mission was appointed to the princely lands. It rapidly secured agreements that the four states formed *daerah istimewa* (special regions) of the Indonesian Republic. Finally the Republican leadership gave priority to winning over the top echelons of the pamong praja at an all-Java conference convened on 30 August. There Sukarno explained the 'gentlemen's agreement' with the Japanese for the transfer of administrative functions to Indonesians. He promised to maintain the status and position of the administrative hierarchy.

Hatta lucidly explained the strategy adopted in these first weeks as 'the seizure of power from within'. The alternative of creating a wholly new government in defiance of the Japanese, he argued,

> would have caused a violent struggle and the victory would not certainly have been ours. It would have created two different government administrations side by side.
>
> ... the administrative structure capable of working effectively would have been allowed to fall into the hands of the Japanese to be handed over to the Allies.

Cogent as this reasoning was, it did not reconcile pemuda enthusiasts to the other side of Sukarno's 'gentlemen's agreement' – his undertaking to curb violent confrontations with the Japanese. Insofar as the pemudas can be said to have had a policy it was one of action, mass mobilization, and intimidation. But the pemudas were short on organization – indeed most of them came to distrust large scale organization of any kind. The leaders in the capital owed their eminence to their pre-war political role and their links with Sukarno, Hatta, Subardjo, and Sjahrir. But more typical pemuda leaders were those in charge of semi-militarized groups during the Japanese occupation, or who for other reasons were able to persuade and inspire a group of followers to join them in the streets. The relationship between pemuda groups was one of example rather than command.

Up to the second week of September pemuda action was mainly directed towards raising red and white flags on public buildings, distributing information and exhortation, and taking over some facilities. By mid-September, however, pemuda militants in the cities had gained both the ability and the determination to organize mass rallies. These had been expressly forbidden by the Japanese because of the danger of violence. For that reason Republican officials also tried to discourage them, though they could not refuse to address them if held. Surabaya was the first city where mass meetings were organized, on 11 and 17 September. It remained the most extreme case in Java where pemudas held the initiative from a rather unimpressive older group. Because of the influence of the Republican leadership Jakarta had no such rally until 19 September, and then only because Sukarno and Hatta were presented with a virtual fait accompli. It was however a massive one. Up to 200,000 people filled the vast central square now called Medan Merdeka. Japanese tanks and guns threatened from every corner of the square. In the briefest of speeches Sukarno pleaded that everyone should trust their leaders and at once go home quietly. The crowd obeyed. Violence was avoided, and Sukarno demonstrated in compelling terms his indispensability to the Japanese or anyone who wished to take their place in Java ...

By the end of September there was throughout Java a government machinery in Indonesian hands, an increasingly violent and well-armed 'revolutionary' pemuda movement, and a top political leadership accepted as legitimate by the great majority of inhabitants. What was lacking was co-ordination between the three. The caution required by Sukarno and Hatta's 'revolution from within' strategy inhibited the political leaders from effectively mediating between the revolutionary movement and the administration. There was, therefore, a general devolution of authority and initiative to the residency or kabupaten ['regency'] level. At each level pemuda enthusiasts and administrators established their own uneasy relationship. A revolutionary process was beginning spontaneously in numerous centres throughout Java.

The Republic outside Java Before the war all the important Indonesian political and social organizations had headquarters in Java and branches throughout the archipelago. All sizeable Indonesian towns were cosmopolitan in population and national in political orientation. In normal times one would have expected developments in Java to be repeated on a smaller scale throughout the archipelago. But the cleavages the Japanese occupation had created between Java, Sumatra, and the Navy-occupied territories [in eastern Indonesia], were not easy to bridge. The objective of isolating the outer islands from the relatively advanced political atmosphere of Java, which had been pursued ineffectively and ambiguously by the Dutch, was achieved almost unwittingly by the Japanese.

Given the separate paths followed by Java, Sumatra, and the Navy-administered area under the Japanese, the factors impeding a vigorous independence movement in the latter two areas could be summarized as follows:

1. Their less concentrated and urbanized population.
2. The strength of traditional monarchies in many areas, allowing the Dutch ample scope for manipulating and intimidating semi-autonomous rulers. The threat of deposition on the grounds of having collaborated with the Japanese was an effective Dutch weapon against many rajas.
3. The more politically repressive and intensive Japanese administration in these areas, showing the pre-war Dutch régime in a better light by contrast.
4. The extremely belated and inadequate Japanese preparations for independence.
5. The substantially greater Japanese troop strength (especially in relation to population) in the outer islands. At the surrender there were over 125,000 Japanese troops in the Navy area, as against about 71,000 in Sumatra and about 50,000 in Java. Not surprisingly, Japanese co-operation with the independence movement after the surrender seemed to be in inverse proportion to Japanese numbers.
6. The earlier Allied presence. General MacArthur's Southwest Pacific Command already occupied Tarakan and Balikpapan (Borneo), Morotai, and parts of New Guinea before the surrender, and Dutch Civil Affairs units were established in all these centres. Admiral Mountbatten's Southeast Asia Command parachuted several units into northern Sumatra in July 1945, as part of the preparation for the invasion of Malaya planned for 7 September. By contrast there had been no Allied preparations for any operations in Java.

The situation confronting the Allies in October might be summarized as follows: in Java a functioning government apparatus accepting the authority of Sukarno's Republican cabinet, though strongly challenged in many areas by pemuda activists; in Sumatra a series of functioning Republican governments in the major residencies, though with little co-ordination between them; in South Sulawesi and Bali Republican governors more or less supported by the local aristocracy; elsewhere no broadly-based Republican movement, although there was a militant anti-Dutch pemuda movement in every sizeable town.

CHAPTER 6

The Independence Settlements:
1. The Immediate Post-war
Settlements

The Karens claim a right of self-determination because they are a national group on a given territory which is their homeland ... In constitutional language they cannot be characterized as a subnational group who cannot expect anything more than what is due from a civilised Government to a minority. (Sau Po Chit, *Karens and the Karen State*)

General features of the post-war period

Although the post-war independence settlements differed widely in their timing and circumstances, certain general features affecting most of the region can nevertheless be distinguished. In the first place, and most important of all, was the overall fact that the events of the Second World War had completely and irreversibly changed the political landscape. Colonial rule – which, before the war, depended on the notion of an overwhelming European power that had increasingly become a bluff rather than a reality – had been swept away when the Japanese army called that bluff. During the period of the Japanese military presence, mass nationalist movements were created that were able to spread their influence and organization throughout the territories concerned. Nationalist power was further consolidated in Vietnam and Indonesia after the Japanese surrender because neither colonial power (France or the Netherlands) had the military muscle at its disposal to reimpose its authority quickly or decisively.

Britain, France and the Netherlands were all aware of the changed political environment of the post-war world. But they were equally certain that the maintenance in one form or another of their imperial framework was vital for the sustaining of their national power and prestige. All of them, therefore, came up at the end of the war with new imperial plans designed to change the relationship between the imperial metropolis and its possessions, while at the same time maintaining the essential link. These imperial plans had the common feature of redefining this imperial link in terms of 'partnership' rather than imperial dominance, but a partnership in which the former imperial power would maintain a substantial degree of ultimate sovereignty and control over the political agenda. The plans also tended to emphasize federalized solutions, or ones that safeguarded the rights of ethnic minorities and peripheral regions. Clearly, this emphasis was designed to weaken the impetus to national unity that had in many cases built up during the war years. It was with such plans – the French plan for a federal Indochina, the Dutch plan for a federal Indonesia, the 1945 British White Paper plan for delayed independence in Burma, and the British Malayan Union plan of 1946 – that the returning colonial powers hoped to slow down the moves to independence, bargain with the respective nationalist forces, and reassert their authority in the region.

There then followed, in general, a period of bargaining accompanied by the threatened or actual use of force on both sides. In Burma, for example, this period lasted roughly from the summer of 1945 to late 1946; in Indonesia, it lasted from mid-1945 to late 1949. The colonial power would often try in these negotiations to seek out weaknesses and areas of division within the nationalist front that it confronted; these weaknesses could be ethnic differences, regional sentiments or – as in France's exploitation after 1946 of the fact that the Vietnamese nationalist movement was dominated by communists – ideological. The nationalist leadership for its part would seek to maintain unity at all costs, and seek to show the returning colonial power that the country concerned was ungovernable without its consent.

Eventually, but within very different time-spans for each country, an equilibrium was reached between the colonial power and the nationalist front, as the colonial power recognized that it no longer had control of the political agenda. This point was reached in mid-1946 by the British in Burma, but only by the early 1950s in the case of the French in Indochina. At that point the colonial power concerned would be inclined to move rapidly towards a settlement that would meet the wishes of the nationalist leadership while at the same time retaining its economic interests and some measure of residual political influence. In other words, in the last stages of independence negotiations, some kind of confluence of interest usually developed between the colonial power and the nationalist leadership. This consensus immeasurably strengthened the position of the nationalist leadership in the period of transition to agreed independence.

During this tortuous transition from colonial–nationalist confrontation to collusion, two major groups within the decolonizing state were to find themselves increasingly marginalized. The first comprised those communities, ethnic minorities and peripheral regions that had often co-operated with the colonial power. In the early stage of the independence negotiations, it was precisely the rights and interests of these groups that were highlighted by the colonial powers. As the balance of negotiations changed, however, these groups were left, in effect, to their own devices in the search for a last-minute accommodation with the dominating nationalist movement. Not surprisingly, therefore, we see a whole range of rebellions between 1945 and 1960, directed by these abandoned groups against the newly independent governments of Southeast Asia (see 'Negotiated independence in Burma', p. 165).

The other group marginalized at this time included certain ideological elements who found themselves in one way or another squeezed out of the centre of power within the nationalist movements as the respective nations approached independence. Those strict Muslim leaders and groups that wished to see the establishment of an Islamic state in Indonesia are a classic example. Between the years 1945 and 1950 it became apparent that the 'secular' nationalists – those who saw Islam as one pillar of the fundamental principles (*pancasila*) of the Indonesian Republic, but nothing more – had gained a firm grip on the political agenda. One Islamic response to this was the outbreak of the so-called Darul Islam (Abode of Islam) revolt, which in 1949 created an Islamic alternative – the Negara Islam Indonesia (Islamic State of Indonesia) – to the Indonesian Republic. This revolt took root in isolated areas throughout Indonesia, and lasted from 1948 to 1962.

More than any other ideological grouping, the communists found themselves edged from the centre of power within the nationalist movements in the immediate post-war period. A number of circumstances conspired to marginalize the communists. First, the nationalist movements themselves needed to build a broad, inclusive political front that would win support from all classes and sections, and thereby weaken the position of the colonial power; second, the nationalists often sought to win international support, particularly from the United States, which was allergic to any kind of link between communism and nationalism; and, finally, there was the fact that the Soviet Union chose in late 1947 to return to a strategy of global confrontation with the West *and* with 'bourgeois'-dominated nationalist movements. In the course of 1948, communist rebellions were stimulated in the Philippines, Burma, Malaya and Indonesia. These were quite as much a challenge to the respective nationalists as they were to the colonial powers, and left a lasting scar on nationalist–communist relations in the region.

The independence settlement in the Philippines

In the Philippines, the United States and the Filipino nationalist elite had already, before the outbreak of the Second World War, agreed on a timetable for a transition to full independence by 1946. Essentially, this timetable was undisturbed by the events of the war. During the course of the war and the Japanese occupation, however, there was a short-lived *froideur* in the relations between the United States and the Filipino elite. This was brought about by the fact that those members of this elite who had not left in the baggage-train of the retreating Filipino and United States armed forces in 1942 not only continued to work under the Japanese, but formed the backbone of the independent Filipino state that was created by the Japanese in 1943. The communist-dominated Hukbalahap movement, on the other hand, played a leading role in guerrilla resistance to the Japanese. When General MacArthur led the United States back into the Philippines in 1945, therefore, there were a number of scores to be settled. There was, first of all, American resentment at the Filipino elite's 'collaboration' with the Japanese, and betrayal of the partnership that had been sustained through the whole colonial period. From the Filipino political perspective, there was the determination of Hukbalahap and other patriots who had resisted the Japanese – along with the Filipino elite leadership who had left the Philippines with the Americans in 1942 – to punish the collaborators and marginalize them politically in the run-up to independence.

The Filipino collaborating elite were too well entrenched, and the elements opposing it too disparate and – particularly given the Hukbalahap presence – too radical, for the Americans to risk any major political upheaval. Helped along by General MacArthur, the Philippines moved rapidly to independence, and the issue of collaboration was pushed to one side. The Philippines emerged in 1946 as an independent state with the power of its traditional governing elite virtually untouched. The US–Philippines relationship was also perpetuated by a series of defence agreements that safeguarded America's strategic position in the region (see 'The independence settlement in the Philippines', p. 155).

The independence settlement in Burma

When the British returned to Burma in the spring of 1945, they outlined their long-term plan for the future of the country: the 1945 White Paper proposals. This plan stipulated a three-year period of tutelage under a British governor, during which economic rehabilitation from the ravages of war was to be consolidated, and the various minorities in the peripheral regions were to be brought into a national consensus on the future shape of a self-governing Burma. Only then, it was envisaged, would the moves to full self-government within the British Commonwealth get under way.

This plan by-passed the mass nationalist movement – the Anti-Fascist People's Freedom League (AFPFL) – that had been created during the war by Aung San, defence minister and armed forces chief in the short-lived independent Burmese government created by the Japanese. The AFPFL contained a wide range of political groupings and had a nation-wide structure, quasi-military formations and access to arms. The British government in Burma soon discovered that Aung San and the AFPFL had the ability to make Burma ungovernable. As neighbouring India, along with its formidable army, moved rapidly towards independence during 1945 and 1946, it became apparent to the British that they had neither the means nor, indeed, the need, to cling to their programme of gradual political evolution in Burma.

Between mid- and late 1946, therefore, Britain reversed its policy, and Burma's political agenda became largely a matter of bilateral negotiation between the British and Aung San's AFPFL. In this critical period, a number of minority groups – particularly the Karens in the southeastern corner of Burma – who had gained secure political positions under the British, but had historically feared ethnic Burmese dominance, found themselves marginalized. The resulting Karen demand for independence from Burma – or at least for a very substantial measure of self-government within the post-colonial state – set in motion a process that, following the independence of Burma, was to result in a whole series of long-lasting separatist rebellions (see 'Negotiated independence in Burma', p. 165).

READINGS

1. The independence settlement in the Philippines

In his classic essay, 'The Philippine "Collaborators": Survival of an Oligarchy', David Steinberg provides an almost textbook case of the inbuilt bias towards continuity in administrative institutions and their personnel, even in times of political change. No political science treatise could make the case so well.

On the face of it, the indictment at the end of the war against those members of the Filipino political elite who had ditched their loyalty to the United States, and had participated in the independent government set up by the Japanese in 1943, was overwhelming. Burmese, Malay or Indonesian 'collaboration' with the Japanese was perfectly explicable: these respective countries were under colonial control, and the Japanese offered them partnership – along with independence in the case of Burma (1943) and Indonesia (1945) – in the struggle against their European oppressors. In Indochina, the French administrators had openly collaborated with the Japanese. For reasons cited in Steinberg's essay, the situation was different in the Philippines. Moreover, many Filipinos had suffered bitterly during the war at the hands of the Japanese. At the end of the war – not to put the case any more strongly – there were a lot of scores to be settled.

The collaborating elite were able, however, to protect their position, and lead the Philippines into full independence in 1946. In the first place, the vast majority of the elite had stayed in the Philippines after the American defeat in 1942: only a small coterie had left with the Americans. The bulk of the elite – excluding those few who took the perilous path of resistance – were consequently implicated in collaboration, and therefore acted collectively to defend their positions and their reputations after the war. Secondly, the post-war situation of near anarchy and economic chaos made it vitally necessary for administrative continuity to be maintained, and not to be disrupted by some sort of attempt at the 'purification' of Filipino society. Finally, the United States was not prepared to hand over power to the forces of revolution and communism embodied in the Hukbalahap movement that had played a key role in the guerrilla war against the Japanese.

The Filipinos themselves were tired of economic chaos and the fratricidal conflict brought about by the guerrilla war against the Japanese. While the leftists and Hukbalahap who had fought the Japanese offered them an endless prospect of political strife, the collaborating elite offered them stability, continuity and a welcome period of political amnesia.

David Steinberg, 'The Philippine "Collaborators": Survival of an Oligarchy', in Josef Silverstein (ed.), *Southeast Asia in World War II: Four Essays* (New Haven, CT: Southeast Asia Studies, Monograph series, No. 7, Yale University, 1960). Excerpts taken from pages 67–78.

The Japanese occupation of the Philippines was a failure for a myriad of reasons. Despite their elaborate propaganda appeal for a 'Co-prosperity Sphere' and for 'Asia for the Asiatics', the Japanese attracted very few Filipinos to their cause. Much of their failure was their own fault. Japanese brutality and plunder soon revealed the enormous gap between promise and practice. Some of the failure was attributable to their lack of time, materiel, and peaceful conditions. However, at the root of their problem was their inability to alter the pattern of Filipino allegiance.

Throughout the war Filipinos continued to give personal allegiance to Manuel Quezon, whose Commonwealth government-in-exile bolstered Philippine resolve to remain true to prewar patterns and institutions. General Douglas MacArthur's [military commander in the Philippines] dramatic flair and charismatic appeal to Filipino emotions personified the United States for many Filipinos, and the promised inevitability of his return lent to it a quality of messianic salvation. Moreover, most Filipinos confidently expected that the United States would honor its independence pledge and, as a result, felt they were participating in the war as equal allies. The psychic drive for a sense of equality with the Caucasians, which reached fruition during the war, was fundamental to the national character. Consequently, few Filipinos saw themselves as trapped pawns in a global struggle, believing instead that they and the Americans were together fighting to defend their mutual independence and democratic ideals. It is immaterial that many of these same Filipinos comprehended the nature of democracy in only a most hazy way, since it was their emotional commitment that determined their response. When during those first months of the war the Filipinos refused to abandon the American cause, even when the struggle was hopeless, they established a pattern of response that was to blossom into the enormous guerrilla movement, embracing, at least passively, almost the total population. In spite of the Japanese attempt to rush independence by the creation of the 1943 Laurel Republic [Philippine Republic, headed by the main collaborator, José P. Laurel], they were never regarded as liberating friends but rather as oppressive conquerors.

A few Filipinos, of course, became genuinely attracted to Japanese institutions or to the opportunities the occupation presented. The society's discontented were encouraged and pampered by the Japanese, who created an organization of militant sympathizers known as the Makapili. By early 1945 the Japanese army had given military training to about 5,000 Makapili activists, who willingly fought and died for the Japanese cause. These Filipinos, who represented a minute fraction of the nation, clearly had shifted their prewar allegiance, and the postwar courts had little trouble determining that these Makapili had violated the national will and were, therefore, culpable ...

The knotty problem, however, was not what should be done with those few Makapili who had clearly demonstrated their allegiance to Japan but how to deal with that larger group whose focus of allegiance was no longer clearly discernible. The Makapili could easily be dismissed as traitors; the so-called 'collaborators' could not be categorized so easily. The word 'collaborators' was used pejoratively but never equated with 'traitor'. Consequently, the attempt to resolve the degree of culpability of these 'collaborators' – political, economic, and social, rather than criminal – has been one of the critical postwar political, juridical, and moral problems of Philippine society.

The most important group of 'collaborators' were those who served in the wartime political governments, a group which at the same time was almost totally identifiable with the prewar oligarchy. The Japanese had achieved one of their few notable successes of the occupation by prevailing on members of this well-entrenched oligarchy, which was fully experienced in the arts of governing and completely in control of the prewar social, economic, and political institutions, to retain office during the war. Playing on the personal and collective fears, vanities, and aspirations of these oligarchs, who by chance were trapped in the country rather than evacuated to Washington, the Japanese were able to maintain a facade of willing cooperation between Filipinos and Japanese and to tap, at least partially, the experience and prestige of these men. After the war Filipinos faced the ticklish task of having to determine the culpability of the most powerful and influential segment of their society.

On first glance, it would appear that the oligarchy flouted the will of the nation, expressed at Bataan and Corregidor [final battles in defence of the Philippines in 1942], by attempting to restore and maintain normality, peace, economic viability, and political solidarity during the Japanese years. Even when these oligarchs felt no personal sense of involvement in the Japanese cause, their participation did put them at variance with most of the rest of the nation. It would have been logical to expect that, after the war, these officials would have been subjected to some sort of societal punishment ranging from removal from office to imprisonment. In fact, however, the oligarchy not only survived the war physically but also retained effective political power into the postwar era. The only member of either wartime government to be tried and convicted for 'political collaboration' was Teofilo

Sison, whose case was the first of some 5,600 postwar indictments to be listed on the docket. No other 'political collaborator' was convicted, and many managed to be re-elected to high office while still under indictment for treason. After that first Sison trial, the specially empowered People's Court reversed itself on almost every point of law, reflecting in large measure – as courts usually do – a decision by the society to pardon the 'collaborators', which was perhaps also revealed by the election of Manuel Roxas [see below].

This remarkable phenomenon raises certain critical questions about Philippine social organization. The survival of the oligarchy is the most lasting fact of the Japanese occupation and, long after the physical damage has been repaired and the personal wounds healed, the ramifications of this survival will continue to operate throughout Philippine life. The occupation pushed the Philippines to the brink of radical social upheaval; the immediate postwar period permitted the society, already dazed by the trauma of the war, to opt for security by retaining its elite. The Japanese period was the crucible in which the oligarchy's paramount position was tempered. The fact that it survived as robustly as it did is convincing evidence that it is the basic element in Philippine social structure. Yet the decision to continue the old leadership in power was not without consequences and it is perhaps now more clear that the society has had to pay a high price for political continuity.

Questions of loyalty or allegiance and the obverse, disloyalty or treason, are inevitably among the most difficult man ever has to face. As nationalists about to receive their independence from the United States, the Filipino leaders certainly could not be held guilty of the same kind of treason to the United States as an American citizen, even though there was such a statutory provision. The only pertinent question was whether these Filipinos had been disloyal to that complex of allegiances which the majority of the nation continued to maintain despite the Japanese presence. Since there is no abstract absolute called patriotism, these wartime leaders explained to the nation that, while they might have served the Japanese, they had served the Filipinos more by mitigating the harshness of the occupation, by preventing 'opportunistic' men from gaining power for selfish reasons, and by working to further the health, welfare, and education of the nation during the occupation, just as before.

The leaders of the oligarchy spoke out with positive assuredness, almost defying others to assert that there had been any alternatives. They claimed to be the true, unsung heroes of the war, because they had taken the most tortuous path. They maintained vehemently that they had not failed the Americans but that, vice versa, the Americans had failed the Philippines by providing not even a modicum of protection in 1941. They had, they said, been given careful instructions by Quezon and MacArthur to serve as a buffer for the nation, authorized to do anything short of taking an oath of allegiance to Japan. Disdaining the role of humble supplicants, they demanded rather than asked the nation to restore them and brooked no doubt about the nation's compelling need for their leadership during the postwar crises. As a result, the oligarchy retained an authoritative position over the society even while nominally on trial. Shrewdly aware of the dynamics of Philippine social organization, these oligarchs insisted that nothing had changed from the prewar era.

Their claims did not go unchallenged. Men like Tomas Confesor, Francisco Delgado, Tomas Cabili, and Lorenzo Tañada, if not President Osmeña [see below] himself, offered the nation an alternative. This small but vocal opposition argued that the Japanese task had been made far easier by oligarchic cooperation and contested the arguments of 'duress' and 'suspended allegiance'. These leaders denied that the nation's suffering had been alleviated in any appreciable way. Pointing instead to the ruined city of Manila, they insisted that the oligarchic arguments were a perversion of the truth, which was that the oligarchy had aided primarily itself. They stated that there was no legal or moral validity to the claim that a man ought to be pardoned for an act merely because someone else might also have committed that act. The Japanese were bound to find some Filipino willing to serve in a Japanese-sponsored government, but the nation was asked whether such Filipinos had to be the established elite of the society. Almost by definition, the nation was reminded, the more distinguished the 'collaborator' the greater his usefulness to the occupying power ...

It was further asserted that political trust demanded of the officeholder greater risks than those of the average citizen since the obligations of office carried liabilities as well as emoluments. The unpleasant reality was that throughout history the prestige of authority had often to be protected by personal sacrifice. Few denied that in January 1942 the prewar officials had a real duty to cushion the impact of the initial military occupation; however, some questioned whether they had to cling to power for the duration of the war. Indeed, the heroic martyrdom of Chief Justice Jose Abad Santos, who absolutely refused to serve the Japanese, was held up as an embarrassing foil to those who claimed they had had no choice but to serve. Abad Santos has never been accorded his legitimate place in the Philippine pantheon because his martyrdom manifested, in Robert Frost's words, 'the road not taken'.

In the face of such arguments, how did the oligarchy survive? During the war, when the issues still seemed clear-cut, the 'collaborators' were adjudged to be traitors by the Americans, whose preoccupation with the concept of total war rendered 'collaboration' one of the most pernicious categories of treason. From the American point of view, this simplistic appraisal of the Filipino 'collaborators' worked well. [President] Roosevelt, Stimson, Ickes, and indeed most Americans believed that the Filipino oligarchy had failed to discharge the demands of continuing loyalty required in war as in peace and, therefore, planned to eliminate these men in the postwar world either by detention or by political purge. Roosevelt flatly declared that 'those who have collaborated with the enemy must be removed from authority and influence in the political and economic life of the country'. Since the United States still theoretically held complete sovereignty over the Philippines, such a course of action was possible. However, American leaders, immersed in the staggering problems of prosecuting a two-front war and building a global peace, failed to determine exactly how this purge was to be implemented.

On becoming president [in exile] in August 1944 following Quezon's death, Sergio Osmeña discovered to his dismay that an atmosphere of mañana permeated Washington's thinking on 'collaboration'. When in October 1944 the Commonwealth government was brought back to the Philippines with MacArthur's invasion of Leyte, Osmeña found himself forced to operate ad hoc with no clear directive from Washington. That Osmeña was allowed to carry this burden without American support was a major blunder by Washington. Unlike Quezon, who was in a very real sense the 'liege' to whom the oligarchy owed allegiance, Osmeña could be regarded as simply another, albeit famous, member of the oligarchy who had had, moreover, the good fortune to be spared the dilemma of 'collaboration' because of his evacuation to Washington. The nebulous American instructions required that he purge his lifelong colleagues but Osmeña realized that, had he remained in the Philippines, the Japanese would have tried to get him to serve as president instead of Laurel – and perhaps succeeded. Two of his sons who had remained in the Islands were accused of 'collaboration'. Osmeña must have been acutely aware of the irony of history which had taken him to the United States in exile only to bring him back more as his peers' prosecutor than as their leader. It was undoubtedly difficult to conceive of these men, many his former protégés, as traitors.

Still, he made an honest attempt to do justice both to the oligarchy and to the United States, his task considerably complicated by MacArthur's lordly attempt to fill the vacuum of leadership from Washington. Although MacArthur landed at Leyte thinking that the oligarchy had been disloyal not only to the United States but to him personally, his attitude shifted in the following months, especially when, with the fall of Manila, he started to evolve a postwar policy for the country. When the American troops captured most of the wartime leaders, MacArthur separated his friend Manuel Roxas from the rest and gave him a fiat pardon. Despite the fact that Roxas had handled himself very circumspectly during the war and was as free of the taint of 'collaboration' as possible in his situation, MacArthur's pardon made a shambles of Osmeña's 'collaboration' policy … MacArthur utilized his enormous authority as returning hero and military commander in chief of a war zone as well as his personal contacts to catapult Roxas toward the presidency. Concomitantly, since Roxas had served to at least some degree in the wartime governments, his pardon was the bridgehead for the restoration of the others.

Osmeña, who had become isolated from the realities of Philippine politics during his enforced exile in America, was suddenly forced to combat not only Roxas personally but the whole of the oligarchic group who had retained local political connections throughout the war. In a continuing effort to find some American counterforce to MacArthur, Osmeña finally gained Roosevelt's attention and a promise of aid, only to have this hope end in Roosevelt's death a week later. [The new president] Truman, uninformed on the Philippines, had too much else to do to undertake a confrontation with MacArthur at that point. Consequently, Osmeña was left to execute singlehandedly Washington's avowed policy of forming a government free of any taint of 'collaboration'. He was able to structure a cabinet of men who had either joined the guerrillas or been in Washington, but in order to get the Manila government functioning again he soon was compelled to recall to service most of the government bureaucrats who had held office during the war. These professional civil servants were too vital to the country to be barred or bypassed.

Moreover, Osmeña soon discovered that as a result of MacArthur's rapid restoration of civilian government, he was obligated to convene a Congress. The critical question was what Congress should be called and who was eligible to be seated. An election had been held in 1941 just prior to the Japanese invasion for a Congress that had never been convened. This gave Osmeña a new dilemma: to summon the Congress elected in 1941 meant calling a legislature most of whose members had served during the war but to elect a new Congress in the chaos of the postwar months seemed all but impossible on practical grounds. He first proposed, rather naively, to screen the postwar body and allow only those who had clean wartime records to take their seats, but he was immediately accused of being a dictator since as president he was constitutionally barred from making such a selection. Roxas, who had been elected a Senator in that 1941 Congress, pressured for summoning it intact until Osmeña, lacking American support, was forced to yield — and thereby also hand Roxas a forum and patronage position from which to rally the opposition. After a brief parliamentary fight by the anti-Roxas forces, who attempted to put up legal barriers, Roxas was elected president of the Senate. From then until the national elections the next year, Roxas contested Osmeña's policies, appointments, and paramountcy. Addressing himself to the 'collaboration' question, Roxas said:

> What is collaboration? There are no puppets or collaborators in this House. I am against every collaborator. I would be the first to bring them to justice. But the mere fact of service under the Japanese is not conclusive evidence of collaboration. Not a single Senator can justly be accused of collaboration.

In time, Roxas openly splintered the monolithic Nacionalista party (the establishment nationalist party) by running for president against Osmeña on the Liberal party ticket. It was during this extended period that the true degree of the destruction of the Philippines became known, and it was far worse than anyone had realized. The 1944–45 crop, only 60 per cent of normal, had been largely consumed by the two armies; transportation was paralyzed; and industrial production had all but stopped. Manila was in rubble with estimates of the damage ranging as high as 85 per cent of the city destroyed. Many were homeless, most were starving, medical and sanitation facilities were destroyed, and of those who did not have war wounds a good percentage had dysentery, malaria, or even cholera. Law and order had collapsed, the black market thrived. With American troops as the only source of hard currency and supplies, the pimp, the whore, and the thief became the only people with steady employment. American emergency food shipments alone staved off chaos, and the Philippine per capita production was perhaps lower in 1945 than it had been in 1899. Damage exceeded several billion dollars.

An understanding of this economic situation is fundamental to any explanation of the survival of the oligarchy. The economic crisis was so severe that national necessities required a change in priorities. Nothing obviously was as important as mere survival and, consequently, all other considerations had to be postponed. Many, including MacArthur and [American] High Commissioner Paul McNutt, believed that the country could not afford to waste the talents of the established leaders or risk leaving the job to untried hands. Men like Rafael Alunan, Antonio de las Alas, and Manuel Roxas, with their wealth of experience in economic affairs, constituted one of the few surviving resources of the country.

Moreover, the death and destruction of the last months of the war so stunned the country that the nation was comatose. That trauma blurred the delineation of loyalties that had seemed so clear but a few months before. Feelings still ran high, but most people were left numb with their personal grief, and vengeance would not restore life. In such chaos, the society very humanely recoiled from hate and closed ranks as the only hope for beginning life again. The horrors of the war were repressed as too grim to remember, and the busy tasks of reconstruction served as a welcome sponge, absorbing energy and attention. It was not an optimum time for the Filipinos to battle the human imperfections of an imperfect world. Thus physical destruction, psychological withdrawal, and Christian charity combined to reduce societal pressure against the oligarchy.

Nevertheless, while Roxas was able to capitalize on the new mood of the nation, Osmeña was left pursuing the original American 'collaboration' policy and, not surprisingly, found himself increasingly isolated, despite his status as a charter member of the oligarchy. In contrast to this image of a tired old man who had lost everyone's confidence in his ability to give dynamic leadership to the rebuilding of the country, Roxas seemed to be looking forward, ready for the new and better future. Cut off from his traditional sources of political power because of his commitment to the American 'collaboration' policy, Osmeña was forced to search for political backing wherever he could find it. Roxas' candidacy made Osmeña accept support from the whole leftist spectrum of nonestablished groups, from the moderate fringes of the oligarchy through the guerrilla leaders to the extreme left. Roxas preached national unity. It was Osmeña who was forced to maintain the guerrilla v. 'collaborator' division into the postwar era.

Among these newfound supporters was the radical guerrilla group, the Hukbalahap. The Huks, who had been rabidly anti-Japanese, represented both a Communist and traditional peasant challenge to the oligarchy. They rallied to Osmeña as their best hope and won for him large majorities in the central plain of Luzon. However, their support came at a terribly high price for Osmeña, who increased the cycle of his alienation by accepting their support. The great moneyed families who underwrite election campaigns quickly turned away from Osmeña in fear and suspicion of his radical supporters. Their privileged economic position was tied, in large measure, to their land holdings, and the Huks certainly could not be counted trustworthy defenders of large land interests.

In his reluctant shift to the left, Osmeña frightened more than the landlords. The Huks worked deliberately to retain the polarization of the society into two camps – the anti-Japanese, democratic, guerrilla, anti-oligarchy versus the reactionary, pro-Japanese, oligarchy. It is important to remember, however, that the oligarchy stood for more things to the nation than the Huks admitted. It stood for stability to many Filipinos, an important link to an earlier and simpler era. Only a relatively few were aware of this consciously, but many were cognizant of it subliminally, and as it became clear that prewar normality would never return more and more Filipinos began to crave this symbol of a more stable period. The Hukbalahap stressed the need to split the fabric of the society even further, but the spectre of civil war was so horrendous to Filipinos that they rallied to the oligarchy despite the taint of 'collaboration'. Thus not only did rich landlords recoil to protect their special interests but also many middle-class Filipinos, confronted with this choice, opted for Roxas rather than risk further social upheaval. Here, too, the postwar realities altered the perspectives of the war. Men like Tañada and Delgado were put in the untenable position of having in effect to endorse the continuing polarization of the society in order to uphold their position on the 'collaboration' issue. They were trapped politically between the Huks and the oligarchy.

It was March 1946 before the Truman Administration became aware that Roosevelt's policy of purging the 'collaborators' had gone awry, by which time American policy objectives were different. Truman refused to follow the recommendations of his specially appointed investigator Walter Hutchinson, who had visited Manila to study ways to implement the 'collaboration' policy. His decision grew in part from the desire to avoid any intervention by the United States that could be considered an infringement on prospective Philippine sovereignty, by now so close at hand, and in part from consideration of strong arguments by MacArthur and NcNutt that nothing be done that would weaken Roxas' chances in the approaching election. However, an even more important factor was increasing American concern over the worldwide Communist threat, which seemed to hang over Greece, Iran, France, Italy, eastern Europe, China, and, also, the Philippines. The American commitment to try the 'collaborators' receded before the exigencies of 'cold war'. American policy posited the Philippines as the American 'showcase of democracy' in the Far East, and Washington realized that the Huk threat was, at the minimum, embarrassing and, at the maximum, disastrous to American aims and prestige. China was in turmoil and Washington knew that, with the wartime destruction and carnage as a dowry, the Philippine bride was entering the state of independence gravely ill. Clearly, among the belated remedial steps, there was little room for a purge. Washington, looking for cures, saw the oligarchy as the only group in the Philippines with the ability to lead the nation into independence and defeat the Huks. The indigenous, legitimate, and non-Communist peasant grievances against the oligarchy were ignored, as Washington saw in the Hukbalahap only another phase of the international Communist conspiracy. American money was soon freely granted to the very men whom Roosevelt had wanted to purge but a few years before.

The net effect of this American reversal was to becloud further an already confused situation. Washington tacitly withdrew its support from Osmeña and those few non-Communists who pursued the 'collaboration' question. This nullified Osmeña's strongest political weapon against the Roxas forces, since ten of Roxas' slate of sixteen had served in the wartime government. This reversal also aborted the early precedents established in the Sison trial, and no subsequent 'political collaborators' were convicted. Indeed, Osmeña had wandered into the pathetic trap of pursuing Washington's policy after Washington had abandoned it.

Osmeña, tired and discouraged, refused to campaign. It was no surprise that Roxas was elected [in April 1946], though his margin seemed surprisingly narrow in view of his vitality, aggressiveness, charisma, support from MacArthur and McNutt, and freedom from all those liabilities under which Osmeña labored. The nation had voted into power those who had remained in office in Manila during the war rather than those who had taken to the hills to fight or gone to Washington ...

There remains the question, at what damage to the health of the society was this restoration made? It can be argued effectively that at least some of the postwar dishonesty, bribery, nepotism, and corruption which has plagued Philippine life is due to the oligarchy's scramble back into power. Obviously such 'social cancers' exist elsewhere and had an hereditary disposition in Philippine social structure dating back to the pre-Spanish era. Still, the postwar period has been characterized by a chronic cynicism, as people at all levels stooped for power. Since the men at the top seemed to get away with it, many others figured that they could succeed similarly. Such cynicism about the dignity of office has had the profoundly deleterious effect of causing the possession of office to seem the only important thing – indicating that José Abad Santos's martyrdom by the Japanese was not only unnecessary but, even worse, perhaps stupid. The oligarchic survival may have contributed to the moral weakening of the nation.

Having discovered that it was still dominant, the oligarchy moved collectively to be generous to its critics. Much of its strength has always rested in its ability to incorporate new members into the power structure, and so men like Tañada were welcomed into full membership, if with the clear but tacit recognition on both sides that thereafter the 'collaboration' question must be quarantined by silence to avoid reopening wounds that might not heal a second time. The wounds did close, leaving some scar tissue as the only visible evidence of the ailment. Still, tacit in the conspiracy of silence was the nagging anxiety that somehow the malady was festering or, far more serious, metastasizing despite the superficial healing of the wound. Like the cancerous lump that is studiously ignored but secretly feared in the naive hope that tumors disappear by themselves, Filipinos have gone to some length to avoid any examination of the 'collaboration' infection even a generation after. The implicit assumption has been that, even if there were a lingering division below the surface, there was no need to have this dragged into the light and exorcised from the body politic, because the new blood of a new generation of political leaders would cure the disorder naturally. The assumption was that 'time heals'. It is a valid assumption provided that metastasis has not carried the infection elsewhere in Philippine life unnoticed.

[Afterword: Steinberg's 'cancer' metaphor at the end of this essay is an allusion to José Rizal's seminal book, *Noli Me Tangere*, which was translated into English by C. Derbyshire under the title *The Social Cancer*.

After the election, the Hukbalahap movement gradually shifted to a strategy of armed rebellion against the new independent Philippine government. By 1950, due largely to the ineffectiveness and corruption of the Philippine government, the Hukbalahap rebellion posed a serious threat to the regime. With American aid, however, and the charismatic leadership of Defence Minister – then, from 1953 to 1957, President – Magsaysay, the back of the rebellion was broken in the early 1950s.]

2. Negotiated independence in Burma

The first article in this section is by Hugh Tinker, and is entitled 'Burma's Struggle for Independence: The Transfer of Power Thesis Re-examined'. The viewpoint of this article is that the rapid road to Burmese independence was not planned by the British, but was essentially the consequence of a cumulative recognition of realities forced on the British by events in India, Burma and Southeast Asia in 1945 and 1946. On the one side, the essentially pre-war vision of Governor Dorman-Smith called for a slow, steady and 'responsible' move to self-government under British tutelage. On the other, Lord Louis Mountbatten, 'supremo' of South-East Asia Command (SEAC), and his subordinate Major-General Hubert Rance – who, as head of Civil Affairs administered Burma while it was under British military control in 1945 – represented those who recognized the new post-war realities: namely, that Britain was too overstretched in the region to be able to impose its will any longer in areas where there was a substantial, organized and armed opposition to British rule.

Aung San's Anti-Fascist People's Freedom League (AFPFL) was just such an armed opposition. Its vast network of local organizations was given teeth by its armed militia, the People's Volunteer Organization (PVO). In the period between summer 1945 and late summer 1946, the British – including Dorman-Smith – were to discover that Aung San and his AFPFL could make Burma ungovernable, unless Britain was prepared to use a degree of force that it discovered it simply did not have at its disposal. In the course of the autumn of 1946, therefore, the British government bowed to the facts of life and entered into negotiations with Aung San for immediate independence. Hugh Tinker's article, based as it is on his authoritative study of the documentation surrounding the negotiations for independence in Burma (see Select Bibliography), is an essential starting-point for understanding Anglo-Burmese relations in the years 1945 to 1948.

In one sense, the concession of independence to Burma can be seen as a triumph of *realpolitik* and statecraft. In the long term, however, the headlong rush to independence that began in January 1947 contributed to problems that Burma has still not resolved. The PVO militia organization may have made Burma ungovernable for the British, but the new Burmese leaders were to find that it could also make Burma ungovernable for the Burmese themselves. The AFPFL remained a united mass movement only while Britain tried to slow down the moves towards independence; once the timetable for independence was agreed, the movement began to fragment as the various factions jostled for power. The assassination of Aung San and some of his closest colleagues in July 1947 revealed the deep fissures in the political leadership. Moreover, in January 1948, Burma embarked on an independent future with an economy that had not recovered from the war, but which was burdened with idealistic plans for creating a vaguely defined form of state socialism.

The most intractable problem that the rush to independence left unresolved was that of the status of the Karens. Having for decades insulated the minority areas from Burma proper, the British effectively reversed policy in the early months of 1947, and left the minority leaders to patch up whatever agreement they could get from the dominant AFPFL leaders. This the bulk of the Karen leadership was not prepared to do. Included below is a pamphlet written in 1947 by an eminent Karen lawyer, Sau (or Saw) Po

Chit, making the case for a Karen state separate from Burma. Partition of existing political entities has never been a popular political solution (witness Bosnia in the 1990s), and the British were certainly not prepared to entertain any such idea in the case of Burma in 1948. The alternative, however, has been something like forty-five years of separatist conflict in the Karen region.

Hugh Tinker, 'Burma's Struggle for Independence: The Transfer of Power Thesis Re-examined', *Modern Asian Studies*, Vol. 20, no. 3 (1986). Excerpts taken from pages 461–81.

On 3 May 1945, British-Indian forces landed in Rangoon. The Japanese had pulled out. The city was liberated. On 16 June there was a victory parade, though the final victory over Japan was still distant and most of their conquests were intact. Admiral Mountbatten, Supreme Allied Commander, took the salute while detachments representing the one million men under his command passed by in massed array ... Watching the parade from the central dais was a young man dressed in the uniform of a Japanese Major-General, though he also wore an arm-band with a conspicuous red star. The outfit was incongruously crowned by a pith sun-helmet – a topi. Probably most foreigners present assumed he was a Chinese officer. He was actually Bogyoke [a Burmese military rank: general] Aung San, commander of the BNA.

When the parade was over, Mountbatten entertained dozens of Rangoon notables at Government House. When they had dispersed, he held a meeting with Aung San, his principal military supporter, Bo Ne Win, and his two chief political associates, the Communists Than Tun and Ba Hein. Removing his topi, Aung San revealed a Japanese army shaven skull (maru cozu). He had prominent bone structure, but most conspicuous were his intense, staring eyes. This was the man Mountbatten recognized as holding the key to the political and military future of Burma.

The meeting was very much at variance with the policy in London, and also that of Sir Reginald Dorman-Smith, the civilian Governor of Burma who had been in exile at Simla [in India]. Until recently, Aung San and his soldiers had been known to the British as the Burma Traitor Army. Mountbatten refused to accept this reading of the situation even though it represented the view of the Cabinet, the Chiefs of Staff, his own C. in C. Allied Land Forces South East Asia, and his own staff at Kandy concerned with military government. He was very conscious that the task of driving the Japanese out of South East Asia had only just begun. He needed a secure base for the hazardous assault upon Malaya. He could not risk a guerrilla rebellion in his rear. More profoundly, Mountbatten perceived that imperial high noon had passed away, with imperial sunset soon to follow. He recognized the urgency for the British to establish friendly relations with the younger generation of Asian nationalists ...

To make his position quite clear, Mountbatten issued an instruction on 'Policy to be adopted towards the Burmans'. This was regarded as very dubious by many of the Civil Affairs Officers, but the Supremo made it clear that anyone who 'sabotaged' his policy could expect to be court martialled. He had already replaced the head of Civil Affairs by a new man flown out from England, Major-General H. E. Rance, who accepted his chief's line whole-heartedly.

The approach of the Cabinet was markedly more cautious. In the statement presented to the House of Commons on 17 May 1945, emphasis was placed on the physical destruction suffered by Burma, and when military government was terminated (not expected then for at least another year) there would be three years of direct rule by the civilian governor before elections were held under the existing 1935 Act. The legislature would then be invited to frame a new constitution, though even then HMG 'would have continuing obligations after the establishment of full self-government in Burma'. Clearly, even under the most optimistic interpretation of this timetable the Burmese could not attain self-government for five to six years, and then the Frontier Areas would still be 'subject to a special regime under the Governor'. This programme had been finalized by the India Committee of the Cabinet whose chairman was Attlee and it continued to command his support after the Coalition [between Conservative and Labour] was dissolved one week later.

The Burmese politicians, even the most moderate, were dismayed. The Japanese had granted them independence (after a fashion) in August 1943. At the hour of liberation almost all political elements were included in the newly formed Anti-Fascist People's Freedom League. Their Supreme Council, meeting on 16 May, had demanded 'that the right of national self-determination shall be applied forthwith to Burma'. How could this be implemented? The overwhelming strength of the British military forces was obvious to all. Hence, Than Tun as Secretary-General of AFPFL issued a directive headed 'Why we should not continue to revolt'. British policy was broadly known from newspaper reports, yet Than Tun argued with prescience that British economic and military strength had been weakened by five years of war. Imperialism would wither. The AFPFL did not directly challenge the British but simply reiterated the demand for 'immediate complete self-government'. In the same document there was a claim that the BNA be incorporated in a new Burma army. Than Tun concluded: 'The Revolutionary Council believes that we will achieve our freedom at the most within two years' – a prediction considerably more accurate than the British government's timetable ...

In the following months, Rance as military governor endeavoured to liquidate the BNA. Its members were offered enlistment in battalions under British control with demobilization for those deemed unfit. Meeting succeeded meeting, but Aung San always produced reasons why they could not proceed immediately. The BNA (now renamed the Patriot Burmese Forces by Mountbatten's decision) was their major asset in any coming struggle against the British ...

On 15 July Mountbatten joined the discussion. Aung San proposed (and this was accepted) that the reorganized regular army would have two 'wings', one formed of ex-BNA soldiers with their own officers, though under British command, and another wing of battalions raised from the tribal levies – Kachin, Chin, and Karen – who had fiercely harassed the retreating Japanese. Dorman-Smith was persuaded to accept this arrangement ...

[When] Japan collapsed, Mountbatten was suddenly confronted by the extension of SEAC's boundaries to include Indonesia and Indo-China. Of more immediate concern, Dorman-Smith bombarded the new Labour government with demands for the resumption of civil government in Burma. He stated he would tender his resignation if refused. This was to be the first ultimatum of several.

The Burmese also were quick to respond to the new situation. Than Tun stepped up the propaganda campaign to get rid of military government. A conference was convened to formulate fresh demands. Some 5,000–6,000 attended and the Rangoon shops were closed for the day. Aung San made the main speech, emphasizing the Burmese contribution to allied victory, pointing to Labour's electoral triumph as a sign that imperialism was on the way out, and warning that '99 per cent of the PBF [Patriotic Burmese Forces] would be unwilling to serve in the fighting forces of a country that was not free'. Tongue-tied when speaking in English, Aung San was an eloquent orator in Burmese. Than Tun followed, presenting a manifesto 'World Peace and Free Burma', in which he proposed the immediate setting up of a Provisional Government with full powers over internal and international affairs ...

In the midst of growing pressures, Mountbatten endeavoured to solve the twin problems of the procrastination of Aung San and the importunity of Dorman-Smith by summoning a high-level conference at Kandy, attended by his military top brass, senior British civil servants ... and a Burmese delegation (still mainly in Japanese uniforms) led by Aung San and Than Tun ...

A programme for an early handover to civil government was agreed with Dorman-Smith, followed by a detailed plan to embody PBF officers and men into the new Burma army. This was spelled out in the 'Kandy Agreement' signed by Aung San and Than Tun on 7 September. One item was the appointment of a Burmese Deputy Inspector General along with one representing the ethnic minorities, both under a British Inspector General. Simultaneously, Mountbatten offered the post to Aung San with the rank of Brigadier. He was far too shrewd to be sidetracked in that way, though the gesture was appreciated ...

The stage was now set for Dorman-Smith's return. A member of the Anglo-Irish ascendancy, a Cabinet Minister under Chamberlain, he alternated between authoritarian aloofness and occasional flashes of insight into the new mood of Burmese nationalism. His real fault was that he operated a 'crony' system of government, listening to advisers, British and Burmese, who were quite out of touch with the new mood. From time to time the real world impinged on his consciousness, but invariably one of his cronies persuaded him to stick to a do-nothing policy.

He announced that he would go further than the White Paper, setting up an advisory council. An invitation went out to AFPFL. They claimed to nominate a majority of members of the Council. This claim was rejected, and Dorman-Smith formed a Council of his cronies (Sir John Wise, Sir Paw Tun, and Sir Htoon Aung Gyaw) and such politicians as he could lure away from AFPFL. He was confident that the League would split into factions. Already there were hints of tension between Aung San and his supporters and Than Tun and the Communists. The policy was to play for time ...

In November 1945, a meeting in New Delhi took a decision which was later to prove the key factor at a critical moment in Burma. British-Indian troops had been sent to Java to rescue POWs and Dutch civilians. They clashed with Indonesian nationalist forces. In Surabaya on 29 October, Brigadier Mallaby was killed and a month of bitter fighting followed. Wavell, as Viceroy, Auchinleck, as Commander in Chief, India, and Mountbatten as Supreme Allied Commander were all agreed that the repercussions on Indian public opinion could be 'very serious'. Suppose that a similar conflict occurred in Burma, where some 79,000 Indian troops were stationed – what then? Mountbatten insisted that the handover to the civil authorities had been premature; the situation was 'deteriorating' ... They could not permit Indian troops to be used to suppress a popular rising. Henceforth, Indian soldiers in Burma were embargoed from intervening in a political confrontation. Neither the AFPFL nor the Cabinet in London knew of this ...

Three battalions of Burma Rifles had been created out of the PBF with former BNA commanders (Bo Ne Win and Bo Zeya) designated as commanding officers. However, the remainder of the former BNA did not simply become civilians; they were organized in the People's Volunteer Organization (*Pyithu Yebaw Tat*: army of comrades) wearing military uniforms under their old officers. They continued to drill and bear arms (of which there were thousands 'underground' throughout Burma). Dorman-Smith dismissed these activities: 'Aung San is a tired and deflated little man', he told London. His report was sent on the eve of another major demonstration below the Shwe Dagon pagoda in January 1946 with 1,200 delegates and a total attendance estimated even by the British at 20,000 to 30,000. Aung San condemned the existing regime, which he described as 'Economic Fascism': the governor was 'the Dictator of Burma'. Than Tun was still General Secretary and drafted AFPFL pronouncements but Aung San had become the undoubted political leader. There were signs that he intended to distance himself from the Communists ...

A second meeting of the AFPFL Supreme Council, 16–23 May, launched a Freedom Fund and called for a one million membership drive. In case their demands were not met, an Executive Committee was set up to prepare for 'the struggle that may lie ahead'. While the Council made its plans, the PVO marched and drilled openly. On 13 May, members of the PVO were arrested at Tantabin, forty miles from Rangoon. On 18 May a procession of 1,000–1,500 marched in protest. The police opened fire: there were several casualties, three being fatal. The governor interviewed Aung San, and those arrested were set free. Despite the explosive atmosphere, no rising followed. Perhaps Aung San believed the situation was drifting his way: certainly the senior British officials felt the governor had been too weak. However, for Dorman-Smith, time had run out. On 11 June he handed over to a temporary governor and left for London. Soon after arrival he learned he would not return …

[The Labour Government in Britain felt that Dorman-Smith had 'lost his grip'. Dorman-Smith's replacement as governor was Major-General Sir H. E. Rance, who had administered Burma during the temporary military administration in 1945.]

What was he [Rance] expected to do? Instructions received just before departure were 'To secure within the scope of the White Paper and the Act of 1935 an Executive Council … broader based and to include if possible a representative team from AFPFL'. As regards any timetable 'there is no advantage in fixing paper dates' while 'we should in general continue to avoid the term "Dominion Status" as the constitutional goal'. As for 'Independence': 'no reference should be made to it'. Bearing these unpromising instructions, Sir Hubert Rance was sworn in on 31 August 1946.

Within one week reality burst in upon him. The Rangoon police went on strike. They had serious grievances; their pay had fallen far behind inflation. Rance rapidly discovered that his present Executive Council was useless and his senior officials out of touch. The strike threatened to spread, and AFPFL moved to exploit the possibilities. On 9 September Rance told Pethick-Lawrence (secretary of state for Burma), 'I am playing a lone hand here': he demanded the resignation of the members of the Council he had inherited and started consultations with Aung San and AFPFL. He did not let them have all they wanted, but they formed a solid bloc in the new Council. One innovation was to designate Aung San as Deputy Chairman (almost at the same time Nehru assumed the same position with Wavell [in India]). Tin Tut took charge of finance, while among non-AFPFL members U Saw [one of the older generation of politicians] became Member for Education and Planning, a post he neither desired, nor filled with any competence.

Aung San successfully negotiated a settlement with the strikers, though at considerable cost. The Communists controlled the All-Burma TUC and sought to exploit the strike situation. The Working Committee of AFPFL struck back: the Communists were expelled. Aung San had to prove that he was just as strongly opposed to imperialism. Within four weeks of taking office the AFPFL on the Council pressed for wider powers. When Rance informed Pethick-Lawrence of their demands the reply was a restatement of the position under the 1935 Government of Burma Act. The Council pressed their case in a detailed memorandum by Tin Tut ... In effect he demanded that Burma's political advance should keep pace with that in India, where the Interim Government was functioning and a Constituent Assembly was due to be convened.

Rance insisted to Pethick-Lawrence: 'we cannot deal with the present situation piecemeal'; he was putting together new proposals. The unhelpful response was 'do your best to put the brake on'. The AFPFL countered with demands made public on 13 November: the British Government must announce before 31 January 1947 that Burma would be free within one year, and simultaneously the Executive Council must be recognized as a national government. Although the Burma Office disliked making concessions to what they called 'a caucus with no electoral mandate', they advised the Cabinet that the situation was 'deteriorating rapidly' and recommended (following Rance's proposals) that a delegation from the Executive Council be invited to discussions in London. This was agreed in principle. Rance transmitted the invitation informally and the reception in Council was favourable. However, after further consideration the AFPFL told Rance that before they could agree to the delegation they required an announcement by HMG that the purpose of the visit was to prepare for an 'Interim Government with full powers', and that the forthcoming general election was not to restore the partial parliamentary set-up under the 1935 Act but to elect a Constituent Assembly 'for the whole of Burma'. This claim was justified because India had been given exactly similar terms. A worried Rance reviewed the demand with Aung San and Tin Tut. He told Pethick-Lawrence that just as the 'White Paper was out of date, so I also consider that the time for equivocation is past. In my opinion HMG must now be prepared to be definite or accept the consequences'. This was strong stuff: too strong for the Cabinet. They fell back on another stalling device: 'to frame a statement not perhaps as specific as that made to India'.

A more blunt appreciation of the gathering crisis was despatched by the GOC in C (Commander in Chief), Burma to the War Office. He reminded London that AFPFL 'having taken office, and taunted as traitors by Communists ... must justify themselves ... hence demands on HMG'. If there was a refusal, then AFPFL would resign, the police and other public services would strike, and there was 'chance of widespread rebellion'. If there was an embargo on the use of Indian troops, then his only resource was three weak British battalions. Massive British reinforcements would be required, including 'very considerable administrative tail'. Rance's comment was that if anything this estimate 'was on the low side'. While the Cabinet hesitated, the governor had to report 'the price has hardened': there were now 'more extensive demands'. When the India and Burma Committee [of the Cabinet] met on

19 December 1946 they first listened to an appreciation from Field Marshal Montgomery. He informed them bleakly that if there was widespread rebellion in Burma 'the situation might require up to two [British] divisions; these did not exist'. The Cabinet were still reluctant to agree; several ministers supported A. V. Alexander in regretting that they had come under pressure: 'There was a danger that His Majesty's Government might find themselves in a humiliating position'. But gradually they all faced up to the inevitable: what was the point in 'attempting to hold the country for a period of years by force' when they were agreed on the eventual goal? 'If the principle of independence was sound for India it was also sound for Burma.' They had left themselves no leeway. Parliament was to rise for Christmas next day, so Attlee had to make an announcement then. His statement effectively put paid to the White Paper. They would 'hasten forward the time when Burma shall realise her independence, either within or without the Commonwealth' ...

Events now moved rapidly. The delegation to visit London, led by Aung San, would include Tin Tut, Ba Pe, Thakin Mya (Home Member), U Saw, and Ba Sein, formerly mentor of Aung San but now a minor rival. Except for their leader, aged thirty, all were men in middle age. The British negotiators were led by Attlee, with Cripps, Pethick-Lawrence, Lord Listowel (soon to take over as Secretary of State), and A. V. Alexander. They were joined by two of the postwar recruits, Arthur Bottomley and Christopher Mayhew. The talks lasted from 13 to 27 January, with ten formal sessions. Each side began to trust the other and a degree of compromise appeared, though the concessions were mainly on the British side. A sticking point seemed to be the Burmese demand that the Frontier areas participate in the constitutional process while the Attlee team clung to the established position that the Frontier peoples were their special responsibility which could not be abandoned. Eventually agreement was reached on a basis approved by Rance: that a committee of enquiry equally representative of the plains Burmese and the hill peoples should ascertain what the latter wanted. A draft agreement was produced by Cripps with his customary skill in steering around difficult corners and a meeting to finalize the agreement was convened at 5.30 pm on Sunday evening, 26 January 1947 ...

Next day Attlee and Aung San formally appended their signatures to the 'Conclusions'. Burma had taken a massive stride towards independence. Although Pethick-Lawrence assured Wavell that these changes did not 'put the Interim Government of Burma in any way in advance of the Indian Interim Government, which might be embarrassing for you' this was not the reality. In India, the question of unity or partition was still quite undecided: in Burma the 'early unification' of plains Burma with the Frontier areas was now 'the agreed objective'. And whereas in India the Viceroy was to preside over the meetings of the Interim Government right up to the transfer of power, henceforth in Burma the governor would only be present at meetings involving his special powers, such as the manner of the phasing out of the

Secretary of State's services. On all other occasions, Aung San was in charge. Effectively, power had been transferred. All that remained was to legitimize this by Treaty and Act of Parliament.

The London negotiations had continued longer than watchful spectators in Burma expected, and some misinterpreted this as meaning there was no progress. The Communists accused AFPFL of a sell-out, and organized a mob invasion of the Secretariat. As a form of reply, AFPFL under the direction of Thakin Nu, acting as Aung San's locum, embarked on strikes among workers in public utilities in Rangoon (though not among the police) and in a few remote places up country there were armed outbreaks where local leaders assumed the Freedom Struggle had begun. It was all an indication of how close to the abyss they had come.

The return of Aung San bearing the news that independence was now assured had a calming effect. Among the Frontier leaders the more shrewd and realistic quickly grasped that there was a new game to be played. Within ten days of the delegation's return a conference was held at Panglong in the Shan States where the leaders of the Shans, Kachins and Chins made a deal with Aung San. They would be represented on the Executive Council by their own Counsellor (Shan) assisted by two Deputy Counsellors (Kachin and Chin). An autonomous Shan state would be formed and also a new Kachin State, within a unified Burma. This agreement was not recognized by the Karens, the largest indigenous minority, whose spokesmen were hopelessly divided over their prospects in the new, unfamiliar AFPFL-dominated politics. Most wanted a separate state, but this was difficult as only one-third of them lived in the hills: the majority dwelt in the Delta surrounded by the Burmese population. No Karen had accompanied the mission to London though two members of the community were members of the Executive Council. A sense of resentment against both Burmese and British began to possess them.

Aung San realized that if he was to succeed in attaining his objective of an independent, unified Burma he must keep ahead, maintaining the initiative he had won. The Karens were restive; the Communists were a menace. There were armed men everywhere.

The next hurdle to be cleared was the general election, held on 9/10 April. The pre-war parties realized the futility of trying to compete. Only the Communists contested the elections on a party basis, and although they commanded solid support in the rural areas of central Burma they were successful only in three of the 91 general constituencies: otherwise it was a clean sweep for AFPFL. The main Karen organizations boycotted the election, thus providing a walkover for the minority of Karens who adhered to AFPFL. Assured of the support of 204 of the 210 elected members of the Constituent Assembly, Aung San could go ahead with the immediate presentation of his proposed constitution.

Before then the Panglong Agreement had been processed (there is no more adequate term) by the [Frontier Areas] Committee of Enquiry set up under the Attlee–Aung San agreement. The Committee went beyond their terms of reference as defined to recommend that Frontier leaders be chosen to take part in the Constituent Assembly. To speak for the hill peoples, 45 members were recruited. The Karens were represented on the Committee and gave evidence but with the confusion of purpose which attended all they did they failed to clarify their demands ...

Aung San informed Attlee that he must announce a date for independence 'early in 1948'. Then he revealed details of the new constitution to an AFPFL Convention assembled in Jubilee Hall (named in honour of the old Queen). The form of the constitution came as a complete surprise to Sir Hubert Rance, while in London the Secretary of State learned about it from The Times. Indicating that Burma would be a republic, Aung San effectively gave notice that his country would leave the Commonwealth: for in May 1947 the notion of accommodating a state which did not accept the Crown as its head was beyond the constitutional considerations of Whitehall ...

On 19 July 1947 occurred the event which might have destroyed the realization of independence by constitutional means. Aung San and his deputy premier, Thakin Mya, his Shan Counsellor, his most loyal Karen colleague, together with five others, were shot as they were assembled in Council. Thakin Nu was also on the death list but his intended assassin found himself unable to press the trigger. When gunned down, the Council were considering the arrest of U Saw who was known to be plotting violent action. Arrested later the same day, Saw was found with an ample stock of arms and ammunition, all drawn from British army depots on false police indents. Rumours of a British plan to kill Aung San and substitute U Saw began to circulate, even among responsible politicians. Rangoon was astir with private armies and the countryside was thick with weapons, Japanese and British, in the hands of self-styled freedom fighters, half bandit, half rebel. It was a highly explosive situation, defused by the prompt action of Rance. With no delay he asked Thakin Nu to form a new AFPFL government. Installed in office, Nu publicly repudiated rumours about British involvement in the assassinations, specially emphasizing the 'close understanding between HMG, HE the Governor, and the Burma Government'. By the end of July the crisis had blown over, though many suspicions remained (and remain to this day).

One by one the landmarks signalling independence were reached. On 29 August a Defence Agreement was concluded between Britain and Burma. On 24 September the Constitution was finally adopted by the Assembly at the end of its third sitting. Nu declared that Burma would be 'Leftist', dedicated to the welfare of the common people. He averred that 'we are now united', and that the various ethnic groups 'have shed the past and are becoming more united than ever before'. It was a brave affirmation, but in truth the Karens were discontented, increasingly alienated from the government, while one section of the Communists (the so-called Red Flags) had already gone underground and their rivals, the White Flags, were only awaiting the best moment to revolt. Also, the PVO and certain of the former BNA army units, now deprived of their commander, Bogyoke Aung San, were increasingly flexing their muscles.

It was far too late for the British to influence developments. Almost all the British administrators and those in the police had already left the country. The few remaining British army units were packing up, as were their Indian army comrades ...

On 17 October a treaty was signed at 10 Downing Street by Attlee and Nu in the presence of Bevin, Cripps, and many others, British and Burmese. Article I read 'The Government of the United Kingdom recognises the Republic of the Union of Burma as a fully independent sovereign state'. This set the tone for the rest of the treaty. Last of all, parliament endorsed the treaty through the Burma Independence Bill. Whereas the Conservatives had not opposed the India Bill – largely because of the Dominion Status formula – Churchill led his depleted followers into the opposition lobby on Burma. The Bill passed by 288 to 114 votes. The Liberals, and also three Conservatives supported the government and a number abstained, including R. A. Butler and Harold Macmillan. Nothing now remained but the final obsequies. The astrologers selected 6 January 1948 as the most auspicious day – then changed their minds and asked for 4 January, naming 04.20 hours as the moment when the new six star flag should be raised. (Later, when things went wrong, it was asserted that neither the timing nor the stellar pattern of the flag were properly calculated.)

Sir Hubert Rance departed with dignity. The new state was launched and Thakin Nu assumed his heavy burden with a humble sense of duty and a saving sense of humour.

This account has tried to demonstrate that the 'Transfer of Power' concept does not fit the realities of the British exit from Burma. Capitulation of power would be a more fitting term. Recent works by Kenneth Harris and Kenneth Morgan have sought to give legitimacy to the version popularized at the time – that the Attlee government carried out a carefully planned programme of decolonization. The reality seems to be that Labour did accept the early attainment by India of full self-government (though far too long underestimating the problem of Pakistan). The plan for Burma, Ceylon and Palestine envisaged a much less compressed timetable. Labour's leaders still accepted the Burkean concept of trusteeship whereby a colonial people should be held in tutelage until they had demonstrated their political maturity. The new generation of Burmese leaders, like the Jewish leaders in Palestine, blew Labour's programme apart.

Sau Po Chit, *Karens and the Karen State* (Burma: Karen National Union, n.d.). in India Office Library: IOR M/4/3023.

It would not be difficult to understand the real nature of the Karen and Burman. They are in fact different and distinct genuses and it is a dream that Karen and Burman can ever evolve a common nationality, and this misconception of one homogeneous Burmese Nation has gone far beyond the limits and is the cause of most of the troubles and will lead Burma to destruction if we fail to revise our notions in time. Originally, Karen and Burman belong to two different racial origins (Mongolian, and Tibeto-Burman), religions, philosophies (Animism and Buddhism), social customs and literature. They belong to two different civilizations which are based mainly on conflicting ideas and conceptions. Their aspect on life and of life are different. It is quite clear that the Karen and Burman derive their inspiration from difference sources of history. They have different epics, (e.g. pastoral Phumawtaw-Htawmepah and Burmanised Rama King), different heroes and different episodes. To yoke together two such nations under a single State, one in numerical minority and the other as a majority, must lead to growing discontent and final destruction of any fabric that may be built up for the Government of such a State. It would be no wisdom to proceed to build for Burma a constitution on the assumption that these differences did not exist.

Karens, a nation not a minority Karens came to Burma as first settlers and spread throughout the length and breadth of the 'Golden Chersonese' – the Indonesian peninsulas between the Bay of Bengal and the South China Sea, and right down to Borneo. Today the millions of Karen in both Burma and Siam represent the largest compact body of Karen population in any single part of the world. It has always been taken for granted mistakenly that the Karens are a minority and of course we have got used to it for such a long time that these settled notions sometimes are very difficult to remove. Karens are a nation according to any definition of a nation. We (the Karens) are a nation with our own distinctive culture and civilization, language, literature, names and nomenclature, sense of value and proportion, customary laws and moral codes, aptitudes and ambitions; in short we have our own distinctive outlook on life and of life. By all Canons of International Law we are a nation.

Burma problem The problem in Burma is not [of] an inter-communal character but manifestly of an international one, and it must be treated as such. So long as this basic and fundamental truth is not realised, any constitution that may be built will result in disaster and will prove destructive and harmful not only to the Karens but to the British and the Burmans also. If the British Government are really in earnest and sincere to secure peace and happiness of the peoples in Burma, the only course to us all is to allow the major nations separate 'homelands' by dividing Burma into 'Autonomous National States'. There is no reason why these States should be antagonistic to each other. On the other hand the rivalry and the national desire and efforts on the part of one to dominate the social order and establish political supremacy over the other in the Government of the country will disappear. It will lead more towards national goodwill by international pacts between them, and they can live in complete harmony with their neighbours. This will lead further to a friendly settlement all the more easily with regard to minorities by reciprocal arrangements and adjustments between Karen-Burma and Burmese-Burma, which will far more adequately and effectively safeguard the rights and interests of the Karens and other minorities.

Democracy in Burma Western Parliamentary Democracy System is unsuitable for Burma. Such Democracy as exists in Western Countries is understandable and possible only there, as there exists [there] a single homogeneous nation and a single cultural and social organised society. But in Burma conditions are entirely different. Here there are two nations and talk of democracy and a single unit is impossible. The meaning of democracy in this country can only be, and an electoral system can only result in, the permanent domination of a Burmese majority over a Karen Society in minority, antagonistic to each other and different in everything that is essential to life. The Burmans and the Karens differ fundamentally.

One central government It would be impossible to have a Unitary Central Government in Burma. Such an arrangement would mean that for every eight representatives in Government, there would be one Karen, or in other words the Burman's will will be forced on the Karens.

Right of self-determination The Karens claim a right of self-determination because they are a national group on a given territory which is their homeland and in the zones where they are in a majority. In constitutional language they cannot be characterised as a subnational group who cannot expect anything more than what is due from a civilised Government to a minority.

Our goal Great Britain wants to rule Burma, the Burmans want to rule Burma and the Karens say that they will not let either the British or the Burmans rule the Karens. We want to be free. We have to define and define beyond doubt, what our goal is. There are many people who either do not understand or misunderstand or do not want to understand. There are ignorant people and it is really amazing how our decisions or resolutions are misinterpreted or misrepresented. In order that there should be no room left for misunderstanding and that no doubt should be left in the mind of any intelligent and sensible people, our position with regards to our goal must be clarified. What is the goal of the All Burma Karen National Union [the main Karen political organization]? What is the ideology and what is its policy? The goal of the All Burma Karen National Union is this – we want the establishment of a completely independent State in the South Eastern Zone of Burma with full control finally of Defence, Foreign Affairs, Communications, Customs, Currency and Exchange, etc. We do not want in any circumstances a constitution of an all Burma character with one Government at the centre. We will never agree to that. If we once agree to that, the Karens will be absolutely wiped out of existence. We will never be tributaries of any power or any Government at the centre so far as the South Eastern Zone of our free national homeland is concerned.

Karen State government Our Government will be the people's Government. You may get it either by force or by agreement. But until you get it, the question of constitution making and the form and the system of Government do not arise. Let us first agree that there shall be two Burmas. Then the constitution making body will be elected by some system from the people, and it is the people who will choose their representatives to go to the constitution making body. The constitution and the Government will be what the people will decide. The system of Government shall be democratic.

Minorities in the Karen State Safeguard for minorities must be provided for wherever there are minorities. No Government will ever succeed without creating a sense of security and confidence in the minorities.

Mons and the Karen State Naturally the Karens always have for the Mons a soft corner in their heart. We have absolutely no designs on our Mon friends. The Mons will get from their traditional Sister – the Karen – inspiration and help for preservation of their race, culture, literature etc. Their zone would be an autonomous unit of the Karen State.

Karenni principalities The Karenni combined principalities may or may not choose either to federate or confederate with the Karen State. Their first consideration should be whether our status is compatible with theirs.

No vivisection Burma is composed of nationalities and surely today she is divided and partitioned by Nature ... Burma is being held by the British power and that is the hand that holds and gives the impression of United Burma and United Government. [A] Burmese nation and Central Government do not exist in as much as the various nationalities in Burma are not homogeneous.

There are no genuine arguments advanced against the Karen State scheme. The Karen National Union wants the two odd millions Karens in Burma to secure and settle in zones which they could justifiably claim as their homelands and develop their own culture and live in a manner suited to their genius. There is nothing unusual in the demand for partition. When two brothers born of the same parents find it difficult to get on with each other the only effective solution lies in partition.

Economical aspect It is argued that a Karen State is not a practical proposition on grounds of economy having regard to the revenue yield of some districts in the eastern borderland. You cannot expect to get handsome revenue unless your taxed area, though rich in resources, is properly developed. Let us not build on sands but let us face facts and figures. Kindly take stock of the revenues of the South Eastern Zone of Burma where revenues are drawn from multifarious sources, e.g. lands, rice, timber, salt, rubber, minerals, sea and land customs, fisheries, income-tax, excise, etc. Further increase of revenues is dependent on the extent of development of the resources and on the security and stability in that country. There is not much to bother about [the] economy so long as we are sensible to cut our coat according to our cloth.

Acceptance of the principle The principle of partitioning Burma must be agreed upon at first, then would come the question as to what ways and means should be adopted to give effect to that decision. The question of details will then arise and with good-will, understanding and statesmanship, we (all the indigenous races) shall, let us hope, settle among ourselves. Where there is a will, there is a way ...

CHAPTER 7

The Independence Settlements:
2. Inter-ethnic Negotiations, Conflict
and the Cold War

If Malaya is to become ultimately one country and one nation, the people born within its confines should have a common citizenship. (Tan Cheng Lock, *Memorandum to British Government*, 1945)

The independence settlement in the Malayan region

In the Malayan region, a number of factors dictated that Britain would move more slowly towards independence than in India or Burma, and that it would be able to maintain control of the political agenda in the transitional period. In effect, with the dashing of Britain's hopes of holding on to anything more than a nominal relationship with an independent India, Malaya now replaced India as the hub of Britain's Asian interests, in terms both of its economic potential and its strategic importance. In addition, while the events of the war had heightened ethnic, political and ideological activity in the Malayan region, along with anti-colonial sentiments, these had not coalesced around a common sense of national identity or a mass multi-ethnic nationalist organization. Rather the reverse: the main confrontation in the Malayan region at the end of the war was not that of nationalism against colonialism, but inter-ethnic conflict between Malays and Chinese.

During the war, the British military in India established contact with Chinese guerrillas of the Malayan Communist Party (MCP), who had, after the fall of Malaya, moved into the jungle fringes of central Malaya and formed the Malayan Peoples Anti-Japanese Army (MPAJA). If the British had had to invade Malaya, it is probable that they would have had to rely on considerable support from these communist guerrillas. The Japanese surrender of August 1945, however, changed the situation. From then on, the Malayan communists were seen not as potential allies against the Japanese, but as a potential threat to the return of British rule.

On their return to Malaya after the Japanese surrender, the immediate priorities of the British were the restoration of law and order, the disarmament and dispersal of the communist guerrillas, and the resuscitation of the paralysed economy. During the course of the war, the British had put together a plan for Malaya designed to create a united Malayan state, which was seen as a necessary precondition for political development in the post-war era. This 'Malayan Union' plan involved the ending of the separate protectorate agreements with the various Malay states of the peninsula; the incorporation of these latter states and the two Straits Settlements of Malacca and Penang into one political entity – the Malayan Union – to be governed as a direct colony of Britain; and the ending of the separate statuses of the Malays and the immigrant communities through the creation of a single citizenship status for all who lived permanently in Malaya. The Straits Settlement of Singapore – because of its size, the impact its large Chinese population would have on the racial balance of Malaya, its tradition of political radicalism, and its vital strategic importance for the British – was, for the time being, left out of the Malayan Union.

In many respects, this Malayan Union plan matched the hope expressed before the war, by the Straits Settlements Chinese business elite, that a united Malaya with equal political and cultural rights for all its inhabitants could eventually be created (see 'Tan Cheng Lock and his plan for a united Malaya', p. 188). At the end of the war, however, the Chinese community was left divided and without effective leadership. Its natural spokesmen among the Straits Chinese business elite were largely concerned at this time with rebuilding their shattered commercial concerns and restoring their depleted authority, which had been greatly weakened during the war. By default, therefore, leadership of the Chinese community was to some extent assumed by the radical sections of the trade union movement and the Chinese-dominated Malayan Communist Party (MCP). These latter, however, rejected any idea of a resumption of British colonial rule, and demanded the immediate creation of an independent socialist republic.

If the Chinese reaction to the Malayan Union plan was muted or even hostile, the Malays of the peninsula united in manner never seen before against a scheme that threatened to destroy the sovereignty of the Malay sultanates and the concept that Malaya was *tanah melayu*, the 'land of the Malays'. No sooner had the Malayan Union been installed in 1946, therefore, than the almost unanimous pressure of the Malay community under their new mass organization formed in May 1946, the United Malays National Organization (UMNO), forced the British to accept that the new constitutional arrangement would simply be unworkable. The hitherto quiescent Malays had entered into modern mass politics in the most spectacular and effective manner.

Put simply, the Malay leadership and its mass organization, UMNO, could 'deliver' in political terms. During 1946 and 1947, while the Chinese-dominated communist movement and its associated organizations were moving towards outright confrontation with the British authorities in Malaya, UMNO and the Malay sultans negotiated with the British to create an acceptable alternative to the Malayan Union. In February 1948, the Malayan Federation replaced the Malayan Union. This federal arrangement restored some degree of authority to the separate Malay states, along with Penang and Malacca; at the same time, while it gave automatic citizenship rights to the Malay community, stringent conditions for citizenship were applied to the other communities. The concept of *tanah melayu* was restored.

The constitutional structure that would lead Malaya to self-government and independence had now been set in place but, in the year 1948, Malaya faced a growing political crisis. By the spring of 1948, the Malayan Communist Party (MCP) came out in open revolt, starting a guerrilla war – known as the 'Emergency' – that officially lasted till 1960. Because the MCP was essentially a Chinese organization, this deepened the ethnic divide between the Malays and the Chinese, and drove a further wedge between the British authorities and the Chinese community as a whole. Under the leadership of Tan Cheng Lock, the Chinese business and political elite at last reasserted itself with the formation of the Malayan Chinese Association (MCA) in early 1949. It was at this juncture, too, that serious negotiations began between the elites of the key ethnic communities of Malaya. The Communities Liaison Committee (CLC), set up by the British, began informal talks in 1949 that set the whole tone for the future of Malayan politics up to and beyond independence (see 'Negotiated independence in Malaya', p. 191).

Negotiations about and preparations for Malayan independence, which effectively lasted from 1949 to 1957, centred on inter-ethnic elite negotiations. The creation of an inter-ethnic political partnership was embodied in the forging of the 'Alliance' between the three main ethnic parties – UMNO, the MCA and the main Indian party, the Malayan Indian Congress (MIC) – in the early 1950s. It could be argued that during these years, an inter-ethnic elite 'deal' was forged in which, while the citizenship regulations were relaxed and the principle of parliamentary democracy was conceded, it was tacitly agreed that continued non-Malay domination of the economy would be traded for ultimate Malay (that is, UMNO) control of the political system. It was on the basis of this tacit understanding that Malaya achieved its independence in August 1957.

With the exception of the oil-rich protectorate of the Brunei sultanate, Britain's other colonial responsibilities in the region – Singapore, Sarawak and North Borneo/Sabah – were in 1963 joined to Malaya in the renamed Federation of Malaysia. Although this arrangement was convenient for Britain as the outgoing power, it dangerously disturbed the ethnic balance in Malaya as well as the equilibrium of the region, as shall be seen.

The independence settlement in Indonesia

In August 1945, a small group of Indonesian nationalists in Jakarta, headed by Sukarno, declared the existence of the independent Republic of Indonesia.

There followed a frantic effort by this leadership to assert the Republic's control over Java, Sumatra and the dispersed islands to the east. At roughly the same time as this declaration, a whole series of local revolts burst into the open – spearheaded normally by *pemuda* (youth) organizations of every kind of ideological hue – directed either against the Japanese or their local collaborators, or both. It is remarkable to note, however, that throughout this period of confusion and conflict, the idea of Indonesian unity was solidly sustained in Java and Sumatra at least. Dutch policy in the period 1945 to 1949 failed to grasp this essential point.

Not long after the Japanese surrender, the Dutch were able to restore civil administration in many of the islands of eastern Indonesia – an area that in any case had had a long and loyal connection with the Dutch empire, and had a large Christian community. During this period, the Dutch also gained toeholds in Java and Sumatra through the bridgeheads established by South-East Asia Command, particularly that in Jakarta. Their immediate concern was to help SEAC locate and release the large number of Dutch soldiers and civilians who had been imprisoned during the war by the Japanese. Ultimately their firm intention was to reassert their authority over the East Indies; they recognized, however, that a new political 'partnership' would have to replace the old colonial structure.

Gradually it became apparent to the Dutch that they did not have the means to brush aside what they considered to be the treasonable and il-legitimate Indonesian Republic. In circumstances where neither the Dutch nor the Republic had the military capacity to impose their will on the other, there then followed a long and extremely confused period of negotiations that lasted from 1945 to the middle of 1947. The main Dutch strategy was to build an alliance of those regions, communities, groups and politicians who feared the apparently revolutionary, unitary and Javanese-dominated character of the Indonesian Republic. They accordingly set up, in the areas that they controlled, a federalized structure based on the unit of the *negara* or semi-autonomous region.

Negotiations faltered in the spring of 1947, and in July of that year the Dutch resorted to military action as a means of entrenching their federal concept and weakening the position of the Republic. This so-called 'Police Action' gave them substantial footholds in Java and Sumatra, and enabled them to establish regional *negara* with the help of local politicians. In fact, the evident administrative and military weakness of the Republic of Indonesia tempted the Dutch into a final decisive military action in December 1948. The Dutch regained control of virtually the whole of Java and Sumatra, and the leaders of the Republic – including President Sukarno – were arrested. It seemed at this point as if the Republic would be swept into oblivion.

While the *institutions* of the Republic were manifestly weak and could be brushed aside by the Dutch, its roots nevertheless ran deep in the Javanese and Sumatran hinterlands. Beneath the apparent divisions between regions, parties, ideologies and militias, there was unity supporting the common purpose of removing Dutch colonialism. Within a very short space of time in early 1949, the Dutch discovered that their newly reconquered territories were ungovernable. They had the means to defeat the poorly trained Indonesian army, but not to pacify a politicized and hostile population. Moreover, the very institutions that they had created as the basis of a federalized Indonesia – the *negara* – began to defect at the moment of victory. The leadership of these *negara*, while they had been prepared to work within a federal rather than a unified Indonesia, were at the same time committed to an *independent* Indonesia. Most of them were not prepared to become Dutch puppets. Finally, Dutch actions unleashed a barrage of international protest, mainly from the Islamic world and India. The Dutch might have resisted this pressure, but for the fact that the United States – feeling as it did that the Dutch could not stabilize Indonesia, and that the Republic of Indonesia might form a reliable regional ally for the Americans – put its weight behind this international pressure.

In the first half of 1949, Dutch policy underwent a startling volte-face. After three-way negotiations in the Netherlands between the Dutch, leaders of the Indonesian Republic and representatives of the *negara*, the Dutch conceded independence in December 1949 to a complex hybrid between the Republic and the Federation that the Dutch had created: the so-called 'Republic of the United States of Indonesia' (RUSI). More to the point, the Dutch were allowed by the independence agreement to retain their economic interests in Indonesia, and Dutch colonial rule was retained over the western section of New Guinea. Negotiations over the future of this region were postponed to a later date. In essence, a classic bilateral deal had been struck between the outgoing colonial power and the dominant nationalist force, in this case the Republic of Indonesia. Supporters of the federal concept and the *negara* soon found themselves abandoned, and the hybrid RUSI structure was swept away within months. In August 1950, five years after the original declaration of independence, the Republic of Indonesia formally resumed its existence.

The independence settlement in Indochina

In March 1945, the uneasy co-existence between the Japanese military and the French administration in Indochina came to an end with the Japanese removal of the colonial government and imprisonment of the French population. The Japanese then turned over responsibility for running independent states in Vietnam, Laos and Cambodia to the monarchs – Sihanouk in Cambodia, Sisavong Vong in Laos and Bao Dai in Vietnam – who had previously worked within the French protectorate system. In reality, a vacuum of power was created that was increasingly filled in Vietnam by the Viet Minh patriotic front. When the Japanese surrendered in August 1945, the

Viet Minh immediately moved to seize power throughout the provinces and set up an independent 'Democratic Republic of Vietnam'. When, a few weeks later, Southeast Asia Command moved into southern Indochina and Chinese nationalist troops took over the north, with a view to supervising the Japanese surrender, the Democratic Republic of Vietnam (DRV) had already entrenched itself solidly in north and central Vietnam, though its position was more fragile in the south.

The Free French government under General de Gaulle – which took over during 1944 from the Vichy government that had collaborated with the Germans – was determined at all costs to reassert control over Indochina. Its general plan for the colony involved the creation of an Indochinese Federation, within which the separate states of Indochina would exercise a measure of self-government under the overall direction of a French-appointed High Commissioner. So far as Cambodia and Laos were concerned, this plan proceeded with reasonable smoothness after 1946. The Cambodian monarchy and political elite under Sihanouk, and the Laotian traditional political elite under the symbolic leadership of King Sisavong Vong, negotiated between 1946 and 1954 for increasing measures of self-government, while the two states at the same time retained a close relationship with the French in matters such as defence, the economy, foreign policy and cultural matters. Although there was a degree of fractiousness and division within the Laotian and Cambodian political elites while this process was taking shape, it was at least possible that stable independent states could have emerged in the mid-1950s. Tragically, both Laos and Cambodia were inevitably drawn into the conflict between Vietnam and France, and both were to become pawns in the Cold War.

The French were quickly to discover, however, that they lacked the military means to eliminate the Democratic Republic of Vietnam. In the south, they were able to establish a foothold in the wake of South-East Asia Command (SEAC) and, from this foothold, they steadily fanned out into the remaining towns of south Vietnam during the latter part of 1945. In the north, however, the leader of the Democratic Republic, Ho Chi Minh – with the help of some very canny footwork – managed to maintain an uneasy co-existence with the Chinese nationalist army that was in temporary occupation as part of the post-surrender arrangements of the Allies. After the Chinese began their gradual evacuation from Vietnam in early 1946, the French were forced by their weak position to reach an agreement with the Viet Minh over the status of north and central Vietnam. This involved a highly ambiguous arrangement whereby the Democratic Republic/Viet Minh recognized the overall authority of the French in Indochina as a whole, and the French in return recognized the autonomous rights of the Democratic Republic. This was clearly no more than an acknowledgement by both sides of their temporary weakness; negotiations between March and September 1946 showed that there was no real common ground between the two sides.

In December 1946, full-scale war broke out between the French and the Viet Minh. During the course of 1946, while the French had been trying to negotiate with the Viet Minh, they had, at the same time, tried to sabotage the position of the Democratic Republic by encouraging separatist sentiments, particularly in the south and in the minority regions in the Central Highlands. After 1947, the French changed tack, and set out to exploit ideological divisions within the Vietnamese nationalist movement itself, playing on the fact that the Viet Minh movement was manifestly communist-dominated. This new strategy, however, suffered from the fact that the French had never given any scope during the colonial period for moderate nationalism to take root or build mass strength. It was only after lengthy and tortuous negotiations that the French gradually established the 'State of Vietnam' as the 'legitimate' nationalist government of Vietnam. The key figure in this state was none other than Bao Dai, the former emperor who had ruled under the French protectorate, and had acted as a figurehead for the Vietnamese government set up by the Japanese.

The transparent objective of the French was to convert an anti-colonial conflict into a civil war between communist and anti-communist Vietnamese states.

It became increasingly evident in the early 1950s, however, that the creation of this new state would not help the French position in Vietnam. Bao Dai and his government could provide neither effective military nor credible political support for the French. Moreover, in the course of 1949 and 1950, the character of the Franco-Viet Minh war was changed from a small-scale guerrilla conflict into a full-scale positional war. Even with the help of the hastily recruited armed forces of Bao Dai's State of Vietnam and of local militias and special forces units, it was clear that the French did not have the manpower to sustain this kind of war. By early 1954 – even without the spectacular defeat of the French at the outpost of Dien Bien Phu – the logic of the situation was pointing to a French withdrawal and the confirmation of the independence and unity of Vietnam under the Democratic Republic.

The Cold War and the Geneva Settlement of 1954

In the early 1950s, however, the situation in Vietnam was drastically affected by the intrusion of the Cold War into the region. In the period between 1945 and 1949, the 'anti-fascist' alliance between the USSR and the West broke down, and was replaced by the so-called Cold War confrontation in Europe. In 1949, this confrontation between the communist world and the West spread to Asia, following the Chinese Communist (CCP) defeat of the Nationalists (Kuomintang) and the establishment of a communist regime in Peking. Cold War tensions mounted even further when, in 1950, the communist regime in North Korea invaded non-communist South Korea. To the

West in general, and the United States in particular, it seemed as if East Asia had become the front-line in the Cold War.

By 1950, therefore, the war in Vietnam acquired a new strategic and ideological dimension. The Democratic Republic of Vietnam openly acknow-ledged its communist identity, and its allegiance to the communist bloc; in response, the United States backed the French in recognizing Bao Dai's State of Vietnam as the legitimate successor to French colonial rule, and the United States began to pour in aid for the French war effort. As a con-sequence, a stalemate began to develop in the Vietnam war. Although the French will to continue the war began steadily to slip in the years 1953 and 1954, the Americans were determined to prevent a Viet Minh victory by all means short of direct military intervention.

By early 1954, it was clear that the stalemates in the Vietnamese and Korean conflicts could be broken only by international negotiations. The international conference convened in Geneva during the spring of 1954 was designed to bring an end to these conflicts and thereby help reduce the alarming level of international tension that had built up by this time. When the powers at the conference began to discuss the Vietnam situation in May 1954, however, it was evident that the Viet Minh's commanding military and political position was matched by the United States' determination to prevent a communist takeover of Vietnam. Agreement was eventually reached that a ceasefire should be followed by a temporary partition of Vietnam into a communist zone in the north and a non-communist ('retained') zone in the south. Neither of these interim political entities was to be given international recognition, but it was agreed that Vietnam should be finally united by vaguely defined democratic procedures that were to take place in two years' time. The independence and integrity of the royal governments of Laos and Cambodia were, however, confirmed by the Final Declaration of the Geneva Conference in July 1954 (see 'The First Indochina War and the partition of Vietnam, 1945–54', p. 202).

READINGS

1. Tan Cheng Lock and his plan for a united Malaya

Tan Cheng Lock was, in many respects, typical of the membership of the Chinese elite of the Straits Settlements of Penang, Malacca and Singapore. Western-educated, a Christian, and with a distinguished lineage in Malacca and the Southeast Asian region, he represented the class upon which the British colonial government in the Straits Settlements colony had increasingly come to rely in the 1920s and 1930s. However, the influence of the Straits Chinese (as they were called) had been informal rather than formal. Increas-ingly, Chinese community leaders like Tan Cheng Lock demanded, first, that the Straits Chinese should have substantial representation in the government and administration of the Straits Settlements; and, second, that the Chinese immigrants throughout the Malay peninsula should be given a greater sense that Malaya was their true home.

When the Japanese occupied Malaya, Tan Cheng Lock fled with the British and set up an 'Oversea-Chinese Association' in his temporary headquarters in Bangalore, south India. The aim of this association was to put pressure on the British government to ensure that the voice of the Chinese community was heard in the planning for the future of Malaya after the war. The forcible expulsion of the British administration in Malaya, the effective ending thereby of the protectorate agreements that had linked Britain to the Malay States, and the new international climate embodied in the formation of the United Nations in 1945, seemed to offer a perfect environment in which to argue for a new political structure in Malaya.

The memorandum below is a frank statement of Tan Cheng Lock's views on the future of Malaya. Three essential objectives stand out: the ending of the administrative division between the Straits Settlements and the Malay States, and thereby the creation of a united Malayan nation; rapid moves towards self-government for Malaya, within the framework of the British empire; and the establishment of equal citizenship rights for all the inhabitants of Malaya. In essence, this plan involved the end of the separate status of the Malay States with their respective sultans, and therefore the end of the concept of Malaya as *tanah melayu*, or 'the land of the Malays'. It is noticeable that the key features of this plan were, in fact, embodied in the Malayan Union scheme introduced in May 1946, although with a significant exception: Singapore – the city that gave the Chinese a majority in the peninsula – was excluded from the Malayan Union.

Tan Cheng Lock, *Malayan Problems from a Chinese Point of View* (Singapore: Tannsco, 1947). Excerpts taken from pages 61–73.

Memorial relating to Malaya submitted to His Majesty's Secretary of State for the Colonies, London, 1945 We, Malayans, from different parts of the country now temporarily residing in India and awaiting the hour of Malaya's liberation to return to what we regard as our homeland to assist in its rehabilitation, wish to express our views and feelings regarding its future and its post-war economic and political re-construction for the consideration of His Majesty's Secretary of State for the Colonies.

We experience deep feelings of anxiety and uneasiness as to what is to be the future of Malaya and its inhabitants owing to the absence of any pronouncement by His Majesty's Government of their intentions and future policy regarding the country, in the formulation of which none of the leaders or representatives of its permanent inhabitants, now available, have yet been consulted as far as our knowledge goes.

It should be within the province and competence of the future Government of Malaya to maintain and foster the inter-racial harmony and friendship existing amongst the mixed communities making up its population and to promote and encourage their active co-operation by all means, especially by a policy of equal treatment, impartiality and justice to all of them alike without discrimination, thereby helping to create a true Malayan spirit and consciousness amongst all its people to the complete elimination of any racial or communal feeling and to bring about a spirit of unity in their attachment to the British Commonwealth and Empire ...

If a policy of 'divide and rule' were attempted in Malaya, and Malays, for instance, were encouraged to dislike Chinese through preference given to the one community at the expense of the other, or *vice versa*, an attempt of this nature would, as experience has proved elsewhere, not only be sterile but also bring about such a state of affairs as would prepare the breeding ground and sow the seeds for the eventual growth of an anti-British sentiment in both communities to the detriment of the whole country.

We are strongly of the opinion that the only safe, sound and wise policy for the future Government of Malaya should be to rally to its support those true Malayans, who passionately love the country as their homeland and those who intend to settle there, and who are united by the legitimate aspiration to achieve by proper and constitutional means the ideal and basic objective of Self-Government for a united Malaya within the British Commonwealth and Empire, in which the individuals of all communities are accorded equal rights and responsibilities, politically and economically, including a balanced representation of the various communities in the Government to ensure that no one community will be in a position to dominate or outvote all the others put together.

The old paternal rule is up to a point good, but to revert to it is essentially a sterile policy; it affords no scope for change and growth; while the connection between the Straits Settlements and the Malay States is so intimate that it would be extremely difficult to set up self-government in the one but not in the other. Further the Straits Settlements Colony, being less than one-thirtieth of the total area of the whole country, comprises a very tiny portion of British Malaya. In consequence self-government in the Straits Settlements but not in the rest of Malaya will not make any appreciable difference to the political status and constitutional advance of the country and its inhabitants as a whole. Hence the imperative necessity of a united Malaya in a political sense. Economically and geographically the country is a unit, and it can only be administered with a maximum of efficiency as a single unit ...

[*The need for a Malayan citizenship and identity*] When the vital and indispensable need of the country was population, Chinese immigrants, who in considerable numbers had been pioneers in developing the tin-mining industry in Perak, Selangor and elsewhere in the Peninsula since 1850, before the time of British intervention in 1874, were encouraged to settle down in the hinterland, where they were practically its sole workers and revenue producers, the taxation of whose industry provided all the money available for its development.

Ever since then Chinese immigrants have been legally admitted into the Malayan mainland to take a major part in its economic development, for which purpose they have proved to be essential with the result that at the time of the Japanese invasion in 1941 the Chinese community was the most numerous section of the population of Malaya [including the Straits Settlements], which as estimated in December 1940 was approximately 5½ millions comprising:-

Malays (indigenous and immigrant)	41%
Chinese (Malaya-born and immigrant)	43%
Indians (Malaya-born and immigrant)	14%
Others	2%

If the Government should enforce a policy aiming at the removal of sectional barriers and the treatment of the different communities on the footing of equal rights and opportunities and duties and responsibilities and on the principle that no single community should be placed in a position to dominate the others, all obstacles in the way of its constitutional progress and development towards self-government should vanish, as has been amply demonstrated in the case of other territories with mixed communities and races.

Conclusion In conclusion the task that lies before His Majesty's Government of finding solutions for the problems and in their efforts to overcome the difficulties indicated above and others that may arise in connection with the re-construction of Malaya, we respectfully venture to offer our services and co-operation, in doing which we are actuated by a sense of love and patriotic attachment to Malaya, and the ambition to help its progress towards the attainment of a status of an equal, worthy and proud partner in the British Commonwealth and Empire, in the defence of which her sons should be made to feel that they have a real stake, such as would compel their willingness and readiness to submit to the supreme sacrifice.

2. Negotiated independence in Malaya

Despite Tan Cheng Lock's advocacy of a united Malaya, the Malayan Union system inaugurated in 1946 was not able to command effective Chinese support, and was met with a unanimous wall of Malay hostility. The British authorities accordingly entered into a virtual 'deal' with the leaders of the United Malays National Organization (UMNO) and the Malay sultans, and created a new Malayan 'Federation' that began operating in February 1948. The new system restored at least some of the powers of the states, and state legislative councils were established, along with settlement legislative councils of equal status for Malacca and Penang. Real power, however, resided in the British High Commissioner of the Federation, who was supported at the centre by an appointed federal executive council and federal legislative council, where representation was weighted in favour of the Malays. Most important of all, perhaps, the citizenship laws of the Federation gave almost automatic federal citizenship rights to Malays, while these rights were tightly restricted for other communities in Malaya.

It was at precisely this time (1948) that the Malayan Communist Party came out in open rebellion against the Federation government. Since the vast bulk of the Malayan communist guerrillas were Chinese, this rebellion had the effect of raising racial tension. This racial tension was further exacerbated by news of Chinese communist victories in the civil war in China itself in 1948 and 1949; these were to culminate in the establishment of the People's Republic of China in October 1949. To the Malays – and to a degree to the British – it seemed as if a gigantic Chinese communist conspiracy was unfolding in East and Southeast Asia.

Against the background described above, inter-ethnic relations in Malaya continued to deteriorate throughout 1948. It was in this context that, in January 1949, Tan Cheng Lock set up the Malayan Chinese Association (MCA), which was essentially designed to act as a mass movement and a pressure group for moderate Chinese who rejected the communist agenda. Although this organization aroused considerable initial suspicion among Malays, the MCA – along with the Indian ethnic political organization, the Malayan Indian Congress (MIC) that had been formed in 1946 – was to form the key to the inter-ethnic elite bargaining that eventually led to the creation of the united Malaya that achieved independence in 1957.

The dynamo that started the process of inter-ethnic elite bargaining was the Communities Liaison Committee, which was set up in 1949 and chaired by Malcolm MacDonald, British 'Commissioner-General' for Southeast Asia, a job that involved considering long-term policy in the region. Although membership fluctuated, the committee usually comprised about six Malays, among them Dato Onn bin Jaafar, founder of UMNO; six Chinese, including Tan Cheng Lock; one European; and two South Asians. Below are selected segments of reports by Malcolm MacDonald on the meetings of the Communities Liaison Committee. The key to the success of this committee was its informality and confidentiality: in such circumstances, frank discussions could take place without being subject to outside communal pressure. As such, the committee's workings could be seen as a model for inter-ethnic bargaining in a political system.

In terms of substance, the main themes of the committee's deliberations should be briefly noted. At the heart of the discussions was the question of identity, and the general acceptance of the idea of forging a Malayan identity and a 'Malayan-mindedness' – a project that required concessions on the part of all ethnic groups. In practical terms, this involved a willingness to redefine federal citizenship in such a way as to open that citizenship to a larger number of non-Malays who were clearly 'Malayan-minded'. This widening of federal citizenship could then open the door for the creation of a broadly defined 'national' citizenship of an independent Malaya.

It is also interesting to note that progress in the development of what Malcolm MacDonald – over-optimistically, no doubt – called an 'inter-racial' Malayan identity was seen by the committee as tied to political progress. In the committee's deliberations, the *process* of moves to self-government was considered, particularly the encouragement of elections at the state, settlement (Penang and Malacca) and municipal levels.

Colonial Office Records relating to the meetings of the Communities Liaison Committee, April 1949 to September 1949: CO 717/183.

Singapore, 22nd April, 1949
From: Commissioner General in S.E.A.
To: Secretary of State for the Colonies (Tel. No. 46)

Communities Liaison Committee held four meetings in Kuala Lumpur on April 19th and 20th. The Committee reached several unanimous agreements on items of policy. It has sent some of those to the Government for their consideration, but it is not repeat not at present publishing any of them. The members feel that it will be better to wait until they have more nearly completed their examination of various aspects of relations between the communities, so that they can then present a report which gives a comprehensive and balanced picture of their conclusions.

Towards the close of this latest series of meetings the Chairman, Thuraisingham, said that he thought that the Committee should consider certain political questions at its next meeting. During the last few weeks, he said, some developments had occurred which were prejudicing the work of the Committee, in that they tend to cause misunderstandings and suspicions between the communities. He mentioned some of the activities of the Malayan Chinese Association and of the Malayan Indian Congress. In further discussion it became clear that some of these developments are having an unfortunate effect. For example, the fact that the membership of the Malayan Chinese Association has been opened to very large numbers of Chinese who cannot be said to owe any loyalty to Malaya has caused resentment amongst the Malays, as well as criticism in some other quarters, including Chinese quarters.

A recent speech by Tan Cheng Lock at a Malayan Chinese Association meeting in which he renewed old criticisms against the Federal Constitution has increased Malay uneasiness. The Malays fear that the Association with its huge membership of alien as well as 'Malayan' Chinese will exert too much political influence on the Federal Government.

Members were unanimous in condemning recent activities by the Malayan Indian Congress, whose leaders look to India rather than to any Malayan source for their political inspiration. This tends to cause friction between the Indian political community and others.

Quite a warm controversy arose in the Committee when those matters were being discussed, especially between the Malay and the Chinese representatives. It was another indication of the delicacy of these political problems, and of the immense tact and care with which they still need handling, if we are to succeed in joining the Malays and Chinese in a truly friendly partnership.

After discussion it was agreed that political relations between the communities should be broached at the next meeting of the Committee, and that the meeting should continue over three consecutive days, so as to give us time to tackle some of the questions fairly thoroughly. The following Agenda of items to be considered was accepted:-

1) Should the ultimate aim of all communities be the creation of a united Malayan nation?
2) What is meant by the 'Special position' of the Malays?
3) Should all Federal citizens, irrespective of race, have equality of status, opportunity and privileges?
4) What should be the qualifications for the ultimate Malayan nationality? (a) allegiance to Malaya, (b) birth, residence and other tests.

You will see that the above Agenda will carry us into the midst of important problems and controversies. We shall certainly have some troublesome discussions, but it is best that the members of the Committee should face these matters frankly and make a real attempt now to reach agreements. The meetings hitherto have established a measure of friendliness and mutual confidence amongst all the members of the Committee which should stand us in good stead. I do not expect that the Committee will be able to reach early or complete agreement on all aspects of the problems posed above, but I hope that we can at least get accord on a number of them and avoid disaster on the others.

[On 12 May, another meeting of the Communities Liaison Committee took place. However, since illness prevented the key community leaders, Tan Cheng Lock and Dato Onn bin Jaafar, from attending, the question of dealing with vital political issues was postponed. Malcolm MacDonald noted in a message for the Secretary of State to the Colonies on 16 May 1949: 'I notice a certain amount of nervousness, among some of the members, about these impending political discussions. The communist victories in China are having an influence in making relations between Malays and Chinese in Malaya more delicate.']

Singapore, 19th August, 1949
From: Commissioner General in South East Asia
To: Secretary of State for the Colonies

After an interval of three months, the Communities Liaison Committee resumed its meetings in Kuala Lumpur on August 13th and 14th. The Committee spent the whole time considering the political aspects of relations between the various communities in Malaya. This, of course, is the most difficult part of its task, and might end in wide disagreements between the members of the Committee. However, remarkable progress was made in these discussions, and a considerable measure of at least tentative agreement was reached amongst all the community leaders present. This is encouraging, though we must keep our fingers crossed.

The following is a summary of the main conclusions of the Committee at this Kuala Lumpur meeting. They are tentative, for it was agreed that no member of the Committee need feel finally bound by his agreement to any of these conclusions until the complete set of conclusions have been reached, and the political picture can be viewed as a whole. This was a necessary proviso, so as not to frighten any of the community leaders into feeling that they were being hustled prematurely into difficult decisions.

(a) It was unanimously agreed that the aim in the Federation of Malaya is the establishment of self-government with sovereign status, and that a nationality should be created for all qualified citizens irrespective of race. DATO ONN endeavoured to have the word 'early', or some similar expression, inserted before the words 'establishment of self-government'. I resisted this proposal, and in the end it was unanimously agreed that it should be dropped. In the course of the discussion TAN CHENG LOCK asked DATO ONN how soon he thought Malaya would be ready for self-government. The DATO replied, 'between 15 and 20 years from now'. This is an interesting expression of his present views. TAN CHENG LOCK made it clear that the Chinese would wish Malaya to stay in the British Commonwealth when it becomes self-governing, and no one objected to this. The point was not discussed further. I judged that it would be a mistake to endeavour to force a specific decision in favour of this so early in the proceedings; though I hope that we can secure this later.

(b) In the course of the discussion on (a) the question of the relations between the Federation and Singapore was raised, with a view to amalgamation of the two being either agreed or rejected. I felt that this controversy would arouse an unfortunate row on the Committee at the present stage, which would prejudice the chance of agreement on other important and, in some ways, more urgent questions touching relations between the communities. I therefore proposed that the discussion for the present should be confined to the problem in the Federation, and that the question of its relations with Singapore should be considered by the Committee at a later stage. I emphasised that decisions taken on the Federation problem should all be regarded as without prejudice to the possibility of the Federation and Singapore being more closely associated. The Committee unanimously agreed to adopt this procedure.

(c) The Committee unanimously agreed that as a first step towards the realisation of self-government immediate consideration should be given to the possibility of introducing legislation for elections to the State and Settlement Councils as early as conditions permit in each case. It was accepted that some States would not be ready for elections for some time to come, but it was felt that if two or three States and Settlements gave a lead, the pace of progress would be speeded throughout the Federation. It was generally agreed that elections in at least some of the States and Settlements, as well as in Municipalities, should precede elections to the Federal Legislative Council, on the grounds that this would give the people of the country experience in popular elections, etc. for 'local' authorities before plunging into this sophisticated democratic practice for the supreme legislative authority in the Federation.

(d) It was generally agreed, though I think no formal 'agreed view' was passed on the subject, that all Federal citizens, without distinction of sex and without the application of any property or literacy tests, who register as voters should be qualified to vote in these State and Settlement elections. Some members of the Committee were inclined to urge that there should be, say, a property qualification, but DATO ONN amongst others resisted this. It was agreed that the question must in each case be decided by the State or Settlement authority concerned, but it was felt that if the first State to introduce such elections based its franchise without qualification on Federal citizenship, the others would be likely to follow that lead ...

(e) The Committee agreed unanimously that the Malays have 'a special position' in the Federation on account of the fact that for centuries Malaya has been their sole home, and that the country includes nine Malay States with Rulers in Treaty relationship with the King, the Rulers and States also being internationally recognised. The Committee agreed that this special position of the Malays should be safe-guarded, the purpose being to ensure that they are not politically dominated in their country, and that as time goes on they also take an increasingly important part in the economic life of the country. The agreement of the Chinese and other non-Malay leaders to this principle is valuable.

(f) Subject to (e) above, which is not regarded as coming into conflict with the principle now enunciated, it was agreed that all Federal citizens (to become nationals in due course) should enjoy equality of status, privileges and opportunities in the Federation, irrespective of race. The agreement of the Malay leaders on the Committee to this is important, and created a very good impression on their non-Malay colleagues. It was at this point that DATO ONN indicated that the members of the Committee should not be hustled too fast into such important decisions, and that I suggested that every decision should be regarded as tentative until the complete picture can be viewed. DATO ONN is unqualified in his support of the principle of equality between all Federal citizens, but is naturally anxious to ensure that the Committee does not propose that so many non-Malays should become Federal citizens that the Malays are swamped.

The Committee are unanimous that provision for the nationality referred to in (a) above should be made as early as is practicable. They recognise, however, that this raised many difficulties, and have postponed further discussion of the matter for the present.

The Committee then considered that difficult question of what should be the qualifications for Federal Citizenship (and ultimately for nationality). A considerable discussion ensued, and the following points emerged:

i. It was unanimously accepted that the principle that only those who owe Malaya their loyalty and regard Malaya as their permanent home should qualify for citizenship.

ii. It was unanimously agreed that 'Loyalty' to Malaya was not quite good enough, and that the conception of 'undivided loyalty' should be a proper guide in considering a person's claim to citizenship.

iii. The Chinese urged that all non-Malays born in the Federation and permanently domiciled there should become citizens automatically by process of law. All the customary arguments in favour of the Chinese proposal were produced in the discussion. The Malays did not, repeat not, flatly oppose the proposal. Indeed, DATO ONN stated that, whereas the Malays would not, repeat not, have considered for a moment any such suggestion three years ago, Malay opinion on the matter had advanced some way since then. He stated emphatically that the Malays accept the idea that everyone, irrespective of race, who really owes 'undivided loyalty to Malaya' and really regards the country as his permanent home, where he will live and die, should be admitted to Federal Citizenship. But he expressed scepticism about the strength of the loyalty of some of the people involved, and indicated that the Malays must have time to consider the proposal very carefully. Partly for tactical reasons I supported him to some extent in this conciliatory but cautious attitude ...

iv. My impression, for what it is worth, is that the Malay leaders are prepared to agree to some measure of relaxation of the Citizenship clauses. On the other hand, their reaction during these discussions may have been (on the spur of the moment and under the influence of the friendly atmosphere in the Committee) more generous than it will turn out to be when they have time for cool reflection ... If they make a reasonably good response to the plea for some relaxation in the Citizenship clauses of the Federal Agreement, the effect on relations between them and the non-Malay communities, especially the Chinese, will of course be excellent. In return, I think we could then get the Chinese leaders to abandon completely any further and more extravagant claims for the admission to citizenship of Chinese immigrants with rather short residence qualifications ...

In the course of the discussion on citizenship, etc. the point was made over and over again that, if a real nation composed of peoples of several races is to develop in Malaya, its citizens should speak a common language. This led to a discussion of education policy in the Federation, and the following two expressions of opinion were unanimously agreed:-

i. The teaching of Malay should be compulsory in all Government and State-aided primary schools.

ii. Every facility should be given for the progressive elimination of communal schools, and the establishment of central schools to be attended by children of all races together, the medium of instruction in these schools being either Malay or English. It was suggested that Malay would probably be the appropriate medium of instruction in rural areas, and English in the urban areas.

The Chinese as well as the other members of the Committee accepted these resolutions without demur. When I urged that the display of pictures of SUN YAT SEN, CHIANG KAI SHEK and MAO TSE TUNG should be prohibited in Chinese schools, and that they should be discouraged also from hanging up the Chinese flag, the Chinese members of the Committee expressed strong agreement with this. This question of education is of course fundamental to the problem of creating an inter-racial nation in Malaya. These tentative decisions of the Committee on the subject go to the root of the matter, and the unanimous consent given to them is encouraging. The Committee realise that it is impossible to implement the policy proposed except by a gradual process, but they attach so much importance to it being adopted and started as early as possible that they decided to appoint a small deputation to see the Director of Education, and if necessary the High Commissioner himself, on the subject. The deputation consists of one Malay, one Chinese, one Ceylonese and one Eurasian.

You will see from the above that the Committee covered a lot of ground and reached several very encouraging conclusions. But I repeat that they are tentative, and that the ultimate result may not mark such a large measure of progress as appeared to be promised in these first discussions. Nevertheless, I think that a lot of the progress registered will be maintained. The discussion was conducted throughout in a most comradely spirit. I feel more confident now than I did when I last reported that the Committee will succeed in making a substantial constructive contribution to political and other problems in Malaya.

Communities Liaison Committee Communiqué, 16 September 1949.
Public Relations, Singapore, Press Release No. SE.49/168.

The Communities Liaison Committee held meetings in Johore Bahru on Wednesday, Thursday and Friday, September the 14th, 15th and 16th respectively. They discussed political aspects of the inter-communal problem in the Federation of Malaya, and reached the following Agreed Views:-

1. It is the Agreed View of the Committee that the aim of the Federation of Malaya should be the attainment of self-Government with sovereign status and the creation therein of a nationality.

2. It is the Agreed View of the Committee that as a first step towards this end, that as soon as circumstances and local conditions permit, legislation be introduced for the election of members to the several legislatures within the Federation of Malaya.

3. It is the Agreed View of the Committee that, in order that the practice of holding elections may be introduced by stages and progressively amongst the peoples of the Federation, Elections should be held first in those Municipalities and States and Settlements which are ready for them. Subsequently Elections for the Federal Legislative Council should be introduced. As the work of preparing an Electoral Law for the Federation will necessarily take a considerable time, it is the Committee's Agreed View that early consideration be given to the subject by the Federal Legislative Council.

4. It is the Agreed View of the Committee that the franchise for elections to the several legislatures in the Federation should be based on Federal citizenship. This is a question to be finally settled, however, in each case by the authorities concerned in the light of local circumstances.

5. It is the Agreed View of the Committee that the teaching of the Malay and English languages should be compulsory in all government and Government-aided primary schools.

They further agreed that the following Memorandum should be issued for publication as an expression of their unanimous views:-

Memorandum

1. In this memorandum the word 'Malayan' is used as a term of convenience and refers to the inhabitants of the Federation of Malaya.

2. The aim of the Federation being to attain sovereign status with Malayan nationality, a beginning should be made to equip it properly for that end. The ultimate loyalty must be an undivided one to the Federation ...

3. The immediate [psychological] problem is to send boys and girls out into the world with a Malayan mind and so strongly Malayan-minded that they will pass it on in due course to their children.

4. Malay and English should be compulsory subjects in every Government and Government-aided primary school, and elementary instruction in the

Constitution and the Malayan way of life should be given in those two languages when children are sufficiently advanced in them to understand what is being said. Every encouragement should be given to the establishment of steadily increasing numbers of Government or Government-aided schools where children of all races attend together, the medium of instruction being Malay and English. In these schools there should be facilities also for teaching to children other languages which are their mother tongues. As such schools increase the numbers of Government and Government-aided communal schools should be progressively reduced.

5. In America every primary school begins the day with the salute to the flag and the singing of the national anthem. Elementary teaching of the constitution and the American way of life is also given. The problems of America are very akin to our own and it must not be forgotten that immigrants and their descendants still maintain their own national customs in America and frequently speak their own national languages in their own homes, and that there are newspapers published in America in the languages of nearly all (if not all) European languages and, we believe, some Asian. Nevertheless, these immigrants and their descendants are whole-heartedly American. This is achieved to a great extent by carefully planned psychological methods, in which the emphasis is placed upon the duties to the country as well as the rights of its citizens.

6. Royal portraits, anthems, flags and memorial days are psychologically important. As long as children in Malaya are brought up to regard non-Malayan national leaders, anthems, flags and memorial days as being of outstanding importance and the government of the Federation as an impersonal outside thing, they will not become Malayan minded. The children of today become the students of tomorrow and the ancestors of the future. It is upon the children in primary schools that we must concentrate first and see that the lessons then taught are continued throughout secondary schools and into colleges and the University of Malaya. Throughout it must be emphasized that … in course of time a nation of Malayans will arise from the Federation, that this nation will be a Government of the people, that they themselves are Malayans and will be the ancestors of the nation to arise, and that the Federal flag is the emblem of all this, of their loyalty to the country in which they are living and of their hopes for the future.

7. Children should be familiarized with the portraits of His Majesty the King [of Britain] and Their Highnesses the Rulers [the State Sultans], and of Her Majesty the Queen and the Rulers' Consorts. The portraits of Their Majesties and the Ruler of the State and his Consort should hang in every Government and Government-aided school in the Federation. It would also be well if children became familiar with the prominent leaders of their own racial groups, not as racial leaders but as prominent Malayans. To this end much could be done by the Public Relations Office through the cinema.

8. In course of time there should be a Federation anthem. If such a

Malayan anthem does come, it will do so better spontaneously than through a prize competition, which usually produces stilted and academic music. Until such an anthem comes into being, children in the two Settlements should use the British national anthem and those in the States the State anthem. A child's loyalty is affected very much by the national anthem, and the habit of standing to attention while it is being sung has a definite psychological effect.

9. At the beginning of each day, while the anthem is being sung, the Federation flag should be saluted and all schools should be provided with it. It would be wise to restrict the public display of flags to that of the Federation, the Union Jack and the State flags. Streets, buildings and public places should not be decked with the flags of foreign nations except upon the national day of that nation or upon buildings owned or occupied by official representatives of foreign nations.

10. Federation Day should be marked with ceremonial in every town and sizeable village throughout the country, not merely with perfunctory ceremonial but with impressiveness, and the people should be taught to regard it as a day of holiday and rejoicing ...

15. When the Federal Agreement was made, there were great fears that the Chinese would swamp the Malays numerically in course of time and the Annual Report on the Federation for 1948 shows that since 1931 the Malays have increased by 30.26 per cent, and the Chinese by 46.67 per cent. It is, however, very doubtful if the Chinese in the Malay States are politically minded and experience in Singapore shows that the building up of democratic institutions and the inculcation of democratic thought will be a slow process in that Colony. It seems, therefore, that for a long time the Malays will not have much to fear politically and, if in the ensuing years, the educated Chinese become Malayan-minded, they will have still less.

16. We think that part XII of the Federal Agreement (Citizenship) should be re-considered [with a view to widening citizenship rights]. If benefits and electoral rights are to be confined to Federal Citizens, justice would seem to require it ... If our future Malayan state is to arise from Federal citizenship, and that would seem to be a sine qua non, then expediency requires it. Moreover, it would seem that a great change of thought has arisen since the negotiations for the Federal Agreement, that all races are now more liberal in their views, and that working in the Federal Council they have discovered how closely linked in reality they are to each other.

17. What we want to do is to bring into the fold of Federal Citizenship people of the type that will build up into a Malayan nation and the more there are of such the better. Under the present law Europeans and Eurasians are very hardly treated. Yet such persons would be most helpful and the trend of economic affairs is such as to make more Europeans likely to make their homes here and educate their children here. The Eurasian of the settled community appears to have exactly the same claim to a special position that a Malay has, since this is his only home and as a rule he is a true Malayan.

The old-established Chinese, Indian and Ceylonese families are so self-evidently Malayan that they could not be ignored. The very genuine desire for the preservation of Malay life and civilisation that is so abundantly clear amongst all races in Malaya should surely remove by now most of the fears that existed when the Federation Agreement was being worked out. We repeat, therefore, that in our view the Citizenship provisions of the Federal Constitutions should be reconsidered and we propose to give attention to this.

3. The First Indochina War and the partition of Vietnam, 1945–54

The war between the Democratic Republic of Vietnam (Viet Minh) and France, which broke out in December 1946 and did not come to an end until July 1954, was an enormously complex event, not least because of the extension of the Cold War to Southeast Asia in the late 1940s and the simultaneous attempt of the French to convert a colonial war into a contest between two Vietnamese governments. The following narrative compiled by the British Central Office of Information in 1965 highlights the essential points with admirable conciseness – although there are, of course, indications of an anti-communist bias.

One element in the history of this conflict that has become clearer with hindsight is the manner in which the political strategy of the Viet Minh/Democratic Republic of Vietnam had evolved prior to the Geneva conference. It must be borne in mind that the Viet Minh was a patriotic front created by an orthodox communist party, the Indochina Communist Party (ICP). In September 1945, the Viet Minh, guided by the ICP, masterminded the creation of an independent state, the Democratic Republic of Vietnam (DRV). When Chinese nationalist (KMT) troops moved into the north of Vietnam, in the same month, to supervise the Japanese surrender, they brought with them pro-KMT Vietnamese politicians – particularly from the Viet Nam Quoc Dan Dang (VNQDD) and Dong Minh Hoi – who had been in exile in China since the 1930s. In order to avert the danger that the Chinese would install these politicians in power and remove the Vietnamese communists, Ho Chi Minh moved with customary flexibility and astuteness. He incorporated VNQDD/Dong Minh Hoi politicians into the DRV government and National Assembly and, in October 1945, declared the dissolution of the Indochina Communist Party (ICP). This move was purely nominal, and the ICP continued to control the DRV secretly. When the KMT eventually left northern Vietnam in spring 1946, the pro-Chinese politicians were rapidly weeded out and, in some cases, liquidated. After the Chinese communist victory in 1949, the ICP re-emerged with the new name of Viet Nam Dang Lao Dong, or Vietnam Workers' Party, and the DRV announced its orthodox communist credentials. Such were the complex machinations of communist politics.

Although the DRV take-over was relatively smooth in the north and centre of Vietnam, in the southern Cochinchina area the Viet Minh had to contend with such regional political forces as the Cao Dai and the Hoa Hao religious movements, which had managed to entrench themselves locally in the prevailing vacuum of power after March 1945. Although the Viet Minh reached a temporary accommodation with these groups in August–September 1945, most of these local agreements had collapsed by 1947. Thereafter, the Cao Dai and the Hoa Hao generally co-operated with the French. Large areas of Cochinchina, therefore, were outside Viet Minh control throughout the 1947–54 period.

It should also be noted that there were, in retrospect, serious flaws in the agreements reached at the Geneva Conference of 1954. Despite the fact that the 'big powers' attended the conference, the substantial agreements were reached between the Viet Minh and the French military commands. When, therefore, the French military evacuated Vietnam in April 1956, there was simply no means of enforcing the decision to hold the 'Vietnam-wide' elections that had been planned for July 1956. The 'Final Declaration' of the Geneva Conference was guaranteed only verbally by the powers. Moreover, neither the United States nor the State of Vietnam (South Vietnam) was prepared even to give its verbal assent to the agreements. All that the Geneva Agreements really achieved was an immediate cease-fire, which allowed the regroupment of the respective forces to the north and south, and the 'temporary' partition of Vietnam into two 'political entities' without international recognition. No structures were put in place to ensure a long-term settlement of Vietnam's future.

The events of 1945 to 1954, complex though they are, provide an essential background for understanding the partition of Vietnam into two competing national governments in 1954, and for understanding the dynamics of American involvement in Indochina.

Central Office of Information (British Information Services), Vietnam
(London: HMSO, 1965). Excerpts taken from pages 1–17.

The 'Democratic Republic of Vietnam' In December 1943 the French Committee of National Liberation [the Free French] had promised Indo-China 'a new political status within the French Community' and, in March 1945, the French Provisional Government issued a declaration providing in general terms for a Federal Indo-China with local autonomy within the French Union [a collectivity roughly equivalent in concept to the British Commonwealth]. France was, at the end of the war, not in a position to send troops immediately to Indo-China and, at the Potsdam Conference (July 1945), it was agreed that, to receive the Japanese surrender, Indo-China north of the 16th parallel should be occupied by Chinese forces, while troops under General Gracey (Britain) were to occupy the south. Between the Japanese surrender and the arrival of these troops, however, events of decisive importance had occurred in North Vietnam.

With the Japanese surrender the Viet Minh moved into the political vacuum existing in North Vietnam. They were by far the most effectively organised group supporting the cause of independence, they derived much prestige from their association with the Allies and they became, for a while, the centre of a broadly based national movement. On 29th August, 1945, a 'provisional government' was proclaimed in Hanoi with Ho Chi Minh as President, and, as Supreme Political Adviser, Bao Dai, who had abdicated as Emperor five days previously. On 2nd September Ho Chi Minh proclaimed the independence of the 'Democratic Republic of Vietnam'.

French rule restored in Cochin-China　In Cochin-China the Viet Minh was by no means in such a strong position as in the north. The Cao Dai and the Hoa Hao had been equipped with arms by the Japanese and left in control of certain areas, and they, together with the Trotskyists and other non-Stalinist nationalist groups, formed a United National Front whose relations with the 'Committee of the South', appointed by the Viet Minh to rule in Cochin-China, were extremely tense. A number of these nationalist leaders were killed by the Viet Minh, including, in the following year, Huynh Phu So, the founder of the Hoa Hao.

In mid-September 1945, when British and Indian troops under General Gracey began to arrive in Saigon, the authority of the Committee of the South was tenuous and Vietnamese bands were engaging in looting and violence against the French. On 23rd September French troops, on the orders of General Gracey, took control of Saigon. This was followed by a Vietnamese rising, and though the French soon established themselves in Saigon, guerrilla warfare continued in the countryside. On 9th October, 1945, an agreement signed in London by the British Foreign Secretary, Mr. Ernest Bevin, and the French Ambassador, M. Massigli, recognised the French civil administration as the only one entitled to direct non-military affairs south of the 16th parallel. British forces were withdrawn from Cochin-China early in 1946.

Chinese occupation in the north　During the Chinese occupation of northern Vietnam, which began in mid-September 1945, the Viet Minh behaved, from necessity, in a conciliatory manner towards the Chinese-supported VNQDD and Dong Minh Hoi ... The dissolution of the Indo-Chinese Communist Party was announced in October 1945. In December 1945 and January 1946 'elections' with little pretence of secrecy or freedom of choice were held for a National Assembly.

On 28th February, 1946, an agreement was reached between France and China by which France gave up her extra-territorial rights in China and granted Chinese goods concessions on the Haiphong–Kunming railway and China agreed to withdraw her troops from Indo-China.

Negotiations between France and the Viet Minh On 6th March, 1946, an agreement was signed at Hanoi between M. Saintény, the French Commissioner in Tongking, and Ho Chi Minh, by which the Vietnamese agreed not to oppose the return of the French army to the north and France recognised the Democratic Republic of Vietnam as 'a free state with its own government, parliament, army and finances, forming part of the Indo-Chinese Federation and the French Union'. After the cessation of local hostilities a referendum would be held to decide whether Tongking, Annam and Cochin-China should be united. Under a military annex to the agreement, French troops, with the possible exception of those guarding bases, were to be withdrawn from Vietnam by 1952.

In April 1946 a conference was convened at Dalat to prepare for a definitive meeting in Paris. At the Dalat meeting it became clear that there were serious difficulties of interpretation as regards the March agreement. Moreover, the Viet Minh queried the honesty of any referendum which might be held under French auspices in Cochin-China, where fighting was, in fact, still continuing. These differences became more acute following the establishment on 1st June by the [French] High Commissioner, Admiral d'Argenlieu, of a provisional government in Cochin-China which was declared to be an independent republic within the Indo-Chinese Federation and the French Union. The Viet Minh regarded this as a breach of the Hanoi Convention.

A delegation led by Ho Chi Minh attended a conference at Fontainebleau which opened on 6th July, but no progress was made, and the Vietnamese delegates withdrew when, at the beginning of August, Admiral d'Argenlieu convened a second conference at Dalat to which delegates of the 'non-Vietnamese peoples in Indo-China' were invited, including delegates from Cochin-China and southern Annam as well as from Laos and Cambodia. On 14th September, however, just before he left France, Ho Chi Minh signed a 'modus vivendi' agreement with the French Government, covering mainly economic matters but including an agreement by both sides to cease 'all hostilities and acts of violence'.

Relations between the French and the Viet Minh, however, continued to deteriorate. Following clashes in Haiphong the French bombarded the city on 23rd November, causing heavy loss of life among Vietnamese civilians. On the night of 19th December the Viet Minh launched a general attack upon the French in Hanoi. This was followed within a few hours by attacks against all French garrisons in north and central Vietnam.

The War of 1946–54 *The communists in the DRV* At the same time as the Viet Minh launched their attack upon the French in Hanoi, Ho Chi Minh and the DRV 'government' took to the jungle. Within a few months the Viet Minh had been driven from the cities in Annam and Tongking, but remained in control of the greater part of the countryside. The resulting military stalemate was to last for nearly eight years. Politically, the period was marked by the emergence of the open dictatorship of the Communist Party in the Viet Minh areas and by the progressive transfer of authority by the French to the administration that had been set up by Bao Dai under their auspices [see below].

The immediate effect of the outbreak of fighting between the Viet Minh and the French seems to have been to slow down the trend towards one-party rule in the DRV. Following the victory of the Chinese Communists at the end of 1949, however, the allegiance of the Viet Minh to the Communist cause was openly proclaimed and the Viet Minh set about the indoctrination of the population with Marxist ideas. In February 1951 the formation was announced of the 'Viet Nam Dang Lao Dong' (Vietnam Workers Party) which announced that its basis was the doctrine of Marx, Engels, Lenin and Mao Tse-tung, adapted to the realities of the Vietnamese revolution. The leadership of this party, as well as its pronouncements, left little doubt that it was a revival of the Indo-Chinese Communist Party. In March 1951 the Viet Minh was incorporated in another national front, the Lien Viet, first formed in 1946. Apart from the Lao Dong, the various other social and political groups tolerated in the Viet Minh zone joined the Lien Viet.

In a speech on 10th January, 1954, Ton Duc Thanh, chairman of the Lien Viet Front, declared: 'In the light of the great October Socialist Revolution and the ideology of Lenin and Stalin and the Soviet Communist Party, the Vietnamese working class and its general staff – the Indo-Chinese Communist Party founded by President Ho Chi Minh – have led the Vietnamese Revolution to the present outstanding achievements ... The Soviet Union was, is, and always will be a bright example which fosters in the heart of every Vietnamese citizen an ironlike confidence. The people of Vietnam regard the Soviet Union as the goal of their struggle and clearly realise that the present Soviet image will be the Vietnamese image of the future.'

The establishment of the Bao Dai regime French contacts with Bao Dai, who was now living in Hong Kong, began early in 1947. During the year, both the Cao Dai and the Hoa Hao (whose founder, Huynh Phu So, had been killed by the Viet Minh), as well as various individual nationalists, broke with the Viet Minh and declared their support for Bao Dai. In May 1948 General Nguyen Van Xuan, one of the founders of the Cochin-Chinese Republic, formed a provisional central government for Vietnam and, with this government, France signed, on 5th June, 1948, an agreement at Ha Long Bay recognising in principle the independence and unity of Vietnam as an Associated State within the French Union. On 8th March, 1949, by an exchange of letters between Bao Dai and the President of France (the Elysée agreements), Bao Dai was recognised as the head of an independent Viet-namese state within the French Union. The independence was, however, qualified by, e.g., provisions for the co-ordination of Vietnamese foreign policy with that laid down by the High Council of the French Union. French Union forces were to retain their bases in Vietnam and to have rights of free passage. A Vietnamese national army was to be established. Certain important functions which had previously been dealt with by France for the Indo-Chinese Union as a whole – including communications, immigration control, customs, foreign trade and various financial matters – were reserved for an inter-state conference.

Under the Elysée agreements the inclusion of Cochin-China in the State of Vietnam was subject to consultation of the population. A territorial assembly for Cochin-China was elected, with the function of voting on this matter and, on 23rd April, 1949, it voted to adhere to Vietnam. This decision was given effect by a vote of the French Assembly on 22nd May.

On 14th June, 1949, Bao Dai, who had returned to Vietnam at the end of April, took up his functions as Head-of-State. The hoped-for rally of nationalist opinion to the new regime did not, however, take place. Ngo Dinh Diem, the leader most respected by the [non-communist] nationalists, declined to accept office, stating that 'The national aspirations of the Vietnamese people will be satisfied only on the day when our nation obtains the same political status which India and Pakistan enjoy'. Bao Dai himself held office as Prime Minister until January 1950, when Nguyen Phan Long was appointed Prime Minister.

The inter-state conference envisaged under the Elysée agreements took place at Pau between June and November 1950 and agreement was reached that, within a framework of inter-state co-ordination, each state of the Indo-Chinese Union was to control its own finances, customs system, foreign trade, immigration, communications and postal system. France, when her interests were affected, was to participate in the economic conferences of the Indo-Chinese states. The transfer of powers to Vietnam was given effect by agreements signed on 23rd December, 1950. In the same month a beginning was made in the creation of a national army under Vietnamese control.

The transfer of power was, however, still viewed with scepticism by Vietnamese opinion. Nguyen Phan Long, who had antagonised the French authorities, was dismissed by Bao Dai in May 1950. His successor, Tran Van Huu, was replaced in June 1952 by Nguyen Van Tam, who had been closely associated with the French administration and prominent in the separatist movement in Cochin-China.

International aspects   On 7th February, 1950, following the formal ratification of the Elysée agreements and of similar agreements between France on the one hand and Cambodia and Laos on the other, Cambodia, Laos and Vietnam were recognised by Britain and the United States. *With the Communist victory in China, the emergence of the unequivocally Communist nature of the Viet Minh, and the French grant, at least in principle, of independence to the Associated States, the civil war in Vietnam was taking on an international significance* [emphasis added]. Already on 18th January the Communist Government in China (followed on 31st January by the Soviet Union) had recognised the Viet Minh regime. In the autumn of 1950 the Viet Minh launched a series of successful attacks on French posts on the Chinese frontier and thus opened up their communications with the Chinese Communists. From this time onwards the Viet Minh received substantial Chinese support both in military supplies and equipment and in the training of Viet Minh forces in Chinese military camps.

In May 1950 it was announced that, to restore security and develop genuine nationalism in Indo-China, the United States Government had agreed to a French request for military and economic aid in the area. This aid would go not only to France but also to each of the Associated States. United States aid was much increased following the invasion of South Korea in June 1950 by Communist forces from the north and the intervention of Chinese Communist 'volunteer' forces in Korea in November. The French budget for 1954 showed that 78 per cent of the cost of the war in Indo-China was found by the United States. Statements were issued by Britain and the United States, warning that grave consequences would ensue if Chinese troops intervened in force in Indo-China.

Military operations, 1951–54 The danger that the Viet Minh might overrun the Red river delta area was temporarily averted under the leadership of General de Lattre de Tassigny, who served as High Commissioner from December 1950 until his death in January 1952. After the failure of their offensive in the delta area, the Viet Minh resorted again, and with growing success, to infiltration tactics. In April 1953 Viet Minh forces invaded Laos in the guise of 'volunteers' supporting a Laotian 'liberation army' whose existence at this stage was extremely doubtful. In December 1953 they resumed the invasion [of Laos], the device of referring to the Viet Minh forces as 'volunteers' being now abandoned. French determination to defend the outpost of Dien Bien Phu on the Tongking side of the Laotian frontier led to the encirclement of 15 battalions, the remnants of which were overwhelmed by the Viet Minh on 8th May, 1954. The success of the attack on Dien Bien Phu showed that the Viet Minh had been much better equipped with artillery by the Chinese than had been supposed ...

The Geneva agreements The heavy casualities suffered by the French Union forces in Indo-China, and the doubtful prospects of bringing the war to any satisfactory conclusion, caused an increasingly large section of French opinion, during 1953 and early 1954, to consider the possibilities of a negotiated peace in Indo-China. On various occasions during 1953 the French Government made it clear that it would consider any reasonable proposal for a 'cease-fire' in the Indo-China area. In an interview with a Swedish newspaper correspondent at the end of November 1953, Ho Chi Minh stated that if the French Government wished to consider an armistice and 'to resolve the question of Vietnam by negotiation' then the people and Government of the 'Democratic Republic' were ready to examine the French proposals.

On 18th February, 1954, at the conclusion of the Berlin conference between France, the Soviet Union, Britain and the United States, it was announced that a conference was to meet at Geneva on 26th April to discuss the settlement of the Korean question and the problem of restoring peace in Indo-China.

No progress was made in sessions of the Geneva conference dealing with Korea. Discussions on Indo-China began on 8th May between delegates of Britain and the USSR (joint chairmen), France, the United States, the Chinese People's Republic, Cambodia, Laos and Vietnam, [i.e. the Associated State of Vietnam], and from the Viet Minh forces [i.e. the DRV]. Dien Bien Phu fell on the same day. During the conference the Laniel government in France resigned and, in the speech which the new Prime Minister, M. Mendès-France, made to the French Assembly on 17th June, he undertook to resign if he had not secured an honourable settlement in Indo-China within one month.

The conference ended on 21st July, 1954, after agreements had been concluded for the cessation of hostilities in Cambodia, Laos and Vietnam. A final declaration was issued taking note of these agreements and of various declarations issued by France, Cambodia and Laos. The United States and Vietnamese [State of Vietnam] Governments did not subscribe to this declaration but made declarations in which they stated, *inter alia*, that they would not use force to oppose the execution of the agreements. The US declaration also indicated that the US 'would view any renewal of the aggression in violation of the ... agreements with grave concern and as seriously threatening international peace and security'. The Vietnamese [State of Vietnam] Government strongly protested against the agreement as entailing the partition of Vietnam.

Cease-fire agreement for Vietnam The agreement concluded between the French Union and Viet Minh commands provided for a withdrawal, within 300 days, of the French Union forces to the south of a military demarcation line fixed at approximately the 17th parallel [and for all communist/DRV forces to move to the north of this demarcation line] (Articles 1 and 2). A demilitarised zone was to be established to a width of not more than 5 kilometres on either side of the demarcation line (Article 1). Both parties were to 'order and enforce the complete cessation of all hostilities in Vietnam' (Article 10). During the period of the regrouping 'any civilians residing in a district controlled by one party who wish to go and live in the zone assigned to the other party shall be permitted and helped to do so by the authorities in that district' (Article 14d). Each party undertook 'to refrain from reprisals or discrimination against persons or organisations on account of their activities during the hostilities and to guarantee their democratic liberties' (Article

14[c]). The entry of additional military personnel was prohibited, although, subject to certain conditions, the rotation of units and the arrival of individual personnel on a temporary duty basis was permitted (Article 16). The introduction of fresh military equipment was prohibited, though worn-out equipment could be replaced (Article 17). No military base under the control of a foreign state was to be established in either zone; 'the two parties shall ensure that the zones assigned to them do not adhere to any military alliance and are not used for the resumption of hostilities or to further an aggressive policy' (Article 19). The agreement applied to all the armed forces of either party. Each was to respect the demilitarised zone and the territory under the military control of the other party, and was to commit no act and undertake no operation against the other party (Article 24). The commanders of the forces of the two parties were to take all steps 'to ensure full compliance with the agreement by all elements and military personnel under their command' (Article 27). A Joint Commission composed of representatives of the commanders of the two parties was to be set up to facilitate the execution of provisions of the agreement concerning joint action by the two parties (Articles 30 and 31). An International Commission, composed of representatives of Canada, India and Poland and presided over by India, was to be set up for the control and supervision of the application of the provisions of the agreement (Article 34).

The final declaration of the Geneva conference provided that 'so far as Vietnam is concerned, the settlement of political problems, effected on the basis of respect for the principles of independence, unity and territorial integrity, shall permit the Vietnamese people to enjoy the fundamental freedoms guaranteed by democratic institutions established as a result of free general elections by secret ballot. In order to ensure that sufficient progress in the restoration of peace has been made, and that all the necessary conditions obtain for free expression of the national will, general elections shall be held in July 1956, under the supervision of an international commission composed of representatives of the member-states of the International Supervisory Commission, referred to in the agreement on the cessation of hostilities. Consultations will be held on this subject between the competent representative authorities of the two zones from 20th July, 1955, onwards ... The provisions of the agreements on the cessation of hostilities intended to ensure the protection of individuals and of property will be most strictly applied and must, in particular, allow everyone in Vietnam to decide freely in which zone he wishes to live.'

The establishment of the Republic of Vietnam [South Vietnam] The

Geneva agreements were rapidly followed by the removal of the remaining restrictions on Vietnamese independence in the area south of the 17th parallel. In September 1954 the security and judicial services and various technical services which had been operated by the French were handed over to Vietnamese control.

In February 1955 the military command in Vietnam was transferred to the Vietnamese authorities, and in April 1956 the French Union High Command there was dissolved and the remaining elements of the expeditionary force left the country.

From the end of 1954 onward, United States economic aid was channelled direct to Vietnam. In November 1954 General Lawton Collins arrived in Vietnam as special envoy of President Eisenhower and, in January 1955, it was announced that, at the request of M. Diem [prime minister of South Vietnam], General Collins had agreed to the United States assuming full responsibility for assisting Vietnam in the organisation and training of its armed forces ...

Refugees, 1954–55 During the period of the military regrouping (up to 19th May, 1955) and during an extension to 20th July, 1955, some 890,000 refugees, the majority of them Catholics, arrived in South Vietnam from the Communist north. Though, politically, the arrival of the refugees assisted the Diem Government by bringing home to opinion, both inside and outside Vietnam, the extent of resistance to the Communist regime, it confronted it with an economic problem of huge dimensions. The movement of refugees took place in the face of systematic obstruction by the DRV authorities, who made little pretence of endeavouring to fulfil Article 14(d) of the cease-fire agreement. The corresponding movement from the southern to the northern zone was relatively very small indeed.

CHAPTER 8

The Decade of Instability,
1954–65

The truth is that guerrilla warfare, mounted from external bases – with rights of sanctuary – is a terrible burden to carry for any government in a society making its way towards modernization. (W. W. Rostow, address to graduating class at the US Army Special Warfare School, Fort Bragg, June 1961)

The Cold War confrontation in mainland Southeast Asia

The agreements reached at Geneva gave the West – the United States in particular – valuable time in which to build up what amounted to an anti-communist 'shield' in mainland Southeast Asia. The cornerstone of this defence strategy was the collective security treaty creating the South-East Asia Treaty Organization (SEATO), concluded in late 1954, which bound together in a mutual defence pact the United States, Australia, France, New Zealand, Pakistan (including what was then East Pakistan, now Bangladesh), the Philippines, Thailand and the United Kingdom. In a sense, however, the importance of this agreement tended to be more symbolic than actual, and the real keys to American strategy in the region were, first, the close Thai–US relationship that had been established during the Second World War; second, the policy of building an anti-communist 'bastion' in Laos, despite the terms of the Geneva Conference, which had envisaged Laos as a neutral zone in the Cold War; and, finally, the attempt to bolster a viable anti-communist regime in South Vietnam. Military aid and advice, strategically focused economic aid, and a measure of political and administrative support and manipulation, all played key roles in this strategy to protect a region that was viewed, by 1950, as a front-line in the Cold War between the West and the global communist threat.

Behind this 'front-line' area, the Philippines – with its air and naval base facilities – and the Malayan region, with its close post-colonial relationship with Britain, Australia and New Zealand, played a crucial 'back-up' role.

Despite the huge American commitment to this security network, it did not in fact command unanimous support in the region. In the first place, the network outlined above was clearly dominated by the United States and the former colonial powers. Many of the states that had recently emerged into independence were understandably reluctant to become involved in what could be seen as a classic example of 'neo-colonialism' in action. In the course of the 1950s, the policy of 'non-alignment' – a decision, that is, to side neither with the United States and the West nor with the communist bloc – held considerable attractions for many of these states. 'Non-alignment' also provided the opportunity – appealing for many 'populist-charismatic' leaders of newly independent states – to play a high-profile role on the world stage. Burma under U Nu, Indonesia under Sukarno, and Cambodia under Sihanouk all adopted a 'non-aligned' position in international affairs, and Indonesia and Cambodia in particular accompanied this non-alignment with rhetoric slanted increasingly against Western 'neo-colonialism'. As a consequence, Indonesian–US and Cambodian–US relations deteriorated sharply through the late 1950s and early 1960s.

Secondly, the United States became increasingly aware during the 1950s that a simple policy of building security blocs of friendly nations around the perimeter of the communist world could not prevent the threat of communist *subversion*. After the death of Stalin in 1953, it had been gradually accepted by the Soviet Union that the global confrontation between the West and communism could not be resolved by war which, in a nuclear age, could only result in mutual destruction, but would have to be pursued by a more subtle contest in the political and economic arena. For both the Soviet Union and the United States, the key zone of this confrontation was not along the barbed-wire perimeters of the communist bloc, but in the whole vast area of the decolonizing world. Throughout this so-called 'Third World' area, newly independent nation-states were struggling, in the 1950s and 1960s, to replace the established regimes of the colonial powers, create efficient administrative structures, and develop economic policies that would lead their populations out of poverty and backwardness. Often, these massive tasks had to be undertaken against a background of war, political chaos, ambitious and unrealistic economic and political programmes, and exaggerated expectations on the part of the newly liberated populations. In short, the Third World – including Southeast Asia – was full of weak and vulnerable states undergoing a delicate process of transition. This made them easy targets for political subversion from within.

The Laos Crisis and regional subversion

A major problem for America's planned security network in Southeast Asia was the inherent weakness and vulnerability of at least two of the states that were regarded as essential to this network: Laos and South Vietnam.

The Geneva Conference had confirmed the independence and the territorial integrity of the Royal Lao government (RLG), but had stipulated that this state should maintain neutrality unless directly threatened by an outside power, and that the government of Laos should enter into immediate negotiations with the rebel, communist-dominated 'Pathet Lao' movement in order to integrate that movement within the state. This Pathet Lao movement, composed of Lao communists and other dissidents, had been put together as a military–political force by the Vietnamese communist leaders in 1950, mainly as a means of undermining the French position in Laos at that time. With Viet Minh help, the Pathet Lao formed a 'revolutionary base' in the northeast frontier between Vietnam and Laos, and also along the eastern frontier of Laos and Vietnam down to Cambodia.

Despite many difficulties, negotiations between the Royal Lao government and the Pathet Lao proceeded between 1954 and 1957, and a settlement was eventually reached that would have involved the military, administrative and political integration of the Pathet Lao. Between 1958 and 1961, however, Laos found itself irresistibly drawn into the Cold War confrontation and the Vietnam conflict. The United States was determined to prevent a coalition agreement that, it felt, would enable the Pathet Lao to subvert the RLG 'from within'. They therefore used their overwhelming influence to bring about the breakdown of the agreement, and encouraged the creation of a strong anti-communist government.

After the breakdown of the coalition agreement in 1958 and 1959, civil war broke out in Laos. The Pathet Lao quickly resumed control of the eastern borders, and were by 1961 threatening the Mekong heartland of the Royal Lao government. By this time the United States had discovered that the RLG was simply too weak to sustain the anti-communist 'bastion' role that American policy had imposed on it. Faced with the bleak alternative of a Pathet Lao–North Vietnamese takeover of Laos or a massive American–SEATO military intervention, the United States, at a hastily recalled international conference in Geneva, forced the RLG to patch together a new coalition agreement in 1962. Within a few months, however, this coalition broke down and, from 1963 to 1975, Laos was divided between a communist-dominated northern and eastern region – including the so-called 'Ho Chi Minh Trail' – and an RLG-dominated Mekong River region (see 'The Laos Crisis, 1958–62', p. 218).

The 'Laos Crisis' of 1958–62 showed the extreme vulnerability of the West's position throughout mainland Southeast Asia. This was due not only to North Vietnam's determination to bring about the destruction of pro-Western South Vietnam, and therefore to maintain a military presence in eastern Laos and Cambodia, but also to the fact that Laos and Burma shared borders with communist China. Burma, like Laos, was a weak state that had since its independence in 1948 faced insurgencies from peripheral separatist movements like those of the Karens, the Kachins and the Chins, and from various communist factions. The fact that Chinese nationalist troops had fled into northeastern Burma at the end of the Chinese civil war, and had established a warlord presence on the Burma–Thailand border, meant that this whole sensitive and ungovernable region was drawn into the confrontation between the United States and communist China. Both sides tried to extend complex networks of influence through the area, and this contest stretched down to northeastern Thailand on the Mekong border region, and even down to the Malaya–Thailand border area. Thailand, the key pro-Western state in mainland Southeast Asia, was surrounded by weak states and threatening insurgencies.

The Vietnam crisis, 1954-65

This situation made the United States all the more determined to prop up the regime in South Vietnam which, by the late 1950s, was showing serious signs of internal weakness after a promising start under Premier (later President) Ngo Dinh Diem, who replaced Bao Dai as head of state in 1955. The difficulties of this regime stemmed ultimately from its origins as a French creation designed to weaken support for the communist Democratic Republic of Vietnam. The inherent lack of 'nationalist credibility' of this state was compounded by Diem's evident reliance on the United States. From 1954 on, the United States and Diem embarked on a forced-pace programme of 'nation-building', the central feature of which was the removal of the patchwork of warlord alliances – including local Cao Dai and Hoa Hao leaders – created by the French between 1945 and 1954. This patchwork of alliances had, for all its evident weakness, been the provincial mainstay of Bao Dai's state. This complex structure was replaced under Ngo Dinh Diem by a highly centralized local government system that stretched right down to the village level.

The Diem government, however, had neither the requisite administrative cadre nor the local networks of support to sustain such a system. Through the years 1954 to 1958, therefore, a vacuum of government was opened up in the rural hinterland of South Vietnam, known after 1955 as the Republic of Vietnam (RVN). Not surprisingly, this vacuum was rapidly filled by the resistance network of the Viet Minh, which had established itself in the south during the period between 1945 and 1954, but had temporarily gone underground when the Geneva Conference designated South Vietnam as a non-communist zone. Diem's launch, after 1956, of an intensive campaign to root out Viet Minh resistance cadres in the countryside merely accelerated the establishment of this resistance network. When the northern communist leadership in Hanoi decided – after some delay – that, first, Diem and the Americans had no intention of negotiating for the unification of Vietnam; secondly, that the Americans would not allow the Diem regime simply to disintegrate; and thirdly, that the local resistance networks in South Vietnam could form an effective base for a co-ordinated resistance against Diem, they openly sanctioned, in 1960, a full-scale 'national-liberation' struggle against the southern regime, to be headed by the National Liberation Front for

South Vietnam (NLFSVN), known colloquially as the 'Viet Cong', or 'Vietnamese Communists'.

In the light of America's determination to prevent subversion in South Vietnam, US aid was gradually stepped up, particularly when the northern regime started providing direct support for the southern resistance. The Americans found themselves, however, pouring in aid to support a regime that appeared to be quite unable to help itself against an ever more effective resistance movement, supplied with men and materials from the north. As the level of United States aid increased and the situation deteriorated, so the Americans became increasingly embroiled in the internal political problems of the Diem regime, particularly in mid- to late 1963.

The United States fell into the trap of believing that the problems of South Vietnam lay not in the nature of the state that had been created by the French, but in the 'misrule' of Diem and his family. When, however, Diem's regime was eventually overthrown by a military junta in November 1963 – with the connivance of the United States – the political and security situation, far from improving, deteriorated at an alarming rate. Military and development aid was poured in as South Vietnam lurched from crisis to crisis, but this aid was countered by troops and armaments funnelled south along the Ho Chi Minh Trail by North Vietnam. By mid-1964, the United States administration had convinced themselves that sustained bombing attacks, directed first against the Ho Chi Minh Trail, and then against key targets in North Vietnam, might force the communists to halt their aid for the southern insurgency. By early 1965, however, it was clear that nothing would prevent the collapse of South Vietnam but the direct injection of US combat troops. Such troops were accordingly dispatched in increasing numbers through 1965. In the same decisive year, the process of 'escalation' reached its culmination when these troops moved from a defensive strategy centred on key US bases, to all-out 'Search and Destroy' operations in the more remote border regions (see 'The insurgency in South Vietnam and United States intervention, 1954–65', p. 227).

Instability in the Indonesian region, 1950–65

Indochina was not the only focus of instability in Southeast Asia during the 1950s and early 1960s. In a remarkable feat of endurance and unity, the Indonesian Republic had managed to survive intact through the period of struggle against the Dutch between 1945 and 1950. However, once a common enemy had been removed, all the fissures – ideological, regional, party-political – that had been papered over during the revolutionary period began to reopen. First, the so-called Darul Islam revolt, which began in West Java in 1948 with the ultimate objective of creating an Indonesian Islamic State (Negara Islam Indonesia) in place of the Republic of Indonesia, spread after 1950 to other islands. Second, after a setback in September 1948, when it became involved in a premature rebellion against the Republic's government, the Partai Komunis Indonesia (PKI) set about developing a long-term political strategy and a mass base under a new and more effective leadership. Third, a number of regional dissatisfactions burst out into the open from 1950 onwards, focused mainly on regional rights and on the issue of the demobilization of the vast number of regional militias that had emerged during the revolutionary period. Finally, at the centre of power, in Jakarta, serious differences emerged between those political leaders who wanted to see the installation of a parliamentary democracy based on the Western model, and those – like the armed forces' leaders and President Sukarno himself – who felt that a more authoritarian and centralized system would better suit Indonesia's traditions and deal with its immediate weaknesses.

In 1955, nation-wide elections were called for the purpose of replacing the unelected 'National Committee' that had governed, on the basis of inter-party elite bargaining, for a decade. These elections, however, far from reducing political instability, substantially increased it. The main parties – the Partai Nasional Indonesia (PNI), the Partai Komunis Indonesia (PKI), and the two Islamic parties, namely Masyumi and Nahdatul Ulama – gained roughly similar levels of support from their respective regional bases. Government, therefore, depended on continual jostling and bargaining between these parties. More seriously still, a clear gap had already, before the elections, begun to develop between the Java-based PKI, PNI and Nahdatul Ulama on one side and, on the other, Masyumi, whose main base of support was in the outer islands, including Sumatra. The period of the 1950s saw a growing split developing between Java and Sumatra in particular, and a growing sense in the outer islands that Indonesia's political and economic policy primarily favoured resource-poor, population-rich Java.

Evidence of this growing regional discontent was provided by the outbreak of a number of revolts in Sumatra and the outer islands in the years 1956 to 1958. These revolts served to unite Sukarno, the PKI, the other 'Javanese' parties and the armed forces in a determined effort to safeguard Indonesian unity. The armed forces in particular tended to ascribe to themselves a special role in Indonesia as the guardians of Indonesia's unity and independence. We should note, however, the ambiguity of the army's position. While its leadership stood firmly against the regional rebellions that broke out in the late 1950s, its regional commanders often sympathized with the fears of the regions, and particularly their anxiety over the lurch to the Left in Jakarta and the growing power of the PKI.

By 1958, the system of constitutional democracy in Indonesia had effectively collapsed. It was replaced in 1959 by a new political system, so-called 'Guided Democracy'. This could be regarded as an early attempt by a Southeast Asian state to discard Western models of government, and replace them with a system based on 'indigenous' values. Guided Democracy was, in essence, an authoritarian system of government with President Sukarno at its hub, into which ideologically sympathetic parties were co-opted, and which was ultimately bolstered, particularly at the regional level, by the power of the armed forces. The elements that made up Guided Democracy were disparate and often mutually antagonistic; all that really held them together was a shared desire to maintain national unity at all costs, and the belief of the main players that they would be able to exploit the political system for their own ends.

The key to Guided Democracy was the personality and the vision of Sukarno. He created what was in effect a model 'charismatic-populist' regime, in which very diverse political and social forces could be balanced and manipulated in a complex power struggle played out in the centre with Sukarno as the supreme 'puppeteer'.

Unity within the regime could be maintained only by a constant sense of internal and external 'threat' and a permanent 'revolutionary dynamic' driven by Sukarno's rhetoric. The keys to the essentially populist ideology of the regime were, first, an emphasis on the 'masses' and 'struggle', but with a careful avoidance of divisive class or economic issues; an emphasis on the unity of the oppressed of the Third World; and a virulent campaign against 'neo-colonialism' in all its regional manifestations and, increasingly, against the West in general.

In practical terms this meant that the manifold instabilities of the Guided Democracy regime were exported to the region as a whole. Centrally directed campaigns were launched in sequence against Dutch and foreign economic interests in Indonesia; against continued Dutch rule in western New Guinea; against the formation by Malaya and Britain in 1963 of the Federation of Malaysia, which linked Malaya, Singapore, Sarawak and Sabah; and, finally, against the United States, the West in general and even against the 'Western-dominated' United Nations. As the internal political tensions increased in Indonesia, so the stakes had to be raised externally. Initially the West tried a policy of appeasement and, in the course of the 1960s, it connived at the transfer of Dutch New Guinea from the colonial power to Indonesia. In 1963, however, Indonesia slid into an undeclared war – the so-called *Konfrontasi* or 'Confrontation' – against Malaysia and Britain in Borneo. An increasingly chaotic regime with a ramshackle economy was ultimately held together by a radical foreign policy that seemed by 1964 to be lurching unmistakably towards the communist bloc (see 'Indonesia and "Guided Democracy": a revolution in search of an Idea', p. 239).

READINGS

1. The Laos Crisis, 1958–62

After the United States embarked on its strategy of containment in Europe in 1947, it relied on the creation of a collective security agreement – the

North Atlantic Treaty Organization (NATO) – backed by nuclear power. The United States also built up a number of security agreements in the Pacific – with the Philippines, Japan, Taiwan, South Korea, and through the ANZUS treaty with Australia and New Zealand – before concluding the SEATO collective security pact in 1954. These security agreements were backed by a clear indication during Eisenhower's presidency (1953–61) that the United States would no longer allow its troops to be bogged down, as they had been in Korea in 1950, in a conflict where the communists had an inherent advantage because of their manpower superiority. In future, communist aggression on the periphery of its land-mass would be met with a 'massive retaliation' directed at the heart of the communist world.

By the time that this strategy was perfected in the mid-1950s, however, it was already in a sense out of date. The new concept of 'Peaceful Co-existence' promoted by Soviet leaders after Stalin's death in 1953 accepted that outright war between the capitalist and communist camps would not lead to the global victory of socialism, but to mutual nuclear destruction. The confrontation between the two 'systems' would therefore have to be fought in the economic and political spheres. (It was argued, however, that the communist military defence shield would have to be kept up because, as the crises of capitalism became more intense, the capitalist world would try to resort to war in order to avoid global defeat.)

In the course of the 1950s, the arena of this struggle shifted to the Third World. A classic example of this Cold War confrontation in the Third World is the 'Laos Crisis' of 1958–62, when the kingdom of Laos sprang briefly into prominence before it was swallowed up by the larger drama of the Vietnam war. The following narrative is written by the compiler of this book. It represents an attempt to compress into a small space not only the events and the significance of the 'Laos Crisis', but also the complex background to those events.

Clive J. Christie, 'The Background to the Laos Crisis, 1958-62'

When J. F. Kennedy took over the American presidency from Eisenhower in January 1961, he was informed that the situation in Laos constituted the gravest immediate international crisis that he faced. In the course of the previous year, American attempts to create a strong anti-communist bastion in Laos had collapsed, and the United States was now faced with the imminent prospect of the communist take-over of a state that was considered to be a key defensive barrier for non-communist Southeast Asia.

How had this situation come about? How was it that this distant and underdeveloped backwater, with a population of around 2–3 million people, had gained such a central status in American strategic thinking?

The answer was to be found in the geopolitical position of Laos during the Cold War era. The kingdom of Laos had borders with communist China, communist North Vietnam, South Vietnam, Cambodia, Thailand and Burma. It had the misfortune, in other words, to lie athwart the main zone of confrontation between the communist and non-communist regions of mainland Southeast Asia. The inherent vulnerability of its geographical position was compounded by the weakness of the independent Lao state that was created after the Second World War, and by the fact that many of the remote and vulnerable border areas were inhabited by a jumble of minority groups, many of whom had a traditionally hostile relationship with the ethnic Lao living in the plains regions, and over whom effective central government control had rarely been exercised, even at the height of French colonial rule.

The historical background to independence   The Lao people are a branch of the ethnic T'ai group that had, from at least the twelfth century onwards, filtered southwards out of southeast China into mainland Southeast Asia, spreading across the northern mountains of Vietnam, and then moving into the Mekong River Valley and the Bangkok plain area. The Lao branch settled along the Mekong River and came to dominate both sides of the Mekong, from the China–Burma–Thailand–Laos border region in the north, to the Khong Falls on the border with modern-day Cambodia. Lao history and identity have been defined by the Mekong River and, although there was a period of relative Lao political unity under the shadowy kingdom of Lan Xang from the fourteenth to the sixteenth centuries, the Laotian area was, after the early eighteenth century, divided into separate principalities stretched along the Mekong. Principal among these were the kingdoms of Luang Prabang, Vientiane (or Vieng Chan) and Champassak. The relationship between these riverine Lao states and the patchwork of mountain minority peoples living in the eastern foothills of the Annamite Cordillera has been marked historically by intense mutual suspicion and – on the part of the Theravada Buddhist Lao people – contempt for their uncivilized neighbours.

The history of modern Laos has been dominated by the fact that the Mekong River area is sandwiched between what became – particularly in the course of the eighteenth century – two powerful regional states: Siam/ Thailand and Vietnam. The mountainous barrier of the Annamite Cordillera, however, generally protected Laos from Vietnamese expansion, and the primary threat to the Lao states in the eighteenth century came from the Chakkri dynasty of Siam. In the course of the late eighteenth century and the nineteenth century, the kingdom of Siam steadily absorbed the Khorat plateau region and the kingdom of Vientiane and established a protectorate over Champassak and, by the later nineteenth century, it had asserted control over the northern Mekong kingdom of Luang Prabang.

This Siamese expansion into the Mekong region increasingly alarmed the French who had, over the years 1858 to 1885, gained control over Vietnam and Cambodia. The French suspected that Siam was effectively a client-state of Great Britain; any expansion of Siamese power, therefore, was perceived by them as a *de facto* expansion of British influence. In order to safeguard their strategic flank in Vietnam, between 1887 and 1895 the French negotiated protectorate agreements with the Lao states and statelets on the east bank of the Mekong, and (in 1893) forced the Siamese to accept this situation. In a subsequent treaty of 1904, the west bank province of Sayaboury and the west bank section of Champassak were also ceded by Siam to France. It has subsequently been argued that, whatever its original motives, French imperialism 'saved' Laos from absorption into the Siamese empire. While there may be some truth in this, it should also be noted that the French seizure of the east bank of the Mekong divided the Lao people, and in particular separated the large Lao population of the Khorat plateau region from their brethren across the Mekong River.

Under the French protectorate, Laos became a sleepy backwater of the French empire. Apart from some plantations and silver-mines in the south of the country, economic activity above the subsistence level was minimal, and a Western education was available only to the tiny membership of the traditional Lao elites of the various pre-colonial kingdoms and principalities.

The era of war, nationalism and independence, 1940–1954 It was the Second World War and the defeat of France by Nazi Germany in the summer of 1940 that threw a wholly unprepared Laos into the arena of international politics. The new vulnerability of France tempted a resurgent, ultra-nationalist regime in Siam (now renamed Thailand) to demand from the French Indochina administration the return of its 'lost' territories in Laos and Cambodia. After brief and inconclusive border skirmishes in December 1940 and January 1941, the Thais were able – with the help of the new regional arbiter, Japan – to regain the two trans-Mekong regions of Sayaboury and Champassak, as well as the westernmost provinces of Cambodia.

Thereafter, from 1941 to 1945, the French were forced to acquiesce in agreements with Japan that enabled the latter to use French Indochina as a military base. The French administration, acutely aware of its vulnerability in a Japanese-dominated Southeast Asia, belatedly set out to establish a new 'partnership' with the indigenous elites of Vietnam, Laos and Cambodia. In the case of Laos, this strategy met with some success, since – stimulated by old historic fears as well as recent events – the Lao elite saw a revanchist Thailand as a real threat to Laos' territorial integrity. During the early 1940s, northern Laos was unified under the kingdom of Luang Prabang, and the 'Lao Renovation Movement' was formed, with the primary objectives of building a sense of national unity, and kindling an interest in Lao history and culture. These first steps towards Laotian political unity and the creation of a modern national identity were actively encouraged by the French administration in Laos.

In March 1945, however, the Japanese military staged its *coup de force* and removed the entire French administration throughout Indochina. It then installed 'independent' governments in Vietnam, Laos and Cambodia under the nominal authority of the respective monarchies that had formerly accepted the French protectorate. Hardly had the King of Luang Prabang reluctantly proclaimed the independence of Laos, however, than the Japanese themselves surrendered in August 1945, leaving a vacuum of authority. The nationalist (Kuomintang) Chinese were allocated responsibility for post-surrender arrangements in northern Laos, and Britain's South-East Asia Command for the south. In practice, however, this brief period of Allied military occupation had little long-term impact. The political future of post-war Laos was to be shaped, first, by the emergence of a new Lao nationalist organization, the Lao Issara ('Free Lao') and, second, by the determination of the French to regain control of all Indochina and dictate the shape of future political developments there.

In the period August–October 1945, the Lao Issara movement proclaimed the independence and unity of Laos, and installed a government, with the primary aim of resisting any return of French authority. The Lao political elite was, however, deeply divided. The split was most clearly revealed in the confrontation between Prince Phetsarath, who as the key figure in the Lao Issara government took a resolutely anti-French stand, and the king of Luang Prabang and Laos, Sisavong Vong, who, along with his son Prince Savang Vatthana, believed that the future safety of Laos lay in maintaining a close relationship with the French.

Using Champassak in the south of Laos as a *point d'appui*, the French gradually began a process of reoccupation that culminated in the retaking of Vientiane in April 1946. The Lao Issara government fled to Bangkok, and the French thereafter set about implementing their political plan for Laos. In essence, this involved an increasingly self-governing Laos within an overall framework of French sovereignty. New institutions of government were gradually put in place and, in 1949, Laos was recognized as an independent state within the 'French Union' – the latter being an organization somewhat akin to the British Commonwealth of the time, but one in which the French retained far greater powers, particularly in the areas of defence and foreign policy. In 1953, Laotian independence was 'perfected', and a fully self-governing Royal Lao government (RLG) officially came into being, although the state was still heavily dependent on France in the areas of defence, foreign policy and the economy.

These developments triggered a split in the Laotian nationalist movement that was to dominate political developments in Laos for the next thirty years. By 1949, the bulk of the members of the Lao Issara group in exile in Bangkok had opted to throw in their lot with the new Royal Lao government that was taking shape under French patronage in Vientiane; among these politicians was the 'father of Lao nationalism' and key figure in the post-war politics of Laos, Prince Souvanna Phouma. Another faction of the Lao Issara, however, had already in 1945 established links with the communist

Viet Minh, and had developed a resistance base in southern Laos. When the final split in the Lao Issara came in 1949, this faction formed the nucleus of a rival, anti-French, pro-Viet Minh government – which went under the overall title of Pathet Lao (Lao Nation) and was dominated by the Neo Lao Issara (Free Laos Front) – set up in August 1950 across the Vietnamese border.

Although the Pathet Lao resistance movement was composed largely of Laotian communists, elite dissidents and anti-French minority leaders, it ultimately depended on the political guidance and the military fortunes of the Vietnamese communists, who were at that time engaged in the war against the French. The question of the extent of Pathet Lao dependence on the Vietnamese communists has been shrouded in mystery and deceit. One thing, however, is clear: the existence of a home-grown anti-French resistance movement in Laos lent a cloak of legitimacy to the Viet Minh invasions of northeastern Laos in April and December 1953. It was these invasions, in addition to parallel Viet Minh–Pathet Lao operations launched from the southern Laos panhandle against the Central Highlands of Vietnam, that decisively shifted the strategic advantage in the war in favour of the Viet Minh. From the point of view of the Pathet Lao, these invasions enabled it to establish firm politico-military bases along the whole Vietnamese–Laotian border.

From the Geneva Conference of 1954 to the 'Laos Crisis'   By the beginning of the Geneva Conference in 1954, therefore, there were two Laotian governments claiming national legitimacy: the Royal Lao government created through negotiations with the French; and the Pathet Lao 'resistance' government created under Vietnamese communist patronage in 1950, with its base in the eastern provinces bordering Vietnam.

In the course of the Geneva Conference, however, the status of the Royal Lao government as the internationally recognized Laotian political entity was confirmed, as was its territorial integrity. It was nevertheless stipulated by the powers at the conference that the Pathet Lao should continue to administer the two northeastern provinces of Phong Saly and Houa Phan until a negotiated settlement could be reached between the RLG and the Pathet Lao for the political, administrative and military integration of these two provinces into the Royal Lao government system. It was also agreed that Laos should neither participate in a military alliance, nor allow foreign powers to establish bases on its territory unless it came under direct foreign threat. Laos was, however, allowed to retain its special relationship with France: indeed, it is possible that communist China in particular saw this as the best possible guarantee that the United States would not be able to gain the same kind of foothold in Laos that it had already established in South Vietnam.

In the ensuing years, between 1954 and 1958, three parallel political developments in Laos were eventually to lead to civil war and the eruption of the so-called 'Laos Crisis'. On the political front, a long, tortuous process of negotiation began between the Royal Lao government and the Pathet Lao – negotiations in which Prince Souvanna Phouma played a commanding role. By the end of 1956, an outline agreement for the creation of a coalition government was reached, and by the end of 1957, this coalition government came into being, and the plan for full administrative and military integration was accordingly accelerated.

Behind the scenes, however, other developments were under way that were to sabotage this agreement. On the one side, the United States was determined in this post-Geneva period to draw Laos into its security net that had been formalized by the creation of the South-East Asia Treaty Organization (SEATO) in September 1954. Although Laos' neutralized status, as agreed at the Geneva Conference, prevented the US from openly including Laos within SEATO, American aid to Laos was steadily stepped up; by the mid-1950s, in fact, the United States was, in practice, taking over from France as the key 'patron' of the Royal Lao government.

On the other side, the Pathet Lao organization increasingly acquired the characteristics of a fully orthodox communist-dominated movement. In March 1955 a Laotian communist party, the Lao People's Party, was secretly formed, along with all the usual panoply of a political bureau and a central committee. In 1956 this secret organization created the Lao Patriotic Front (Neo Lao Hak Sat) which was to operate in the open as a leftist 'patriotic' organization, although it was at all times under the control of the Lao People's Party. The steady march towards the creation of a communist Laos in the image of North Vietnam was under way.

In short, all the hopes for the creation of a non-aligned, ideologically neutral, united Laos – hopes that were embodied in the political career of Prince Souvanna Phouma – were crushed between the communist and American agendas. Following the communist coup d'état in Czechoslovakia in 1948, the United States was mistrustful of coalitions that included communists. It therefore regarded the Laotian coalition of November 1957 as the first stage of a communist take-over, from within, of the Laotian government itself. In 1958 and 1959, the Americans, along with their Thai allies who had considerable links with the Lao elite, forced the resignation of Souvanna Phouma, the collapse of the coalition government, and the entrenching of the power of right-wing factions within the political arena and – more important – within the armed forces. In the period from summer 1959 to the spring of 1960, the United States encouraged the creation in Laos of the embryo of the same kind of anti-communist 'bastion' state that had already emerged in Thailand, South Korea and Taiwan. As a consequence of these developments, the civil war in Laos resumed in the summer of 1959, with the Pathet Lao once again seizing exclusive control of their eastern strongholds. By this date, the communist leadership in North Vietnam had decided to embark on a full-scale struggle for the unification of Vietnam.

Since North Vietnam needed to ensure support for, and control over, the insurgency in the south, it needed to secure the access routes running from North to South Vietnam via southern Laos – the 'Ho Chi Minh Trail'.

The Laos Crisis American policy in Laos in the late 1950s was primarily driven by the fear that the Pathet Lao would be able to stage a coup within the Royal Lao government, and therefore ensure that the country would fall to communism virtually without a shot being fired. Counsels were divided, however, over the best policy to ensure the maintenance of a non-communist Laos. This division of opinion centred on the question of the ability of the right wing in Laos to sustain the 'bastion' role that the United States had ascribed to it. The Laotian government and army were perfectly happy to consolidate their political power and absorb ever-increasing doses of American aid; they proved to be remarkably reluctant, however, to confront or check the Pathet Lao. In August 1960, the inherent weakness of the Vientiane regime was further revealed when a neutralist faction in the Royal Lao Army seized power and reinstated Souvanna Phouma.

There now existed three factions in Laos: the Pathet Lao with their headquarters in the northeast; the neutralist government in Vientiane; and the remnants of the previous right-wing regime that had assembled in Savannakhet in south Laos. These developments divided United States policy-makers between those who advocated an attempt to work through Souvanna Phouma to create a new political consensus, and those – particularly the Central Intelligence Agency (CIA) – who advocated full-scale support for the right-wing faction in Savannakhet. The latter policy prevailed, however, and, with considerable logistic help from Thailand, the right-wing faction had by the end of 1960 blasted the neutralists out of Vientiane with the aid of an indiscriminate artillery barrage across the Mekong River.

The recapture of Vientiane proved to be a hollow victory, since it merely had the effect of drawing the neutralists and the Pathet Lao together in a tactical alliance. In the early months of 1961, the neutralist–Pathet Lao coalition seized control of large swathes of territory throughout Laos.

This was the crisis that J. F. Kennedy confronted when he became president. By April 1961, it had become manifestly obvious that the Royal Lao government, though it had the means, did not have the will to resist the Pathet Lao–neutralist alliance. Kennedy's administration was faced with the unpalatable alternatives either of permitting the collapse of the pro-American government, or of initiating a massive intervention by SEATO forces, with American troops playing the key role.

There were two dimensions to the crisis that the United States faced. At the regional, Asian level, developments in Laos proved that pro-Western governments in Asia were as vulnerable to internal subversion and their own inherent weaknesses as they were to Korean War-style invasion. This raised a question-mark over the whole tendency of the United States to rely on 'top-down' nation-building strategies. It gave credence to the view among Kennedy's closest advisers that, if the Americans were to win the struggle for support in the Third World, they would have to use more subtle, localized strategies based on the needs of the rural hinterland rather than on the selfish interests of unstable and often corrupt elites.

At the international level of the global confrontation with the USSR and the communist world, the United States found itself trapped in a position roughly analogous to that of the Soviet Union in the Cuban Missile Crisis about a year and a half later. The United States had committed itself to a position in Laos that it could not maintain without taking a massive military gamble with unforeseeable consequences. This they were not, in the end, prepared to do; they were not prepared to risk global confrontation – possibly war – in order to sustain a corrupt and inept regime in Laos.

The only escape from the dismal alternatives of war or humiliation was negotiation. In May 1961, the Geneva Conference was reconvened with the remit of finding a solution to the Laos Crisis. Since the Soviet Union and China were as reluctant as the United States to allow the situation in Laos to blow up into a full-scale global conflict, a consensus rapidly built up behind the idea of putting together a new coalition government in which rightists, neutralists and the Pathet Lao would be represented, and of reaffirming Laos' neutral status. With the help of a considerable amount of offstage American sabre-rattling – which was directed against the Pathet Lao *and* a recalcitrant right-wing faction that could not bring itself to believe that it had lost American favour – a settlement along these lines was eventually reached in July 1962. Cynics could not help observing that – after all the alarums and excursions of American policy – the settlement looked remarkably similar to the coalition that the Americans had helped to destroy in 1958–59.

Laos and the Vietnam War The coalition agreement reached in July 1962 was an apparent triumph for Souvanna Phouma and that significant section of educated Lao opinion that wanted to see a united, ideologically neutral Laos, insulated from the Cold War, and protected from the machinations of its predatory neighbours.

The tragedy for Laos was that the kind of settlement the Geneva agreements tried to create in Laos had been overtaken by events long before the final arrangements were made in mid-1962. By 1962, the insurgency in South Vietnam was already seriously threatening the survival of the regime there. The 'Ho Chi Minh Trail' through the mountains of eastern Laos was firmly established, and the main priority for the North Vietnamese patrons of the Pathet Lao was the maintenance of firm and exclusive control of the eastern provinces of Laos. In return, the North Vietnamese were tacitly – not openly – prepared to acquiesce in effective American control of the Mekong river area in Laos – an area that was seen by the United States as strategically vital for the security of Thailand.

Between the strategic priorities of the United States and North Vietnam, as they geared up for full-scale conflict in South Vietnam, the Laotian neutralists were squeezed out of existence. Laotian neutralist politicians and their armed force units gradually slid either into the Royal Lao or the Pathet Lao camps. In the same period (1963–64) the coalition government once again broke up, and the condition of *de facto* partition and civil war was resumed. Against his inclinations, but bowing to the irresistible realities of the Indochina situation, Souvanna Phouma now presided over a Royal Lao government that was, in all but name, an American protectorate. Conversely, the Pathet Lao region, particularly the 'Ho Chi Minh Trail' area, had become a strategic adjunct of North Vietnam's war effort. The fate of Laos – that 'Shangri-La' for those who had witnessed its unearthly beauty before it had fallen victim to ideology and geopolitics – would now be decided by the outcome of the Vietnam War.

2. The insurgency in South Vietnam and United States intervention, 1954–65

In June 1954, Ngo Dinh Diem was appointed prime minister of the State of Vietnam – what could now be called South Vietnam. Between 1954 and 1956, Diem consolidated his regime with considerable American help. But from 1956 to 1960, remnants of the old Viet Minh insurgency in the south, along with other local dissident elements, waged an increasingly effective war against the Diem regime. The United States accelerated its aid to the regime between 1960 and 1963, but decided by the latter date that the major impediment to improvements in the south lay in Diem's regime itself. After the assassination of Diem in November 1963, the situation did not improve, however, but deteriorated: ever-expanding insurgency in the provinces was matched by political instability in Saigon, where military juntas alternated with short-lived civilian governments. In 1964, the United States tried to retrieve the situation by an expanded bombing campaign directed against the 'Ho Chi Minh Trail' in Laos, and then against the North itself. The aim of this campaign was to force the North to stop its aid for the insurgency in the South, and thus give South Vietnam time to stabilize politically and gradually gain control of the provinces. By early 1965, however, it was clear that nothing short of a direct American take-over of the war could save South Vietnam and, by the end of 1965, around 150,000 American troops were in South Vietnam.

Bernard B. Fall was an academic and journalist who saw these events unfolding. It is the good fortune of historians that they can be wise after the event; indeed, that is their job. It is less usual to be, like Bernard Fall, wise during the event. In the following article, he gets to the heart of the problem that was faced by the Americans and the South Vietnamese: the battle for control of the villages and hamlets. His article is followed by a US

Department of State 'White Paper' (a government document for public consumption, justifying government policy), produced in February 1965, and giving the official American version of the history of South Vietnam after 1954. It was designed, of course, to provide a justification for United States bombing of the North, and for greater American military intervention in the South. It is interesting to compare these two versions of events.

One point that should be noted is the key role that communist China played in American strategy towards Vietnam. When American troops came too near to the Chinese frontier during the Korean War in 1950, Chinese troops massively intervened. It was fully anticipated that the same thing would happen if, for example, the United States directly invaded North Vietnam. Throughout the period from 1958 to the end of the 1960s, China was regarded as an unpredictable power, driven by an extremist anti-Western ideology. It was China, not the USSR, that was seen by the United States as the global 'rogue power' during this period.

Bernard B. Fall, 'The Roots of Conflict' (January 1965), in B. B. Fall, *Vietnam Witness 1953–1966* (London: Pall Mall Press, 1966). Excerpts taken from pages 275–92.

As this article is written, an insurgent group which originally had engaged in little else but lightly armed banditry has blossomed out into a full-fledged national liberation movement; and, as ten years earlier, its effects have outstripped by far its own Vietnamese national context to affect the whole Indochinese peninsula, including Thailand.

Much has been written, on both sides of the ideological fence, about the Vietnamese emergency that is wholly or partly inaccurate. The present situation in Viet-Nam is not due entirely to North Vietnamese aggressiveness, nor can the blame be laid fully at the feet of the oppressive and woefully inefficient Ngo Dinh Diem regime. The truth, as almost always in such cases, lies somewhere in between. A case can probably be made for the assertion that the mistakes of the Diem regime gave rise to enough discontent for the ever-watchful North Vietnamese Communists to attempt to give that discontent a shape and dimension which would turn the situation to their advantage. And that they would succeed so well at their enterprise as they have so far must be credited to the erroneous estimates of the Indochina situation made in many Western chanceries since 1954 ...

The Final Declaration ... stipulated that Viet-Nam as a whole would be reunified through 'general elections [to] be held in July, 1956, under the supervision of an international commission'. But almost from the start the Ngo Dinh Diem government in Saigon repeatedly declared itself 'not bound by the Geneva agreement signed in contempt' of Vietnamese national interests. The dissolution of the French High Command in Indochina – that is, the actual signatory of the cease-fire – on April 26, 1956 (before the July,

1956, deadline) provided some grounds for Saigon's argument that it was not bound by the obligations signed by a French general on its behalf ...

After the July, 1956, deadline the North Vietnamese Communist regime had little reason to treat South Viet-Nam with kid gloves. What could have possibly deterred it from beginning an extended campaign of subversion was what deterred similar attempts in the other two divided countries, Germany and Korea. In the former, that deterrent was the solidity of the German economic and political fabric even before the re-birth of West German armed might; and in the latter it is a 600,000-man standing army of such strength (and directly backed up by U.S. ground forces on the cease-fire line) as to make any attempt at undermining it through pinprick attacks a fairly hopeless enterprise.

Viet-Nam south of the 17th parallel at first possessed neither of those two assets, but the acquiring of economic and political stability was within her power, and provision of an adequate military shield for her was within the means of her allies. In the end, she was to get neither. Contrary to all the mythology on the subject – for instance, that 'the years 1956 to 1960 produced something close to an economic miracle' – South Viet-Nam's economic recovery had floundered badly. In the words of Denis Warner, an Australian observer who was otherwise inclined to view events in South Viet-Nam with considerable optimism: 'The much-vaunted rural help program did not exist. Land reform was a flop. Industry was insignificant.' Administratively, South Viet-Nam's government purely and simply resisted any deep seated reforms. In spite of extensive American help in that field, the Vietnamese bureaucracy remained largely mandarin in outlook, and the overlay of corruption and political favoritism which emanated from the Ngo Dinh family only made matters worse. And finally, there was the matter of the poor, misled, badly equipped and badly trained Army of the Republic of Viet-Nam (ARVN).

The departing and beaten French had left the ARVN a shambles, despite the fact that some of its units had fought heroically (and many say, better than now) alongside the French to the bitter end. Until 1954, most of the technical and staff services of the ARVN had been handled directly by the French Union Forces, and no Vietnamese officer had actually commanded more than a regiment in combat. With the changeover to American advisers and matériel, the ARVN also changed its whole military purpose. Until 1961, the defense of South Viet-Nam was based on the assumption of a Korean-like across-the-parallel attack. The secondary assumption then was that, as in Korea, such an open onslaught would have to be dealt with by the SEATO coalition specifically created in September, 1954, for that purpose – if not by the United Nations. In such a case, the mission of the ARVN was simply to delay the advance of the Communist invaders long enough for the Allied counterthrust to come into play; say two to three weeks. That, so the assumption went, could be handled by a 100,000-strong Vietnamese force abundantly provided with armor and artillery. Paramilitary forces needed for the control of the countryside were either disbanded or left without American aid or training.

The effects of what I have elsewhere called the 'Korean trauma' were not long in coming and also aroused the concern of other observers. Colonel H. C. B. Cook, a former British military attaché in Saigon, wrote in 1962 that Vietnamese officers talked to him about the 'American-type war we train for and the Indo-China war we will have to fight' ...

What is being faced in Viet-Nam is *revolutionary warfare*. In revolutionary warfare, small-war tactics are being used as the physical environment warrants, but for a political purpose and in a highly politicized environment. That is why the British 'won' (after thirteen years) in Malaya and decisively 'lost' in Cyprus and Palestine. In the case of Malaya (or the Mau-Mau case [in Kenya], for that matter) the insurgents had not truly succeeded in politicizing their civilian environment in their favor. Thus, tactics used in Malaya were not successful in Cyprus and are not, to all appearances, in South Viet-Nam, as the near-disastrous experience with the 'strategic hamlets' [see Glossary] showed. The Communist adversary, on the other hand, had made his judgment very early in the game on what particular target within the South Vietnamese body politic would yield him the highest dividends in *effective population control* – not military supremacy. And that target, as during the First Indochina War, was the village administration, since 85 per cent of the Vietnamese population lives in village units of about a thousand souls ...

Personal investigations showed that in May, 1953, the 180,000 French Union troops in North Viet-Nam fully controlled 1,803 villages and towns out of a total of approximately 5,780; another 1,843 were considered 'unsafe', and the remaining 2,143 were under effective Communist control. In the province of Hung-Yen, located in the center of the Tongking Delta, three townships out of 511 were in French-Nationalist [State of Vietnam] hands by March, 1954. Those villages had by and large been wrested from non-Communist control through a variety of tactics ranging from the assassination of the village chiefs to friendly persuasion of the villagers.

The same efficient tactics were employed four years later against South Viet-Nam, and with the same resounding success. The fact that this was not recognized in time is the great tragedy of South Viet-Nam's present plight. Yet, the signs were clearly visible for everyone who wanted to see them. Field research in South Viet-Nam in 1957 already showed disquieting evidence of a deliberate 'kill-pattern' of village chiefs and officials; they were not killed in random fashion – as in the case of widespread banditry or lawlessness – but in certain key provinces obviously destined to become 'resistance bases'. I was to report in 1958 that 'guerrilla activities in South Viet-Nam during 1957 and 1958 no longer represent a last-ditch fight of dispersed sect or Communist rebel remnants. On the contrary, they have taken on a pattern of their own (including) gradual "insulation" of the central authorities from direct contact with the grass roots.'

That this view was far from being accepted is shown by many statements made then and later by many experts in Vietnamese affairs. Professor Wesley Fishel, an American former senior civilian adviser to the late President Diem, averred in August, 1958, that South Viet-Nam 'can be classed as one of the most stable and peaceful countries of Asia today'. Another adviser, Wolf Ladejinsky, dismissed the insurgent effort as being the work of 'local Viet-Minh agents in remote areas'. A highly reputable British observer, Mr. P. J. Honey, stated as late as 1963 that 'by 1959 ... President Diem had consolidated his position and effectively silenced most of the opposition to his regime'. What had indeed been silenced was what could have become the 'loyal opposition' in Viet-Nam; the Communist cadres on the other hand, were playing havoc with the local administration. A few figures will give an idea of what is meant. During the year 1957, a total of 472 small officials were killed by the Communists, according to a statement made by President Diem himself. That figure about doubled during 1958–59, and, according to a conservative American source, 'since the middle of January [1960], terrorists led by Communists have been killing on the average fifteen government officials of South Viet-Nam each week'. On May 25, 1961, the late President Kennedy, in an address to both Houses of Congress, stated that the Communists (Viet-Cong) in South Viet-Nam had killed '4,000 civil officers' during the previous year, or more than ten a day.

In other words, by the time the VC became an open military challenge to the South Vietnamese regime and its American advisers, they had literally taken over effective control of much of the South Vietnamese hinterland from the legal government. This was also confirmed by a former U.S. government adviser in Viet-Nam, Professor Robert Scigliano, who stated that by late 1962, 'the Communists had in fact extended their influence, in varying degrees, to about 80 per cent of the Vietnamese countryside'. It is, therefore, highly immaterial to attempt to trace back Communist intentions at subverting South Viet-Nam to a particular meeting of the North Vietnamese Communist Party [Lao Dong] Central Committee in May, 1959, or to a particular resolution of the same party's Third National congress, held in Hanoi in September, 1960. Long before those dates the Second Indochina War had assumed its basic pattern ... By applying civilian rather than unrealistic military standards of effective control – such as in the field of taxation – the present situation in South Viet-Nam appears to show striking parallels to the situation which prevailed in the Tongking Delta under French aegis in 1953 ...

In the face of that kind of generalized threat, the actual military threat was comparatively secondary, despite its more spectacular and newsworthy aspects. Here again, as ten years earlier, the military setbacks assumed a certain gravity only because they occurred against a background of political disintegration. Dien Bien Phu, as a military setback, involved only 4 per cent of the French battle force and the equipment lost was replaced by U.S. aid deliveries even before the battle was over. But what made Dien Bien Phu the disaster it became was that the Vietnamese civil administration was then, as now, on the verge of countrywide collapse ...

This estimate of the South Vietnamese situation, based on verifiable data rather than wishful thinking or personal opinions, has deliberately avoided taking into account such unassessable elements as rivalries between Vietnamese generals and civilian politicians, or the possible negative influence of Buddhism or of the South Vietnamese trade unions. Yet, on the basis of the known and verifiable facts alone, it can be stated that the chances of a Western success in South Viet-Nam similar to that achieved by Britain in Malaya or by the United States in the Philippines [in association with the Philippines Government against the Hukbalahap communists in the early 1950s] are, for the time being, somewhat remote. In both Malaya and the Philippines there was a very early recognition of the nature of the problem, and a fairly rapid build-up of economic, social, and political counterforces. In Viet-Nam, such recognition was absent, and similar steps now being taken there meet with commensurately little success.

Realization of that fact has produced a new strategy designed to re-establish, through military means, the security conditions necessary for the various civilian reforms to become established. There is nothing basically new about that strategy. Many other specialists in that field have advocated variants of it in the past. But in the past it has required a ratio of pacification forces versus insurgents that is simply not available in Viet-Nam today. In Malaya, British and Malayan forces had achieved a superiority ratio of 50 to 1; in Cyprus, British forces had achieved a 110 to 1 ratio, and in Algeria the French had reached 10 to 1. The present ratio in South Viet-Nam is 4.5 to 1; and the French ratio in the First Indochina War was an incredibly low 1.2 to 1, which (all other matters being equal) would suffice to explain France's ultimate defeat.

Obviously, then, an unconditional surrender victory over the Viet-Cong – if that is what is contemplated – will sooner or later require *political* decisions in Washington ... as to how the South Vietnamese war theater is to be provided with the requisite troop ratio if South Viet-Nam's manpower and, above all, cadre reservoir, cannot provide it.

This leaves the political or military observer of the Vietnamese scene with the temptation to look for solutions that might perhaps be less costly in manpower, such as naval or air intervention against North Viet-Nam. The temptation, assuredly, is great, for North Viet-Nam is no guerrilla base but an organized state with conventional targets such as cities, industries, and railroads. But such a policy raises two questions, at least: (1) would not such a policy have the net effect of 'unleashing' upon sorely pressed South Viet-Nam a large part of North Viet-Nam's regular combat divisions, whose deadly effectiveness needs no additional substantiation, and (2) could such an operation be attempted without a Red Chinese counterescalation which, in turn, could bring Russia into the conflict as an albeit reluctant supporter of her Asian Communist allies? All firm answers to both questions are hardly more than wishful thinking.

There are indications that North Viet-Nam, and perhaps even Communist China, are betting on a possible internal collapse of organized government in South Viet-Nam, in which case that country may well fall into the hands of a National Liberation Front regime by default. The example of the collapse of the Chinese Nationalist regime on the mainland in the autumn of 1949 serves as a grim reminder that countries can be lost to revolutionary warfare even without having been first negotiated away at the conference table.

US Department of State, 'White Paper' (Department of State, publication 7839, February 1965).

A brief history of Hanoi's campaign of aggression against South Viet-Nam While negotiating an end to the Indochina War at Geneva in 1954, the Communists were making plans to take over all former French territory in Southeast Asia. When Viet-Nam was partitioned, thousands of carefully selected party members were ordered to remain in place in the South and keep their secret apparatus intact to help promote Hanoi's cause. Arms and ammunition were stored away for future use. Guerrilla fighters rejoined their families to await the party's call. Others withdrew to remote jungle and mountain hideouts. The majority – an estimated 90,000 – were moved to North Viet-Nam.

Hanoi's original calculation was that all of Viet-Nam would fall under its control without resort to force. For this purpose, Communist cadres were ordered to penetrate official and non-official agencies, to propagandize and sow confusion, and generally to use all means short of open violence to aggravate war-torn conditions and to weaken South Viet-Nam's government and social fabric.

South Viet-Nam's refusal to fall in with Hanoi's scheme for peaceful takeover came as a heavy blow to the Communists. Meantime, the Government had stepped up efforts to blunt Viet-Cong subversion and to expose Communist agents. Morale in the Communist organization in the South dropped sharply. Defections were numerous.

Among South Vietnamese, hope rose that their nation could have a peaceful and independent future, free of Communist domination. The country went to work. The years after 1955 were a period of steady progress and growing prosperity.

Food production levels of the prewar years were reached and surpassed. While per capita food output was dropping 10 per cent in the North from 1956 to 1960, it rose 20 per cent in the South. By 1963, it had risen 30 per cent – despite the disruption in the countryside caused by intensified Viet-Cong military attacks and terrorism. The authorities in the North admitted openly to continuing annual failures to achieve food production goals.

Production of textiles increased in the South more than 20 per cent in one year (1958). In the same year, South Viet-Nam's sugar crop increased more than 100 per cent. Despite North Viet-Nam's vastly larger industrial complex, South Viet-Nam's per capita gross national product in 1960 was estimated at $110 a person while it was only $70 in the North.

More than 900,000 refugees who had fled from Communist rule in the North were successfully settled in South Viet-Nam. An agrarian reform program was instituted. The elementary school population nearly quadrupled between 1956 and 1960. And so it went – a record of steady improvement in the lives of the people. It was intolerable for the rulers in Hanoi; under peaceful conditions, the South was outstripping the North. They were losing the battle of peaceful competition and decided to use violence and terror to gain their ends.

After 1956 Hanoi rebuilt, reorganized, and expanded its covert political and military machinery in the South. Defectors were replaced by trained personnel from party ranks in the North. Military units and political cells were enlarged and were given new leaders, equipment, and intensified training. Recruitment was pushed. In short, Hanoi and its forces in the South prepared to take by force and violence what they had failed to achieve by other means.

By 1958 the use of terror by the Viet-Cong increased appreciably. It was used both to win prestige and to back up demands for support from the people, support that political and propaganda appeals had failed to produce. It was also designed to embarrass the Government in Saigon and raise doubts about its ability to maintain internal order and to assure the personal security of its people. From 1959 through 1961, the pace of Viet-Cong terrorism and armed attacks accelerated substantially.

The situation at the end of 1961 was so grave that the Government of the Republic of Viet-Nam asked the United States for increased military assistance. That request was met. Meantime, the program of strategic hamlets, designed to improve the peasant's livelihood and give him some protection against Viet-Cong harassment and pressure, was pushed energetically.

But the Viet-Cong did not stand still. To meet the changing situation, they tightened their organization and adopted new tactics, with increasing emphasis on terrorism, sabotage, and armed attacks by small groups. They also introduced from the North technicians in fields such as armor and antiaircraft. Heavier weapons were sent in to the regular guerrilla forces.

The military and insurgency situation was complicated by a quite separate internal political struggle in South Viet-Nam, which led in November, 1963, to the removal of the Diem government and its replacement with a new one. Effective power was placed in the hands of a Military Revolutionary Council. There have been a number of changes in the leadership and composition of the Government in Saigon in the ensuing period.

These internal developments and distractions gave the Viet-Cong an invaluable opportunity, and they took advantage of it ...

North Viet-Nam: base for conquest of the South   The Third Lao Dong Party Congress in Hanoi in September, 1960, set forth two tasks for its members: 'to carry out the socialist revolution in North Viet-Nam' and 'to liberate South Viet-Nam'.

The resolutions of the congress described the effort to destroy the legal Government in South Viet-Nam as follows: 'The revolution in the South is a protracted, hard, and complex process of struggle, combining many forms of struggle of great activity and flexibility, ranging from lower to higher, and taking as its basis the building, consolidation, and development of the revolutionary power of the masses.'

At the September meeting the Communist leaders in the North called for [the] formation of 'a broad national united front'. Three months later Hanoi announced [the] creation of the 'Front for Liberation of the South'. This is the organization that communist propaganda now credits with guiding the forces of subversion in the South; it is pictured as an organization established and run by the people in the South themselves. At the 1960 Lao Dong Party Congress the tone was different. Then, even before the front existed, the Communist leaders were issuing orders for the group that was being organized behind the scenes in Hanoi. 'This front must rally ...'; 'The aims of its struggle are ... '; 'The front must carry out ... '; – this is the way Hanoi and the Communist Party addressed the 'Liberation Front' even before its founding.

The Liberation Front is Hanoi's creation; it is neither independent nor southern, and what it seeks is not liberation but subjugation of the South ...

Organization, direction, command, and control of the attack on South Viet-Nam are centered in Hanoi   The VC [Viet Cong] military and political apparatus in South Viet-Nam is an extension of an elaborate military and political structure in North Viet-Nam which directs and supplies it with the tools for conquest. The Ho Chi Minh regime has shown that it is ready to allocate every resource that can be spared – whether it be personnel, funds, or equipment – to the cause of overthrowing the legitimate Government in South Viet-Nam and of bringing all Viet-Nam under Communist rule.

Political direction and control of the Viet-Cong is supplied by the Lao Dong Party, i.e., the Communist Party, led by Ho Chi Minh. Party agents are responsible for indoctrination, recruitment, political training, propaganda, anti-Government demonstrations, and other activities of a political nature. The considerable intelligence-gathering facilities of the party are also at the disposal of the Viet-Cong.

Over-all direction of the VC movement is the responsibility of the Central Committee of the Lao Dong Party. Within the Central Committee a special Reunification Department has been established. This has replaced the 'Committee for Supervision of the South' mentioned in intelligence reports two years ago. It lays down broad strategy for the movement to conquer South Viet-Nam.

Until March, 1962, there were two principal administrative divisions in the VC structure in the South. One was the Inter-zone of South-Central Viet-Nam (sometimes called Interzone 5); the other was the Nambo [Southern] Region. In a 1962 reorganization these were merged into one, called the Central Office for South Viet-Nam [COSVN]. The Central Committee, through its Reunification Department, issues directives to the Central Office, which translates them into specific orders for the appropriate subordinate command.

Under the Central Office are six regional units (V through IX) plus the special zone of Saigon/Cholon/Gia Dinh. A regional committee responsible to the Central Office directs VC activities in each region. Each regional committee has specialized units responsible for liaison, propaganda, training, personnel, subversive activities, espionage, military bases, and the like.

Below each regional committee are similarly structured units at the province and district levels. At the base of the Communist pyramid are the individual party cells, which may be organized on a geographic base or within social or occupational groups. The elaborateness of the party unit and the extent to which it operates openly or underground is determined mainly by the extent of VC control over the area concerned ...

Hanoi supplies the key personnel for the armed aggression against South Viet-Nam   The hard core of the Communist forces attacking South Viet-Nam are men trained in North Viet-Nam. They are ordered into the South and remain under the military discipline of the Military High Command in Hanoi. Special training camps operated by the North Vietnamese army give political and military training to the infiltrators. Increasingly the forces sent into the South are native North Vietnamese who have never seen South Viet-Nam. A special infiltration unit, the 70th Transportation Group, is responsible for moving men from North Viet-Nam into the South via infiltration trails through Laos. Another special unit, the maritime infiltration group, sends weapons and supplies and agents by sea into the South.

The infiltration rate has been increasing. From 1959 to 1960, when Hanoi was establishing its infiltration pipeline, at least 1,800 men, and possibly 2,700 more, moved into South Viet-Nam from the North. The flow increased to a minimum of 3,700 in 1961 and at least 5,400 in 1962. There was a modest decrease in 1963 to 4,200 confirmed infiltrators, though later evidence is likely to raise this figure.

For 1964 the evidence is still incomplete. However, it already shows that a minimum of 4,400 infiltrators entered the South, and it is estimated more than 3,000 others were sent in.

There is usually a time lag between the entry of infiltrating troops and the discovery of clear evidence they have entered. This fact, plus collateral evidence of increased use of the infiltration routes, suggests strongly that 1964 was probably the year of greatest infiltration so far.

Thus, since 1959, nearly 20,000 VC officers, soldiers, and technicians are known to have entered South Viet-Nam under orders from Hanoi. Additional information indicates that an estimated 17,000 more infiltrators were dispatched to the South by the regime in Hanoi during the past six years. It can reasonably be assumed that still other infiltration groups have entered the South for which there is no evidence yet available.

To some the level of infiltration from the North may seem modest in comparison with the total size of the Armed Forces of the Republic of Viet-Nam. But one-for-one calculations are totally misleading in the kind of warfare going on in Viet-Nam. First, a high proportion of infiltrators from the North are well-trained officers, cadres, and specialists. Second, it has long been realized that in guerrilla combat the burdens of defense are vastly heavier than those of attack. In Malaysia, the Philippines, and elsewhere a ratio of at least 10-to-1 in favor of the forces of order was required to meet successfully the threat of the guerrillas' hit-and-run tactics.

In the calculus of guerrilla warfare the scale of North Vietnamese infiltration into the South takes on a very different meaning. For the infiltration of 5,000 guerrilla fighters in a given year is the equivalent of marching perhaps 50,000 regular troops across the border, in terms of the burden placed on the defenders.

Above all, the number of proved and probable infiltrators from the North should be seen in relation to the size of the VC forces. It is now estimated that the Viet-Cong number approximately 35,000 so-called hard-core forces, and another 60,000–80,000 local forces. It is thus apparent that infiltrators from the North – allowing for casualties – make up the majority of the so-called hard-core Viet-Cong. *Personnel from the North, in short, are now and have always been the backbone of the entire VC operation* [emphasis added].

It is true that many of the lower-level elements of the VC forces are recruited within South Viet-Nam. However, the thousands of reported cases of VC kidnappings and terrorism make it abundantly clear that threats and other pressures by the Viet-Cong play a major party in such recruitment.

The infiltration process The infiltration routes supply hard-core units with most of their officers and noncommissioned personnel. This source helps fill the gaps left by battle casualties, illness, and defection and insures continued control by Hanoi. Also, as the nature of the conflict has changed, North Viet-Nam has supplied the Viet-Cong with technical specialists via the infiltration routes. These have included men trained in armor and ordnance, antiaircraft, and communications as well as medical corpsmen and transport experts.

There is no single infiltration route from the North to South Viet-Nam. But by far the biggest percentage of infiltrators follow the same general course. The principal training center for North Vietnamese army men assigned to join the Viet-Cong has been at Xuan Mai near Hanoi. Recently captured

Viet-Cong have also reported an infiltration training camp at Thanh Hoa. After completion of their training course – which involves political and propaganda work as well as military subjects – infiltrating units are moved to Vinh on the east coast. Many have made stopovers at a staging area in Dong Hoi where additional training is conducted. From there they go by truck to the Laos border.

Then, usually after several days' rest, infiltrators move southward through Laos. Generally they move along the Laos–South Viet-Nam border. Responsibility for infiltration from North Viet-Nam through Laos belongs to the 70th Transportation Group of the North Vietnamese army. After a time the infiltration groups turn eastward, entering South Viet-Nam in Quang Nam, Quang Tri, Thua Thien, Kontum, or another of the border provinces.

The Communists have established regular lanes for infiltration with way-stations established about one day's march apart. The way-stations are equipped to quarter and feed the Viet-Cong passing through. Infiltrators who suffer from malaria or other illnesses stay at the stations until they recover sufficiently to join another passing group moving south.

Conclusion   The evidence presented in this report could be multiplied many times with similar examples of the drive of the Hanoi regime to extend its rule over South Viet-Nam.

The record is conclusive. It establishes beyond question that North Viet-Nam is carrying out a carefully conceived plan of aggression against the South. It shows that North Viet-Nam has intensified its efforts in the years since it was condemned by the International Control Commission [set up by the Geneva Conference]. It proves that Hanoi continues to press its systematic program of armed aggression into South Viet-Nam. This aggression violates the United Nations Charter. It is directly contrary to the Geneva Accords of 1954 and of 1962 to which North Viet-Nam is a party. It shatters the peace of Southeast Asia. It is a fundamental threat to the freedom and security of South Viet-Nam.

The people of South Viet-Nam have chosen to resist this threat. At their request, the United States has taken its place beside them in their defensive struggle.

The United States seeks no territory, no military bases, no favored position. But we have learned the meaning of aggression elsewhere in the postwar world, and we have met it.

If peace can be restored in South Viet-Nam, the United States will be ready at once to reduce its military involvement. But it will not abandon friends who want to remain free. It will do what must be done to help them. The choice now between peace and continued and increasingly destructive conflict is one for the authorities in Hanoi to make.

3. Indonesia and 'Guided Democracy': a revolution in search of an Idea

In 1959, President Sukarno formally inaugurated his 'Guided Democracy' regime. In constitutional terms, this involved the ending of the parliamentary democracy structure that had fitfully operated since the elections of 1955; the imposition of a state of martial law throughout the country; and a return to the 1945 constitution that essentially concentrated power in the presidency. Using his charismatic status as much as his formal powers, Sukarno relied on an appointed cabinet, a supreme advisory council and a national planning council as bodies that would represent all the political and social forces in Indonesia without the destructive party conflict brought about by elections. At least in the early years of 'Guided Democracy', however, the armed forces provided the vital glue that held the system together, particularly in the regions.

This authoritarian structure was, nevertheless, designed to serve a dynamic and revolutionary process. Sukarno's ultimate objective, as became clearer in the years after 1959, was to use a centralized system to mobilize all 'progressive' political and social forces in the country against 'reactionary' elements, both within and beyond Indonesia. At the core of Sukarno's thinking was his belief that the unity of Indonesia could be maintained only if the spirit of revolution and struggle that had been generated in 1945 could be recaptured and harnessed for the solution of Indonesia's current problems.

Sukarno's Independence Day speech in August 1964 is in many senses a classic statement of his political concepts. Like many of Sukarno's speeches, the cold words on the page deprived of Sukarno's oratorical skills give an impression of rambling and repetition. The following selected excerpts will, however, attempt to extract the essential themes.

This speech by Sukarno is important in itself, since it encapsulates many of the central themes of 'Guided Democracy': themes which were – though often expressed in less extreme terms – the common currency of the rhetoric of anti-colonialist populism at the time. It also indicates the significant shift that Sukarno took to the radical Left in the period between 1963 and 1965.

President Sukarno, 'A Year of Living Dangerously' (*Tahun 'Vivere Pericoloso'*). Extract from an address given on 17 August 1964 (Djakarta: Department of Information, 1964).

Sisters and Brothers!

Today is the 17th August 1964.

Every 17th August has its own significance, its own special significance. Amongst the twelve months of the year, August is the most sacred for us. America and France hold the month of July sacred, China and the Soviet Union the month of October – we hold the month of August sacred, the month of the Proclamation [of Independence]. And in rhythm to the roar of the waves of history, every 17th of August has its own distinctive traits, its own reverberation, its own significance ...

Lessons from past experiences and the direction for what lies ahead, these two matters are of the utmost importance in a Revolution which is still taking place – Revolution which at bottom is a course, a process, a moving. *Even more* for a Revolution which is being encircled, like our Revolution at present, a Revolution which people are trying to destroy, a Revolution which must keep its head above the ocean of subversion and intervention from the imperialists and colonialists – a Revolution which has to save its body and its soul from the most appalling attacks from all directions – from without, from within, from right, from left, from above, from below. Such are the conditions we are experiencing, such is the test we are passing through! The imperialists' batterings go on persistently, the dogs and wolves around us bark and bay! But the Indonesian Revolution *must march on*, and *indeed, does march on*! We deal with the imperialists' batterings. We take no notice of the bayings of dogs and wolves. We are not afraid of anything! Never mind about the barking of dogs, even a crack of thunder from the skies does not make a single one of our hairs stand on end!

Yes! History marches on. Has history ever come to a stop? The Indonesian Revolution too marches on. The Indonesian Revolution is not going to come to a stop. Imperialism will be shattered to pieces, the dogs and wolves will be silent, but the Indonesian Revolution is going to march on, and will be *victorious*! In Jogjakarta in '48, when imperialism was pounding at the Republic of Indonesia, in Jogjakarta in 1948, under the flickering light of a candle I once wrote that the Indonesian Revolution is 'razende inspiratie van de Indonesische geschiedenis' – the raving inspiration of Indonesian history. Whoever could put History to death, whoever could put the Indonesian Revolution to death, that raving inspiration of History? ...

No Revolution can truly rage if its People do not carry out that Revolution with *romanticist* notions. No Revolution can keep its soul if its People cannot take enemy attacks as the romanticism of Revolution, and parry enemy attacks and pound the enemy to pieces as the romanticism of Revolution. No Revolution can continue to hold its head high if its People are not prepared to make the necessary sacrifices, with their heads also held high, even with a smile on their lips because they consider those sacrifices the romanticism of Revolution. Revolution is a chain of events of striking and being struck, a chain of events of pounding and being pounded, a chain of events of destruction and construction. Striking and being struck, pounding and being pounded, destroying and constructing – this alternation must be felt as the rhythm of the romanticism of Revolution ...

The rhythm of Revolution! Yes, it was this notion that brought me to the idea of the *Romanticism of Revolution*. The romanticism of my own personal struggle also. But in the very first place romanticism of the national struggle, the romanticism of the struggle of mankind in The Universal Revolution of Man, the romanticism of every great struggle that is revolutionary. How Great is God who gave that sense of the romanticism of struggle to me, when I as a youth, physically sitting on a grass mat under the flickering rays of a rushlight, conducted a mental dialogue in the metaphysical world with the great strugglers of many different nations, with the thinkers of all nations who steered the course of history! Thus when, in consequence of that mental dialogue, I reached the conviction that no great struggle could be carried out without the sense of the romanticism of struggle, I never ceased from transferring that feeling of the romanticism of struggle to the People of Indonesia. All rising and falling tides of the struggle, all blows which we gave and all blows which we took are the rhythm of struggle, the *rhythm of Revolution.* 'Strike a blow – come on, march ahead! Struck by a blow – come on, march ahead!' The thunder of Revolution, sometimes resounding as shouts of applause, sometimes voicing suffering and sorrow, as a whole we hear as a song, a symphony, a chorus, like the roar of the waves of the tumultuous ocean pounding on the shore which we hear as a mighty chorus to God ...

Revolution calls for three absolute conditions: romanticism, dynamism, and dialecticalism [see Glossary]. Romanticism, dynamism, and dialecticalism which have their home not only in the hearts of the leaders, but which burn in all the hearts of the People – which electrify every atom of the bodies of the People from Sabang to Merauke [i.e. from Aceh in north Sumatra to New Guinea in the east]. Without a romanticism that electrifies the whole of the People, the Revolution will have no stamina. Without a dynamism that is as though it bewitches the whole of the People, the Revolution will get stuck half way along the road. Without a dialecticalism joined onto the aspirations of the whole of the People, the People will not be at one with the rising demands of the Revolution, and the Revolution will slowly vanish in a waste of apathy, as a river is sometimes lost, sunk in a desert before it reaches the waters of the ocean ...

Yes, we *once did* let that romanticism go. We *once did* let that dynamism go. We *once did* let that dialecticalism go. That time was before 1959. At that time many of our leaders had already been poisoned by liberalism ...

I was most apprehensive at that time. Most apprehensive! But, praise be to God, before it was too late, we *'slammed the wheel round'*, in the direction of the original course of the Revolution. Stop the crazy excesses! Stop the deviations and irregularities! Return to the '45 Constitution! Return to the romanticism, dynamism, dialecticalism of the Revolution! Return to the Mandate of the Sufferings of the People! Return! Return!

Imagine what it would have been like had we not quickly turned the wheel! Imagine what it would have been like if we had not quickly brought the People back to the romanticism, dynamism and dialecticalism of Revolution! Surely there would have been no bounds to the disaster! The destruction of the Revolution was on the threshold! Of that time I said in the 17th August address last year:

> Perhaps we should be getting more and more adrift, more and more without direction, even more and more sinking again into the delta mud of *exploitation de nation par nation* and the delta mud of *exploitation de l'homme par l'homme*. And history would have written: there, between the continent of Asia and the continent of Australia, between the Pacific Ocean and the Indonesian Ocean, there lives a nation that first tried to revive itself as a Nation, but eventually became again a coolie among the nations – became again 'a nation of coolies and a coolie among the nations'.

Yes, indeed it is true that before 1959 our Revolution did go 'adrift'. It did get off its course. It did drift without direction. It did go astray circling around.

And what was the reason for that? Because many of our leaders did not understand the meaning of Modern Revolution in the second half of the twentieth century, that is, the age of *modern imperialism* and *monopoly capitalism*. They, those leaders, assumed that revolution was only: seizing independence, organising a National Government, replacing the foreign civil servants with civil servants of their own nation, and after that: organising every single thing in keeping with the Western examples given in their textbooks. Such leaders as that even pushed it down our throats that 'the revolution is already ended', and that 'colonialism-imperialism are already dead!'

'The revolution is already ended' – that's what they said! Thus, they wanted to kill the romanticism of the Revolution. They wanted to kill the dynamism of the Revolution, whilst we ought to be saying: 'Keep feeding the fire of the romanticism of Revolution until the Mandate of the Sufferings of the People has been fulfilled! Keep on shaking up the dynamism of Revolution until the Message of the Sufferings of the People has been fulfilled! ...

Our Revolution was not merely to evict the Dutch Government from Indonesia. Our Revolution proceeds further yet than that. The Indonesian Revolution proceeds towards three well known objectives. The Indonesian Revolution proceeds towards *Socialism!* The Indonesian Revolution proceeds towards a *New World* without *exploitation de l'homme par l'homme* and *exploitation de nation par nation!* How is it that such a Revolution was to be brought to a standstill with the words 'the revolution has already ended'? How is it that such a Revolution can be made to keep going without romanticism, without dynamism, without dialecticalism? ...

[The key to 'restoring the revolution' was the 'Political Manifesto', or MANIPOL, which was proclaimed on Independence Day, 1959, by Sukarno. This called for a revival of the 'spirit of the Revolution', for social justice and for a process of 'revolutionizing' by political education all the main institutions of government. Later the acronym USDEK was added to MANIPOL creating the overall ideological formula and slogan MANIPOL-

USDEK. USDEK stood for: restoring the 1945 constitution; the Indonesian road to socialism; guided democracy; guided economy; and building Indonesian identity.]

It was with the Political Manifesto [of 1959] that I, and all of us, slammed the wheel around and shouted stop! stop! to all deviations, and fixed our determination firmly upon continuing the Revolution along *the proper rails*, and upon continuing the Revolution on and on and on until the end, until it won complete victory, namely a new Indonesia, a just and prosperous Indonesia, a socialist Indonesia, the creation of the hands and mind of the Indonesian people themselves ...

Now we need no more waste our energy in debating whether the Political Manifesto is right or wrong, good or bad, profitable or detrimental. Indeed, although the greater majority of our people immediately supported the Political Manifesto, at the time of its birth, however, our Political Manifesto underwent ridicule, insult, criticism, and curses. I allowed those conditions to continue for a year, during which time I still tolerated the rightwing opposition newspapers, during which time I still let the rightwing opposition parties go their way, while observing them, following them, keeping an eye on them. But they were truly reactionaries! They thought that my toleration was a sign of weakness. Then, they became less and less able to control themselves, they became more and more unbridled and did as they liked. Their trumpet, the yellow press, howled and barked as they wished, interspersed with explosions of grenades and pistol shots, even of machine-gun fire from land and from the air, all aimed at *me, but in fact they were aimed at democracy and freedom itself.* Not only were calculated attempts made in case I was off guard, the mouths of cannon were even directed against me, but thanks to the protection of God I remained calm, I rejected what had to be rejected, namely, playing the fascist. However, one year after the Political Manifesto ... I made it clear that we 'should not be halfhearted' and that 'based on revolutionary morals and the moral of the Revolution it is *the duty* of the authorities *to attack and to destroy* every power, whether foreign or not, native or not, endangering the security or the continuation of the Revolution'. Then, expressing the voice of the heart of the People which demanded justice and democracy, I prohibited the reactionary parties, Masjumi and P.S.I. [see Glossary], and I also ordered that a number of yellow papers which liked to act at will were *also prohibited.* These actions objectively strengthened National Unity and made it healthier.

And please do not think that Sukarno is a clairvoyant person. Do not think that Sukarno is in the possession of some magic power! No! Whenever I predict this or that, my prediction is based on my knowledge of the objective laws of the history of society. If there is any 'magic' in my possession – it is because I know the Message of the Sufferings of the People, because I know conditions, and because I know a science which is efficacious, namely Marxism. Therefore when I ordered the ban on those reactionary parties and newspapers, I imagined that the leftist-progressive people would be even more convinced of the correctness of the Political Manifesto, the 'middle-of-the-roaders' would be able to see the truth of my policy, while the right-wing people would not dare to be *openly* hostile to it anymore ...

I have been accused of bringing advantage to one group only among our big national family. My answer here is, yes. Yes, I am giving advantage to one group only, namely – the *revolutionary group*! I am a friend of the nationalists, but only the *revolutionary* nationalist! I am a friend of the religious group, but the *revolutionary* religious group! I am a friend of the Communists, because the Communists are *revolutionary* ...

It is true that in the Political Manifesto I spoke of 'the evil of the multiparty system', but I have never been hostile towards political parties *as such*, not only because I know the merits of the political parties since before the war, I even set up a political party myself, and was chairman of a political party [the Partai Nasional Indonesia, formed by Sukarno in 1927]. Those very political parties took part in preparing and later serving the Revolution. What I do not like are the political parties that are reactionary, and we have dissolved them, and if they rise again I will get rid of them ...

[*The international situation*]   Now, how is it with our confrontation with 'Malaysia'? We cannot talk about 'Malaysia' without talking about the situation in South-East Asia and the whole of Asia in general. We cannot, I said, because South-East Asia has now in fact become the focal point of world contradictions. Contradictions between socialism and capitalism are to be found in this part of the world, in their sharpest forms. Also contradictions between labour and capital ... Above all contradictions between the newly-independent nations, the colonised and semi-colonised nations with imperialism – it is here in South-East Asia that these contradictions are sharpest. Moreover, these contradictions, the settlement of which means *cutting the life-line* of world imperialism, these contradictions are *the most critical, the most decisive*, in our present world ...

[In 1949] China became free, throwing the imperialist power from the country, and the People of China became master of their own house and of their own fate. Not only People's China but also People's [North] Korea is building socialism in Asia, and also People's Viet Nam, whose Chairman of Parliament, Truong Chinh, representative of 'Paman [Uncle] Ho', is also present at today's celebrations. And today also Cambodia and Indonesia are building Socialism in Asia. Today I am announcing to the whole world, to all friends and foes, that no evil spirits, no jinn, no devil can prevent Korea, Viet Nam, Cambodia and Indonesia from becoming friends and uniting in the march towards a New World without *exploitation de l'homme par l'homme*!

With the liberation of West Irian [Dutch New Guinea], is the Republic of Indonesia already safe and free from imperialist threats? No, far from it!

'Malaysia' is still being 'installed' in front of our door. 'Malaysia' is still spreading itself out as a watch-dog of imperialism in front of the house of the Republic of Indonesia. Military pacts which surround us, have also recently joined in discussions of our affairs, but without our permission! We are being openly encircled by the imperialists from all directions!

But we are not shaken, we do not fear. Indeed, Sisters and Brothers, do not be shaken, do not fear! March forward, keep on pounding away, keep on crushing that 'Malaysia', although it be helped and aided by ten imperialists at once! ...

Yes, Sisters and Brothers, we are at present being encircled! But I call upon you, the entire Indonesian people, to sharpen and keep sharpening the *keris* [Malay/Indonesian dagger] of your love-for-country, to sharpen and continue sharpening the *rentjong* [Acehnese dagger] of your vigilance, to strike and continue striking the hammer of your unity ...

To the Volunteers, both men and women, I give the command to execute all national–patriotic tasks with a spirit of exalted sacrifice and to give their maximum share to our great struggle, our holy struggle to crush the neo-colonialism of 'Malaysia'! ...

[**Conclusion**] The Indonesian People have to be politics-*conscious* and revolution-*conscious*. Conscious! Yes, conscious! All the People! *Everybody!* *Everyone* must be politics-conscious. *Everyone* must be revolution-conscious. To borrow a saying by Lenin, even every *cook* should understand politics and understand revolution – live in politics and live in Revolution.

Allah be praised! Such is indeed the case with the Indonesian People!

Their hearts are always on fire. Their minds forever active. Their spirit always 'obsessed'. Obsessed as if by angelic inspiration! Obsessed by ideals. Obsessed by an Idea. Obsessed by the objective of the struggle. Obsessed by freedom. Obsessed by the idea of a just and prosperous society. Obsessed to see the eradication of *exploitation de l'homme par l'homme*. Obsessed to see the elimination of *exploitation de nation par nation*. Obsessed by an irrevocable hatred of imperialism and colonialism. Obsessed by a life of struggle. *Obsessed,* yes *obsessed* and it is for that reason that they are unceasingly engaged in *action* ...

So as to enable our opponents to hear it, I will now once more proclaim what I have said time and time again: 'Go to hell with your "Indonesia's economy is going to collapse"'! Go to hell with your tale of Indonesia's economic destruction. *Go to hell!* Your psy-war [psychological warfare] is not effective! We consider your psy-war the barking of a dog. Tens of times you have claimed that Indonesia under Sukarno would flounder, would collapse, would be destroyed, but we are immune to your psy-war! Last year they 'predicted' that at the beginning of 1964 the Indonesian economy would collapse. But at the beginning of 1964 Indonesia did not collapse! And they are saying again that in October of this year Indonesia will 'collapse'. *Go to hell!* Indonesia will never collapse – God willing, Indonesia will never collapse.

The seasons of scarcity in 1962 and in 1963 did not cause the collapse of Indonesia's economy. Much less in 1964, when our crops are successful all over the country – Indonesia will never collapse!

Sisters and Brothers who stand in front of me in Merdeka Square, and Sisters and Brothers who are listening to my speech throughout all parts of our country. You are all happy today at commemorating the anniversary of our Proclamation of Independence. With a new determination and refreshed vigour, in addition to a more mature way of thinking through having digested all our past experiences and having contemplated all the paths we must take, we are now entering into the twentieth year of our Independence. My Message to you now is the same as the message I once gave you before: 'Flow on, O river of the Indonesian Revolution, flow on down to the Sea, do not stop, for in flowing out to the Sea you are being loyal to your source!'

As for myself – each time I have finished delivering a 17th of August Address to the People, after I have returned to Merdeka Palace, I invariably sit down in silent contemplation for a few minutes – first of all to express my *deepfelt gratitude* to God and secondly in *admiring my Indonesian People.* You, my People of Indonesia, you, who are waging revolution within your own nation, and you too, who are waging revolution to transform the conditions of all mankind! Allahu Akbar – how persevering you are, how great are your powers of resistance! How sturdy and firm is your step! With a People like you I can make our battlecry resound all over the face of the earth: 'Freedom – Socialism – A New World', and I can thunder into the ears of all the world's imperialists: 'Here am I, where are you!' and I can repeat what I have stated abroad: *'The Indonesian People can take everything for the sake of Revolution. The Indonesian Revolution can crush anything that is thrown in its way!!'*

Truly: You are not a nation of worms, you are a Nation with the traits of the Banteng bull!

> Come on, march on! Go on tearing down!
> Keep on building! Vivere pericoloso (Live Dangerously)!
> Ever onward, never retreat!
> Victory is surely ours.

CHAPTER 9

The Era of Stabilization in
Southeast Asia, 1965–75

The war in Viet Nam has for so long dominated our field of vision that it has distorted our picture of Asia. A small country on the rim of the continent has filled the screen of our minds; but it does not fill the map. Sometimes dramatically, but more often quietly, the rest of Asia has been undergoing a profound, an exciting and on balance an extraordinarily promising transformation. (Richard M. Nixon, 'Asia after Viet Nam', *Foreign Affairs*, Vol. 1, no. 46), [1967]: 111–25)

The paradox: the United States' failure in Vietnam

How can one talk of 'stabilization' in Southeast Asia during the period between 1965 and 1975, when this decade witnessed a war raging in Vietnam, a war that moreover engulfed Laos and then, in 1970, Cambodia? By the late 1960s, Americans were arguing that this war, however damaging its immediate impact, had acted as a 'lightning rod', concentrating and diverting the energies of communism and revolutionary subversion in the region. The argument went that the American military commitment to Vietnam gave the rest of Southeast Asia precious time in which to stabilize.

This, however, was not the perspective in 1965, when the United States was forced to intervene directly in Vietnam in order to avert the collapse of the South Vietnamese regime. There was a natural inclination on the part of the American military bureaucracy to believe that, once they were fully involved, they would be able to impose their military will and reduce the insurgency in South Vietnam to manageable proportions, if not stifle it altogether. A debate, however, still centred around the extent to which American policy-makers as a whole at this time were driven by an 'optimistic' or a 'pessimistic' vision in forming their Vietnam policy. Was the American intervention in South Vietnam, and eventual take-over of the war, based on a clear view of political goals that could be achieved, or was it the result of a cumulation of makeshift, short-term expedients designed to avoid the disintegration of the South Vietnamese regime and the humiliation of the United States?

Throughout this period, American policy in Vietnam was influenced by two vital constraints that served to limit its military, political and diplomatic options. On the one hand, no American administration of either party could afford another *débâcle* like the victory of communism in China in 1949; on the other, after the bloody and costly military stalemate of the Korean War of 1950–53, it had become an axiom of American policy that the United States should never again become bogged down in a ground war in Asia, particularly an unwinnable ground-war confrontation with communist China. As a consequence, President Lyndon Johnson and his administration always placed strict limits on the strategic dimensions of the Vietnam conflict, avoiding in particular any extension of the war that might invite Chinese intervention or Soviet retaliation – for example, an invasion of North Vietnam, or of the strategically vital regions of eastern Cambodia and southeastern Laos, or direct bombing of Haiphong harbour, the main conduit for Soviet military aid. In a sense, the intensity of the bombing campaign in North Vietnam – directed, however, against restricted targets – was an attempt to compensate for this strategic self-limitation. The result was that the United States found itself fighting a war that by definition was geared not towards 'victory' but towards complex and blurred political goals. By 1967, as the 'unwinnable' nature of the war became more apparent (but so, on the other hand, did the unacceptable dangers of expanding its strategic scope), pessimism began to creep in and infect government thinking. It is noteworthy, however, that the American intervention *had*, by 1967, stabilized the political situation in South Vietnam under the leadership of President Nguyen Van Thieu.

Although by late 1967 serious long-term doubts about the war had crept in, at the same time political and military gains appeared to be sufficiently visible to justify a continuation of policy along existing lines. But then, during the Vietnamese New Year ('Tet') holiday in late January 1968, North Vietnam and the southern insurgents launched their major offensive. The Tet offensive was designed primarily to demoralize and disintegrate the foundations of the government of South Vietnam. Overall, it failed in this primary objective, and the National Liberation Front (NLF) in particular suffered massive and irreparable military losses. What this offensive did do, however, was bring home to a large segment of the American public the feeling that the war was unwinnable – just at the beginning of a presidential campaigning season. It also brought out into the open and crystallized the pessimism about the war that had been steadily growing among the policy-makers in Washington (see '1968: The turning-point in the Vietnam war', p. 254).

The year 1968 saw a shift of policy that was marked by the imposition of an upward limit in the number of American troops being sent to Vietnam. This was matched by a bombing halt, progressively widened through the year to cover the whole of North Vietnam; and the initiation of talks in Paris designed to lead to 'de-escalation' of the war, and ultimately to a cease-fire and a mutually acceptable political settlement in the South.

The ceiling placed on American troops to be committed to the war set the scene for a new policy – a reversion, in effect, to the pre-1965 situation – in which South Vietnamese troops were expected gradually to take over more and more of the military burden. This policy was given concrete shape in 1969 by the 'Nixon Doctrine' – in effect, a global policy of 'backing up' rather than 'substituting for' allies in regional conflicts – and 'Vietnamization', that is, the training and arming of Vietnamese troops so that they could take over the front-line role of American troops.

During President Nixon's first term of office, between 1969 and 1973, his main objective, and that of his principal foreign policy adviser Henry Kissinger, was to bring the war to a negotiated conclusion while at the same time ensuring that the United States was not seen to be suffering a humiliating defeat. The principal ingredients of their policy were secret negotiations with the North Vietnamese leadership, removed from public scrutiny or pressure; and an attempt to make the South Vietnamese regime stronger and more self-reliant through the 'Vietnamization' plan and 'intensified pacification' in the provinces. In order to have credibility, this policy of trying to strengthen South Vietnam had to be backed by American military force. Between 1969 and 1972, this force was used in a more incisive and focused way than hitherto, breaking through political and diplomatic constraints that had held the previous Democratic administration in check. In 1969, North Vietnamese and NLF sanctuaries along the Cambodian border were systematically bombed; in spring 1970, a joint American–South Vietnamese 'incursion' was launched against these sanctuary areas inside Cambodia; in 1971, South Vietnamese ground troops were sent into southern Laos in a failed attempt to block the Ho Chi Minh Trail; and at Easter and Christmas 1972, massive bombing raids were launched against, among other targets, Hanoi and Haiphong.

Given this demonstration of continuing and effective American military commitment to South Vietnam, a point was reached in early 1973 when both sides had, as it were, exhausted their military options. A cease-fire was therefore concluded with the reluctant consent of the South Vietnamese government. It was agreed that, within South Vietnam, there should be an 'in-place' cease-fire and the creation of a patchwork of de facto communist and government zones. Although a complex machinery was set in place to facilitate a negotiated political settlement between the communists and the government in South Vietnam, the essential gain for the Americans was that the South Vietnamese regime remained intact. The main – and ultimately decisive – negotiating gain for the North Vietnamese was that their army was allowed to remain in South Vietnam, while the Americans were to complete their military withdrawal.

This agreement enabled the United States to slide out of a conflict that was no longer of importance in the context of the complex global situation that had developed – particularly because of the Sino-Soviet confrontation – in the early 1970s. By this time, the war had not only devastated North and

South Vietnam, but had also condemned Laos to a state of permanent civil war, along with relentless American bombing of sensitive strategic areas like the Ho Chi Minh Trail and the Plain of Jars.

The genesis of the Cambodian tragedy

Up to 1970, Prince Sihanouk had maintained some semblance of stability in Cambodia by a number of difficult balancing acts. In foreign relations, he adopted a position of neutrality between the Western and the communist blocs; in practice, however, he 'leaned' towards North Vietnam and China, and turned a blind eye to the communist 'sanctuaries' in Cambodia from which the North Vietnamese operated against South Vietnam. This stemmed from a simple calculation that the communist side would eventually be victorious in Vietnam. Internally, he tried to maintain a balance between the pro-Western right wing and leftist groupings including the Khmer communists or 'Khmer Rouge'. These positions helped secure him from Vietnamese communist attempts to destabilize his regime. Like Sukarno, however, he ran a highly personalized system of government, and in the early 1960s his rhetoric had also taken on an increasingly populist, anti-Western tone. As a result, by the late 1960s, the threads that held the regime together were beginning to unravel. In 1970, the right-wing elite in the administration and the armed forces ousted Sihanouk and established the 'Khmer Republic'. Since this new regime abandoned neutrality and took an openly pro-American stance, North Vietnam and China responded by giving unrestricted support to the Khmer Rouge. Cambodia was thereafter plunged into a devastating civil war that lasted from 1970 to 1975, and from which the country has never fully recovered.

The rest of Southeast Asia: the ending of the 'independence regimes'

Whatever the horrors of the Indochina war, there *is* a case for arguing that this 'bought time' for the non-communist regimes of the rest of Southeast Asia. The role of outside influence in the whole process of political stabilization and economic growth that took place at this time remains a matter of considerable debate, and invites the following questions that have yet to be satisfactorily answered: To what extent did the United States in particular provide a basis for political stability, and thereby provide an essential precondition for economic confidence and growth? More specifically, to what extent did American military and economic aid relieve Thailand, their key ally in Southeast Asia, of impossible defence burdens and provide a necessary boost for economic development within a free enterprise framework? At the same time – from another and even more politically sensitive perspective – to what extent could it be argued that Southeast Asian economic development that occurred in this period – for example, in Malaysia, Singapore, Thailand, the Philippines and Indonesia – was primarily powered by Overseas Chinese trading networks, and that the degree of economic prosperity that these nations achieved was dependent on the extent to which particular states gave these networks a free rein?

Although the above questions remain open, it is clear that one partial contribution to regional stability and prosperity was the general trend in the region in the 1960s and early 1970s towards the removal or severe modification of the regimes that had brought the countries of the region to independence after the Second World War. During this period we see a military coup in Burma in 1962; a military coup in South Vietnam in 1963; a military coup in Indonesia in 1965; a restructuring of the political system in Malaysia in 1969; a coup in Cambodia in 1970, in which the military played a significant part; and a declaration of martial law in the Philippines in 1972. Overall – though not invariably – these changes saw the replacement of the charismatic leaders and mass political movements that had brought the respective countries to independence by more authoritarian regimes tightly controlled by an administrative elite and the armed forces.

Despite the fact that these regime changes often involved no more than an entrenching of the power of one segment of the existing political elite (particularly the armed forces), many of them – those in Thailand in 1958 and in Burma in 1962, for instance – made great use of the term 'revolution'. In part, this reflected the fact that 'revolution' was a fashionable slogan of the time, useful for conferring legitimacy on political actions, but with little or no concrete meaning. ('When *I* use a word', Humpty-Dumpty said, in a rather scornful tone, 'it means just what I want it to mean – neither more nor less.')

The special, guiding role that the armed forces played in these political changes should also be noted. If these were 'revolutions', they were emphatically revolutions from above. But this military role was not merely a reflection of the concentration of power that the armed forces could muster in a weak state. In three countries in particular – Indonesia, Burma and Thailand – the armed forces had played a key role as a political force, in the Indonesian and Burmese movements for independence, and in the Thai Revolution of 1932. As such, the respective armed forces of these countries regarded themselves not merely as instruments of the state, but as guardians of the nation and ultimate trustees of the nation's destiny.

The ending of the 'independence regimes': Cambodia, Burma and the Philippines

This process of regime change did not always bring about greater political stability, or provide the basis for greater economic prosperity. In Cambodia, the Khmer Republic was formed at the precise time (1970) that the United

States was poised to abandon its Indochina commitment, and was therefore doomed to destruction from its inception. The Khmer Republic could be seen in retrospect as an expendable rearguard covering America's retreat from the region.

In Burma, the continued and indeed accelerated problems brought about by internal weakness and dissension, and the persistence of separatist revolts in the border regions, led to a temporary military take-over in 1958 and the imposition of permanent military rule in 1962. One immediate consequence was the firm establishment of a unitary state that completely excluded the idea of granting autonomous rights to minority regions. After a long gestation period, a new political 'concept' was put in place, emphasizing one-party rule dominated by the army, and almost complete socialist-based national 'self-reliance' or autarky. In practical terms, this led to steep economic decline and ever-intensifying military dictatorship, while at the same time the separatist rebellions continued unabated (see 'The military take-over in Burma in 1962', p. 265).

In the Philippines, too, the 'independence regime' had reached a state of collapse by the late 1960s. The elite-dominated quasi-democratic system had degenerated into a morass of gangster politics marked by corruption and violence; in these conditions, communist and (Muslim) separatist rebellions were able to flourish. President Ferdinand Marcos' declaration of martial law in 1972 was, therefore, initially welcomed by many as a necessary measure. Marcos' emergency rule did not, however, lay the foundations for a new and more stable political system. In some areas, in fact – for example, political corruption – the defects of the old regime were if anything multiplied.

The special case of Thailand

Post-Second World War Thailand provided a successful example of the kind of anti-communist 'bastion' that the United States so signally failed to build in Laos or South Vietnam. The United States provided security for Thailand within the SEATO defence treaty network and, more importantly, bolstered the regime with significant military and development aid. Like the other successful 'bastion' regimes on the periphery of Communist China – Taiwan and South Korea – the military dominated the Thai political system in the post-war decades. Indeed, it could be argued that, since the so-called 'Revolution' of 1932 directed against the monarchy (setting aside the initial period of joint civilian–military rule in the period between 1932 and 1938), Thailand had almost without interruption been governed by some form of military rule, with only a fig-leaf of constitutional structures. However, a significant change in *ideology* was brought about by the regime of Field Marshal Sarit Thanarat in 1958. The importance of the Sarit regime lay in the fact that it based itself on a paternalistic 'Thai'-based ideology – however vague its formulations – that explicitly rejected the Western political norms that had, in theory at least, underpinned the 1932 Revolution. The Thai regime of the time was, like the Burmese military and Sukarno's 'Guided Democracy' regimes, attempting to replace what were seen to be unsatisfactory Western ideological imports with a system based on indigenous political traditions.

Malaysia: the new political settlement after 1969

The Malayan region endured a series of shocks during the period between 1957 and the early 1970s. In 1963, independent Malaya was merged with Singapore, Sarawak and North Borneo (later Sabah) to form the new Malaysian Federation – a classic instance of Britain's mania for 'tidying-up' colonial remnants. The new state, however, found itself immediately embroiled in a series of disputes with its neighbours, Indonesia and the Philippines. The territorial dispute with the Philippines relating to Sabah proved to be only a minor inconvenience; more threatening was Indonesia's determination to 'crush' what it considered a neo-colonial 'puppet' state designed to perpetuate British influence in the region. Tension between Indonesia and Malaysia, supported by Britain, rapidly escalated into an undeclared war in Borneo on the border between Sarawak and Indonesian Kalimantan – the so-called 'Confrontation' or *Konfrontasi* – which eventually petered out in the mid-1960s.

Another problem the new Malaysian Federation faced was the fact that Singapore rapidly proved to be 'indigestible' within the Federation framework. The addition of a dynamic Chinese city, with an ambitious political leadership to match, seriously upset the delicate ethnic, political and economic balance that had been created at the time of the formation of Malaya in 1957. In 1965, after growing political tensions, Singapore was finally ejected from the Federation. The whole unhappy experience of co-existence in the period from 1963 to 1965 left a residue of ethnic bitterness and tension. The *de facto* inter-ethnic 'deal' that had been encouraged by the departing British, in which Malays were understood ultimately to dominate the state and the political system while the Chinese were given a free rein in the economic sphere, began to fray at the edges. The 1969 federal elections in Malaysia allowed these tensions to burst into the open with serious inter-communal riots. In response to these events, the Malay-dominated state apparatus – the UMNO leadership, the bureaucracy and the security forces – seized emergency powers and initiated new inter-ethnic negotiations within what was in effect a strict framework of Malay control.

The resulting national consensus formed in 1970 decisively changed the former elite 'deal' of 1957. Malay control of the state and political system was maintained and indeed strengthened. In addition, the whole weight of government policy and resources was directed towards the economic advancement, education and urbanization of the Malays and other indigenous communities through a policy of positive discrimination. If this had led to

a concurrent restriction and discouragement of Chinese private sector economic enterprise, the new policy could have had severe economic as well as
communal repercussions for Malaysia. The policy was based, however, not
so much on state restraint of the Chinese sector as on encouragement of –
indeed, dependence on – a general policy of rapid overall economic growth.
In effect, what could be described as a 'regulated' democratic structure,
ultimately dominated by a Malay-controlled state apparatus and national
ideology, relied on sustained economic growth to guarantee general levels of
prosperity that would be the key to inter-ethnic peace.

Indonesia in 1965: Guided Democracy, the PKI, the armed forces and the 'New Order'

The most extreme and violent case of regime change came in Indonesia in
1965. By this date, the 'revolutionary dynamic' provided by Sukarno's populist
rhetoric could no longer hold Guided Democracy together. Sukarno's balancing act between the PKI on one side and the armed forces on the other
was clearly coming to an end in 1964, with what appeared to be a decisive
tilt towards the PKI and the communist bloc. A premature and badly
organized coup d'état attempted by a leftist faction in the armed forces in
late September 1965 brought the confrontation between the armed forces
and the PKI to a head. The *de facto* seizure of power by the armed forces
and the neutralization of Sukarno that followed set the scene for the
wholesale elimination of the PKI – leadership, grass-roots supporters and
sympathisers – throughout Indonesia. In some senses this mass slaughter –
a necessary catharsis in the eyes of military and Islamic leaders – marked an
absolute break with the structure and ideologies that had dominated Indonesia
since 1945. The new emphasis was on order, development, accommodation
with the West and Indonesia's neighbours, a sharply anti-communist foreign
policy and, above all, a political system dominated by the armed forces. In
another sense, however, there were strong elements of continuity: the *pancasila*
principles remained the key ideological focus of the state, and Islamic hopes
for a shift to a greater religious emphasis in the state ideology were not
realized; Javanese domination of the political system, via Javanese domination
of the armed forces, was maintained, as was the priority of protecting
Indonesian unity at all costs (see '"Gestapu" and the installation of military
rule in Indonesia', p. 272).

READINGS
1. The turning-point in the Vietnam war: 1968

On 31 January 1968, during the Vietnamese New Year ('Tet') holiday, the
NLF and the North Vietnamese launched a series of co-ordinated attacks on

Saigon and the provincial capitals of South Vietnam. These attacks were beaten back, the South Vietnamese army (ARVN) held firm, and NLF military units were crippled as a fighting force till the end of the war in 1975. The attacks, however, crystallized all the fears and doubts about the war that had accumulated in America through 1967, and had even been expressed, though privately, by Secretary for Defense Robert McNamara. Undoubtedly, Tet was a turning-point in the war, even though American participation continued until early 1973.

The first of the extracts below comes from an essay by Henry Kissinger, published in 1968. It is a masterly, concise analysis of the faults of American policy up to the Tet offensive, and echoes from a different perspective the points made by Bernard Fall in his earlier essay (see Chapter 8). The second article is by Clark Clifford, who took over from Robert McNamara as secretary of state for defense on 1 March 1968, just after the Tet offensive. It is essentially the story of an erstwhile 'hawk' who, as he tried to frame a post-Tet policy for Vietnam, was converted to the view that the existing direction of policy in Vietnam was leading to a cul-de-sac and was, moreover, distorting American foreign policy, weakening the economy and fragmenting American society.

Although Tet was undoubtedly a turning-point, it is important to note that doubts about the direction of the war had been building up in Congress, in the media, in academia and even within the administration, during 1966 and 1967. The importance of Tet lay in the fact that it shifted the balance of the argument in favour of the 'doves'. It is equally important to note the continuity between the policy of the Johnson presidency between March 1968 and January 1969, and the Nixon presidency that replaced it. Nixon's policy of 'Vietnamizing' the war, shifting the emphasis towards negotiations, and refocusing American military strategy towards a 'back-up' role – particularly with air-power – was prefigured by Clark Clifford in 1968, as his article shows.

Henry A. Kissinger, 'The Vietnam Negotiations', in *American Foreign Policy: Three Essays* (New York: Norton, 1969). Excerpts taken from pages 101–8.

The situation within South Vietnam prior to negotiations The sequence of events that led to negotiations probably started with General Westmoreland's [commander of US forces in Vietnam] visit to Washington in November 1967. On that occasion, General Westmoreland told a Joint Session of Congress that the war was being militarily won. He outlined 'indicators' of progress and stated that a limited withdrawal of United States combat forces might be undertaken beginning late in 1968. On January 17, 1968, President Johnson, in his State of the Union address, emphasized that the pacification program – the extension of the control of Saigon into the countryside – was progressing satisfactorily. Sixty-seven percent of the population of Vietnam lived in relatively secure areas; the figure was expected to rise. A week later, the Tet offensive overthrew the assumptions of American strategy.

What had gone wrong? The basic problem has been conceptual: the tendency to apply traditional maxims of both strategy and 'nation-building' to a situation which they did not fit.

American military strategy followed the classic doctrine that victory depended on a combination of control of territory and attrition of the opponent. Therefore, the majority of the American forces were deployed along the frontiers of South Vietnam to prevent enemy infiltration and in the Central Highlands where most of the North Vietnamese main force units — those units organized along traditional military lines — were concentrated. The theory was that defeat of the main forces would cause the guerrillas to wither on the vine. Victory would depend on inflicting casualties substantially greater than what we suffered until Hanoi's losses became 'unacceptable'.

This strategy suffered from two disabilities: (a) the nature of guerrilla warfare, (b) the asymmetry in the definition of what constituted unacceptable losses. A guerrilla war differs from traditional military operations because its key prize is not control of territory but control of the population. This depends, in part, on psychological criteria, especially a sense of security. No positive program can succeed unless the population feels safe from terror or reprisal. Guerrillas rarely seek to hold real estate; their tactic is to use terror and intimidation to discourage cooperation with constituted authority.

The distribution of the population in Vietnam makes this problem particularly acute. Over ninety percent of the population lives in the coastal plain and the Mekong Delta; the Central Highlands and the frontiers, on the other hand, are essentially unpopulated. Eighty percent of American forces came to be concentrated in areas containing less than four percent of the population; the locale of military operations was geographically removed from that of the guerrilla conflict. As North Vietnamese theoretical writings never tired of pointing out, the United States could not hold territory and protect the population simultaneously. By opting for military victory through attrition, the United States strategy produced what came to be the characteristic feature of the Vietnamese war: military successes that could not be translated into permanent political advantage. (Even the goal of stopping infiltration was very hard to implement in the trackless, nearly impenetrable jungles along the Cambodian and Laotian frontiers.)

As a result, the American concept of security came to have little in common with the experience of the Vietnamese villagers. American maps classified areas by three categories of control, neatly shown in various colors: government, contested and Viet Cong. The formal criteria were complicated, and depended to an unusual extent on reports by officers whose short term of duty (barely twelve months) made it next to impossible for them to grasp the intangibles and nuances which constitute the real elements of control in the Vietnamese countryside. In essence, the first category included all villages which contained some governmental authority; 'contested' referred to areas slated to be entered by governmental cadres. The American notion of security was a reflection of Western administrative theory; control was assumed to be in the hands of one of the contestants more or less exclusively.

But the actual situation in Vietnam was quite different; a realistic security map would have shown few areas of exclusive jurisdiction; the pervasive experience of the Vietnamese villages was the ubiquitousness of both sides. Saigon controlled much of the country in the daytime, in the sense that government troops could move anywhere if they went in sufficient force; the Viet Cong dominated a large part of the same population at night. For the villagers, the presence of government during the day had to be weighed against its absence after dark when Saigon's cadres almost invariably withdrew into the district or provincial capitals. If armed teams of administrators considered the villages unsafe at night, the villagers could hardly be expected to resist the guerrillas. Thus, the typical pattern in Vietnam has been dual control, with the villages complying with whatever force was dominant during a particular part of the day.

The political impact of this dual control was far from symmetrical, however. To be effective, the government had to demonstrate a very great capacity to provide protection, probably well over ninety percent. The guerrillas' aim was largely negative: to prevent the consolidation of governmental authority. They did not need to destroy all governmental programs – indeed in some areas they made no effort to interfere with them. They did have to demonstrate a capability to punish individuals who threw in their lot with Saigon. An occasional assassination or raid served to shake confidence for months afterwards.

The North Vietnamese and the Viet Cong had another advantage which they used skillfully. The North Vietnamese and the Viet Cong, fighting in their own country, needed merely to keep in being forces sufficiently strong to dominate the population after the United States tired of the war. We fought a military war; our opponents fought a political one. We sought physical attrition; our opponents aimed for our psychological exhaustion. In the process, we lost sight of one of the cardinal maxims of guerrilla war: the guerrilla wins if he does not lose; the conventional army loses if it does not win. The North Vietnamese used their main forces the way a bullfighter uses his cape – to keep us lunging into areas of marginal political importance.

The United States strategy of attrition failed to reduce the guerrillas and was in difficulty even with respect to the North Vietnamese main forces. Since Hanoi made no attempt to hold any territory, and since the terrain of the Central Highlands cloaked North Vietnamese movements, it proved difficult to make the opposing forces fight except at places which they chose. Indeed, a considerable majority of engagements came to be initiated by the other side; this enabled Hanoi to regulate its casualties (and ours) at least within certain limits. The so-called 'kill-ratios' of United States to North

Vietnamese casualties became highly unreliable indicators. They were falsified further because the level of what was 'unacceptable' to Americans fighting thousands of miles from home turned out to be much lower than that of Hanoi fighting on Vietnamese soil.

All this caused our military operations to have little relationship to our declared political objectives. Progress in establishing a political base was excruciatingly slow; our diplomacy and our strategy were conducted in isolation from each other. President Johnson had announced repeatedly that we would be ready to negotiate, unconditionally, at any moment, anywhere. This, in effect, left the timing of negotiations to the other side. But short of a complete collapse of the opponent, our military deployment was not well designed to support a negotiation. For purposes of negotiations, we would have been better off with one hundred percent control over sixty percent of the country (to give us a bargaining counter), than with sixty percent control of one hundred percent of the country.

The effort to strengthen Saigon's political control faced other problems. To be meaningful, the so-called pacification program had to meet two conditions: (a) it had to provide security for the population, (b) it had to establish a political and institutional link between the villages and Saigon. Neither condition was ever met: impatience to show 'progress' in the strategy of attrition caused us to give low priority to protection of the population; in any event, there was no concept as to how to bring about a political framework relating Saigon to the countryside. As a result, economic programs had to carry an excessive load. Economic programs had produced stability in Europe (after the Second World War) because existing political and administrative structures were threatened above all by the gap between expectations and reality. In Vietnam – as in most developing countries – the overwhelming problem is not to *buttress* but to *develop* a political framework. Economic progress, by undermining the existing patterns of obligation – which are generally personal or feudal – serves to accentuate the need for political institutions. One ironic aspect of the war in Vietnam is that while we profess an idealistic philosophy, our failures have been due to an excessive reliance on material factors. The Communists, by contrast, holding to a materialistic interpretation, owe many of their successes to their ability to supply an answer to the question of the nature and foundations of political authority.

The Tet offensive brought the compounded weaknesses – or, as the North Vietnamese would say, the internal contradictions – of the American position to a head. To be sure, from a strictly military point of view, the offensive was an American victory. Viet Cong casualties were very large; in many provinces, the Viet Cong infrastructure of guerrillas and shadow administrators surfaced and could be severely mauled by American forces. But in a guerrilla war, purely military considerations are not decisive: psychological and political factors loom at least as large.

On that level the Tet offensive was a political defeat in the countryside for Saigon and the United States. Two claims had been pressed on the villages. The United States and Saigon had promised that they would be able to protect an ever larger number of villages. The Viet Cong had never claimed that they were able to provide permanent protection; they had claimed that they were the real power and presence in the villages and they threatened those who collaborated with Saigon or the United States with retribution.

As happened so often in the past, the Viet Cong made their claim stick. Some twenty provincial capitals were occupied. Though the Viet Cong held none (except Hue) for more than a few days, they were there long enough to execute hundreds of Vietnamese on the basis of previously prepared lists. While the words 'secure area' never had the same significance for Vietnamese civilians as for Americans, it applied most meaningfully to the provincial and district capitals. This was precisely where the Tet offensive took its most severe toll. The Viet Cong had made a point whose importance far transcends military considerations: there are no secure areas for Vietnamese civilians. This has compounded the already great tendency of the Vietnamese population to await developments and not to commit itself irrevocably to the Saigon government. The withdrawal of government troops from the countryside to protect cities and the consequent increase in Viet Cong activity in the villages even in the daytime has served to strengthen this trend.

For all these reasons, the Tet offensive marked the watershed of the American effort. Henceforth, no matter how effective our actions, the prevalent strategy could no longer achieve its objectives in a [stated] period or with force levels politically acceptable to the American people. This realization caused Washington, for the first time, to put a ceiling on the number of troops for Vietnam. Denied the very large additional forces requested, the military command in Vietnam felt obliged to begin a gradual change of its peripheral strategy to one of concentrating on the protection of the populated areas. This made inevitable an eventual commitment to a political solution and marked the beginning of the quest for a negotiated settlement. Thus, the stage was set for President Johnson's speech of March 31 [1968], which ushered in the current negotiations.

Clark Clifford, 'A Vietnam Reappraisal', *Foreign Affairs*, Vol. 47, no. 4 (July 1969). Excerpts taken from pages 609–22.

I took office [as US Secretary of State for Defense] on March 1, 1968. The enemy's Tet offensive of late January and early February had been beaten back at great cost. The confidence of the American people had been badly shaken. The ability of the South Vietnamese Government to restore order and morale in the populace, and discipline and esprit in the armed forces, was being questioned. At the President's direction, General Earle G. Wheeler, Chairman of the Joint Chiefs of Staff, had flown to Viet Nam in late February for an on-the-spot conference with General Westmoreland. He had just returned and presented the military's request that over 200,000 troops be prepared for deployment to Viet Nam. These troops would be in addition to the 525,000 previously authorized. I was directed, as my first assignment, to chair a task force named by the President to determine how this new requirement could be met. We were not instructed to assess the need for substantial increases in men and matériel; we were to devise the means by which they could be provided.

My work was cut out. The task force included Secretary (of State) Rusk, Secretary Henry Fowler, Under Secretary of State Nicholas Katzenbach, Deputy Secretary of Defense Paul Nitze, General Wheeler, CIA Director Richard Helms, the President's Special Assistant, Walt Rostow, General Maxwell Taylor and other skilled and highly capable officials. All of them had had long and direct experience with Vietnamese problems. I had not. I had attended various meetings in the past several years and I had been to Viet Nam three times, but it was quickly apparent to me how little one knows if he has been on the periphery of a problem and not truly in it. Until the day-long sessions of early March, I had never had the opportunity of intensive analysis and fact-finding. Now I was thrust into a vigorous, ruthlessly frank assessment of our situation by the men who knew the most about it. Try though we would to stay with the assignment of devising means to meet the military's requests, fundamental questions began to recur over and over.

It is, of course, not possible to recall all the questions that were asked nor all the answers that were given ... All that is pertinent to this essay are the impressions that I formed, and the conclusions I ultimately reached in those days of exhausting scrutiny. In the colloquial style of those meetings, here are some of the principal issues raised and some of the answers as I understood them:

'Will 200,000 more men do the job?' I found no assurance that they would.

'If not, how many more might be needed – and when?' There was no way of knowing.

'What would be involved in committing 200,000 more men to Viet Nam?' A reserve call-up of approximately 280,000, an increased draft call and an extension of tours of duty of most men then in service.

'Can the enemy respond with a build-up of his own?' He could and he probably would.

'What are the estimated costs of the latest requests?' First calculations were on the order of $2 billion for the remaining four months of that fiscal year, and an increase of $10 to $12 billion for the year beginning July 1, 1968.

'What will be the impact on the economy?' So great that we would face the possibility of credit restrictions, a tax increase and even wage and price controls. The balance of payments would be worsened by at least half a billion dollars a year.

'Can bombing stop the war?' Never by itself. It was inflicting heavy personnel and matériel losses, but bombing by itself would not stop the war.

'Will stepping up the bombing decrease American casualties?' Very little, if at all. Our casualties were due to the intensity of the ground fighting in the South. We had already dropped a heavier tonnage of bombs than in all the theaters of World War II. During 1967, an estimated 90,000 North Vietnamese had infiltrated into South Viet Nam. In the opening weeks of 1968, infiltrators were coming in at three to four times the rate of a year earlier, despite the ferocity and intensity of our campaign of aerial interdiction.

'How long must we keep on sending our men and carrying the main burden of the combat?' The South Vietnamese were doing better, but they were not ready yet to replace our troops and we did not know when they would be.

When I asked for a presentation of the military plan for attaining victory in Viet Nam, I was told that there was no plan for victory in the historic American sense. Why not? Because our forces were operating under three major political restrictions: the President had forbidden the invasion of North Viet Nam because this could trigger the mutual assistance pact between North Viet Nam and China; the President had forbidden the mining of the harbor at Haiphong, the principal port through which the North received military supplies, because a Soviet vessel might be sunk; the President had forbidden our forces to pursue the enemy into Laos and Cambodia, for to do so would spread the war, politically and geographically, with no discernible advantage. These and other restrictions which precluded an all-out, no-holds-barred military effort were wisely designed to prevent our being drawn into a larger war. We had no inclination to recommend to the President their cancellation.

'Given these circumstances, how can we win?' We would, I was told, continue to evidence our superiority over the enemy; we would continue to attack in the belief that he would reach the stage where he would find it inadvisable to go on with the war. He could not afford the attrition we were inflicting on him. And we were improving our posture all the time.

I then asked, 'What is the best estimate as to how long this course of action will take? Six months? One year? Two years?' There was no agreement on an answer. Not only was there no agreement, I could find no one willing to express any confidence in his guesses. Certainly, none of us was willing to assert that he could see 'light at the end of the tunnel' or that American troops would be coming home by the end of the year.

After days of this type of analysis, my concern had greatly deepened. I could not find out when the war was going to end; I could not find out the manner in which it was going to end; I could not find out whether the new requests for men and equipment were going to be enough, or whether it would take more and, if more, when and how much; I could not find out how soon the South Vietnamese forces would be ready to take over. All I had was the statement, given with too little self-assurance to be comforting, that if we persisted for an indeterminate length of time, the enemy would choose not to go on.

And so I asked, 'Does anyone see any diminution in the will of the enemy after four years of our having been there, after enormous casualties and after massive destruction from our bombing?'

The answer was that there appeared to be no diminution in the will of the enemy. This reply was doubly impressive, because I was more conscious each day of domestic unrest in our own country. Draft card burnings, marches in the streets, problems on school campuses, bitterness and divisiveness were rampant. Just as disturbing to me were the economic implications of a struggle to be indefinitely continued at ever-increasing cost. The dollar was already in trouble, prices were escalating far too fast and emergency controls on foreign investment imposed on New Year's Day would be only a prelude to more stringent controls, if we were to add another $12 billion to Viet Nam spending – with perhaps still more to follow.

I was also conscious of our obligations and involvements elsewhere in the world. There were certain hopeful signs in our relations with the Soviet Union, but both nations were hampered in moving toward vitally important talks on the limitation of strategic weapons so long as the United States was committed to a military solution in Viet Nam. We could not afford to disregard our interests in the Middle East, South Asia, Africa, Western Europe and elsewhere. Even accepting the validity of our objective in Viet Nam, that objective had to be viewed in the context of our overall national interest, and could not sensibly be pursued at a price so high as to impair our ability to achieve other, and perhaps even more important, foreign policy objectives.

Also, I could not free myself from the continuing nagging doubt ... that if the nations living in the shadow of Viet Nam were not persuaded by the domino theory, perhaps it was time for us to take another look. Our efforts had given the nations in that area a number of years following independence to organize and build their security. I could see no reason at this time for us to continue to add to our commitment. Finally, there was no assurance that a 40 percent increase in American troops would place us within the next few weeks, months or even years in any substantially better military position than we were in then. All that could be predicted accurately was that more troops would raise the level of combat and automatically raise the level of casualties on both sides.

And so, after these exhausting days, I was convinced that the military course we were pursuing was not only endless, but hopeless. A further substantial increase in American forces could only increase the devastation and the Americanization of the war, and thus leave us even further from our goal of a peace that would permit the people of South Viet Nam to fashion their own political and economic institutions. Henceforth, I was also convinced, our primary goal should be to level off our involvement, and to work toward gradual disengagement.

To reach a conclusion and to implement it are not the same, especially when one does not have the ultimate power of decision. It now became my purpose to emphasize to my colleagues and to the President, that the United States had entered Viet Nam with a limited aim – to prevent its subjugation by the North and to enable the people of South Viet Nam to determine their own future. I also argued that we had largely accomplished that objective. Nothing required us to remain until the North had been ejected from the South, and the Saigon government had been established in complete military control of all South Vietnam. An increase of over 200,000 in troop strength would mean that American forces would be twice the size of the regular South Vietnamese Army at that time. Our goal of building a stronger South Vietnamese Government, and an effective military force capable of ultimately taking over from us, would be frustrated rather than furthered. The more we continued to do in South Viet Nam, the less likely the South Vietnamese were to shoulder their own burden.

The debate continued at the White House for days. President Johnson encouraged me to report my findings and my views with total candour, but he was equally insistent on hearing the views of others. Finally, the President, in the closing hours of March, made his decisions and reported them to the people on the evening of the 31st. Three related directly to the month's review of the war. First, the President announced he was establishing a ceiling of 549,500 in the American commitment to Viet Nam; the only new troops going out would be support troops previously promised. Second, we would speed up our aid to the South Vietnamese armed forces. We would equip and train them to take over major combat responsibilities from us on a much accelerated schedule. Third, speaking to Hanoi, the President stated he was greatly restricting American bombing of the North as an invitation and an inducement to begin peace talks. We would no longer bomb north of the Twentieth Parallel. By this act of unilateral restraint, nearly 80 percent of the territory of North Viet Nam would no longer be subjected to our bombing ...

[*Analysis of the changing regional situation in 1968*] In 1965, the forces supported by North Viet Nam were on the verge of a military take-over of South Viet Nam. Only by sending large numbers of American troops was it possible to prevent this from happening. The South Vietnamese were militarily weak and politically demoralized. They could not, at that time, be expected to preserve for themselves the right to determine their own future. Communist China had recently proclaimed its intention to implement the doctrine of 'wars of national liberation'. Khrushchev's fall from power the preceding October and [Prime Minister of China] Chou En-Lai's visit to Moscow in November 1964 posed the dire possibility of the two communist giants working together to spread disruption throughout the underdeveloped nations of the world. Indonesia, under Sukarno, presented a posture of implacable hostility towards Malaysia, and was a destabilizing element in the entire Pacific picture. Malaysia itself, as well as Thailand and Singapore, needed time for their governmental institutions to mature. Apparent American indifference to developments in Asia might, at that time, have had a disastrous impact on the independent countries of that area.

During the past four years, the situation has altered dramatically. The armed forces of South Viet Nam have increased in size and proficiency. The political situation there has become more stable, and the governmental institutions more representative. Elsewhere in Asia, conditions of greater security exist. The bloody defeat of the attempted communist coup in Indonesia removed Sukarno from power and changed the confrontation with Malaysia to cooperation between the two countries. The governments of Thailand and Singapore have made good use of these four years to increase their popular support. Australia and New Zealand have moved toward closer regional defense ties, while Japan, the Republic of Korea and Taiwan have exhibited a rate of economic growth and an improvement in living standards that discredit the teachings of Chairman Mao.

Of at least equal significance is the fact that, since 1965, relations between Russia and China have steadily worsened. The schism between these two powers is one of the watershed events of our time. Ironically, their joint support of Hanoi has contributed to the acrimony between them. It has brought into focus their competition for leadership in the communist camp ... The Cultural Revolution and the depredations of the Red Guards have created in China a situation of unrest that presently preoccupies China's military forces. The recent border clashes on the Ussuri River [between China and the USSR in early 1969] further decrease the likelihood that China will, in the near future, be able to devote its attention and resources to the export of revolution.

These considerations are augmented by another. It seems clear that the necessity to devote more of our minds and our means to our pressing domestic problems requires that we set a chronological limit on our Vietnamese involvement.

A year ago [1968], we placed a numerical limit on this involvement, and did so without lessening the effectiveness of the total military effort. There will, undeniably, be many problems inherent in the replacement of American combat forces with South Vietnamese forces. But whatever these problems, they must be faced. There is no way to achieve our goal of creating the conditions that will allow the South Vietnamese to determine their own future unless we begin, and begin promptly, to turn over to them the major responsibility for their own defense. This ability to defend themselves can never be developed so long as we continue to bear the brunt of the battle. Sooner or later, the test must be whether the South Vietnamese will serve their own country sufficiently well to guarantee its national survival. In my view, this test must be made sooner, rather than later ...

In the long run, the security of the Pacific region will depend upon the ability of the countries there to meet the legitimate growing demands of their own people. No military strength we can bring to bear can give them internal stability or popular acceptance. In Southeast Asia, and elsewhere in the less developed regions of the world, our ability to understand and to control the basic forces that are at play is a very limited one. We can advise, we can urge, we can furnish economic aid. But American military power cannot build nations, any more than it can solve the social and economic problems that face us here at home.

This, then, is the case history of the evolution of one individual's thinking regarding Viet Nam. Throughout this entire period it has been difficult to cling closely to reality because of the constant recurrence of optimistic predictions that our task was nearly over, and that better times were just around the corner, or just over the top of the next hill.

We cannot afford to lose sight of the fact that this is a limited war, for limited aims and employing limited power. The forces we now have deployed and the human and material costs we are now incurring have become, in my opinion, out of all proportion to our purpose. The present scale of military effort can bring us no closer to meaningful victory. It can only continue to devastate the countryside and to prolong the suffering of the Vietnamese people of every political persuasion.

Unless we have the imagination and the courage to adopt a different course, I am convinced that we will be in no better, and no different, a position a year from now than we are today.

At current casualty rates, 10,000 more American boys will have lost their lives.

We should reduce American casualties by reducing American combat forces. We should do so in accordance with a definite schedule and with a specified end point.

Let us start to bring our men home – and let us start *now*.

2. The military take-over in Burma in 1962

The Anti-Fascist People's Freedom League (AFPFL) that led Burma to independence in January 1948 was more a mass movement than a cohesive party. It accommodated a broad spectrum of ideological groupings and factions and had, until his assassination in July 1947, depended very heavily on the charismatic leadership of Aung San. Its programme for an independent Burma combined an emphasis upon parliamentary democracy (necessary to reassure the outgoing British), with broadly state-socialist objectives in the area of the economy (necessary to placate the communist factions on the left of the AFPFL), and (in order to mollify the anxieties of the minorities) a federalized structure of government that gave certain guarantees to the Shans, Kachins, Chins and Karens. The fact, however, that independent Burma declared itself a republic, and therefore accepted exclusion from the British Commonwealth, reflected a desire to make a clean break with the colonial state, and reassert a full Burmese identity.

The following decade of independence, however, revealed the weaknesses of this new state. A case could be made for arguing that Burma was not sufficiently prepared for self-government, particularly in the light of the wartime devastation inflicted on the society and the economy. In the event, the attempt to build a socialist-orientated economy did not avert communist rebellions in 1947 and 1948; and the carefully constructed federal structure did not prevent separatist minority rebellions, starting with the Arakanese in 1948. The fact that Burma's northeastern frontier with China and Laos made it a front-line in the Asian Cold War, meant that both the communist and the separatist rebellions were embroiled in, and prolonged by, the wider conflicts of the region. In the domestic arena, the state was far too weak to implement any ambitious economic plans, and even a limited degree of state intervention resulted in stagnation and unlimited opportunities for corruption. Under these circumstances, the fragile unity of the AFPFL was tested to destruction. In 1958, the AFPFL broke up into two main factions.

U Nu's principal solution to the tendencies towards fragmentation that afflicted Burma during this period was to try to bring Buddhism into the heart of the state ideology and identity. Buddhist scholarship and education were expanded and enhanced under state patronage, and U Nu planned to make Buddhism the official state religion. This was in line with a wider trend towards the 'politicization' of Buddhism in the 1950s and early 1960s that affected Sri Lanka, Laos, Thailand and South Vietnam, as well as Burma. At the same time, U Nu was inclined to grant greater autonomous powers to the minorities as a means of resolving the deepening separatist crises of the early 1960s.

Not only did the Buddhist strategy fail to bind the nation together, but U Nu's permissive attitude towards the minorities appeared to threaten the unity of Burma itself. In 1958, the armed forces had stepped in for a while during a particularly acute political crisis, but had then allowed the civilian politicians to resume power. In March 1962, however, Ne Win and the army staged another coup. The regime that was then established has controlled Burma to the present day. In the following extract, Robert Taylor outlines the fundamental ideology and political strategy that was gradually set up after that coup d'état. It is an important analysis of the birth of the military regime in Burma, and illustrates the caution with which the regime moved towards its political goals.

Robert H. Taylor, *The State in Burma* (London: Hurst, 1987). Excerpts taken from pages 291–300.

The Consequences of the March 2nd Coup The ouster of the civilian government of Prime Minister Nu and his Union Party by a military Revolutionary Council headed by General Ne Win on March 2, 1962 was not seen at the time to be a particularly momentous event. Foreign observers saw the coup as a reassertion of the disciplined government of the 1958–1960 [military] caretaker period, and therefore primarily as an attempt to restore order in an increasingly chaotic political situation. It evoked no outward manifestations of public opposition in either Rangoon or in the central and peripheral regions of the state. The coup, conducted with the loss of one life, began with the arrest of the President, the Prime Minister [U Nu], five other cabinet ministers, the Chief Justice and some thirty politicians and former *Sawbwas* [local hereditary rulers] from the Shan and Kayah [Karenni] States. Though it took place during a strike by Rangoon's importers and retail traders against government plans to turn more trade over to citizens, this apparently had no bearing on the decision by the army to replace the civilian government.

Rather, the army justified its action in the name of ensuring the continued unity of the nation. Nu's policies since 1960, especially the establishment of Buddhism as the state religion, the organization of administrations for new Mon and Arakan States, and the continuing negotiations with politicians from the Shan and Kayah States over increasing regional autonomy, raised the prospect to the army and to many others of increasing disunity in the state and of the possible loss of independence. The examples of Laos and South Vietnam, both then riven by civil war and consequently under foreign domination, were very much alive in the minds of many people, including the coup leaders.

The issue of federalism and the possibility of trying to apportion state sovereignty were intimately related to other central questions. The granting of greater autonomy to the states would have allowed them to pursue different patterns of economic development and would have further under-mined socialism, which was of decreasing importance to Nu anyway. The possibility of the secession of the Shan and Kayah States raised the prospect of independent foreign policies for these regions and, should they have elected to do so, of their entry into an alliance with an outside power such as the United States. This would have posed a major threat to the security of the remainder of the state, with the possibility of direct conflict between China and the United States extending beyond Laos and Vietnam to the heart of Burma. Such possibilities were not considered fanciful in 1962.

The federal issue was part of a general critique, widely shared within the army, of the nature of parliamentary democracy as it had been practised in Burma. Federalism and multi-party democracy were considered open to abuse by politicians representing landlords and capitalists and others seeking power and wealth for personal rather than public ends. This critique subsequently became not only the justification for the coup but also the justification for the changes in the nature of the state that followed from military rule. It soon became clear as a result of this critique that the consequences of the coup for the state and society were more significant than just the temporary replacement of one set of rulers by another. The weakness of the post-colonial state was attributed to parliamentary democracy and federalism, and therefore it seemed obvious that their abolition was necessary in order for the state to reassert itself over other institutions in civil society.

Though the Revolutionary Council did not initially phrase its seizure of power in the name of state reassertion, it did so twelve years later when formally passing power to the new legislative body, the *Pyithu Hluttaw* or People's Assembly, formed under the constitution inaugurated on March 2, 1974. In a detailed but unpublished report of its stewardship of the state, the Revolutionary Council wrote that after it 'took responsibility for the condition of the state (*naingngantaw*), it began a transitional revolution with the intention of establishing a socialist society of affluence and without human exploitation, with a strong governing power, and the long term independence for the state' ...

In the two years between the coup and March 1964, by which time the bulk of the economy had been nationalized, the Revolutionary Council declared illegal all political opposition, took over the direct management of most educational and cultural organizations, and established the nucleus of a political party with ancillary mass organizations and its own ideology through which support for the state would be organized. The process required the demobilization of institutions which had rivalled the state for allegiance during the previous two decades and necessitated the creation of institutional substitutes tied directly to the state.

After organizing itself as a government of eight members and after issuing its announcement on foreign policy, on March 3 the Revolutionary Council eliminated the major organs established by the 1947 constitution, including the central legislature and the councils set up as the putative governments of the Kachin, Shan, Karen, and Kayah states and the Chin Special Division ... Two days later, on March 5, all legislative, judicial and executive powers of state were placed in the hands of the Chairman of the Revolutionary Council. As both head of state and of government, Chairman Ne Win in theory possessed all state power and thus achieved a position of formal dominance within the state unprecedented since 1885. However, an attempt was made to suggest the collective nature of the Revolutionary Council government by substituting the designation 'Chairman' for 'Prime Minister'.

Revealing the Revolutionary Council's initial desire to gain the cooperation of other political groups in its attempts to recast the structures of the state, Council Chairman Ne Win met with the leaders of the civilian political parties on a number of occasions. Not surprisingly, the leadership of the political groups which had been consistently denied state power during the previous fourteen years pledged their support for the Revolutionary Council, whereas the groups which had held power previously refused to cooperate for fear of losing their independence or because they believed that the military government would not last long. In meetings in April and May, the civilian party leaders refused to join with the Revolutionary Council in forming a single political party under its leadership.

In the initial months of the Revolutionary Council the state-centred and comparatively radical socialist economic policies subsequently instituted were little in evidence. Though the Revolutionary Council made it clear that one of the purposes of the coup was to put the economy back on the road to the socialist goals of the original AFPFL, within six days of the coup the Minister for Trade, the 'pragmatic' Brigadier Aung Gyi (then considered the second most influential member of the coup group), reversing the policy of the previous government, stated that any plans for the nationalization of import trade would be postponed for at least two years. Not until August 1, when Imperial Chemical Industries was nationalized, was a major economic measure taken. Evidence of what was to come became clear in November when the government abolished the ten-year guarantee against the expropriation of foreign investments. More radical economic policies were not, however, introduced until after the resignation of Aung Gyi from the Revolutionary Council on February 8, 1963. The departure of Aung Gyi was probably necessary for the abrupt change in economic and political policy which followed.

But the change in economic policy in early 1963 lay in more than just a clash of wills between Aung Gyi's supporters and those of the chairman in the Revolutionary Council. During the preceding ten months the Revolutionary Council had sought, but from the perspective of its more ardently socialist members had not received, the cooperation of party leaders and national businessmen. Thus a majority of the government felt they would have to pursue their goals without the cooperation of other institutions and groups. A week after Aung Gyi's resignation the chairman announced thoroughgoing policies to nationalize both foreign and domestic trade as well as banking and manufacturing.

Earlier, however, the intention of the Revolutionary Council to intervene in aspects of society previously considered private was apparent. In a series of orders issued in March 1962 it was announced that horse racing would be banned in one year's time, that beauty contests and all government-sponsored music, song and dance competitions would be prohibited, and that gambling was to be banned in the Shan State. The state assumed direct control of the universities on May 14 but divorced itself formally from the Buddhist faith on May 17 by dissolving the Buddhist Sasana Council. In the next month the American Ford and Asia Foundations and the Fulbright programme as well as British and American language training schemes were closed and from then on only governments or international agencies (having been granted state approval) were permitted to train Burmese nationals. In August, the state assumed control over all publishing by establishing a system of registered printers. By these moves, and others, such as an officially sponsored National Literary Conference in November, the state began to seal Burmese culture from outside influences and to focus public attention on state-sanctioned cultural activities. At the same time, the state was distancing itself from social and religious issues which in its frame of reference were too politically threatening for the state to attempt to control, and which had, in the past, led to dissatisfaction among followers of different religious faiths.

The Revolutionary Council was aware of the utility of a state ideology around which the populace could focus its beliefs and loyalties, and which could be used as a means of mobilizing popular support for the state. The experiences of the military leadership during the anti-fascist resistance of the 1940s had convinced them of the need for a form of 'united front'-style organization to direct popular energies. A first step in the direction of shaping public opinion was taken on April 30 with the publication of the Revolutionary Council's policy statement, 'The Burmese Way to Socialism'. To be useful for the state as a long-term doctrine, this statement had to be sufficiently vague not to tie the government to an explicit set of policies, but sufficiently emotive to appeal to public sentiment. Following the failure of the major civilian political party leaders to join them in forming a new national front, the Revolutionary Council launched its own party, the Burma Socialist Programme Party (BSPP), on July 4, thirty years to the day since the founding of the *Do Bama Asiayon*. Indeed, many of the Revolutionary Council's ideas and much of its style echoed the *Do Bama Asiayon*'s prewar manifesto and evoked much the same response from established interests. At first the Party was composed only of members of the Revolutionary Council, although other politicians, especially of the left, became involved in its early organization. A philosophical underpinning of the Party's ideology was issued the following January as the *System of Correlation of Man and His Environment* ...

The BSPP was to be the party of all the working people and therefore the Revolutionary Council and the post-coup state claimed a different class bias from its left- and right-wing predecessors. As made explicit in a document called the 'Specific Characteristics of the Burmese Way to Socialism', published on September 4, 1964, the Revolutionary Council, in an attempt to defend itself from charges of being Communist and anti-religious in its orientation, argued that the state had now become based not upon the narrow capitalist and landlord class which had primarily benefited from independence, nor that class's enemy, the Communist Party, but rather upon all the people.

The development of these ideological expressions stem from two characteristics of the coup group. First, the major figures of the period had been raised on the anti-imperialist and anti-capitalist rhetoric of the *Do Bama Asiayon* and of the Anti-Fascist Organization. During the war organizers from the Communist movement had worked among the Japanese-trained officer corps, instilling the rhetoric of Marxist-Leninist politics. Secondly, some former Communists and others of the left were among the first civilians to express support for the Revolutionary Council, and their skills with language and propaganda were thus used by the state. But unlike previous political movements in recent Burmese history the Revolutionary Council did not want to use the rhetoric of its ideology to mobilize one class against another in revolution or elections, but rather wanted to unite the entire nation by demonstrating that all classes had made their contribution to the national effort, but that, due to improper leadership, the revolution had gone astray.

The rhetoric of the Revolutionary Council belied its early appearance and behaviour. Though it said it was conducting a revolution, efforts were made to gain the cooperation of both previously legal and illegal political groups, and, initially, few political opponents were arrested. In the first months after the coup life went on much as normal for most Burmese, and even when sweeping economic changes were introduced they tended to be implemented piecemeal. For example, though the press came under effective government control as early as August 1962, the Burmese-language papers *Hanthawaddy* and *Myanma Alin* were not nationalized until January 1969.

What most determined the style of the Revolutionary Council and has consequently become characteristic of the style of the state since 1962 is that a majority of its leading personnel have had their formative administrative and political experiences within the army. Thus, the army-style of command and planning has tended to become that of the state. Military analogies and examples most readily come to the minds of the senior leaders. Three years after the coup, for example, General Ne Win described his position as the leader of the Revolutionary Council in military terms: 'Like the commander of a military unit in disarray, I am faced with the problem of how to mobilise and regroup the people in order to set up an organisation that will serve the interests of the country in a spirit of unity.' The leadership's working concept of a socialist economy was more like a system of military post exchanges than of a complex national organization of production and commerce. Again, a phrase from General Ne Win is suggestive: 'Internal trade is our real problem. I say trade only by convention. Internal distribution may be more appropriate for socialism.' Military metaphors are common in state and party documents also. For example, in describing the first year of nation-wide monopoly paddy purchasing by the state, the Revolutionary Council's un-published report to the first *Pyithu Hluttaw* noted that the local administrative committees 'supervised the whole process effectively in the form of a military operation'.

Since 1962 the state has appeared to much of the rest of the world as isolated and *sui generis*. By the mid-1960s the economy was becoming less and less involved in world trade. Whereas in the 1950s the ratio of Burma's foreign trade (imports plus exports) to gross domestic product, a common indicator of an economy's external development, was 40 per cent, it fell to 26 per cent between 1960 and 1970, and to 13 per cent between 1970 and 1977, one of the lowest among developing economies. There has been little change since. The state's radical economic autarky and general disengagement from the world, including in 1979 leaving the Non-Aligned Movement, has been exceptional. Its domestic economic policies – which appear to have been intended to reduce the economic level of the cities to that of the countryside rather than the reverse, which is the normal pattern in the rest of non-Communist Asia – have seemed perverse to observers who judge 'development' and well-being in terms of international hotels and 'GNP per capita in US dollar' terms. Indeed, some of their policies such as the 1964 edict which 'unified retail rice prices throughout the Union at the prices ruling in the Delta' had to be abandoned because of their economic impracticability. Why then, did the Revolutionary Council propose policies that seemed to fly in the face of 'common sense'?

Faced with what they perceived to be an obligation to strengthen and perpetuate the state, and having abandoned the option of turning to the outside world for material support, the Revolutionary Council had no option but to turn inwards and restructure the relationship of the state with the institutions of civil society. The post-colonial state stood, as it were, weak and suspended between the world economy, dominated by Western financial institutions, markets and states, and its own population. Rejecting the threats to security and independence that an outside alliance would have entailed, they turned to find means of gaining the cooperation and support of the largest section of the population, the peasantry. Unlike the state-builders of Western Europe or North America, they sought not to please an entrepreneurial class of manufacturers or traders. No significant bourgeoisie existed in Burma. Rather, the only internal group powerful enough to bring down the state was the peasantry, and so this class's inherent and historical antipathy toward the state and its exactions had to be overcome.

3. 'Gestapu' and the installation of military rule in Indonesia

In his concept of Guided Democracy, Sukarno envisaged a dynamic tension between political and social forces in Indonesia, but within an authoritarian framework 'guided' by himself. The 'revolutionary' energies thus generated would be directed against external enemies – Western imperialism and their local Asian supporters – and internal 'reactionary' elements. Sukarno's rhetoric shifted decisively to the left in the last years of Guided Democracy (see Chapter 8), and the Indonesian Communist Party (PKI) increasingly became the central ideological force in the regime, while at the same time it was building a formidable and openly organized mass base. By 1965, it seemed that only the implacable opposition of most of the armed forces leadership and Sukarno's apparent objective of maintaining a 'balance' of political forces stood between the PKI and a gradual, or violent, attempt to take over power.

Sukarno's regime thrived on rumour, and by 1965 these rumours had reached a pitch where some kind of confrontation between Left and Right in Indonesia seemed inevitable. There has been much debate over the background to the events of the night of 30 September 1965. It seems that Sukarno was more deeply involved than the PKI in the early stages of the coup directed against the armed forces leadership, and it seems highly unlikely that the PKI would have planned such an incompetent operation as the murder and attempted murder of the army leadership in Jakarta. What was probably intended by the coup leaders was not a full-scale coup d'état, but a shift in the balance of forces within the armed forces, 'helped along' by a few exemplary murders. Whatever the initial role of the PKI, however, the PKI newspaper, *Harian Rakyat*, put its full weight behind the coup on the morning of 1 October 1965. This fact alone sealed the fate of the communists and sympathetic leftists in Indonesia.

Below is a concise summary of the 'Gestapu' events and their aftermath, and an analysis of the centrality of these events in the whole epoch of post-colonial Indonesian history. In effect, an army that had since its inception during the Japanese occupation been a political as well as a military force took over the political system, and has dominated it ever since.

Michael van Langenburg, 'Gestapu and State Power in Indonesia', in Robert Cribb (ed.), *The Indonesian Killings of 1965–1966: Studies from Java and Bali* (Clayton, Victoria: Monash Papers on Southeast Asia, Centre of Southeast Asian Studies, Monash University, 1990). Excerpts taken from pages 45–61.

The usual image of the establishment of Indonesia's 'New Order' (*Orde Baru*) and Suharto's rise to political power is one of gradual, 'slow but sure' progress. But, in fact, the political process which actually replaced the 'Old' order of Guided Democracy with the 'New' had been carried out effectively within six months of the outbreak of the so-called Gestapu affair of 30 September/1 October 1965. The basic power structure of the New Order state was put in place between 1 October 1965 and mid-March 1966. This was possible principally because the violence of mass killings in late 1965 permitted the speedy elimination of political opponents and the restoration of order upon which future hegemony could be built.

The Gestapu affair erupted on the night of 30 September 1965 with the abduction and murder of six senior members of the military high command and an adjutant to the Defence Minister. This was ostensibly part of an attempted transfer of state power to a Revolutionary Council (Dewan Revol-usi), appointed by a '30 September Movement' (Gerakan 30 September). In fewer than twenty-four hours, however, the attempted seizure of power had been crushed by military forces led by the commander of the Army's Strategic Command (KOSTRAD), Major-General Suharto.

The Suharto-led military command did not merely crush the attempted 'coup', but also set about seizing political power. The defeated Movement was dubbed with the acronym *Gestapu* (for Gerakan September Tiga Puluh, Movement of September 30) ... presumably with the intention of investing it with the aura of evil associated with the term 'Gestapo'. On 2 October 1965, the army's Supreme Operational Command (Komando Operasi Ter-tinggi, KOTI) established an Action Front to Crush the Gestapu (KAP [Komando Aksi Pengganyangan]–Gestapu), an alliance of militant young anti-communist leaders in Jakarta. In the meantime, the corpses of the seven murdered officers were recovered from a well in the Lubang Buaya (Crocodile Hole) district at the Halim Perdanakusumah Air Force base outside Jakarta. Five days after the recovery of the bodies, KAP–Gestapu held a mass rally in Jakarta which climaxed with an attack on the headquarters of the Indonesian Communist Party (PKI). The building was ransacked and burned. In the next few days, an Operational Command for the Restoration of Security and Order (Komando Operasi Pemulihan Keamanan, KOPKAMTIB) was formed under Suharto's command to identify, arrest and investigate all those responsible for and involved in the 30 September Movement. KOPKAMTIB's powers were undefined, other than to 'restore order and security', and effectively unlimited by any juridical restraint. Almost immediately afterwards, in the province of Aceh, troops from the regional military command joined militant Islamic youth in a massacre of PKI supporters. On 17 October Suharto, in an instruction to all army personnel, declared the PKI to be 'traitorous' and announced that 1 October, the day on which the 30 September Movement had been crushed, would henceforth be celebrated as Sacred Pancasila Memorial Day (Hari Peringatan Pancasila Sakti).

Within days of the failure of the 30 September Movement, the commanders of the army strategic reserve, KOSTRAD, and of the paracommando unit RPKAD, together with their allies embarked on a deliberate campaign to promote a climate of fear and retribution. A crucial element was a propaganda campaign, especially during October and November, aimed at creating popular fear and loathing of the PKI and its supporters. Photographs of the grisly exhumation of the bodies of the seven slain officers were displayed prominently in most of the print media. These were accompanied by lurid accounts of the murdered officers having been sexually assaulted and mutilated by members of the PKI women's movement, Gerwani. The murder of General Nasution's infant daughter, fatally wounded in the course of the attempt to abduct Nasution himself on 30 September, was publicized to its maximum tragic extent. The state funerals of the seven slain officers and of Nasution's young daughter were held with pomp and ceremony, and wide media exposure. The populace was urged to have little mercy on the perpetrators of the Gestapu affair who were principally identified as being the PKI. They were publically vilified as 'traitors' (*pengkhianat*), 'devils' (*setan*), child-murderers and sexually dissolute women. Published reports and rumours spread widely that the nation had only just escaped a massive purge of anti-communists, planned by the PKI, in the wake of the Gestapu. From the popular media, from military commanders and from anti-communist political leaders, the crushing of 'Gestapu–PKI' was urged on with the urgency of 'kill or be killed'. The 'kill or be killed' atmosphere was heightened soon after Gestapu by the appearance in virtually all regions where mass killings later occurred, of alleged death lists, purported to have been drawn up the PKI in preparation for a post-coup extermination of anti-communists.

In the second half of October 1965, groups of anti-communist youth in

Central and East Java, mostly belonging to Islamic and Christian organizations, began mass killings of alleged PKI sympathisers. Simultaneously, RPKAD (paracommando) units began moving through Central Java, with instructions from Jakarta to restore order and crush the remnants of the 30 September Movement. The Movement as such no longer had organized form, but its remnants were identified as being members and alleged sympathisers of the PKI. In Java the RPKAD armed and trained anti-communist youth groups for the specific purpose of crushing the PKI. Similar activity was under way in northern Sumatra, where KOSTRAD (Strategic Reserve) special units and others from the regional military command promoted and supported the mass killing of PKI sympathisers by local anti-communist youth.

Under army supervision, and with army participation, large-scale massacres took place in Central and East Java, Bali and northern Sumatra. Class interests, religious fervour, communal hatreds, deep ideological differences were all mobilized in the anti-communist violence. Thousands of vigilante groups, supported by military units and frequently directed by military commanders, spread through the regions, killing or arresting alleged PKI sympathisers. Tens of thousands were placed under military detention. The PKI, which in early 1965 had claimed some three million party members with another fifteen million in affiliated organizations, was destroyed as a political force.

By early December, the bloodbath, having claimed at least a quarter of a million victims, began to lose the 'momentum' of the previous two months. The institutional instrument for the exercise of state power on behalf of the new regime, the KOPKAMTIB, was in place. The consolidation of power now demanded a restoration of order. The military high command moved to bring the mass violence to an end, restraining vigilante actions by militant anti-communist groups. KOPKAMTIB, as an intelligence and security command network extending from Suharto, as commander, down to local military commanders at village level, was utilized for this purpose. All military commanders within the national territorial military command structure were made responsible for carrying out the KOPKAMTIB tasks of intelligence and internal security. In particular, KOPKAMTIB was made responsible for purging the civil service of persons alleged to have been involved in the 30 September Movement. Suharto, the KOPKAMTIB commander, was promoted to Minister/Army Commander. On 6 December, a presidential decision expanded KOPKAMTIB activities to 'restore the authority of the Government by means of physical–military and mental operations'. The Army general staff was made the staff command for KOPKAMTIB, with power to co-opt assistance from the navy, air force and police. Special operations by KOPKAMTIB could, in addition, draw on the resources of all government departments, as required. Finally, all military units in the country, from the inter-regional and provincial commands down to village level, were made operational units of KOPKAMTIB.

Between December 1965 and March 1966 the state's management of violence shifted from military-promoted killings at the local level to much more centrally-directed arrests and detention of Old Order remnants, carried out through the KOPKAMTIB apparatus. At the same time, the transfer of state power was completed. In March 1966, President Sukarno was compelled to sign the now famous instruction of 11 March (Surat Perintah Sebelas Maret) or Supersemar, empowering Suharto, newly appointed as Minister/Army Commander, to:

> Take all measures considered necessary to ensure peace and order
> and stability of the Revolution ... in the interests of the Nation and
> State of the Republic of Indonesia ...

This acknowledged that effective control of state power was in the hands of Suharto and his military command. The next day, Suharto issued a decree in the name of the President declaring the PKI illegal, and ordering the dissolution of the party and all its affiliated organizations.

Within a week of Supersemar, on Suharto's orders, fifteen ministers were removed from Sukarno's presidential cabinet. Twelve of them, including two of the four deputy prime ministers, were placed under arrest by KOPKAMTIB. In the next few weeks further purges took place. More cabinet ministers were removed. PKI and Sukarnoist sympathisers in the state bureaucracy were purged. Over three hundred Air Force officers were arrested. Purges were extended rapidly to the other armed services and the police. In June 1966 the new military command convened a session of the Provisional People's Consultative Assembly (Majelis Permusyawaratan Rakyat Sementara, MPRS), purged of its PKI members and their supporters. This New Order MPRS endorsed the legality of the Supersemar and drastically curtailed Sukarno's powers as president, including rescinding his appointment as president-for-life.

The power of the New Order state was consolidated and expanded during the next five years. By the middle of 1966, state power was effectively in the hands of a new military-dominated oligarchy, headed by General Suharto. Nine months later, by the end of March 1967, virtually the entire state apparatus (civilian and military), purged of 'Old Order' elements, was under the control of this oligarchy. Suharto was appointed Acting President by the MPRS. Several senior members of the former regime were put on trial for treason, and convicted ... Drastic changes in economic policy were under way. The army swiftly completed the formulation and issue of a long-standing doctrine asserting its permanent role in Indonesian socio-political life. The command structure of the armed forces was re-organized, centralized, and brought under Suharto's authority. Construction was begun of a new state-controlled, 'non-party' political organization. The nucleus for this was the army-sponsored Joint Secretariat of Functional Groups (Sekbar Golkar) which had been set up in 1964, as an anti-Communist popular front, to coordinate anti-PKI organizations within the National Front (Front Nasional). In 1969, the implementation of the first Five Year Development Plan (Rencana Pembangunan Lima Tahun, Repelita), saw a major program of state-directed economic reconstruction under way. Within a further three years, following a successfully managed general election, state power was considerably more centralized and more functionally effective over the civil society at large than at any time since 1942.

Before Gestapu, a dominating feature in the history both of Indonesian nationalism and of the Indonesian national polity had been the defining of Indonesian national identity. The building of state power was intrinsically absorbed within, and took second place to, struggles to construct a nationalist polity. After the declaration of Indonesian independence in 1945, the major forces competing for control of the national state were primarily concerned with establishing a nationalist legitimacy to govern. The struggles were for the *control of*, rather than the *building of*, state power. Since Gestapu, it is the growth and centralization of state power that has dominated the national polity. Before Gestapu the building of state power was intrinsically absorbed within struggles to construct a nationalist polity. Since Gestapu these priorities have been reversed. From this perspective, the image of continuity of state power through the twentieth century needs to be qualified. There has undoubtedly been continuity in state apparatus from the colonial state to the present – such as institutions of civil administration or organized religion. But this does not mean the same thing as continuity of state power. On the contrary, the conditions of state power have varied drastically during this century. Throughout the twenty-three years from the termination of Dutch colonial rule by the Japanese in 1942 until the collapse of Guided Democracy in 1965, the power of the state was considerably diminished if compared both with the preceding forty years of Dutch colonial rule and the subsequent era of the New Order since Gestapu.

Neither has the consolidation of state power in the post-Gestapu era been simply a continuity between pre-World War II 'colonial' and contemporary 'post-colonial' state systems: broken briefly by a 'deviant' period of immediate post-independence upheaval. Rather, the New Order is a distinctive product of the dialectic between national identity and state power that has dominated a half century of Indonesian national politics. That dialectic, important in the national discourse of the 1920s and 1930s, became even more prominent after the Japanese occupation of the Indies in 1942. Since then, the emergence of the military as an important institutional base for Indonesian nationalism has seen even more overt assertions of authoritarian models contributed to the debates about the ideal Indonesian nation-state.

As political disorders developed within the Indonesian polity between 1945 and 1965, contradictions between the needs of state power and the search for national identity increased. The establishment of the system of Guided Democracy in 1959 was itself an attempt on the part of Sukarno

and some other national leaders to resolve just such contradictions. Guided
Democracy sought resolution through compromise, even consensus, directed
by an authoritarian state. However, the two generations of conflict within
Indonesian nationalism had made compromise, let alone consensus, increasingly unlikely. The political divisions of the nationalist discourse continued
to prevail over the consolidation of state power ...

The political debates and conflicts within the Guided Democracy political
system had spread widely during the early 1960s into the villages and small
towns of Indonesia. Ideological and communal hatreds reached high emotional
levels. Simultaneously, a powerful 'alliance' of political forces – consisting of
military officers, bureaucrats, intelligentsia, entrepreneurs, politicians and
community leaders – emerged, anxious to see an end to political upheaval.
Most were intensely anti-Communist. They wanted a more regulated civil
society, orderly and, importantly, one orientated towards economic development. In the conditions prevailing by mid-1965 this could not be achieved
without some final resolution of political conflicts. There was no longer any
room for political compromise, such as had occurred frequently since 1945.
Resolution would have to mean a clear victory for the victors, and overwhelming defeat for the losers. Just that occurred between October 1965 and
March 1966. The result has been the construction of a powerful state system
that has engendered manifold changes in the structural patterns of civil
society.

The mass violence that had occurred in the wake of the failure of the 30
September Movement was crucial in the consolidation and expansion of state
power under the New Order regime. It served three important purposes.
First was the elimination of the leadership of the PKI and the destruction
of its mass cadre structure. Second, it issued an unequivocal warning to those
who might consider a challenge to the new ruling elite. Third, it created a
dramatic historical break, a break since made part of the hegemonic ideology
of the state system with the official celebration of 1 October as Hari
Peringatan Pancasila Sakti (Sacred Pancasila Memorial Day). The sheer scale
of the killings particularly was important in facilitating state hegemony ...

Irrespective of what percentage of the massacres may have been 'spontaneous', as distinct from being deliberately directed by state authorities, the
total scale of the social trauma of the killings made the main instruments of
this hegemony – KOPKAMTIB, fear of Communism, the acceptance of
order and stability (*ketertiban* and *stabilitas*) in the interests of economic
development (*pembangunan*) – much more easily utilized by the state. Put
crudely, the deaths of a mere 1000 would not have provided KOPKAMTIB
and Supersemar with the legitimacy in the restoration of order that the
deaths of over 100,000 did. The massacres endorsed the military as a powerful
and ruthless instrument of state power. They endorsed Communism as an
instrument of chaos and disorder ...

The legitimacy of the New Order has been built on its role as the restorer of order. The scale of the killings has served to consolidate in the public mind an image of the Old Order as a period of chaos and disorder. The New Order has used the historical memory of the killings in the establishment of its own legitimacy. The killings themselves are not given any prominence in the official histories of the New Order. They are certainly not justified solely as retribution by the New Order against the Old. Where retribution is suggested, it is usually presented as being that of the spontaneous actions by the 'People' against 'Communist' treachery. This places ultimate responsibility for the mass violence at the feet of the PKI and its political allies: making that violence a consequence of the chaos of the Old Order, not the beginning of the New. In the years since 1966, it is the memory of past disorder, and not the details of the mass killings themselves, which the official discourse of the New Order regime has emphasized. If the engineered climate of fear and retribution in the immediate aftermath of Gestapu was important to the seizure of state power itself, the historical memory of disorder has been crucial in the subsequent consolidation of that power ...

Establishing a contrast with the disorder of the past is, therefore, a crucial need. In the dominant ideology and political iconography of the New Order, the mass killings are a consequence of the Old Order, a signifier of an especially distasteful past. The heroes of the New Order are the seven officers who fell victim to that disorder (killed by the 30 September Movement) and those who brought that disorder to an end. The term Gestapu has been coined by the victors to emphasize the demonic forces of the Old Order, from which the nation has been rescued. The chief satanic enemy is identified as 'Gestapu/PKI' or 'G–30–S/PKI'. Formulations about Pancasila, Undang-undang Dasar '45 (the 1945 State Constitution), and Dwifungsi/ABRI (the civil–military 'dual function' of the armed forces) are used to stress constitutional order, political stability and cultural cohesion as products of the New Order state. Implicit, is that these will protect the nation from political chaos such as that of 1960–65.

Since 1966, the term Gestapu has come to signify chaos and disorder. In contrast, Supersemar signifies social order and stability. The two 'icons' of the New Order state, the Monumen Pancasila Sakti (Sacred Pancasila Monument), erected on the site of the 'Crocodile Hole' well in which the bodies of the seven murdered officers were found in October 1965, and the Super-semar document itself, emphasize this. In the discourse of both, nationalism is subordinated to assertions of state power. Whilst nationalistic sentiment has certainly not disappeared from public political rhetoric since October 1965, it has been subordinated to the interests of the state. During the pre-Gestapu Guided Democracy years, it was nationalism that had been the driving force in a popular rhetoric of revolution and anti-imperialism. Since Gestapu, nationalism has been made part of a hegemony of order and stability, and put to the service of a corporate, managerial state ...

The Gestapu affair initiated the greatest outbreak of violence in modern

Indonesian history. The many thousands who resorted to violence in 1965 and the few who utilized it to build a strong state system were all responding in some sense to circumstances arising from the intense internecine conflicts that had beset Indonesian nationalism for over half a century. Prominent in those conflicts were struggles between 'Marxism' and 'anti-Communism', tied in with, and mostly determined by, primordial factors of cultural identity and religious belief. This long struggle was called upon to motivate and justify the violent seizure of state power in 1965/66. Both God (Tuhan/Allah/Dewa) and cultural traditions (ethnic identity, traditional values, etc.) were invoked to combat Communism as 'atheistic' and 'foreign' ...

The Gestapu affair and its consequences is significant well beyond the history of modern Indonesia alone. It could be argued that apart from Indonesia, only in the Soviet Union, China and Spain in this century has mass violence on a huge scale within the national polity also been utilized to build a state system vastly more powerful than before; and, in consequence, so markedly change the civil society within a generation.

CHAPTER 10

1975: The Crossroads and Beyond

[A]n independent Singapore survives and will survive because it has established a relationship of interdependence in the rapidly expanding global economic system. (S. Rajaratnam, 'Singapore: Global City', 1972)

[T]he victory of Vietnam has opened a new stage of development, extremely favourable, for the world revolutionary movement. (Le Duan, 'Forward to the Future', 1975)

Regime resilience and regional security

The turbulent period of the 1960s and early 1970s, during which the regimes that had achieved independence in Southeast Asia were either removed or severely modified, has been followed by an era of relative political stability and continuity. In Burma and Indonesia, the armed forces that took over power in the 1960s remain the dominant forces in their respective nations. After the political uncertainties of the 1960s, the two ruling parties of Malaysia and Singapore – UMNO and the People's Action Party (PAP) – have kept an iron grip on the political system. In Vietnam and Laos, the communist parties have, since their victories in 1975, maintained complete control over the whole state apparatus. Leaving to one side the special case of Cambodia, the only countries where 'regime continuity' does not appear to have been maintained are Thailand and the Philippines. Through the 1970s and early 1980s, Thailand underwent a period of considerable political turmoil, marked by the inability of either military or civilian-parliamentary regimes to achieve lasting stability. In the Philippines, Marcos' regime began to crumble in the early 1980s, and its eventual collapse in 1906 was followed by years of uncertainty, punctuated by a number of attempted military coups. In both cases, however, it is noticeable that these intervals of turmoil have followed similar patterns: namely, a gradual reduction of military control over the political system, and a steady entrenchment of democratic political institutions.

These regime changes were, from the mid-1960s onwards, accompanied by a heightened awareness of the threats to regional security. After the fall of Sukarno and the destruction of the PKI in Indonesia, the 'Confrontation' border war in Sarawak between Indonesia and the Malaysian Federation rapidly came to an end. The general threat that all the states of the region faced from communist subversion – encouraged by either the Chinese or Vietnamese Communists – forced the regimes of the region to recognize that their survival and stability depended on a subordination of cross-border claims and conflicts to the general mutual need for regional security. This sense of common purpose lay behind the creation in 1967 of ASEAN, the Association of South-East Asian Nations. Although this emphasized loosely defined cooperation rather than a tight concept of mutual security, it was nevertheless highly significant in that it was a strictly regional pact that was not bolstered by the ex-colonial powers or the United States; and in that it joined together the core nations – Malaysia, Indonesia, Thailand, the Philippines and Singapore – of the region, many of which had hitherto been identified with different Western 'patrons'. A 'post-colonial' logic of regional security was now replacing the security structures of the era of colonialism and decolonization. This tendency was reinforced by the enunciation in 1969 of the so-called 'Nixon Doctrine' by the newly elected American president, in which it was made clear that the United States expected its regional allies – including those in Asia – to bear the primary burden of maintaining their security against external and internal threats. The United States would from now on play a 'back-up' rather than the kind of 'substitute' role they had played in Vietnam.

It seemed that 'regional resilience', therefore, was being built up along with 'regime resilience'; but in some ways, the perspective of the Southeast Asian states and economies was already, by the 1970s, becoming global as well as regional. The most remarkable example of this was the Republic of Singapore. In 1965, Singapore was ejected from the Federation of Malaysia, because its ethnic composition and its political culture had seriously disturbed the overall stability of the state. Singapore now had to embark on an uncertain future, in which its very 'viability' as an independent state appeared to be doubtful. As a Chinese city surrounded by an overwhelmingly Malayo-Islamic region, an entrepôt without a hinterland or access to natural resources, with a political system and society that had since colonial times been honeycombed by communist organizations, Singapore faced massive problems.

In fact, it was this very sense of risk and threat surrounding Singapore in its early years – in addition to the atmosphere of brinkmanship that its leadership generated – that was the dynamo which gave the economy and society its essential energy. By the early 1970s, with the internal security of the regime assured, the regional constraints on the Singapore economy forced its leaders to look beyond the region and 'think globally' (see 'Singapore and the global economy', p. 285).

The communist victory in Indochina and its impact

Paradoxically, this new Southeast Asian era was consolidating at precisely the time that Marxism-Leninism finally triumphed in Indochina.

The most important results of the Indochina cease-fire agreements of 1973 were, first, that the non-communist regimes of Laos and South Vietnam were allowed to remain intact; but, second, that the United States removed its direct military presence. Unless, therefore, the United States was prepared in the future to reintroduce direct military support for the non-communist regimes in Indochina, the military balance had tilted decisively to the communist side.

As far as Cambodia was concerned, the fact that the Khmer Rouge did not accept the 1973 truce agreement meant that the civil war between the Khmer Rouge and the Khmer Republic continued unabated, a civil war in which the non-communist side was severely weakened after summer 1973, when the United States was forced by Congress to end its bombing support. Rejection of the truce agreement also gave an early indication of the divergence of policy between the Vietnamese and Lao communists on one side, and the more militant and dogmatic Khmer Rouge on the other.

By 1974, it was apparent to the communist leadership in North Vietnam that a political settlement favourable to the communist side could not be reached through negotiations. The cease-fire, moreover, had given the South Vietnamese regime the chance to consolidate. It was therefore decided to resume military action, which began in earnest in early 1975. By this time, the United States was so embroiled in the internal crisis caused by the Watergate scandal and the resignation of President Nixon in 1974, and so traumatized by the whole Vietnam war experience, that a military recommitment to South Vietnam had become a political impossibility.

When the North Vietnamese began their assault on the Central Highlands in March 1975, the South Vietnamese regime simply unravelled, first in the Central Highlands, then in the northern and central coastal provinces, and finally in Saigon and the Mekong Delta. By the end of April, the South Vietnamese state had disappeared. The Royal Lao government rapidly disintegrated in the wake of these events in Vietnam. By the spring of 1975, the Cambodian civil war also came to its inevitable and grisly conclusion with the Khmer Rouge seizure of Phnom Penh on 17 April.

Many explanations for the spectacular collapse of South Vietnam have been offered, but the simple explanation is that the anti-communist regime had never, following its creation by the French after the Second World War, had 'nationalist legitimacy' or been self-sustaining in military, administrative or economic terms. After 1954, its survival had depended on the life-support machine of American aid; when that plug was pulled, the demise of the regime was only a matter of time.

Thus came to an end a conflict that had cast a shadow over the Southeast Asian region for thirty years. For the Vietnamese communists, it was a stunning victory, a vindication of years of struggle and endurance (see 'Vision of victory: Vietnam in 1975', p. 291). For the rest of Southeast Asia, however, the victory of communism in Indochina caused alarm and uncertainty. The immediate excesses of the Khmer Rouge regime – in particular the forced evacuation of Phnom Penh – provided no reassurance concerning the character of these new communist states. And, although the initial statements and behaviour of the communist parties in Vietnam and Laos were more conciliatory, the programme for unification was pushed forward rapidly in Vietnam after 1975, as also were the forced-pace programmes for the 'socialization' of the economies in both Vietnam and Laos. It was evident, in other words, that Indochina was moving deliberately along an entirely different ideological, political and economic track from that of the rest of Southeast Asia. Clearly, although it was apparent that these regimes would for the foreseeable future be preoccupied with the tasks of internal reconstruction, the expansionist dynamic implicit in communist ideology, along with the sheer military power of Vietnam and the instinctive tendencies of its leaders to resort to armed force ('struggle') as a means of resolving conflicts, were likely to make them unwelcome and difficult neighbours.

The communist implosion

The communist regimes of Indochina did indeed reveal a tendency to resort quickly to the use of military force after 1975. Unexpectedly, however, they directed this violence against each other rather than outwards towards the rest of Southeast Asia. The source of the confrontation between the Vietnamese and Cambodian (Kampuchean) regimes between 1975 and 1978 was historical, ideological and strategic.

Cambodia has had good historical reasons for fearing the expansionist tendencies of Vietnam, and has therefore tended to rely on big-power 'patrons' to protect its position. To some extent, France had fulfilled this role in the colonial period; after 1954, Sihanouk increasingly hinged his foreign policy on a close relationship with communist China; the ill-fated Khmer Republic that lasted from 1970 to 1975 relied on the United States; and the Khmer Rouge resumed Sihanouk's close links with China. This link was reinforced by the fact that the Khmer Rouge – or at least the most prominent faction within it – closely followed the 'Maoist' line both in internal and international matters. This Maoist line could be described simply as the view that the lineaments of the old society, its culture, its religions and its social structure, had to be obliterated before a new socialist society could come into being.

Cambodia's historic fear of Vietnam is matched by Vietnam's historic fear of China. This mistrust always lay under the surface in the post-1945 period, despite the fact that, after 1949, both countries' regimes were communist. The divide between the Vietnamese and Chinese communist parties acquired an ideological dimension in the 1960s, when the North Vietnamese refused to follow China along the Maoist route and stuck to the ideological and international 'line' of the Soviet Union. Given the growing confrontation in the decolonized world in the 1960s and 1970s between the Soviet Union and China, these historical and ideological divisions help explain the natural emergence of a Vietnam–Soviet axis and a China–Cambodia axis.

Growing internal dissensions within the Khmer Rouge regime in 1977 and 1978, coupled with escalating border incidents, eventually led to outright war between Vietnam and Cambodia/Kampuchea in December 1978, which was followed by a brief border war between Vietnam and China. The rapid military takeover by Vietnam of Cambodia in 1978 and 1979, and the installation of a puppet regime, seemed to confirm the worst fears in the region about Vietnam's innate expansionist tendencies (see 'Communist "implosion" in Indochina', p. 295).

Emerging intact

Despite the lack of a hard-and-fast collective security agreement, and despite considerable differences of view as to whether China or Vietnam constituted the major long-term threat in the region, ASEAN provided a framework for a combined and coherent Southeast Asian response to the Indochina crisis during this period. ASEAN benefited, also, from propitious international circumstances, particularly the strategic link between the USA and China against what was seen to be the regional and global threat posed by the USSR–Vietnam link.

There were unpalatable side effects to this struggle for regional security which drew, and continue to draw, international attention. In 1975, Indonesia's fear of what it saw as an imminent communist takeover in Portuguese Timor in the wake of the collapse of the Portuguese empire, coupled with its instinctive tendency towards expansionism in the region, led it into an attempt to annex East Timor and incorporate it within the Indonesian state. Ever since that date, intermittent conflict has persisted in East Timor – a conflict that has been marked, moreover, by exceptional brutality. Another unpalatable side effect was the recognition and, to a degree, support that ASEAN gave through the 1980s to the remnants of the Khmer Rouge who had installed themselves on the Thai–Cambodian border.

However, whether or not the discipline of regional security required complicity in these unpalatable actions, the fundamental fact was that the region as a whole emerged intact, indeed substantially strengthened, from the crisis of the period of 1975 to 1980 (see 'Security and insecurity in the ASEAN region', p. 305)

READINGS

1. Singapore and the global economy

Below is an excerpt from an address given in 1972 by the then foreign minister of the Republic of Singapore, S. Rajaratnam. The general plan for

Singapore's survival outlined here looks nowadays like a standard blueprint for economic development. At the time, however, it was an innovative – perhaps even genuinely revolutionary – strategy. It had not been formulated as a result of leisurely long-term planning, but as a reaction to circumstances that had been imposed on Singapore's leadership after the city had, in effect, been expelled from the Federation of Malaysia in 1965. As such, it illustrates the main characteristics of the first generation of independent Singapore's leadership: adaptability and pragmatism.

Rather like Israel after 1948, Singapore after 1965 saw itself as a state whose secret weapon was that it had 'no alternative'. The vulnerability of Singapore meant that its leadership could not afford the luxury of harbouring illusions, and did not have the scope to make mistakes in policy.

The 'global' strategy outlined below depended on two essential factors. In the first place, it required a framework of regional stability. Secondly, it required a strong government and a disciplined 'rugged' society capable of warding off external threats, and of maintaining internal cohesion.

S. Rajaratnam, 'Singapore: The Global City', in Wee Teong-Boo (ed.), *The Future of Singapore: The Global City* (Singapore: University Education Press, 1975). Excerpts taken from pages 15–24 (text of an address to the Singapore Press Club, 6 February 1972).

The survival of Singapore What I propose to do is to elucidate an inexplicable mystery about Singapore – a mystery which some people find worrying and others somewhat irritating. And the mystery is this: Why has not an independent Singapore as yet collapsed? Worse still, why instead of things getting progressively worse are things getting better? Is all the progress and economic buoyancy an illusion created by a cunning arrangement of mirrors? Or can the whole thing be attributed to good luck and happy accidents, such as the war in Vietnam and the political and economic difficulties of neighbouring countries?

Some people appear to think so. That is why from time to time, some people, including otherwise perceptive journalists, become anxious every time Singapore hits an air-pocket. The higher Singapore flies the greater, the fear is, will be the fall. Immediately after separation [from Malaysia in 1965] the prognosis for Singapore was a gradual relapse into economic decay and mounting political turbulence.

When this did not happen the fears gradually subsided.

Then came the announcement [in 1969] that the British were going to liquidate their bases and with it the substantial contributions they made to our economy. The general feeling was that this time Singapore really (had) had it. Again the worst did not happen

More recently some of our neighbours quite understandably instituted measures to dispense with some aspects of Singapore's entrepôt trade.

Predictably the professional mourners appeared before the wailing wall proclaiming doomsday. True, our entrepôt earnings dropped by 4.5 per cent (or $30 million) in 1970. In fact it has been dropping since 1960 when it constituted 19 per cent of our Gross Domestic Product (GDP) to 11 per cent in 1970. The indications are that our entrepôt trade will continue to form a smaller and smaller percentage of our Gross National Product.

But despite the decline in our entrepôt trade and the run-down of the British base, our GDP increased by 15 per cent in 1970. Investments have flowed in, and unemployment, traditionally Singapore's sword of Damocles, instead of increasing, has decreased to the point that some sectors of our economy have to be manned by imported labour.

However, the jittery pessimist has not stopped biting his finger nails. As he sees it, facts and logic indicate that an independent Singapore cannot be viable. And let me say that the case against an independent Singapore is, at first sight, a formidable one.

As a matter of fact, I and my colleagues believed in it once – believed in it strongly enough to successfully bring about a merger between Singapore and Malaysia. I do not wish to spell out the case, as most of you are familiar with it. Briefly the case is that a small city state, without a natural hinterland, without a large domestic market and no raw materials to speak of, has a near-zero chance of survival politically, economically or militarily.

What then is wrong with the case against the survival of an independent Singapore? Where is the basic flaw?

One easy explanation offered is that we have thrived on happy accidents. For example, it is said that Singapore's prosperity is the consequence of the failure of our neighbours to realise their full economic potentialities. When they do then they would dispense with the services that Singapore has traditionally performed. Then it will be curtains for Singapore.

My contention, which I shall elaborate in a little while, is that the opposite is true. The more prosperous our neighbours become, the greater will be the chance of Singapore's survival, the better our economic prospects. Our economic relationship with them will of course be different. We cannot, as before, live by importing and re-exporting their raw produce. As I remarked earlier, the entrepôt trade will constitute a declining percentage of our economy as our neighbours take over much of the trade themselves.

Nor can we, as we do now, live by selling them cheap textiles, shoes, slippers, chocolates and things of that order ...

Times are changing and there will be less and less demand for the traditional type of entrepôt services Singapore has rendered for well over a century. Its role as the trading city of South-East Asia, the market place of the region, will become less and less important.

The Global City This is because it is transforming itself into a new kind of city – the Global City. It is a new form of human organization and settlement that has, as the historian Arnold Toynbee says, no precedent in mankind's past history ...

It is this global character which distinguishes the World City from the cities of the past. Earlier cities were isolated centres of local civilizations and regional empires. They were in comparison with Global Cities somewhat parochial with an extremely limited range of influence. They were either capital cities or cities of prestige, holy cities, city states and even capitals of convenience.

But the Global City, now in its infancy, is the child of modern technology. It is the city that electronic communications, supersonic planes, giant tankers and industrial organization have made inevitable. Whether the Global City would be a happier place than the megalopolis out of whose crumbling ruins it is emerging will depend on how wisely and boldly we shape its direction and growth.

By and large men have made a mess of their cities. They have yet to learn how to cope with cities. In the West and more so in Asia most cities are unpleasant places to live in. Many of them are dirty, crime ridden, anarchic and often violence prone. In many Western cities the trend is for the well-to-do minority to flee to the outskirts of the city, while the rural poor swarm into the heart of the already congested cities.

One writer has described this process as the gradual conversion of many a once-proud metropolis into a necropolis – a dumping ground for unwanted motor cars and unwanted human beings.

Whether cities are good or bad the trend towards urbanisation is irreversible. Individual cities may decay and eventually pass out of history. But since remote time, however much we may denounce them, the cities have been the creators and sustainers of civilisation, culture, technology and wealth. The slogan about the countryside surrounding the cities [used by 'Maoist' Chinese communists, emphasizing the 'leading' role of the peasantry in Third World revolutions] is no more than the defiant cry of agrarian romantics as they watch the countryside being swallowed up relentlessly by the cities. This process has been accelerated cataclysmically in Asia since World War II.

Population in Asian cities has doubled or even trebled during the past decade. Nearly two-thirds of the world's increase in urban population during the past decade took place in the Third World. Nearly half of the world's population today live in cities. The coming decades will see the further urbanization of the world's population. For most of Asia this uncontrolled growth of cities is posing serious social, economic and political problems.

But nothing short of a total collapse of world civilisation can halt the take-over of the world by the cities. It is against this background that the Global City should be viewed.

The Global Cities, unlike earlier cities, are linked intimately with one another. Because they are more alike they reach out to one another through the tentacles of technology. Linked together they form a chain of cities which today shape and direct, in varying degrees of importance, a world-wide system of economics. It is my contention that Singapore is becoming a component of that system – not a major component but a growingly important one. It is in this sense that I have chosen to describe Singapore as a Global City.

That is why all the gloomy predictions about the future of an independent Singapore have been proved wrong. The pessimistic scenario was written on the assumption that an independent Singapore would be a self-contained city state; that it would, at the most, be a regional city and therefore its fate and fortunes would depend wholly on the economic climate in the region. The economic climate of the region is no doubt important to us and what happens in the region would have consequences for us economically, politically and militarily.

But we are more than a regional city. We draw sustenance not only from the region but also from the international economic system to which as a Global City we belong and which will be the final arbiter of whether we prosper or decline.

If we view Singapore's future not as a regional city but as a Global City then the smallness of Singapore, the absence of a hinterland, or raw materials and a large domestic market are not fatal or insurmountable handicaps. It would explain why, since independence, we have been successful economically and, consequently, have ensured political and social stability.

Let me, as an example, deal with the question of hinterland. We have, it is true, no hinterland of our own. Were we a self-contained regional city and nothing more we would be in serious trouble. The pessimists would have been proved correct.

But once you see Singapore as a Global City the problem of hinterland becomes unimportant because for a Global City the world is its hinterland. This is no hopeful theory. Our shipping statistics show clearly that the world is our hinterland. In 1959 some 9,500 ships brought 14 million tons of cargo into Singapore. Some 10 years later, in 1970, the number of ships had doubled and the cargo trebled. The ships came from all parts of the world, carrying goods to and from all parts of the world.

Our port is not merely a regional port but a global port. Our port makes the world our hinterland. We can get all the raw materials we lack cheaply and quickly because the sea remains the most economic way of transporting bulk cargo. You do not have to spend vast sums of money building roads and railroads to open up the sea. The sea is all highway. All you need is a ship to get to Singapore. The sea gives us ready access to other Global Cities.

Singapore is linked in other ways to other Global Cities. We are in constant and instantaneous contact, through cable and satellite communications, with some 140 countries ...

[But] Singapore's claim to being a Global City does not rest on its communications network alone. We are also being connected to other Global Cities through the international financial network. We have become an important gold market centre. The Asian Dollar Market has become an important aspect of our banking system ... The establishment in Singapore of a still growing number of foreign banks and merchant banks whose operations are world-wide is yet another indication of the fact that we are becoming a Global City.

The strongest evidence of Singapore's absorption into the emerging system of Global Cities is its link-up, more and more, with international and multi-national corporations. We have been aware for a long time that consumption is no longer wholly a national matter. Economic nationalism has not prevented people from buying and consuming goods from all parts of the world.

But now production itself is becoming an international matter. The conventional idea that goods move internationally but that factors of production do not is being eroded by new realities. Internationalisation of production through the world-wide expansion of international and multi-national corporations is moving forward at amazing speed ...

Internationalised production is only in its infancy. At the moment the Americans are in the vanguard of this movement, though in certain sectors of internationalised production the Europeans are equally prominent. But whatever the final shape of internationalised production it will be the major channel of international trade, commerce and production in the decades ahead.

By linking up with international and multi-national corporations Singapore not only comes within the framework of a world economy but is offered a shortcut to catch up or at least keep pace with the most advanced industrial and technological societies. By plugging-in in this way we can achieve in 20 or 30 years what otherwise would have taken us a century or more to achieve.

This is because the international and multi-national corporations introduce us to high technology, complex managerial and marketing skills in addition to bringing in investments. They start complex industries for which we have neither the capital resources nor the expertise to initiate ourselves. Whether the host countries can absorb and utilise the opportunities offered will depend on whether the peoples concerned respond rationally or irrationally to these mammoth and occasionally unfeeling institutions.

There are admittedly grave political and economic dangers implicit in the entry of powerful foreign concerns into weak and underdeveloped countries. I believe that many of the men who control these big concerns from remote Global Cities are not idealists. They may not even understand that the institutions they have created may be powerful instruments for shaping the world economy our vastly shrunken world demands.

But Singapore must be prepared to undertake these risks simply because the alternative to not moving into the global economic system is, for a small Singapore, certain death. We can, if we have the will and the intelligence, create the necessary anti-bodies within our social system to give us immunity against the many dangers that close association with giant foreign corporations could bring.

But they also provide, as I said, shortcuts to enable us to catch up with the advanced societies. It will ensure that when the 21st century dawns those Singaporeans living then would be men of the 21st century – this means well over half the Singaporeans now living.

As a matter of fact we are already plugged into the 21st century through these foreign corporations. In manufacturing, which is the leading growth sector of our economy, the more substantial investments have come from international and multi-national corporations. Most of the $1,700 million now invested in industries have come from international firms. Their presence will partly explain how Singapore has been able to expand industrially despite its small domestic market. The reason is that these international and multi-national concerns simultaneously bring not only industries but also established markets. For these firms the world is their hinterland; the world is their market and through them we are automatically linked to the world hinterland and world markets that would on our own be unavailable to us.

I hope I have elucidated somewhat the mystery why an independent Singapore, far from collapsing as many expected, continues to make progress. The gist of this possibly lengthy discourse is that an independent Singapore survives and will survive because it has established a relationship of interdependence in the rapidly expanding global economic system. Singapore's economic future will, as the years go by, become more and more rooted in this global system. It will grow and prosper.

2. Vision of victory: Vietnam in 1975

Below is the speech delivered by Le Duan, then general secretary of the Vietnamese Communist Party (known through its previous history as the Indochina Communist Party and then the Vietnamese Workers' Party, or Lao Dong), after the collapse of South Vietnam in the spring of 1975. Technically, victory belonged to the National Liberation Front for South Vietnam (NLFSVN), which had in 1969 formed a government known as the People's Revolutionary Government (PRG) for South Vietnam. Very quickly, however, the elaborate façade that the northern communists were only lending 'fraternal support' for a southern insurgency, and that the unity of Vietnam would come about only through negotiation between North and South, was removed, and Vietnam was unified in 1976 as the Socialist Republic of Vietnam. Independence and unity, the two goals first temporarily achieved by Ho Chi Minh in the August 1945 revolution, were now finally secured.

The victory of Vietnamese – indeed, Indochinese – communism in 1975 pointed to a very different future for Asia than that outlined by Singapore's Foreign Minister Rajaratnam a few years' earlier. As the speech below shows, this victory was seen by the Vietnamese leadership as a step forward for the whole global communist movement, and for the principles of the Bolshevik Revolution of 1917. It seemed that United States imperialism had not only been defeated in Vietnam, but was in retreat globally. It is one of the ironies of modern international history that this sense that the global advantage lay with Soviet communism led the Soviet Union into a highly adventurist foreign policy in Asia and Africa in the 1970s and early 1980s. As a consequence, the Russians found themselves wasting money and (in Afghanistan) blood in support of Third World regimes that had nothing to offer the Soviet Union but their ideological loyalty. The events of 1975 in Indochina were to encourage a communist hubris that contributed not a little to the nemesis of 1989 and 1990.

In this speech, Le Duan offered the South Vietnamese a new and bright socialist future cleansed of the corrupting influence of American imperialism. In fact, even though in the end the United States could not sustain the South Vietnamese state, it had created in the government-held areas a war-generated, modern urban-enclave economy. The urban South Vietnamese population had tasted the fruit of the Tree of Knowledge of capitalism and, in the ensuing decade, simply could not be integrated into a socialist, planned economy. This divergence between North and South Vietnam – as much cultural as economic – has remained a problem for a unified Vietnam ever since.

Also in his speech, Le Duan looked forward to a solid fraternal relationship between the three socialist regimes of Indochina: Vietnam, Laos and Cambodia/Kampuchea. In fact, three and a half years later, these regimes would be plunged into war.

Beneath the rhetoric, Vietnam emerged in 1975 as a Spartan, wholly militarized state, and its liberated citizens could look forward only to an endless vista of 'struggle' on both the domestic and foreign fronts.

Le Duan, 'Forward to the Future'. Extract from victory speech given on 15 May 1975, in Le Duan, *Selected Writings* (Hanoi: Foreign Languages Publishing House, 1977). Excerpts taken from pages 527–40.

Today, with boundless joy, throughout the country our 45 million people are jubilantly celebrating the great victory we have won in the general offensive and uprising this Spring of 1975, in completely defeating the war of aggression and the neocolonialist rule of US imperialism, liberating the whole of the southern half of our country so dear to our hearts, and gloriously ending the longest, most difficult, and greatest patriotic war ever waged in the history of our people's struggle against foreign aggression.

We hail our glorious Fatherland from now on definitively rid of the slavery of foreign domination and the scourge of partition. We hail the beautiful land of Viet Nam from Lang Son to the Cape of Ca Mau, from now on completely independent and free, and independent and free forever.

We hail the new era in our nation's 4000-year history – an era of brilliant

prospects for the development of a peaceful, independent, reunified, democratic, prosperous and strong Viet Nam, an era in which the labouring people
have become the complete masters of their destiny and will pool their physical
and mental efforts to build a plentiful and happy life for themselves and for
thousands of generations to come ...

The victory of our war of resistance against the US aggressors and for
national salvation is the victory of the banner of *national independence*, the
victory of a patriotism forged by thousands of years of glorious effort to
build and defend our nation and now raised to a new height by the Party of
the working class. 'Nothing is more precious than independence and freedom.'
This truth has served as the bugle-call urging our people, generation after
generation, to rush forward and chase out all invaders and traitors. From it
our people have drawn the irresistible strength to break the fetters of old
colonialism and, today, the yoke of neo-colonialism.

This victory is the victory of *socialism*, the highest ideal of mankind and
the most profound aspiration of the labouring people, which has become a
reality over half of our country as well as for one-third of mankind, a
system in which the people have become the real masters, free from the
exploitation of man by man, a system in which everyone lives in independence
and freedom, has enough food and clothing, receives proper education and
enjoys a rich and healthy moral life. Such a system is indeed the source of
the inexhaustible strength of the people in the North, and a great stimulus
to our compatriots in the South.

There can be no genuine independence and freedom for the nation unless
the labouring people are freed from oppression and exploitation. Likewise,
the labouring people cannot be freed from the yoke of oppression and
exploitation so long as national independence and freedom have not been
achieved. For the Vietnamese people, the bright road to independence,
freedom and socialism was opened up by the triumph of the August Revolution [of 1945] and then by the historic victory of Dien Bien Phu. However,
US imperialism, the international gendarme, alarmed by the mounting might
of socialism and the national liberation movement throughout the world,
ousted the French colonialists and invaded the southern part of our country,
turning it into a US neo-colony and military base. The scheme of US
imperialism was to erase the gains of national independence and socialism
of our people and, by so doing, to contain and eventually put down the
national liberation movement, contain and push back socialism in this part
of the world. As the US aggressors themselves have admitted, Viet Nam
became the testing ground for the power and prestige of US imperialism.
Viet Nam became the area of the fiercest historic confrontation between the
most warlike, the most stubborn aggressive imperialism with the most powerful economic and military potential on one side, and the forces of national
independence, democracy and socialism of which the Vietnamese people are
the shock force in this region on the other.

The victory of Viet Nam, therefore, is not only a victory of national independence and socialism in Viet Nam, but has also a great international significance, and an epoch-making character. It has upset the global strategy of US imperialism. It has proved that the three revolutionary torrents of our times are on the offensive [in the socialist world, in the West, and in the Third World] repulsing imperialism step by step and overthrowing it part by part. Today, imperialism, even US imperialism, cannot grab a single square inch of any socialist country; neither can it push back the movement for national independence in the world, nor hinder the advance toward socialism of various countries. In this context, the victory of Viet Nam has opened a new stage of development, extremely favourable, for the world revolutionary movement. Together with the great victories of the fraternal Lao and Cambodian peoples, our victory has made a positive contribution to strengthening the forces of world socialism and created new favourable conditions for the safeguarding of peace and national independence in Indochina and Southeast Asia ...

We will do our best to strengthen solidarity and increase mutual support and assistance with the fraternal socialist countries and the international communist and workers' movement in the spirit of proletarian internationalism, in order to win ever more splendid successes for the lofty ideal of Marxism-Leninism.

We pledge to strengthen the unshakeable militant friendship between the Vietnamese people and the people in our two fraternal neighbour countries – Laos and Cambodia – on the basis of respect for each other's independence, sovereignty and territorial integrity, for the sake of the security, growth and prosperity of each people, and for lasting and stable peace in this part of the world.

We will persist in our policy of strengthening solidarity and friendship with our neighbours in Southeast Asia and the countries of the third World in the struggle to regain and maintain national independence, consolidate sovereignty and oppose all schemes and manoeuvres of imperialism and old and new colonialism ...

In the four thousand years of our nation's history, the last hundred years were the hardest and the fiercest period of struggle against foreign aggression, but they were at the same time the period of our most glorious victories. Our people have overthrown the domination of the Japanese fascists, defeated the old colonialism of France and have now completely defeated the neo-colonialism of the United States. By those splendid exploits, our nation has joined the ranks of the vanguard nations of the world and has won the affection and esteem of the whole of progressive mankind. A nation which has recorded such splendid exploits deserves to enjoy peace, freedom and happiness. Such a nation surely has enough determination and energy, strength and talent to overcome all difficulties and reach the great heights of our times, to turn a poor and backward country heavily devastated by war, in which US imperialism has perpetrated so many crimes, into a civilized, prosperous and powerful country, an impregnable bastion of national independence, democracy and socialism in Indochina and Southeast Asia.

3. Communist 'implosion' in Indochina

In April 1975, the Khmer Rouge or Communist Party of Kampuchea (CPK) achieved victory in a five-year civil war against the American-supported Khmer Republic. There then followed a horrific three-and-a-half-year period of government by a regime that simply eliminated all who were deemed to be political, class or ethnic enemies. The regime of Pol Pot was sustained by an ideology that combined extreme isolationist xenophobia with a simplistic version of Maoism; a dogma that called for the literal elimination of all 'feudal' or 'bourgeois' traces in the society, and, on the basis of a purged population, the creation, from the ground up, of a new socialist society.

Both the ideology and the inherent instability of the Khmer Rouge regime led to confrontation with Cambodia's/Kampuchea's neighbours. By the end of 1978, this had blown up into a full-scale war between Democratic Kampuchea (as the Khmer Rouge called their regime) and the newly united Socialist Republic of Vietnam. Vietnam achieved a rapid victory and then installed a new regime — the People's Republic of Kampuchea, or PRK — headed by Heng Samrin and other dissident Cambodian communists. In retaliation for the Vietnamese defeat of their Khmer Rouge allies, China in February 1979 launched an attack on the northern Vietnamese border regions. This was beaten off, and revealed the weakness of China's poorly equipped Red Army.

These developments appeared to confirm the fears of many in the region and beyond that Vietnam had now achieved a long-held ambition to create a Vietnamese-dominated communist Indochina. To this was linked the further anxiety that the Vietnamese alliance with the Soviet Union — both strategic and ideological — would mean that Vietnamese expansion would help project Soviet power into the region. A formidable informal alliance, comprising the United States, China and the ASEAN states (see below), came together in the region after 1978, designed to block Vietnamese and, by proxy, Soviet ambitions. Although the Cambodian regime installed by the Vietnamese remained intact through the decade of the 1980s, the strain of maintaining its military occupation — in addition to the growing inability of the Soviet Union to sustain its world role by the end of that decade — forced the Vietnamese to withdraw from Cambodia in 1989. After that date, the Cambodian situation became 'internationalized', with the imposition by the United Nations of a compromise between the main political opponents in Cambodia.

A succinct and persuasive analysis of the origin of these events is given in the extract below, which is taken from the conclusion to Grant Evans and Kelvin Rowley's book, *Red Brotherhood at War: Indochina since the Fall of Saigon*. It was published in 1984, while the Cambodian crisis was still at its height.

Grant Evans and Kelvin Rowley, *Red Brotherhood at War: Indochina since the Fall of Saigon* (London: Verso, 1984). Excerpts taken from pages 281–95.

One of the central claims of supporters of the regimes in Saigon, Phnom Penh and Vientiane during the Second Indochina War was that they were fighting to protect the independence of their nations from conquest by 'international Communism'. The Vietnamese Communists were accused of being lackeys of either Moscow or Peking, rather than nationalists, and the Khmer and Lao Communists were in turn accused of being puppets of Hanoi. Events after the Communist victory have shown how totally misconceived these ideas were. Triumphant nationalism has torn asunder the international solidarity of the 'Red Brotherhood' within three years.

Some commentators have tried to explain this as the triumph of 'traditional' nationalist passions over the ideology of proletarian internationalism, but this is not very persuasive. In Indochina, as elsewhere, nationalism is a modern phenomenon. Nor was Communism the creation of an internationalistic proletariat. The Communist movements of Indochina have their roots in the nationalist revolt against Western colonialism, and the Third Indochina War has its basis in the dynamics of that revolt rather than in a mysterious revival of ancient antagonisms. Viewed from this angle, the events since 1975 are less surprising: this is by no means the first occasion on which victorious nationalists have turned on each other once foreign domination has been overturned.

The main driving force for revolutionary change in Indochina as a whole was the cataclysmic upheaval in the most developed and populous country, Vietnam. It was inevitable that Vietnamese influence was deeply imprinted on the Communist movements of Laos and Cambodia after these countries gained independence. But Communism in Laos and Cambodia was never simply controlled by Hanoi – rather, they were indigenous movements, which, especially in their early stages, looked to the Viet Minh as a model for their own revolutionary movements. But, as they developed a social and political base of their own, they adapted to different national political environments, and their paths diverged. The Communists in Laos and Cambodia found themselves operating in a milieu that was much less touched by modernizing forces than Vietnam, and this in turn rebounded on their relations with Hanoi.

As a consequence of the strength of royalism in Cambodia in the 1950s and 1960s, Hanoi's main concern was to cultivate good relations with Sihanouk's regime. The strains thus created between Hanoi and a handful of 'ultra-leftists' in the CPK [Communist Party of Kampuchea] seemed of little importance at the time – but they were to boomerang on the Vietnamese after Pol Pot's group came to power in 1975. By contrast, in Laos the weak RLG [Royal Lao Government] provided Hanoi with no comparable temptations. The interests of Hanoi and the Pathet Lao leadership never diverged significantly, and the result was that their alliance endured well beyond 1975.

The conflicts that erupted after 1975 were an outcome of the dynamic established by these divergent but intertwined paths of nationalist–Communist revolution. The view, popular among Western and Chinese commentators, that Vietnam embarked on a course of 'expansionism', seeking to subjugate Laos, Cambodia, and beyond that, perhaps all of Southeast Asia, is no more than propaganda. What positive evidence there is points in the opposite direction. The leadership in Hanoi wanted to concentrate on the internal tasks of economic development and modernization.

But, the exponents of this view claim, the proof of the pudding is in the eating: the proof of the 'hegemonistic' ambitions of Vietnam lies in its subjugation of Laos and Cambodia. If Hanoi did not will this, they ask, why did it happen? The answer to this is that the realities of international relations are considerably more complex than these theorists assume – Hanoi's decisions were not made in a vacuum. In the wake of the victories of 1975, instead of the peaceful international context it had assumed, Hanoi found itself under increasing pressure from China, and with its expected opening to the West blocked by the United States. As the pressure mounted, the Vietnamese leadership reacted by switching its attention from economic development to national security. And as this became the preoccupation in Hanoi, the geography of the region ensured that the Vietnamese would become increasingly concerned over their relations with the governments in Phnom Penh and Vientiane ...

It was in relation to Cambodia that the post-1975 crisis in Indochina erupted, and there the critics of Vietnam appear to be on stronger ground. After all, Pol Pot and his colleagues explain the Vietnam–Cambodia war in terms of their heroic resistance to Vietnam's drive to 'colonize' Cambodia. But are they truthful witnesses?

Once again, a closer examination of the available evidence undermines the thesis of a Vietnamese expansionist urge. Hanoi undoubtedly wanted friendly relations with the new regime in Phnom Penh, just as it had sought them with Laos – and, for that matter, with Sihanouk. To this end, Hanoi was willing to turn a blind eye to the atrocities perpetrated by the new regime, both within Cambodia and on the Vietnam border. When Pol Pot spurned the offer of a treaty of friendship, the Vietnamese reluctantly accepted this. While Hanoi preferred a sympathetic government in Phnom Penh, it was willing to accept an unsympathetic one provided it did not constitute a threat to Vietnam itself.

The immediate catalyst of the Third Indochina War was not any expansionist drive on the part of Vietnam, but the violent and provocative conduct of Pol Pot's regime – if Hanoi can be criticized on any count in this connection, it should be for its willingness to acquiesce to the most barbaric behaviour just across the border in the sacred name of 'national independence'. But in the quest for an unattainable 'perfect sovereignty', Pol Pot's regime not only slaughtered its own citizens, it also turned issues of no intrinsic importance into the basis of a major confrontation on the Vietnam–Cambodia border. No government can reasonably be expected to tolerate military actions of the sort to which Vietnam was subjected by Pol Pot's regime in 1977–8. Hanoi was especially sensitive because of the disruptive impact of Phnom Penh's assaults on an already fragile situation in southern Vietnam.

Nevertheless, Hanoi's initial response was moderate. While it made no concessions to Phnom Penh's unilateral demands over the border, it did try to contain the conflict and find a diplomatic solution. It was in the face of Pol Pot's repeated rejections of such a solution that the Vietnamese escalated their military response, and eventually decided to overthrow the Pol Pot regime by force of arms. Perhaps the decision to invade can be criticized as an excessive response to Pol Pot's border war. But it is clear that it was the actions of the regime in Phnom Penh that started the war; Hanoi's actions ended it.

It is thus on the nature of the DK [Democratic Kampuchea, or the Khmer Rouge] regime rather than on the alleged regional ambitions of Vietnam that we have to focus if we wish to understand the genesis of the Third Indochina War. Here the arguments advanced by Hanoi and the Heng Samrin government it installed in Phnom Penh are politically convenient and not very persuasive. They argue that the leadership of an authentic people's revolution was 'usurped' by a group of Maoist fanatics, led by Pol Pot. These usurpers then smashed all urban life because of their 'anti-working class, poor peasant line' and proceeded to turn Cambodia into a forward base for Chinese expansion in Southeast Asia. All in all, it stands as a terrible warning to any Communists inclined to adopt a sympathetic attitude towards China.

But the Vietnamese are unclear on just how it was possible for the leadership of an authentic people's revolution to be usurped in this fashion. Nor is it very clear what Cambodia's 'true Communists' were doing all the while. Precedents can be found in Maoist theories for the anti-urban orientation of Pol Pot's regime, but hardly for their utter extremism. The thuggery of Mao's Red Guards [during China's Cultural Revolution of the mid-1960s] was child's play compared to the actions of the death squads unleashed by Pol Pot. Nor were Pol Pot and Ieng Sary puppets dancing on strings pulled in China – although it was their regime's main supporter, Peking probably had little more control over them than Hanoi did.

The standard clichés of Western commentary are not very helpful either. Journalists usually describe the internal politics of Communist regimes in terms of a conflict between 'pragmatists' (the moderates and rightwingers) and 'ideologues' (the extreme leftwing). But Pol Pot does not seem to have been an ideologue; rather, like Stalin, he prided himself on his pragmatism. In 1978 he boasted of building 'socialism without a model', based on 'the experience gained in the course of the liberation struggle'. Considerations based on general theories or the experiences of other countries in building socialism were contemptuously dismissed.

If the extremism of Pol Pot's regime thus has pragmatic roots, it is in the practical circumstances of the Cambodian revolution that its explanation is to be found. In the chaos that followed the overthrow of Sihanouk, the Khmers Rouges rose from extreme isolation to state power in only five years. The essence of Pol Pot's ideology was the glorification of the self-sacrifice and military heroism that made this possible. After his victory in 1975, the entire nation was to be remade on the spartan model of an isolated guerrilla encampment.

When they came to power in 1975 the Khmers Rouges lacked the educated cadres needed to staff the administrative apparatus of a modern state. The backwardness of the social structure as a whole, and the rapidity of the growth of the movement, meant that the cadres of Khmer Communism were drawn heavily from the ranks of poorly educated peasant soldiers. Most were young and inexperienced, with little understanding of the world beyond the village and the war, easily manipulated by those who were more sophisticated, and ready to use brute force to solve problems they did not understand. Perhaps, with a united, flexible and sophisticated leadership, the CPK [Communist Party of Kampuchea] would have been able to overcome these problems with time. But all these things, too, were lacking in Cambodia in 1975.

It was the inability of such a political apparatus to deal with the problems of running Cambodia's refugee-swollen cities that explains the extraordinary decision [in April 1975] to disperse the urban population and subject it to a campaign of terror. As in earlier revolutions, the resort to terrorist methods of rule was a symptom of weakness and insecurity rather than strength. By these 'pragmatic' methods Pol Pot was able to by-pass the whole problem of constructing a modern bureaucratic state.

The Khmer Rouge movement was by no means united in 1975, and the course pursued by the Pol Pot leadership only added to its internal tensions. Then Pol Pot used the secret police and loyal military factions to carry out an ever-widening series of purges to crush his opponents, both in the central government and in the entrenched regional structures of the party and government. Out of this there emerged a highly centralized military-police-state, headed by a small family clique, which cultivated nationalist delirium in a desperate attempt to establish its legitimacy.

An extreme backwoods chauvinism could be 'pragmatically' exploited in terms of Cambodian internal politics. But externally it locked Pol Pot and his group on a dangerous course. They probably did not have clear-cut expansionist ambitions, but they were certainly irascible neighbours. Incidents erupted all around the country as the Khmers Rouges tried to seal Cambodia's ill-defined borders to stem the flight of refugees and the infiltration of 'enemy agents'. The fact that the most obvious external influence on Cambodian Communism was Vietnamese meant that Vietnam became the main focus of Pol Pot's xenophobia. Thus the campaign to annihilate rival groups within Cambodia went hand-in-hand with escalating violence against Vietnam ...

Pol Pot never accepted the traditional notion of a border as a porous and shifting zone of contact between states that ruled over diverse populations (nor, for that matter, did Lon Nol or Sihanouk). He insisted on a territorial state with sharply demarcated borders and a homogeneous, united population, hallmarks of modern nationalism. Nor did he accept the emphasis of traditional statecraft on compromise and the submission of small states (no matter how absolute their internal despotism may be) to more powerful ones. On the contrary, he was motivated by the distinctly modern ideal of 'perfect sovereignty' for a small state. Realism had made the traditional Khmer kings adept at balancing the demands of their neighbours, and playing them off against one another to maximize their own freedom of manoeuvre. Sihanouk tried to continue this style of diplomacy, but like Lon Nol, Pol Pot believed that it was a failure, and was responsible for the decline of Cambodia. He attempted to meet the demands of all his neighbours with force. Pol Pot's excursions into history were not those of a political leader steeped in traditional lore – they were attempts to bestow legitimacy on present policies by re-writing the past. In short, Pol Pot was not a prisoner of Cambodia's traditions. He was a modern nationalist, albeit a particularly crude and brutal one.

Thus it was neither Vietnamese expansion nor the tragic traditions of Cambodia that made the Vietnam–Cambodia war inevitable. It was the actions of Pol Pot as the leader of a modern revolution that destroyed itself. The revolution succeeded in smashing the framework of Sihanouk's patrimonial traditionalism, but not in establishing a new institutional framework in its place. The war with Vietnam was in a sense simply the external projection of the instability, bellicosity and violence of the Pol Pot regime within Cambodia. The war was not precipitated by any expansionist acts on the part of the Vietnamese; they merely had the misfortune to be standing nearby – preoccupied with their own problems – when Cambodia's revolution blew up in their faces.

This is not to say that they did not have an abiding interest in what happened in a neighbouring country. They were deeply interested in Cambodia and Laos, just as the Thais were. Our point is simply that the available evidence indicates that the Vietnamese sought to peacefully develop friendly relations with Phnom Penh, and that it was Pol Pot's forces that started the war between the two countries.

It might be objected that it was suicidally irrational for Pol Pot's regime to provoke a war with a more powerful state such as Vietnam (or Thailand, with which it came close to war in 1977). This is true, but what it proves is not that Pol Pot could not have attacked Vietnam, but that his foreign policy was irrational ...

The international dimension It is clear that those commentators who emphasized the local roots of the Vietnam–Cambodia war are right. It is not to be understood, as President Carter's secretary of state, Zbigniew Brzezinski, depicted it in 1979, as a 'proxy war' between the Soviet Union and China ... Yet the local conflict was aggravated by, and exploited by, great powers outside the region. Of these, the most important has been China. Without a consideration of this global dimension as well as the local roots, it is impossible to understand the outcome of the conflict ...

The Communist victories in Indochina from 1975 fundamentally recast the balance of power in the whole Southeast Asian region. American power was on the retreat – with Thailand, and even the Philippines to some extent, rethinking the whole question of American military bases on their soil in the wake of the debacles in Cambodia, South Vietnam and Laos ... Communist China aspired to establish itself as the dominant power in the region as American influence waned, and saw the USSR as its main rival. China's drive to open diplomatic and trade relations with Southeast Asian nations met with considerable success – more so than the parallel efforts of the Soviet Union. As an ally to which Peking had given substantial support, Vietnam was naturally expected to submit to Chinese hegemony. The pressure on Hanoi began even before the fall of Saigon, with the occupation of the Spratly Islands in 1974, and intensified rapidly thereafter.

Yet most Western commentators have been curiously blind to China's assertive policies from 1975. In the 1950s there had been much talk of Peking's 'expansionist policies' – at a time when China was actually weak and cautious in its behaviour. It was in these terms that American intervention in Korea and Indochina had been justified at the time. Of course, China was then an ally of the Soviet Union – on the wrong side in the cold war, from Washington's point of view. But one of the first consequences of China's assertion of its aspirations to independent great power status was the shattering of the Sino-Soviet alliance; and by the late 1970s American leaders were anxious to play the 'China card' against the Soviet Union. In this context, Western commentators benignly overlooked a considerable growth of Chinese influence, while flying into a major panic over any sign of Soviet 'expansionism'. Thus a major shift in the international balance of power occurred with surprisingly little comment. But it was a shift of the first order of importance for Indochina.

It was, ironically, in Communist Vietnam that Chinese hegemony met with the most resistance. Hanoi's leaders had long struggled to maximize their own freedom of manoeuvre by carefully balancing the demands of their Chinese and Soviet patrons. In this way they had managed to carry on a war about which neither of the Communist great powers were happy through to a victorious conclusion. But from 1975 China's new assertiveness made such a balancing act increasingly difficult. While the non-Communist countries of Southeast Asia were able to balance Chinese influence with

American influence, this course was not open to a government that had only recently defeated American military intervention. Hanoi's efforts to develop an opening to the West were frustrated by US hostility. As its options diminished, Hanoi had little choice but to align itself with Moscow and gird itself for a long struggle with China.

Faced with such a stark choice between Moscow and Peking, Hanoi had sound reasons for choosing Moscow. For a leadership anxious to modernize a backward country, Peking could offer little by way of sophisticated technology, economic aid, or successful development planning. And, for a country plunging once again into a perilous international situation, Moscow could offer more sophisticated weapons. Unable to compete with Moscow's blandishments, Peking resorted to crudely coercive measures – threatening Hanoi, cutting off aid, and stepping up the military pressure on the Sino-Vietnamese border. At each step, Peking's influence in Hanoi shrank; by 1978 the VCP leadership had decided that China had become 'the main enemy of the Vietnamese revolution'. At the same time, Peking was becoming increasingly apprehensive about the ties between its southern neighbour and its antagonist to the north, the Soviet Union.

The outcome was bitter rivalry between Vietnam and China for influence in Indochina. Vietnam began pressing Laos and Cambodia for a 'special relationship' that would, in effect, exclude Chinese influence. Laos went along with this, but in Cambodia it only inflamed the antagonism of Pol Pot's regime toward Vietnam. In non-Communist Southeast Asia, ties with China had already become considerable, and no one wished to jeopardize them by siding with Vietnam. And Hanoi's sudden enthusiasm for excluding great power influences from the region was inevitably viewed with scepticism, given its growing relationship with Moscow.

Pol Pot's group provided China with its only diplomatic triumph in Indochina. From 1975 Peking became the main foreign patron of the Democratic Kampuchea regime, and used it to step up its pressure on Hanoi. As the Vietnam–Cambodia war unfolded, Peking openly threw its weight behind Phnom Penh. China's preference was for a protracted conflict, sufficiently low-key to 'bleed' Vietnam without provoking effective retaliation, but such subtleties were beyond the capabilities of the Pol Pot regime. Peking appears to have sought to restrain some of DK's most suicidal excesses in 1978, but in vain. While characters like Pol Pot were unloved in Deng Xiaoping's Peking, Deng could hardly stand by idly when the Vietnamese overthrew a regime to whose protection China had committed itself. But, given Soviet backing for Vietnam, military intervention by China was a dangerous option. The Peking leadership was divided over the issue, and in this context America's attitude proved decisive. By strongly condemning Vietnam's actions in Cambodia and making it clear that an attempt to 'teach Vietnam a lesson' would not interrupt the process of Sino-American rapprochement in any way, Washington helped tilt the scales decisively in favour of intervention. But, even so, the final decision was made only after Deng had been reassured by his visit to the USA in January 1979.

China's invasion of Vietnam in February 1979 proved unsuccessful. Much damage was done to northern Vietnam, but the Chinese troops performed poorly, and sustained heavy casualties. Hanoi was able to rebuff the invasion without either supporting action from the Soviets or without withdrawing troops from Cambodia. Far from being cowed by China's actions, the Hanoi leadership became more resolute than ever. And, after the first failure, threats of 'another lesson' rang hollow.

While keeping the situation tense on the Sino-Vietnamese border and giving backing to the anti-Vietnamese guerrillas operating in Cambodia, China concentrated on bringing maximum diplomatic pressure to bear on Vietnam. In this it had the backing of the USA, and achieved considerable success. The Vietnamese intervention was almost universally condemned by countries outside the Soviet bloc (and by some within it). What Western aid had been flowing into Vietnam was cut off, adding to the economic disruption and the demoralization within the country. In 1979 Hanoi found itself under more effective siege than at any time during the Second Indochina War.

Vietnam responded to these pressures by moving further into the Soviet orbit, by readjusting its economic policies at home, and by consolidating its ties with Laos and the new regime it had installed in Phnom Penh. The economic ties between the Soviet bloc and Vietnam were further strengthened, and the Soviets were granted access to Cam Ranh Bay – to the great annoyance of Peking and Washington. The more moderate economic policies adopted in 1979 meant scaling down the VCP's plans for rapid modernization, but they did succeed in lifting the Vietnamese economy out of the acute crisis situation of 1979–80. In this, they were helped by more favourable weather conditions in the early 1980s. By 1983 it was clear that the strategy of economic coercion had failed – Vietnam remained mired in acute poverty, but the prospect of the Hanoi leadership capitulating on matters it regarded as vital to the country's security because of economic pressure was becoming more remote than ever.

Meanwhile, Communist Indochina was emerging as a political and military bloc under Vietnamese leadership. Laos quickly established relations with Heng Samrin's PRK [Peoples Republic of Kampuchea] government, and in February 1979 Vietnam signed a treaty of friendship with Cambodia paralleling its 1977 treaty with Laos. The 'militant solidarity of Laos, Vietnam and Cambodia' became a stock phrase in political rhetoric, and the three countries adopted a common stance on the Cambodia issue. To Chinese commentators, this was a vindication of Pol Pot's charge that Hanoi aspired to establish an 'Indochina Federation'. In reality, Chinese pressure was a major factor in catalysing Hanoi's drive to strengthen its regional alliances.

In Cambodia, the Vietnamese faced immense problems. Contrary to some claims, military resistance was not one of them. The Khmers Rouges did not surrender, but within six months they had been largely confined to remote and unpopulated areas of the country, where the Vietnamese attempted to starve them into submission. With Chinese and Western aid, Pol Pot was able to rebuild his forces in enclaves along the Thai–Cambodian border but he was not able to mount any serious challenge to the Vietnamese military presence in Cambodia, either by conventional or guerrilla warfare. The wholesale brutality of his regime in power meant that his forces did not have the minimum level of popular support (or even tolerance) necessary for effective guerrilla warfare.

Behind the protective shield of the Vietnamese military, their Cambodian allies attempted to build up a new administration. Here they faced problems of staggering dimensions. After Pol Pot's terror, there was little left of the educated middle class needed to run the government; and those willing to work with the PRK were frequently still traumatized, dispirited, and of uncertain political loyalties. Inevitably, the new administration was at first heavily dependent on Vietnamese advisers. However, as the number of trained Khmer officials rose, the PRK became increasingly capable of standing on its own feet, and the Vietnamese advisers were largely withdrawn. Not surprisingly, the new government was dominated by Khmer Communists who had fled to Vietnam to escape Pol Pot's purges, and was organized along the lines of the Vietnamese bureaucratic model.

The collapse of the Pol Pot dictatorship left behind an uprooted and exhausted population, and a devastated economy. The country urgently needed a massive injection of outside aid to stave off famine. But the effort to aid Cambodia was quickly embroiled in the international conflict surrounding Vietnam's intervention. Soviet bloc aid came quickly, but the Americans were reluctant to send aid that would shore up the PRK and ease the pressure on Vietnam – and the USA was a major donor to the international aid agencies through which most aid would be channelled. In the end, they agreed to send aid to Phnom Penh, but engaged in a campaign to blacken the PRK's handling of aid, and insisted that much of it be distributed on the Thai–Cambodian border. Here, under the guise of 'humanitarianism', aid could be channelled to the Khmers Rouges and other insurgents, and used as a magnet to attract population from the PRK-controlled zones into the insurgent-controlled zones.

Over the next three years, conditions within Cambodia gradually returned to normal. This was due in large part to the 1980 decision of the aid agencies to concentrate during the dry season on bringing in seed rice and agricultural implements, thus facilitating the rehabilitation of the country's productive capacity. This inevitably rebounded to the benefit of the PRK and was heavily criticized as 'political' rather than 'humanitarian' aid. Western aid via Phnom Penh was cut back and eventually stopped, and the West concentrated its 'humanitarian' efforts on the areas in the hands of anti-Vietnamese insurgents on the Thai–Cambodian border.

Thus, by 1983, Vietnam's Khmer allies had built up a stable administrative structure, with effective control of most of the territory and population of Cambodia. But it faced insurgency on the Thai border, sustained by Chinese and Western aid efforts, and it remained dependent on the military shield provided by the presence of 150,000 Vietnamese troops. It had become a pillar of Hanoi's anti-Chinese Indochina bloc, and the focus of international controversy.

4. Security and insecurity in the ASEAN region

Below is a summary of the factors of stability and potential instability that face the original members of the Association of South-East Asian Nations (ASEAN), formed in 1967, in addition to the Sultanate of Brunei, which joined in 1984, shortly after its long-standing protectorate agreement with the British ended. With the Vietnamese withdrawal from Cambodia in 1989, and the evaporation of the global communist threat, the stage was set for the development of a new relationship between ASEAN and the communist states of Indochina. Vietnam joined ASEAN in 1995, and it is very likely that Laos, Burma and Cambodia will shortly follow.

Thus it would seem that ASEAN has become a truly regional organization, uniting rather than dividing Southeast Asia. Tim Huxley, however, expresses certain reservations in the following extract about the long-term regional stability of Southeast Asia: first, concerning the viability of the more sprawling maritime states of Southeast Asia – Indonesia and Malaysia – that have potentially serious 'centre–periphery' problems; and secondly, about the capacity of ASEAN to transform itself into a genuine 'security community'. A 'security community' is the description of a region in which such a level of mutual interdependence has developed between the states involved that it would no longer be conceivable for disputes between those states to be converted into open conflict – as, for example, Western Europe or North America.

Tim J. Huxley, *Insecurity in the ASEAN Region* (London: Royal United Services Institute for Defence Studies [RUSI], 1993). Excerpts taken from pages 4–16.

In 1967, when the Association of South-East Asian Nations (ASEAN) was inaugurated, its members (then Indonesia, Malaysia, the Philippines, Singapore and Thailand; Brunei joined in 1984) faced a wide range of security threats. These included domestic insurgencies, latent bilateral disputes between the new Association's own members, the potential impact of communist victories in the continuing war in Indochina, and the danger of interference by extra-regional powers. ASEAN's members were economically and militarily weak developing states in an unstable and conflict-ridden region. While ASEAN was never supposed to be the basis for a *defence* community, from the beginning the Association held a variety of ambitions – the unkind might say 'pretensions' – in relation to the resolution of its members' security problems. To a significant degree, these security objectives have been inter-related, both conceptually and practically. But while ASEAN was always intended to perform a variety of security roles, and has been called an 'emerging security regime with a tendency towards community', its record in achieving its security-related ambitions has been mixed. Strictly speaking, even in the early 1990s ASEAN constitutes only a limited security regime and is – at best – many years away from becoming a security community.

National resilience Since ASEAN was established, there has been a wide-spread acknowledgement among its member governments of the validity of the Indonesian concept of 'national resilience', which involves the use of economic and social development to undermine any impetus for radical political change. Thus the Association's primary declaratory objective of furthering its members' economic growth and social progress was aimed particularly at eliminating the socio-economic deprivation which had so enhanced the appeal of communist revolution, and to a lesser extent ethnically-based separatism, amongst large segments of its members' popula-tions. There has also been consensus between leaders of ASEAN's members that the attainment of 'resilience' at the national level in each of the ASEAN countries will contribute to a wider 'regional resilience' which will eventually form the basis for Southeast Asia's security against external as well as internal threats. The collapse of the non-communist Indochinese regimes in 1975 reinforced the ASEAN members' commitment to the idea that economic and social development were essential weapons in the continuing struggle against the communist threat. This consensus was reflected in the formal public statement issued by ASEAN's heads of government following their first summit meeting in 1976. The Treaty of Amity and Cooperation in Southeast Asia expressed a determination to strengthen 'national resilience' in 'political, economic, socio-cultural as well as security fields' and to 'co-operate in all fields for the promotion of regional resilience'.

ASEAN's most widely-perceived significance in security terms has been related to its function as a device for controlling intra-regional conflict (both between its own members, and more widely within Southeast Asia) and to its potential role in the broader management of regional security through the ZOPFAN (Zone of Peace, Freedom and Neutrality) concept. However, the ASEAN states' failure to implement more wholeheartedly policies in support of its most fundamental, but often overlooked, security objective – the creation of 'national resilience' – may have undermined progress towards achieving ASEAN's wider security aims.

Rapid growth characterized the ASEAN countries' economies for most the 1970s and 1980s, although there has been a long-term depression in the Philippines since the early 1980s, and a short-lived region-wide recession in the mid-eighties. Economic dynamism and growing prosperity has continued to be one of the most striking features of most ASEAN members in the early 1990s. GDP growth figures for Indonesia, Malaysia, Singapore and Thailand in 1992 were all in the 5–8 per cent range, and authoritative forecasts suggest that they will remain there for at least the rest of the decade. Singapore is now essentially a developed country, and has been ranked ahead of Britain and the Netherlands in a recent comparative assessment of living standards. Malaysia, followed by Thailand, are both approaching Newly Industrialised Country status. Even the Philippines' stagnant economy is expected to recover during the next several years, perhaps achieving 4–5 per cent growth by the mid-late 1990s. Brunei is wealthy on the scale of the smaller Gulf states, and in theory its whole population could live comfortably off the interest from investments indefinitely even after the Sultanate's massive oil and natural gas reserves are exhausted.

The economic prosperity of most ASEAN members can only marginally be ascribed to the success of ASEAN policies aimed at enhancing regional economic cooperation. 'Cooperative enterprise directed against protectionist practice by industrialised states' has become more important with the rise of nascent trading blocs since the 1980s, and has certainly had a positive impact on ASEAN members' economic development. But, in general, attempts at economic cooperation within ASEAN have not been either far-reaching or successful. The ASEAN region's prosperity is largely the result of economic policies pursued at the national level by individual governments.

Despite the striking economic success of most of ASEAN's members in terms of rapid rates of GDP growth, these impressive aggregate figures tend to camouflage the continued existence of significant levels of socio-economic inequity between both classes and regions in economically booming Malaysia and Thailand and relatively prosperous Indonesia, as well as in the depressed Philippines. The attainment of 'national resilience' will require a much greater degree of social justice – especially in the sense of a funda-mental amelioration of the basic rural problems of landlessness, indebtedness and underemployment, and of urban poverty – in the four largest ASEAN countries.

The spatial dimension to poverty has particularly serious implications for 'national resilience'. Socio-economic inequality between regions has always been a problem for the governments of the larger ASEAN states, and undoubtedly contributed in the past to insurgencies in areas such as Thailand's northeast and Mindanao in the southern Philippines. Since the 1980s there have been indications that unfair development policies – manifested in the form of a 'resource drain', whereby higher than average regional GDP based on exploitation of local primary resources is paralleled by a higher than average incidence of poverty – have accentuated pre-existing centre–periphery tensions based on ethnic and political differences. In Indonesia, economic grievances rooted in the perception that the local community was deriving little or no benefit from the massive exploitation of natural gas resources was almost certainly the trigger for the large-scale armed revolt by an Islamic separatist movement in Aceh (the northernmost part of Sumatra) in 1990. The problem of Aceh may foreshadow long-term problems for the Indonesian regime's efforts to maintain national unity. The memory of previous severe difficulties in centre–periphery relations, particularly in the late 1950s, has inclined the Suharto regime to over-centralise power, which has seriously impeded development outside Java, especially in the eastern islands such as Sulawesi. A continuation of the present policy of centralising political power and economic decision-making could, over a 15–20 year period, lead to Indonesia becoming 'a reluctant union held together by military force'. Rather similarly, tensions in Malaysia between the two resource-rich, but relatively impoverished Borneo states of Sabah and Sarawak and the federal government have become increasingly serious since the late 1980s ...

But the most fundamental problem in relation to the widely-recognised need to improve the 'national resilience' of the four largest ASEAN countries is that the very nature of their regimes has often tended to impede the implementation of policies which are clearly necessary in order to ameliorate tensions between classes and between regions. In very broad terms, these regimes' rather narrow power bases have been located principally in the military, business, landowning, bureaucratic and technocratic elites. These elites have often seen their interests as coincidental with the maintenance of a social, economic and political status quo which tolerates exploitation and corruption. Given that the regimes have depended for their survival on the support of these elite elements rather than the population as a whole, there has often been little incentive to undertake fundamental reforms. As one commentator observed with reference to Thailand over a decade ago, 'public policy tends to be shaped by the interests of small, usually urban-based higher-income groups, rather than the declared social and economic priorities of the nation'.

Political development, in the sense of building more democratic and responsive political structures, is clearly necessary if the eradication of poverty and the resolution of centre–periphery tensions in the larger ASEAN states are to remain feasible objectives. But the problem is that the sort of fundamental political change which is probably necessary to ensure the attainment of social justice and fair treatment of peripheral regions has never been on the agenda of either individual ASEAN regimes or ASEAN as an organisation. Indeed, the very concept of 'national resilience' revolves around the use of performance legitimacy – based on tangible improvements in aggregate living standards – to maintain the existing ASEAN regimes' hold on power. There is certainly much truth in the argument that the ASEAN states' economic successes have owed much to the firm direction which could probably only have been provided by authoritarian regimes. But there is also a strong argument that the necessity of responding to the sectional and regional pressures which would result from a broadening of effective political participation would help to overcome some of the ASEAN states' serious socio-economic problems. It is also true, though, that such a degree of political change would necessitate a radical curtailment of the privileges of the elite groups which presently dominate the larger ASEAN states' political systems.

Regional Stability in Southeast Asia

The main guarantor of regional stability in Southeast Asia is the institution of the nation-state. In mainland Southeast Asia, nationalism had a ready-made framework on which it could build, given the existence of the strong pre-colonial identities of the Burmese, Thai, Vietnamese and Cambodian states. In maritime Southeast Asia, however, nation-states had to be created out of a multiplicity of islands, pre-colonial states, cultures and ethnic groups. In the end, it was the colonial state that created the borders of the modern nation-states. Remarkably, the integrity of these borders has been maintained despite separatist insurgencies, communist subversion, irredentist revolts – as, for example, in the Patani-Malay region of Thailand, or the Muslim regions of the Philippines – and complex territorial claims between neighbours. The only clear violation of the territorial disposition created by the colonial period has been Indonesia's seizure of Portuguese Timor.

There has been, in other words, a consensus in favour of the view that disputes between the states of Southeast Asia must be subordinated to the common interest of preserving stability in the region. It is this consensus – embodied in ASEAN – that forms the true basis of the stability of the region; regional stability is, in turn, the precondition for regional security and prosperity.

On the face of it, Southeast Asia could be described as extremely diverse in terms of culture, religion, language, historical influences, ethnic make-up and geography. Perhaps it is precisely this underlying disunity that has decisively contributed to the successful statecraft that has provided up till now a remarkable degree of harmony for the region. The region is faced by permanent external as well as internal threats; it is, after all, composed of a number of relatively small or dispersed states surrounded by larger and more cohesive states, and regions that have an enormous potential for conflict and instability – one only has to think of South Asia and its record of recent conflict, or the tensions in the China–Taiwan–Korea–Japan theatre to appreciate this.

Because of this environment of threat, government in Southeast Asia tends to have the air of permanent crisis management. The statements of regional leaders are permeated by a sense of threat, and a sense that – in order to survive – the region must not only be politically alert, but economically dynamic, ever sensitive to the global trends of the future. There is the sense that, only by keeping ahead of these global trends can the region avoid being overtaken by them.

There can be little doubt that this sense of threat is, to a degree, embedded in the thinking of society as a whole – a fact that encourages a remarkable degree of political consensus. A culture of economic enterprise and self-reliance is, in fact, matched by a political culture of risk-avoidance. There is a danger, however, that the exploitation of the generalized desire for a politically stable environment may lead to institutionalized corruption, stasis and eventual sclerosis. Although many of the states of the region have demonstrated 'regime resilience', the real challenge is that of creating a long-term institutional stability in the political system – something that transcends regime resilience. Paradoxically, the as yet undiscovered key to enduring political stability and firmly rooted economic strength may lie in the ability to ensure peaceful political change.

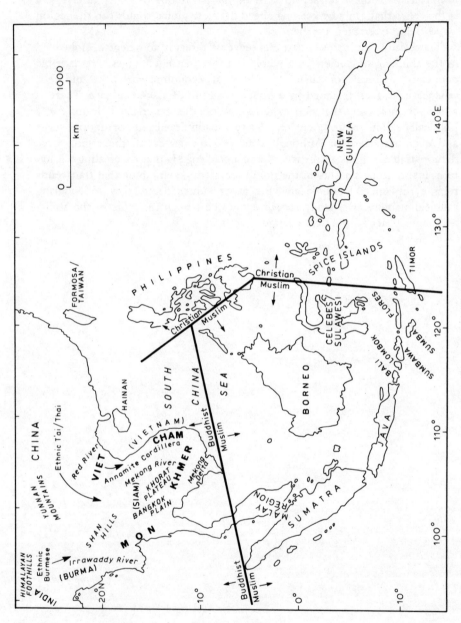

I. Pre-Colonial Southeast Asia

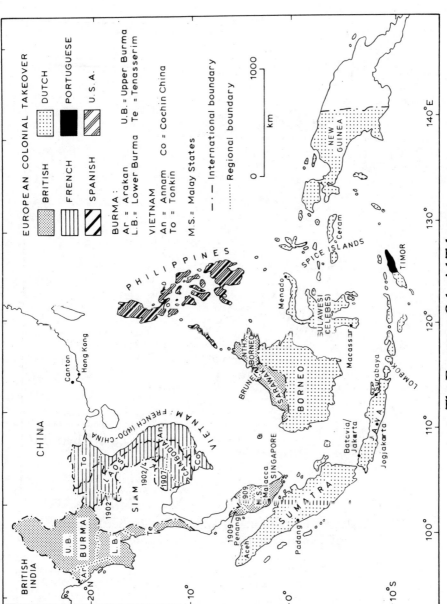

2. The European Colonial Takeover

EUROPEAN COLONIAL TAKEOVER

BRITISH
DUTCH
FRENCH
PORTUGUESE
SPANISH
U.S.A.

BURMA:
Ar = Arakan   U.B. = Upper Burma
L.B.= Lower Burma   Te = Tenasserim

VIETNAM
An = Annam   Co = Cochin China
To = Tonkin

M.S.: Malay States

— · — International boundary
········· Regional boundary

km

0   1000

CHINA

Canton
Hong Kong

BRITISH INDIA

BURMA
U.B.
Ar
L.B.
Te

SIAM

VIETNAM (FRENCH INDO-CHINA)

To
LAOS
1902
1902/
1907
CAMBODIA
Co
An

PHILIPPINES

SUMATRA

Aceh
1909
Penang
M.S.
Malacca
1909
SINGAPORE
Padang

BORNEO

BRUNEI
SARAWAK
NTH. BORNEO

SULAWESI
(CELEBES)
Menado
Macassar

SPICE ISLANDS
Ceram

NEW GUINEA

Batavia/
Jakarta
JAVA
Surabaya
Jogjakarta
LOMBOK

TIMOR

20°N
10°
0°
10°S

100°
110°
120°
130°
140°E

3. The Malay States/Sultanates and the Straits Settlements of Penang, Malacca and Singapore

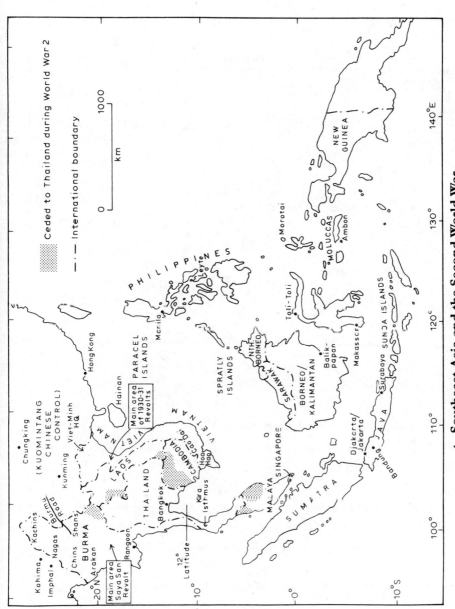

4. Southeast Asia and the Second World War

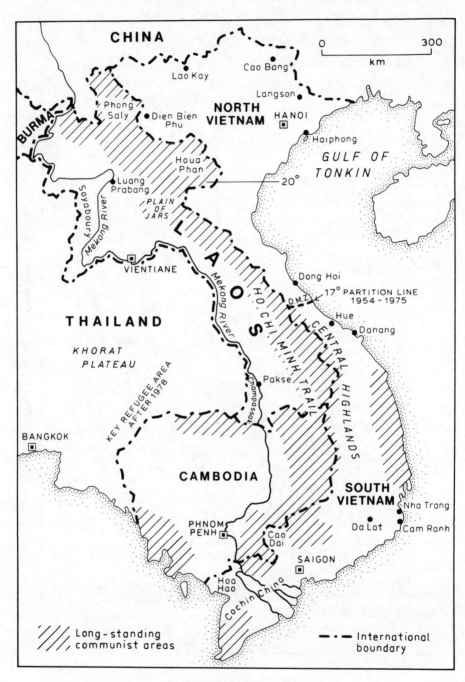

5. Indochina, 1954–75

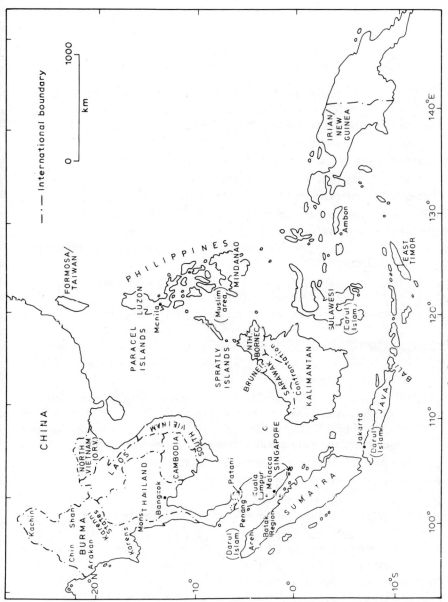

6. Southeast Asia, 1945–75

Glossary

ABRI: (Indonesian) Angkatan Bersendjata Republik Indonesia (Armed Forces of the Republic of Indonesia).

adat: (Indonesian, from Arabic) Pre-Islamic custom, often subsumed into Islam.

Al-Azhar: Chief mosque and university in Cairo.

Al-Imam: (Arabic) 'The Leader'; see *imam*.

ASEAN: The Association of South-East Asian Nations.

BKR: (Indonesian) Badan Keamanan Rakyat (People's Security Body).

BPKI: (Indonesian) Badan Penyelidik Usaha Persiapan Kemerdekaan Indonesia (Body to Investigate Measures for the Preparation for Indonesian Independence).

Brest-Litovsk Treaty: Punitive peace treaty imposed on the Bolsheviks by the Germans in 1918, after the collapse of Russia in the First World War.

bupati: (Javanese) Traditional local regent or regency (kebupaten) official, co-opted by the Dutch into the colonial administration.

Caliphate: The successors to Muhammad: leader of the Islamic empire.

Can Vuong: (Vietnamese) 'Aid the King' rebel movement against the French in Vietnam, begun in 1885.

Cao Dai: (Vietnamese) The Cao Dai religious movement combines elements of Confucianism, Daoism, Buddhism and Christianity. It was (and is) dominated by a strictly graded religious hierarchy. In essence, Cao Dai was designed to synthesize and supersede the main religions of Vietnam.

Cuu Quoc Hoi: (Vietnamese) National Salvation Associations.

daerah istimewa: (Indonesian) special regions.

Darul Islam: (Arabic) Abode of Islam.

dato/datu: (Malay/Indonesian) Local chieftain, honorary title.

'dialecticalism': Briefly, the notion that progress in the natural world and in human history depends upon the dynamism created by conflict between natural phenomena or political and social forces.

Dó-bama Asiayone: (Burmese) 'We Burmans Association'.

Dwifungsi ABRI: (Indonesian) The 'dual role' ('dwifungsi') of the Indonesian armed forces in civilian and military matters.

fatwa: (Arabic/Islam) Religious or judicial decision given by a qualified Islamic leader.

Galon Associations: Paramilitary nationalist organizations in colonial Burma.

Gerwani: (Indonesian) Gerakan Wanita Indonesia (Indonesian Women's Movement). PKI women's movement.

Gestapu: (Indonesian) Gerakan September Tiga Puluh (30th of September Movement).

Golkar: (Indonesian) Golongan Karya (Functional Group).

hadith: (Arabic/Islam) The collected reported sayings of Muhammad.

haji: (Arabic/Islam) One who has undertaken the pilgrimage to Mekka.

Hari Peringatan Pancasila Sakti: (Indonesian) Sacred Pancasila Memorial Day.

Hoa Hao: A radical, millenarian Buddhist sect formed in 1939 by Huynh Phu So in western Cochinchina.

Ho Chi Minh: Vietnamese nationalist leader, born in 1890; joined the French Communist Party in 1920; thereafter became an agent of Comintern; founded the ICP in 1930. Until the beginning of the Second World War, he was mainly absent from Vietnam. His earlier pseudonym was *Nguyen Ai Quoc.*

Ilustrado: Educated elite of the Philippines.

imam: (Arabic/Islam) The leader of prayer in a mosque.

KAP-Gestapu: (Indonesian) Komando Aksi Pengganyangan Gestapu (The Action Front to Crush the Gestapu).

Kaum Muda: (Malay/Indonesian) see *Muhammadiyah;* Islamic modernizers in Malaya and Indonesia.

Kaum Tua: (Malay/Indonesian) see *Nahdatul Ulama;* Islamic traditionalists in Malaya and Indonesia.

KNIP: (Indonesian) Komite Nasional Indonesia Pusat (Central Indonesian National Committee).

KOPKAMTIB: (Indonesian) Komando Operasi Pemulihan Keamanan dan Ketertiban (Operational Command for the Restoration of Security and Order).

KOSTRAD: (Indonesian) Komando Strategis Angkatan Darat (Army Strategic Command).

KOTI: (Indonesian) Komando Operasi Tertinggi (Supreme Operational Command).

Lao Dong: (Vietnamese) Vietnam Dang Lao Dong (Vietnam Workers' Party).

Lao Issara: (Lao) Free Lao movement and government.

League of Nations: An international organization – precursor of the United Nations – set up in the wake of the First World War.

Lubang Buaya: (Indonesian) 'Crocodile Hole'.

madrasah: (Arabic) An Islamic religious school.

Majapahit (Modjopahit): The great Hindu–Buddhist/pre-Muslim kingdom centred in east Java, that dominated Java, Bali, southern Sumatra and southern Kalimantan (Borneo) during the fourteenth and fifteenth centuries, and extended its sphere of economic and political influence into eastern Indonesia as well.

Manipol: (Indonesian) Manifesto Politik (Political Manifesto).

Masyumi (Masjumi): (Indonesian) Majlis Syuro Muslimin Indonesia (Consultative Council of Indonesian Muslims), founded during the Second World War; was closely connected to Sumatran unrest in the 1950s, and was banned (along with the pro-Western PSI, or Partai Sosialis Indonesia) in 1960, during Guided Democracy.

Mataram (Later Mataram): The central Javanese sultanate that dominated much of Java and parts of neighbouring islands during the seventeenth and early eighteenth centuries, named after the first major state of Java, founded in the eighth century.

'moral economy ethic': The notion that the peasantry in traditional societies generally do not try to change or improve their condition, because of the risks/catastrophe that could attend failure; rather, their economic/social strategy is that of risk avoidance.

MPRS: (Indonesian) Majlis Permusyawaratan Rakyat Sementara (Provisional People's Consultative Assembly).

mufti: (Arabic/Islam) Officer who expounds Islamic law and issues fatwas.

Muhammadiyah: (Arabic/Indonesian) The Way of Muhammad, founded by members of the *Kaum Muda* ('youth group') in Java in 1912 as an Islamic reformist movement.

Nahdatul Ulama: (Arabic/Indonesian) Muslim Scholars' Association, formed in 1926 by the *Kaum Tua* ('elder group') to defend religious tradition in the face of pressure for reform from the *Muhammadiyah* movement formed by the *Kaum Muda* ('young group') in early twentieth-century Javanese Muslim circles.

Nakshabandi Sufism: (Arabic) An ascetic Sufi order, with a large following in Southeast Asia, founded in the fourteenth century.

Negara Islam Indonesia (NII): (Indonesian) Islamic State of Indonesia.

Orde Baru: (Indonesian) New Order.

pamong praja: (Indonesian) civil service.

pancasila: (Indonesian) The 'Five Principles' of the independent Indonesian state.

Pemuda: (Indonesian) 'Youth'; a number of nationalist Pemuda organizations emerged during the Indonesian Revolution.

PKI: (Indonesian) Partai Komunis Indonesia (Indonesian Communist Party).

'plural society': A term used by J. S. Furnivall to describe a society in which different races and cultures live separately and fulfil different functions within the economy – a common feature of colonial societies.

PNI: (Indonesian) Partai Nasional Indonesia (Indonesian National Party); founded by Sukarno and other young nationalist intellectuals in 1927;

a new PNI was formed in 1945 by the leaders of the Indonesian Revolution.

pondok: (Indonesian) A village (Islamic) religious school, providing mostly religious-based elementary education.

PPKI: (Indonesian) Panita Persiapan Kemerdekaan Indonesia (Committee for the Preparation of Indonesian Independence).

priyayi (prijaji): (Javanese) Traditional administrative elite, co-opted into the Dutch colonial administration; see *bupati*.

PSI: (Indonesian) Partai Sosialis Indonesia (Indonesian Socialist Party); moderate socialist political party associated with the educated elite, banned by Sukarno under the Guided Democracy regime.

ratu adil: (Javanese) The 'Just King', who, according to traditional Javanese messianic expectations, will appear, bringing with him an era of justice and economic welfare for the people.

Renan, Ernest: A French theologian and philosopher. In 1882 he wrote a key essay on the concept of the nation and its historical foundations, entitled 'What is a Nation?'

résident: (French) Head of a province in French Indochina.

résident-general: (French) Head of a region of French Indochina – e.g. Annam, Tonkin, Laos.

riba: (Arabic) Usury.

RPKAD: (Indonesian) Resimen Para Komando Angkatan Darat (Army Para-Commando Regiment).

Sarekat Islam: (Indonesian) Islamic Association; the first mass nationalist organization in Indonesia. Originally formed in 1909 as the Sarekat Dagang Islam (Islamic Traders' Association), it was transformed into Sarekat Islam in 1912, with more overtly nationalist and anti-colonial objectives.

shaykh ul-Islam: (Arabic) Religious leader.

Sriwijaja (Srivijaya): The major early trading state that dominated the coasts of Sumatra and the Malay peninsula facing the Malacca Straits for much of the period between the late seventh and the early thirteenth century. Its size and political power may have been inflated in the rhetoric of such Indonesian nationalists as Sukarno, as was that of *Mujupahit*.

'strategic hamlets': The name attached to village organizations formed in an attempt by the regime of Ngo Dinh Diem in South Vietnam to consolidate the rural population of the Mekong Delta into defensible units that could be protected from communist infiltration and assault.

Supersemar: (Indonesian) Surat Perintah Sebelas Maret (11th of March Letter of Instruction).

surau: (Arabic) A small Muslim prayer-house.

talkin (talqin): (Arabic) Instruction or exhortation given at the grave of a departed Muslim by a religious teacher.

Tayson: Name given to the leaders of the major late eighteenth-century rebellion in Vietnam, who united and ruled Vietnam briefly before being defeated by the Nguyen dynasty in 1802.

thakin (thahkin): (Burmese) A title of respect normally accorded to Europeans in colonial Burma, used symbolically by young Burmese nationalists in the 1930s.

Tran Trong Kim: Prime Minister appointed by Emperor Bao Dai after the Japanese handed over independence to Vietnam in March 1945.

ulama: (Arabic) Islamic scholar or teacher.

umat: (Arabic) A people, nation, or religious community, including *umat Islam*, the whole community of Islam.

VNQDD: (Vietnamese) Viet Nam Quoc Dan Dang. The Vietnamese Nationalist Party, founded in 1927. Modelled closely on the Chinese Nationalist Party, or Kuomintang.

Volksraad: (Dutch) People's Council.

Wahhabi: A movement of strict Islamic reformists, with its centre in eastern Arabia; linked to the Saud family who founded the state of Saudi Arabia in 1924.

Watergate scandal: This term encompassed a whole series of scandals relating to the improper and unconstitutional actions of the Office of President Nixon, that were designed to aid the re-election of Nixon in 1972 by discrediting political enemies, including members of the anti-Vietnam-war movement.

Select Bibliography

General

Alagappa, Muthiah (ed.) (1996) *Political Legitimacy in Southeast Asia: The Quest for Moral Authority* (Cambridge: Cambridge University Press).

Anderson, Benedict L. R. O'G. (1991) *Imagined Communities: Reflections on the Origins and Spread of Nationalism* (London: Verso). (Contains Southeast Asian examples of the role of literature in the development of a national identity.)

Brown, David (1994) *The State and Ethnic Politics in Southeast Asia* (London: Routledge).

Buszynski, Leszek (1988) *ASEAN: Security Issues of the 1990s* (Canberra: ANU).

Christie, Clive J. (1996) *A Modern History of Southeast Asia: Decolonization, Nationalism and Separatism* (London: I.B.Tauris).

Elsbree, Willard H. (1970) *Japan's Role in Southeast Asian Nationalist Movements, 1940 to 1945* (New York: Russell).

Far Eastern Economic Review (Hong Kong). (A vital source of information on political and economic developments in Southeast Asia in the post-Second World War period.)

Fifield, Russell H. (1968) *The Diplomacy of Southeast Asia* (Hamden, CT: Archon Books).

Gregor, A. James (1986) *In the Shadow of Giants: The Major Powers and the Security of Southeast Asia* (Stanford, CA: Hoover Institution Press).

Hall, D. G. E. (1968) *A History of South-East Asia* (London: Macmillan).

Hangga, Heiner (1991) *ASEAN and the Zopfan Concept* (Singapore: ISEAS).

Hooker, M. B. (ed.) (1983) *Islam in South-East Asia* (Leiden: E. J. Brill).

Hourani, Albert (1970) *Arabic Thought in the Liberal Age 1798–1939* (London: Oxford University Press). (A classic study of the impact of the Islamic reform movement.)

— (1991) *A History of the Arab Peoples* (Cambridge, MA: Harvard University Press).

Huxley, T. J. (1993) *Insecurity in the ASEAN Region* (London: Royal United Services Institute for Defence Studies).

Huxley, T J and Mohammed Talib (eds) (1996) *An Introduction to Southeast Asian Studies* (London: I.B.Tauris).

Kahin G. McT. (1956) *The Asian–African Conference, Bandung, Indonesia* (Ithaca, NY: Cornell University Press).

Lebar, Frank M. (ed.) (1972) *Ethnic Groups in Insular Southeast Asia* (New Haven, CT: Human Relations Area Files).

Lebar, Frank, Gerald C. Hickey and John K. Musgrave (eds) (1964) *Ethnic Groups in Mainland Southeast Asia* (New Haven, CT: Human Relations Area Files).

Lebra, Joyce C. (1974) *Japan's Greater East Asian Co-Prosperity Sphere in World War 2* (Kuala Lumpur: Oxford University Press).

— (1977) *Japanese-Trained Armies in Southeast Asia: Independence and Volunteer Forces in World War II* (London: Heinemann).

Leifer, Michael (1995) *Dictionary of the Modern Politics of South-East Asia* (London: Routledge).

Ling, Trevor (1979) *Buddhism, Imperialism and War* (London: George Allen and Unwin).

Louis, William Roger (1971) *British Strategy in the Far East 1919–1939* (London: Oxford University Press).

McLane, Charles B. (1966) *Soviet Strategies in Southeast Asia: An Exploration of Eastern Policy Under Lenin and Stalin* (Princeton, NJ: Princeton University Press).

Osborne, Milton E. (1970) *Region of Revolt: Focus on Southeast Asia* (Rushcutters Bay, NSW and Oxford: Pergamon Press).

Palmer, Ronald D. and Thomas R. Reckford (1987) *Building ASEAN: 20 Years of Southeast Asian Cooperation* (New York: Praeger).

Pluvier, J. M. (1974) *South-East Asia from Colonialism to Independence* (Kuala Lumpur: Oxford University Press).

Purcell, Victor (1965) *South and East Asia since 1800* (Cambridge: Cambridge University Press).

Sardesai, D.R. (1989) *Southeast Asia, Past and Present* (Basingstoke: Macmillan).

Silverstein, Josef (ed.) (1960) *Southeast Asia in World War II: Four Essays* (New Haven, CT: Southeast Asia Studies, Monograph Series, No. 7; Yale University).

Ssu-yu Teng and John K. Fairbank (eds) (1969) *China's Response to the West: A Documentary Survey 1839–1923* (New York: Athenaeum).

Steinberg, Joel et al. (1987) *In Search of Southeast Asia: A Modern History* (Honolulu: University of Hawaii Press).

Tarling, Nicholas (1993) *The Fall of Imperial Britain in Southeast Asia* (Singapore: Oxford University Press).

— (1995) *Britain, Southeast Asia and the Onset of the Pacific War* (Cambridge: Cambridge University Press).

— (ed.) (1992) *The Cambridge History of Southeast Asia*, Vol. 2 (Cambridge: Cambridge University Press).

Thompson, Virginia and Richard Adloff (1955) *Minority Problems in Southeast Asia* (Stanford, CA: Stanford University Press).

Thorne, Christopher (1978) *Allies of a Kind: The United States, Britain and the War against Japan 1941–1945* (London: Hamish Hamilton).

— (1986) *Far Eastern War: States and Societies 1941–1945* (London: Unwin).

Vatikiotis, Michael R. J. (1996) *Political Change In Southeast Asia; Trimming the Banyan Tree* (London: Routledge).

Wijerawardene, Gehan (1990) *Ethnic Groups across National Boundaries in Mainland Southeast Asia* (Singapore: ISEAS).

Wurfel, David (1990) *The Political Economy of Foreign Policy in Southeast Asia* (Basingstoke: Macmillan).

Wurfel, David and Bruce Borton (eds) (1996) *Southeast Asia in the New World Order: The Political Economy of a Dynamic Region* (Basingstoke: Macmillan).

Brunei

Franz, J. C. (1990) *The Sultanate of Brunei: Oil Wealth and Problems of Development* (Nuernberg: Friedrich Alexander Universitaet).

Horton, A. V. M. (1984) *The British Residency in Brunei 1906–1959* (Hull: Centre for Southeast Asian Studies, University of Hull).

— (1995) *A New Sketch of the History of Negara Brunei Darussalam* (Bordesley, Worcs: Horton).

— (1995) *Turun Temurun: A Dissection of Negara Brunei Darussalam* (Bordesley, Worcs: Horton).

Hussainmya, B. A. (1996) *Sultan Omar Ali Saifuddin III and Britain: The Making of Brunei Darussalam* (Oxford: Oxford University Press).

King, V. T. and A. V. M. Horton (1995) *From Buckfast to Borneo: Essays Presented to Father Robert Nicholl on the 85th Anniversary of his Birth, 27 March 1995* (Hull: University of Hull).

Saunders, Graham (1994) *A History of Brunei* (Kuala Lumpur: Oxford University Press).

Burma

The colonial era

Adas, Michael (1974) *The Burma Delta: Economic Development and Social Change on an Asian Rice Frontier 1852–1941* (Madison, WI: University of Wisconsin Press).

— (1979) *Prophets of Rebellion: Millenarian Protest Movements Against the European Colonial Order* (Chapel Hill, NC: University of North Carolina Press).

Donnison, F. S. V. (1953) *Public Administration in Burma: A Study of Development during the British Connexion* (London: Royal Institute of International Affairs).

— (1970) *Burma* (London: Benn).

Furnivall, J. S. (1956) *Colonial Policy and Practice: A Comparative Study of Burma and Netherlands India* (New York: New York University Press).

Herbert, Patricia (1982) *The Hsaya San Rebellion (1930–1932) Reappraised* (Melbourne: Monash University).

Khun Yi (1988) *The Dobama Movement in Burma 1930–1938* (Ithaca, NY: Cornell University Press).

Moscotti, A. D. (1974) *British Policy and the Nationalist Movement in Burma 1917–1937* (Honolulu: University Press of Hawaii).

Orwell, George (1949) *Burmese Days* (London: Secker and Warburg). (A classic novel about British colonial society in Burma.)

Po, San C. (1928) *Burma and the Karens* (London: Elliot Stock).

Sarkisyanz, E. (1965) *Buddhist Backgrounds of the Burmese Revolution* (The Hague: Martinus Nijhoff).

Scott, James C. (1978) *The Moral Economy of the Peasant: Rebellion and Subsistence in Southeast Asia* (New Haven, CT: Yale University Press).

— (1985) *Weapons of the Weak: Everyday Forms of Peasant Resistance* (New Haven, CT: Yale University Press).

Secretary of State for India (1931) *Report on the Rebellion in Burma up to 3rd. May 1931*, presented by the Secretary of State for India to Parliament, June 1931, Cmd. 3900 (London: HMSO).

Smeaton, Donald M. (1887) *The Loyal Karens of Burma* (London: Kegan Paul Trench and Co.).

Solomon, R. L. (1969) 'Saya San and the Burmese Rebellion', *Modern Asian Studies*, Vol. 3, no. 3.

Warren, C. V. (1937) *Burmese Interlude*, (London: Skeffington). (Contains section on the Saya San revolt.)

The Second World War and independence

Allen, Louis (1984) *Burma: The Longest War 1941 1945* (London. Dent).

Ba Maw (1968) *Breakthrough in Burma* (New Haven, CT: Yale University Press).

Ba U (1959) *My Burma* (New York: Taplinger).

Burma Revolutionary Council (1962) *The Burmese Way to Socialism: The Policy Declaration of the Revolutionary Council* (Rangoon: Revolutionary Council).

Cady, J. F. (1958) *A History of Modern Burma* (Ithaca, NY: Cornell University Press).

— (1976) *The United States and Burma* (Cambridge, MA, Harvard University Press).

Chakravarti, N. R. (1971) *The Indian Minority in Burma: The Rise and Decline of an Immigrant Minority* (London: Oxford University Press).

Collis, Maurice (1956) *Last and First in Burma 1941–1948* (London: Faber).

Cruickshank, Charles (1983) *SOE in the Far East* (London: Oxford University Press).

Donnison, F. S. V. (1956) *British Military Administration in the Far East 1943–1946* (London: HMSO).

Irwin, Anthony (1945) *Burmese Outpost* (London: Collins).

Kirby, S. W. (1957–69) *The War against Japan*, 5 vols (London: HMSO).

Lintner, Bertil (1990) *The Rise and Fall of the Communist Party of Burma (CPB)* (Ithaca, NY: Southeast Asia Program, Cornell University).

McEnery, John H. (1990) *Epilogue in Burma 1945–1948: The Military Dimension of British Withdrawal* (Tunbridge Wells: Spellmount).

Maung Maung, U (1989) *Burmese Nationalist Movements 1940–1948* (Edinburgh: Kiscadale).

Nu, Thakin (U) (1954) *Burma under the Japanese* (London: Macmillan).

Nu (U) (1975) *U Nu: Saturday's Son: Memoirs of the Former Prime Minister of Burma* (New Haven, CT, Yale University Press).

Owen, Frank (1946) *The Campaign in Burma* (London: HMSO).

Po Chit (Sau) (n.d.) *Karens and the Karen State* (Burma: Karen National Union), in India Office Library, IOR M/4/3023.

Selth, Andrew (1986) 'Race and Resistance in Burma 1942–1945', *Modern Asian Studies*, Vol. 20, no. 3: 483–95.

Silverstein, Josef (1977) *Burma: Military Rule and the Politics of Stagnation* (Ithaca, NY, Cornell University Press).

— (1980) *Burmese Politics: The Dilemma of National Unity* (New Brunswick, NJ: Rutgers University Press).

— (ed.) (1972) *The Political Legacy of Aung San* (Ithaca, NY: Southeast Asia Program, Cornell University).

— (ed.) (1989) *Independent Burma at Forty Years: Six Assessments* (Ithaca, NY: Southeast Asia Program, Cornell University).

Smith, Donald Eugene (1965) *Religion and Politics in Burma* (Princeton, NJ: Princeton University Press).

Smith, Martin (1991) *Burma: Insurgency and the Politics of Ethnicity* (London: Zed Books).

Taylor, Robert H. (1987) *The State in Burma* (London: Hurst).

Tinker, Hugh (ed.) (1983/1986) *Burma: The Struggle for Independence 1944–1948*, 2 vols (London: HMSO).

Trager, Frank N. (1957) *Building a Welfare State in Burma, 1948–1956* (New York: Institute of Pacific Relations).

— (ed.) (1971) *Burma: Japanese Military Administration: Selected Documents, 1941–1945* (Philadelphia: University of Pennsylvania Press).

Yoon, W. Z. (1973) *Japan's Scheme for the Liberation of Burma: the role of the Minami Kikan and the 'Thirty Comrades'* (Athens, OH: Ohio University Papers in Southeast Asian Studies).

Cambodia

Chandler, David P. (1991) *The Tragedy of Cambodian History: Politics, War and Revolution since 1945* (Newhaven, CT: Yale University Press).

— (1992) *A History of Cambodia* (Boulder, CO: Westview Press).

Chandler, David P. and Ben Kiernan (eds) (1983) *Revolution and its Aftermath in Kampuchea: Eight Essays* (New Haven, CT: Southeast Asia Studies, Yale University).

Evans, Grant and Kelvin Rowley (1984) *Red Brotherhood at War: Indochina since the Fall of Saigon* (London: Verso).

Heder, Stephen R. (1991) *Pol Pot and Khieu Samphan* (Clayton, Victoria: Centre of Southeast Asian Studies, Monash University).

— (1991) *Reflections on Cambodian History: Backgrounds to Recent Developments* (Canberra: Australian National University, Strategic and Defence Studies Centre).

Kiernan, Ben (1996) *The Pol Pot Regime: Race, Power and Genocide in Cambodia Under the Khmer Rouge 1975–1979* (New Haven, CT: Yale University Press).

— (ed.) (1993) *Genocide and Democracy in Cambodia: The Khmer Rouge, the United Nations and the International Community* (New Haven, CT: Southeast Asia Studies, Yale University).

Leifer, Michael (1967) *Cambodia: The Search for Security* (New York: Praeger).

— (1983). *Cambodia's Foreign Policy* (London: Allen and Unwin).

Mabbett, Ian W. and David Chandler (1995) *The Khmers* (Oxford: Basil Blackwell).

Osborne, Milton (1979) *Before Kampuchea: Preludes to Tragedy* (London: Allen and Unwin).

— (1994), *Sihanouk: Prince of Light, Prince of Darkness* (Sydney: Allen and Unwin).

Reddi, V. M. (1970) *A History of the Cambodian Independence Movement 1863–1955* (Tirupati: Sri Venkateswara University).

Shawcross, William (1980) *Sideshow: Kissinger, Nixon and the Destruction of Cambodia* (London: Hogarth Press).

— (1984) *The Quality of Mercy: Cambodia, Holocaust and Modern Conscience* (London: Deutsch).

Sopiee, Mohamed Noordin (1989) *The Cambodian Conflict 1978–1989* (Kuala Lumpur: Institute of Strategic and International Studies).

Vickery, Michael (1984) *Cambodia 1975–1982* (Sydney: Allen and Unwin).

— (1986), *Kampuchea: Politics, Economics and Society* (London: Pinter).

Indonesia

Indonesia in the era of colonialism

Alfian (1989) *Muhammadijah: The Political Behaviour of a Muslim Modernist Organization Under Dutch Colonialism* (Yogyakarta: Gadjah Mada University Press).

Alisjahbana, Sutan Takdir (1966) *Indonesia: Social and Cultural Revolution* (Kuala Lumpur: Oxford University Press).

Anderson, Benedict R. O'G. (1990) *Language and Power: Exploring Political Cultures in Indonesia* (Ithaca, NY: Cornell University Press).

Benda, Harry J. and Ruth T. McVey (eds) (1960) *The Communist Uprisings of 1926–1927 in Indonesia: Key Documents* (Ithaca, NY: Modern Indonesia Project, Cornell University).

Cribb, Robert (1992) *Historical Dictionary of Indonesia* (Metuchen, NJ: Scarecrow Press).

— (ed.) (1994) *The Late Colonial State in Indonesia: Political and Economic Foundations of the Netherlands Indies 1880–1942* (Leiden: KITLV Press).

Dahm, Bernard (1969) *Sukarno and the Struggle for Indonesian Independence* (Ithaca, NY: Cornell University Press).

— (1971) *History of Indonesia in the Twentieth Century* (London: Pall Mall Press).

Doran, Christine (ed.) (1987) *Indonesian Politics: A Reader* (Townsville, Queensland: James Cook University of North Queensland).

Freidus, Joy Alberta (1977) *Sumatran Contributions to the Development of Indonesian Literature 1920–1942* (Honolulu: University of Hawaii Press).

Hatta, Mohammad (1972) *Portrait of a Patriot: Selected Writings* (The Hague: Mouton).

Ingleson, John (1979) *Road to Exile: The Indonesian Nationalist Movement, 1927–1934* (Singapore: Heinemann).

Kartini, Raden Adjeng (1992) *Letters from Kartini: An Indonesian Feminist 1900–1904* (translated by Joost Cote) (Clayton, Victoria: Monash University).

Legge, J. D. (1972) *Sukarno: A Political Biography* (London: Allen Lane).

— (1977) *Indonesia* (Sydney: Prentice-Hall).

McVey, Ruth T. (1965) *The Rise of Indonesian Communism* (Ithaca, NY: Cornell University Press).

— (1969) *Sukarno: Nationalism, Islam and Marxism* (Ithaca, NY: Cornell University Press).

Noer, Deliar (1972) *The Modernist Muslim Movement in Indonesia 1900–1942* (Kuala Lumpur: Oxford University Press).

Penders, C. L. M. (1977) *Indonesia: Selected Documents on Colonialism and Nationalism 1830–1942* (St. Lucia: University of Queensland Press).

Reid, Anthony (1969) *The Contest for North Sumatra: Atjeh, the Netherlands and Britain 1858– 1898* (Kuala Lumpur: University of Malaya Press).

Ricklefs, M. C. (1993) *A History of Modern Indonesia since c.1300* (Basingstoke: Macmillan).

Shiraishi, Takashi (1990), *An Age in Motion: Popular Radicalism in Java 1912–1926* (Ithaca, NY: Cornell University Press).

Sjahrir, Soetan (1949) *Out of Exile* (New York: Day).

Steenbrink, Karel (1993) *Dutch Colonialism and Indonesian Islam: Contacts and Conflicts 1591– 1950* (Amsterdam: Editions RODOPI).

Sutherland, Heather (1979) *The Making of a Bureaucratic Elite: The Colonial Transformation of the Javanese Prijaji* (Singapore: Heinemann).

Taufiq, Abdullah (1971) *Schools and Politics: The Kaum Muda Movement in West Sumatra 1927– 1933* (Ithaca, NY: Cornell University Press).

Tsuchiya, Kenji (1988) *Democracy and Leadership: The Rise of the Taman Siswa Movement in Indonesia* (translated by P. Hawkes) (Honolulu: University of Hawaii Press).

Selected Indonesian literature associated with the twentieth century nationalist movement and cultural revolution, in various editions

Abdul Muis, *Salah Asuhan* ('Wasted Education') (1928).

Amir Hamzah, *Nyanyi Sunyi* ('Songs of Loneliness') (1935).

Armijn Pané, *Belenggu* ('Chains') (1940).

Marah Rusli, *Sitti Nurbaya* (1922).

S. Takdir Alisjahbana, *Layar Terkembang* ('With sails unfurled') (1937).

The Second World War and revolution, 1939–50

Anderson, Benedict R. O'G. (1972) *Java in a Time of Revolution* (Ithaca, NY: Cornell University Press).

Benda, H. J. (1958) *The Crescent and the Rising Sun; Indonesian Islam under the Japanese Occupation 1942–1945* (The Hague: Van Hoeve).

Benda, H. J. and J. K. Irikura et al. (eds) (1965) *Japanese Military Administration in Indonesia: Selected Documents* (New Haven, CT: Yale University Press).

Cribb, Robert (1991) *Gangsters and Revolutionaries: the Jakarta People's Militia and the Indonesian Revolution 1945–1949* (Kensington, Australia: Asian Studies Association of Australia, Allen and Unwin).

Frederick, W. H. (1989) *Visions and Heat: The Making of the Indonesian Revolution* (Athens, OH: Ohio University Press).

Kahin, George McT. (1970) *Nationalism and Revolution in Indonesia* (Ithaca, NY: Cornell University Press).

Ken'ichi, Goto (1995) 'Caught in the Middle: Japanese Attitudes Towards Indonesian Independence in 1945', *Journal of Southeast Asian Studies*, Vol. 27, no. 1.

Lucas, Anton (1991) *One Soul, One Struggle: Region and Revolution in Indonesia* (Sydney: Allen and Unwin).

McMahon, R. J. (1981) *Colonialism and Cold War: The United States and the Struggle for Indonesian Independence* (Ithaca, NY: Cornell University Press).

Malaka, Tan (1991) From *Jail to Jail* (edited and translated by H. Jarvis) (Athens, OH: Ohio University Press).

Mook, H. J. van (1944) *The Netherlands Indies and Japan: Their Relations 1940–1941* (London: Allen and Unwin).

Mook, H. J. van (1950) *The Stakes of Democracy in Southeast Asia* (London: Allen and Unwin).

Mrazek, Rudolf (1994) *Sjahrir: Politics and Exile in Indonesia* (Ithaca, NY: Cornell University, Southeast Asia Program).

Reid, Anthony (1974) *The Indonesian National Revolution 1945–1950* (Hawthorn, Victoria: Longman).

— (1979) *The Blood of the People: Revolution and the End of Traditional Rule in Sumatra* (London: Oxford University Press).

— (ed.) (1986) *The Japanese Experience in Indonesia: Selected Memoirs of 1942–1945* (Athens, OH: Ohio University Press).

Rose, Mavis (1987) *Indonesia Free: A Political Biography of Mohammad Hatta* (Ithaca, NY: Cornell University Press).

Said, Salim (1994) *Genesis of Power: General Sudirman and the Indonesian Military in Politics 1945–1949* (Singapore: ISEAS).

Sjahrir, Soetan (1968) *Our Struggle* (Ithaca, NY: Cornell University Press).

Sluimers, Laszlo (1996) 'The Japanese Military and Indonesian Independence', *Journal of Southeast Asian Studies*, Vol. 27, no. 1.

Smail, John R. W. (1964) *Bandung in the Early Revolution, 1945–1946: A Study in the Social History of the Indonesian Revolution* (Ithaca, NY: Cornell University Press).

Swift, Ann (1989) *The Road to Madiun: The Indonesian Communist Uprising of 1948* (Ithaca, NY: Cornell University Press).

Tarling, Nicholas (1996) 'Britain, Portugal and East Timor in 1941', in *Journal of Southeast Asian Studies*, Vol. 27, no.1.

Touwen-Bouwsma (1996) 'The Indonesian Nationalists and the Japanese "Liberation" of Indonesia: Visions and Reactions', *Journal of Southeast Asian Studies*, Vol. 27, no.1.

Indonesia 1950–65 and beyond

Boland, B. J. (1971) *The Struggle of Islam in Modern Indonesia* (s'-Gravenhage: Smits).

Budiardjo, Carmel (1995) *Surviving Indonesia's Gulag* (London: Cassell).

Carey, Peter and G. Carter Bentley (eds) (1995) *East Timor at the Crossroads: The Forging of a Nation* (London: Cassell).

Cribb, Robert (ed.) (1990) *The Indonesian Killings of 1965–1966: Studies from Java and Bali* (Calyton, Victoria: Monash University).

Cribb, Robert and Colin Brown (1995) *Modern Indonesia: A History since 1945* (Harlow, Longman).

Crouch, Harold (1978) *The Army and Politics in Indonesia* (Ithaca, NY: Cornell University Press).

Dijk, C. van (1981) *Rebellion under the Banner of Islam: The Darul Islam in Indonesia* (The Hague: Martinus Nijhoff).

Edman, Peter G. G. (1987) *Communism à la Aidit: The Indonesian Communist Party under D. N. Aidit, 1950–1964* (Townsville, Queensland: James Cook University of North Queensland).

Feith, Herbert (1962) *The Decline of Constitutional Democracy in Indonesia* (Ithaca, NY: Cornell University Press).

Feith, Herbert and Lance Castles (eds) (1970) *Indonesian Political Thinking* (Ithaca, NY: Cornell University Press).

Gunn, G. with Jefferson Lee (1994) *A Critical View of Western Journalism and Scholarship on East Timor* (Manila: Journal of Contemporary Asia Publishers).

Hering, B. B. (ed.) (n.d.) *The PKI's Aborted Revolt: Some Selected Documents* (Townsville, Queensland, James Cook University of North Queensland).

Hughes, John (1967) *Indonesian Upheaval* (New York: McKay).

Hughes, John (1968) *The End of Sukarno: A Coup that Misfired* (London: Angus and Robertson).

Indonesia, Departemen Penerangan (1960) *The Indonesian Revolution: Basic Documents and the Idea of Guided Democracy Issued by the Department of Information* (Djakarta: Department of Information).

Jolliffe, Jill (1978) *East Timor: Nationalism and Colonialism* (St. Lucia: University of Queensland Press).

Kahin, Audrey R. and George McT. Kahin (1995) *Subversion and Foreign Policy: The Secret Eisenhower and Dulles Debacle in Indonesia* (New York: New Press).

Nazaruddin Sjamsuddin (1985) *The Republican Revolt: A Study of the Acehnese Rebellion* (Singapore: ISEAS).

Robinson, Geoffrey Basil (1994): *The Politics of Violence in Modern Bali 1882–1966* (Ann Arbor, MI: University of Michigan Press).

Sudjatmiko, Iwan Gardono (1992) *The Destruction of the Indonesian Communist Party (PKI): A Comparative Analysis of East Java and Bali* (Ann Arbor, MI: University of Michigan Press).

Taylor, John G. (1991) *Indonesia's Forgotten War: The Hidden History of East Timor* (London: Zed Books).

Vatikiotis, Michael R. J. (1994) *Indonesian Politics under Suharto* (London: Routledge).

Laos

Deuve, Jean (1984) *Le royaume du Laos 1949–1965: histoire événementielle de l'indépendance à la guerre américaine* (Paris, EFEO).

Dommen, A. J. (1971) *Conflict in Laos: The Politics of Neutralization* (New York: Praeger).

— (1985) *Laos: Keystone of Indochina* (Boulder, CO: Westview Press).

Dommen, A. J. and George W. Dalley (1991) 'The OSS in Laos: The 1945 Raven Mission and American Policy', *Journal of Southeast Asian Studies*, Vol. 22, no. 2: 327–46.

Fall, Bernard B. (1969) *Anatomy of a Crisis: The Laotian Crisis of 1960–1961* (Garden City, NY, Doubleday).

Goldstein, M. E. (1973) *American Policy towards Laos* (Rutherford, NJ: Fairleigh Dickinson University Press).

Gunn, Geoffrey (1990) *Rebellion in Laos: Peasants and Politics in a Colonial Backwater* (Boulder, CO: Westview Press).

— (1992) 'Prince Souphanouvong: Revolutionary and Intellectual', *Journal of Contemporary Asia*, Vol 22, no. 1): 94–103.

Haney, W. (1971) 'The Pentagon Papers and the United States' Involvement in Laos', in Noam Chomsky (ed.), *The Pentagon Papers: the Defense Department History of the United States' Decision-making on Vietnam* (Boston, MA: Beacon Press).

Hilsman, Roger (1964) *To Move a Nation: The Politics of Foreign Policy in the Administration of John F. Kennedy* (New York: Delta).

Lederer, W. J. (1961) *A Nation of Sheep* (London: Cassell) (chapter 1).

Levy, Paul (1974) *Histoire du Laos* (Paris: Presses Universitaires de France).

McCoy, A. W. (1973) *The Politics of Heroin in Southeast Asia* (New York: Harper and Row).

Pavie, Auguste (1947) *A la conquête des coeurs* (Paris: Presses Universitaires de France). (Memoirs of the first stages of French intervention in Laos – a classic.)

Sananikone, Oun (1975) *Lao Issara: The Memoirs of Oun Sananikone* (edited by D. K.Wyatt) (Ithaca, NY: Cornell University Press).

Stuart-Fox, Martin (1986) *Laos: Politics, Economics and Society* (London: Frances Pinter).
— (1992) *Historical Dictionary of Laos* (Metuchen, NJ: Scarecrow Press).
Toye, Hugh (1968) *Laos: Buffer-State or Battleground?* (London: Oxford University Press).
Zasloff, J. J. (1969) *Revolution in Laos: The North Vietnamese and the Pathet Lao* (Santa Monica, CA: RAND Corporation).
— (1973) *The Pathet Lao: Leadership and Organization* (Lexington: Lexington Books).
— and Leonard Unger (1991) *Laos: Beyond the Revolution* (Basingstoke: Macmillan).

Malaya/Malaysia and Singapore

Malaya and Singapore/Straits Settlements before the Second World War

Andaya, Barbara Watson and Leonard Y. Andaya (1982) *A History of Malaysia* (Basingstoke: Macmillan).
Blythe, W. (1969) *The Impact of Chinese Secret Societies in Malaya: A Historical Study* (London: Oxford University Press).
Cheah Boon Kheng (1992) *From PKI to Comintern, 1924–1941: The Apprenticeship of the Malayan Communist Party: Selected Documents and Discussion* (Ithaca, NY: Cornell University Press).
Emerson, Rupert (1964) *Malaysia: A Study in Direct and Indirect Rule* (Kuala Lumpur: University of Malaya Press).
Gullick, J. M. (1964) *Malaya* (London: Benn).
— (1965) *Indigenous Political Systems of Western Malaya* (London: The Athlone Press).
— (1981) *Malaysia: Economic Expansion and National Unity* (London: Benn).
Heussler, Robert (1981), *British Rule in Malaya: The Malayan Civil Service and its Predecessors 1867–1942* (Oxford: Clio).
Jagjit Singh Sindhu (1980) *Administration in the Federated Malay States 1896–1920* (Kuala Lumpur: Oxford University Press).
Lee, Edwin (1991) *The British as Rulers Governing Multiracial Singapore, 1867–1914* (Singapore: The University of Singapore Press).
Milner, Anthony (1994) *The Invention of Politics in Colonial Malaya: Contesting Nationalism and the Expansion of the Public Sphere* (Cambridge: Cambridge University Press).
Roff, William R. (1967) *The Origins of Malay Nationalism* (New Haven, CT and London: Yale University Press).
Song Ong Siang (1967) *One Hundred Years' History of the Chinese in Singapore* (Singapore: University of Malaya Press).
Tregonning, K.G. (1964) *A History of Modern Malaya* (London: Eastern Universities Press).
— (1967) *Malaysian Historical Sources* (Singapore: University of Singapore Press).
Turnbull, Constance M. (1989) *A History of Singapore 1819–1988* (Singapore: Oxford University Press).
Vaughan, J. D. (1971) *The Manners and Customs of the Chinese of the Straits Settlements* (Kuala Lumpur: Oxford University Press).
Wang Gung Wu (1991) *China and the Chinese Overseas* (Singapore: Times Academic Press).
Winstedt, Richard (1981) *The Malays: A Cultural History* (updated by Tham Seong Chee) (Singapore: Graham Brash).
Yeo Kim Wah (1982) *The Politics of Decentralization: Colonial Controversy in Malaya 1920–1929* (Kuala Lumpur: Oxford University Press).
Yong, C. F. and R. B. McKenna (1990) *The Kuomintang Movement in British Malaya 1912–1949* (Singapore: University of Singapore Press).

Malaya/Malaysia and Singapore in the era of the Second World War and independence

Allen, Louis (1977) *Singapore 1941–1942* (London: Davis-Poynter).

Allen, Richard (1968) *Malaysia: Prospect and Retrospect* (London: Oxford University Press).

Ampalavanar, Rajeswary (1981) *The Indian Minority and Political Change in Malaya 1945–1957* (Kuala Lumpur: Oxford University Press).

Barraclough, Simon (1988) *A Dictionary of Malaysian Politics* (Singapore: Heinemann Asia).

Brown, Ian and Rajeswary A. Brown (compilers) (1986) *Malaysia* (Oxford: Clio).

Cheah Boon Kheng (1979) *The Masked Comrades: A Study of the Communist United Front in Malaya, 1945–1948* (Singapore: Times Books International).

— (1983) *Red Star over Malaya: Resistance and Social Conflict During and After the Japanese Occupation of Malaya 1941–1946* (Singapore: University of Singapore Press).

Chin, K. W. (1983) *The Defence of Malaysia and Singapore: The Transformation of a Security System 1957–1971* (Cambridge: Cambridge University Press).

Elphick, Peter (1995) *Singapore: The Pregnable Fortress: A Study in Deception, Discord and Desertion* (London: Hodder and Stoughton).

Funston, N. John (1980) *Malay Politics in Malaysia: A Study of the United Malays National Organization and Partai Islam* (Kuala Lumpur: Heinemann Educational).

Heng Pek Koon (1988) *Chinese Politics in Malaysia: A History of the Malaysian Chinese Association* (Singapore: Oxford University Press).

Heussler, R. (1985) *British Rule in Malaya 1942–1957* (Singapore: Heinemann Asia).

Jackson, Robert (1991) *The Malayan Emergency: The Commonwealth's Wars 1948–1966* (London: Routledge).

Josey, Alex (1980) *Lee Kuan Yew: The Crucial Years* (Singapore: Times Books International).

Khon Kim Hoong (1984) *Merdeka! British Rule and the Struggle for Independence in Malaya 1945–1957* (Petaling Jaya: Institute for Social Analysis).

King, Frank Henry Haviland (1957) *The New Malayan Nation: A Study of Communalism and Nationalism* (New York: Institute of Pacific Relations).

Lau, Albert (1991) *The Malayan Union Controversy 1942–1948* (Singapore: Oxford University Press).

Leary, John (1989) *The Importance of the Orang Asli in the Malayan Emergency 1948–1960* (Clayton, Victoria: Monash University).

Lee Kuan Yew (1966) *Socialism and Reconstruction in Asia* (Singapore: Ministry of Culture).

— (1967), *Social Revolution in Singapore; Text of a Speech to a British Labour Party Rally, 1 October 1967* (Singapore: Government Printing Office).

Mahathir bin Mohamed (1989) *The Malay Dilemma* (Singapore: Times Books International).

Means, G. P. (1970) *Malaysian Politics* (London: University of London Press).

— (1991), *Malaysian Politics: The Second Generation* (Singapore: Oxford University Press).

Minchin, Samuel (1990) *No Man is an Island: a portrait of Singapore's Lee Kuan Yew* (Sydney: Allen and Unwin).

Mohamed Noordin Sopiee (1974) *From Malaysian Union to Singapore Separation: Political Unification in the Malaysian Region, 1945–1965* (Kuala Lumpur, University of Malaya Press).

Mulliner, K. and Lian The-Mulliner (1991) *Historical Dictionary of Singapore* (Metuchen, NJ: Scarecrow Press).

Munro-Kua, Anne (1996) *Authoritarian Populism in Malaysia* (Basingstoke: Macmillan).

Percival, A.E. (1949) *The War in Malaya* (London: Eyre and Spottiswoode).

Purcell, Victor (1975) *The Chinese in Malaya* (London: Oxford University Press).

Rayner, Leonard (1991) *Emergency Years: Malaya 1951–1954* (Singapore, Heinemann).

Sandhu, K. S. and A. Mani (eds) (1993) *Indian Communities in Southeast Asia* (Singapore: ISEAS/Times Academic Press).

Scott-Ross, Alice (1990) *Tun Dato Sir Cheng Lock Tan: A Personal Profile* (Singapore: A. Scott-Ross).

Short, Anthony (1975) *The Communist Insurrection in Malaya, 1948–1960* (London: Muller).

Silcock, T. H. and Abdul Aziz (1950) *Nationalism in Malaya* (New York: Institute of Pacific Relations).

Simandjuntak, B. (1969) *Malayan Federalism 1945–1963* (Kuala Lumpur: Oxford University Press).

Soh Eng Lim (1960) 'Tan Cheng-Lock: His Leadership of the Malayan Chinese', *Journal of Southeast Asian History*, Vol. 1, no. 1: 34–6.

Stockwell, A. J. (1979) *British Policy and Malay Politics during the Malayan Union Experiment 1945–1948* (Kuala Lumpur: Malaysian Branch of the Royal Asiatic Society).

— (1984) 'British Imperial Policy and Decolonization in Malay 1942–1952', *Journal of Imperial and Commonwealth History*, Vol. 13, no.1: 68–87.

— (ed.) (1995) *British Documents on the End of Empire*; vol. 3, Series B, Malaya: 1. *The Malayan Union Experiment 1942–1948*; 2. *The Communist Insurrection 1948–1953*; 3. *The Alliance Route to Independence 1953–1957*. (London: HMSO).

Stubbs, Richard (1989) *Hearts and Minds in Guerilla Warfare: The Malayan Emergency 1948–1960* (Singapore: Oxford University Press).

Tan Cheng Lock (1947) *Malayan Problems from a Chinese Point of View* (Singapore: Tannsco).

Wan Hashim (1983) *Race Relations in Malaysia* (Kuala Lumpur: Heinemann).

The Philippines

The Colonial Period

Achutegui, Pedro S. de and Miguel A. Bernad (1972) *Aguinaldo and the Revolution of 1896: A Documentary History* (Quezon City: Ateneo de Manila).

Agoncillo, Teodoro A. (1956) *The Revolt of the Masses: The Story of Bonifacio and the Katipunan* (Quezon City: University of the Philippines Press).

— (1973) *History of the Filipino People* (Quezon City: R. P. Garcia).

— (1974) *Filipino Nationalism 1872–1970* (Quezon City: R. P. Garcia).

Blount, James H. (1968) *The American Occupation of the Philippines 1898–1912* (Quezon City: Malaya Books).

Friend, Theodore (1965) *Between Two Empires: The Ordeal of the Philippines 1929–1946* (New Haven, CT: Yale University Press).

Gates, John Morgan (1973) *School Books and Krags: The United States Army in the Philippines, 1898–1902* (Westport, CT: Greenwood Press).

Gowing, Peter (1977) *Mandate in Moroland: The American Government of Muslim Filipinos, 1899–1920* (Quezon City: University of the Philippines Press).

Hayden, J. R. (1942) *The Philippines: A Study in National Development* (New York: Macmillan).

Ileto, Reynaldo (1979) *Pasyon and Revolution: Popular Movements in the Philippines 1840–1910* (Quezon City: Ateneo de Manila University Press).

Kalaw, T. M. (1969) *The Philippine Revolution* (Kawilihan: Jorge B. Vargas Filipiniana Foundation).

Karnow, Stanley (1989) *In Our Image: America's Empire in the Philippines* (New York: Random House).

Mahajani, Usha (1971) *Philippine Nationalism: External Challenge and Filipino Response* (St. Lucia: University of Queensland Press).

Majul, Cesar A. (1967) *The Political and Constitutional Ideas of the Philippine Revolution* (Quezon City: University of the Philippines Press).

May, Ernest R. (1973) *Imperial Democracy: The Emergence of America as a Great Power* (New York: Harper and Row).

Ofreneo, René E. (1980) *Capitalism in Philippine Agriculture* (Quezon City: Foundation for Nationalist Studies).

Onorato, M. P. (1969) *Leonard Wood as Governor-General* (Manila: MCS Enterprise).

Owen, Norman G. (ed.) (1971) *Compadre Colonialism: Studies on the Philippines under American Rule* (Ann Arbor, MI: Michigan Papers on South and Southeast Asia, no. 3, University of Michigan).

Salamanca, Bonifacio S. (1968) *The Filipino Reaction to American Rule 1901–1913* (Hander, CT: Shoe String Press).

Stanley, Peter W. (1974) *A Nation in the Making: the Philippines and the United States 1899–1921* (Cambridge, MA: Harvard University Press).

— (1984) *Reappraising an Empire: New Perspectives on Philippine–American History* (Cambridge, MA: Harvard University).

Sturtevant, David R. (1976) *Popular Uprisings in the Philippines 1840–1940* (Ithaca, NY: Cornell University Press).

Books by José Rizal

— (1956) *The Reign of Greed (El Filibusterismo)* (translated by Charles E. Derbyshire) (Manila: Philippine Education Co.).

— (1961) *The Lost Eden (Noli Me Tangere)* (translated by Leon Guerrero) (Bloomington, IN: Indiana University Press) (also translated in 1912 by Charles E. Derbyshire as *The Social Cancer*).

The Philippines: war, independence and the post-colonial era

Agoncillo, Teodoro A. (1965) *The Fateful Years: Japan's Adventure in the Philippines 1941–1945*, 2 vols (Quezon City: R. P. Garcia).

Boyce, James K. (1993) *The Philippines: The Political Economy of Growth and Impoverishment in the Marcos Era* (Honolulu: University of Hawaii Press).

Che Man, W. K. (1990) *Muslim Separatism: The Moros of Southern Philippines and the Malays of Southern Thailand* (Singapore: Oxford University Press).

Davis, L. F. (1989) *Revolutionary Struggle in the Philippines* (Basingstoke: Macmillan).

George, T. J. S. (1980) *Revolt in Mindanao: the Rise of Islam in Philippine Politics* (Kuala Lumpur: Oxford University Press).

Gowing, Peter G. (1979) *Muslim-Filipinos – Heritage and Horizon* (Quezon City: New Day).

— (1988) *Understanding Islam and Muslims in the Philippines* (Quezon City: New Day).

Greenberg, Lawrence M. (1987) *The Hukbalahap Insurrection: A Case Study of a Successful Anti-insurgency Operation in the Philippines 1946–1955* (Washington DC: US Army Center of Military History).

Hartendop, A. V. H. (1967) *The Japanese Occupation of the Philippines*, 2 vols (Manila: Bookmark).

Kerkvliet, B. J. (1977) *The Huk Rebellion: A Study of Peasant Revolt in the Philippines* (Berkeley, CA: University of California Press).

Kessler, Richard John (1989) *Rebellion and Repression in the Philippines* (New Haven, CT: Yale University Press).

Lachica, Eduardo (1971) *Huk: Philippine Agrarian Society in Revolt* (Manila: Solidaridad).

Lande, Carl M. (1965) *Leaders, Factions and Parties: the structure of Philippine Politics* (New Haven, CT: Yale University Press).

Lansdale, Edward G. (1972) *In the Midst of Wars: An American Mission to Southeast Asia* (New York: Harper and Row).

Lederer, William J. and Eugene Burdick (1960) *The Ugly American* (London: Corgi) (especially chapter 10).

McCoy, Alfred W. (ed.) (1980) *Southeast Asia under Japanese Occupation: transition and transformation* (New Haven, CT: Southeast Asia Series, Yale University).

Majul, C. A. (1985) *The Contemporary Muslim Movement in the Philippines* (Berkeley, CA: Mizan Press).

Putzel, James (1992) *A Captive Land: The Politics of Agrarian Reform in the Philippines* (London: Monthly Review Press).

Steinberg, David J. (1964–1965) 'José P. Laurel: A "Collaborator" Misunderstood', *Journal of Asian Studies*, Vol. 24: 651–5.

— (1967) *Philippine Collaboration in World War II* (Anne Arbor, MI: University of Michigan Press).

Wurfel, D. (1988) *Filipino Politics: Development and Decay* (Ithaca, NY: Cornell University Press).

Yu-José, Lydia N. (1996) 'World War II and the Japanese in the pre-war Philippines', *Journal of Southeast Asian Studies*, Vol. 27, no. 1.

Siam/Thailand

Siam/Thailand before the Second World War

Aldrich, Richard J. (1993) *The Key to the South: Britain, the United States and Thailand during the Approach of the Pacific War 1929–1942* (Basingstoke: Macmillan).

Batson, B. A. (1984) *The End of the Absolute Monarchy in Siam* (Singapore: Oxford University Press).

Chula Chakrabongse (1967) *Lords of Life: A History of the Kings of Thailand* (London: Redman).

Flood, E. T. (1967) *Japan's Relations with Thailand 1929–1941* (Seattle: University of Washington Press).

Kobkua Suwannathat-Pian (1995) *Thailand's Durable Premier: Phibun through Three Decades 1932–1957* (Singapore: Oxford University Press).

Landon, Kenneth P. (1968) *Siam in Transition* (New York, Greenwood Press).

Likhit Dhiravegin (1975) *Siam and Colonialism 1855–1909: An Analysis of Diplomatic Relations* (Bangkok: Thai Watana Panich).

— (1992) *Demi-Democracy: The Evolution of the Thai Political System* (Singapore: Times Academic Press).

Morell, David and Chai Anand Samudavanija (1981) *Political Conflict in Thailand: Reform, Reaction, Revolution* (Cambridge, MA: np).

Sivaram, M (1981) *The New Siam in the Making: A Survey of the Political Transition in Siam, 1932–1936* (New York: AMS Press).

Thak Chaloemtiarana, Charnvit Kaset-Siri and Thinaphan Nakhata (eds) (1978) *Thai Politics: Extracts and Documents* (Bangkok: Social Science Association of Thailand).

Thawatt Mokarapong (1972) *History of the Thai Revolution: Study in Political Behaviour* (Bangkok, Chalermnit).

Thompson, Virginia (1967) *Thailand: The New Siam* (New York: Paragon).

Vella, Walter F. (1978) *Chaiyo! King Vajiravudh and the Development of Thai Nationalism* (Honolulu: University Press of Hawaii).

Wyatt, David K. (1969) *The Politics of Reform in Thailand: Education in the Reign of King Chulalongkorn* (New Haven, CT: Yale University Press).

Wyatt, David K. (1982) *Thailand: A Short History* (New Haven, CT: Yale University Press).

Thailand in the Second World War and after

Barmé, Scot (1993) *Luang Wichit Wathakan and the Creation of Thai Identity* (Singapore: ISEAS).

Batson, Benjamin A. (1990) *'The Tragedy of Wanit': A Japanese Account of Wartime Thai Politics* (Singapore: NUS).

Brailey, Nigel J. (1986) *Thailand and the Fall of Singapore: A Frustrated Asian Revolution* (Boulder, CO: Westview Press).

Chatri Ritharom (1981) *The Making of the Thai–US Military Alliance and the SEATO Treaty of 1954* (Ann Arbor, MI: University Microfilms).

Chinvanno, Anuson (1992) *Thailand's Policies Towards China, 1949–1954* (Basingstoke: Macmillan).

Crosby, Josiah (1945) *Siam: The Crossroads* (London: Hollis and Carter).

Haseman, John B. (1979) *The Thai Resistance Movement during the Second World War* (DeKalb, Ill: Centre for Southeast Asian Studies, Northern Illinois University).

Jackson, Karl D. (ed.) (1986) *United States–Thailand Relations* (Berkeley, CA: University of California Press).

Keyes, Charles F. (1987) *Thailand: Buddhist Kingdom as Modern Nation-State* (Boulder, CO: Westview Press).

Kobkua Suwannathat-Pian (1996) 'Thai Wartime Leadership Reconsidered: Phibun and Pridi', *Journal of Southeast Asian Studies*, Vol. 27, no. 1.

Kruger, Rayne (1964) *The Devil's Discus* (London: Cassell).

Nuechterlein, Donald E. (1965) *Thailand and the Struggle for Southeast Asia* (Ithaca, NY: Cornell University Press).

Pitsuwan, Surin (1985) *Islam and Malay Nationalism: A Case Study of the Malay-Muslims of Southern Thailand* (Bangkok: Thai Khadi Research Institute, Thammasat University).

Reynolds, Craig J. (1991) *National Identity and its Defenders: Thailand 1939–1989* (Clayton, Victoria: Monash University).

Reynolds, E. Bruce (1994) *Thailand and Japan's Southern Advance, 1940–1945* (London: Macmillan).

Riggs, Fred W. (1966) *Thailand: The Modernization of a Bureaucratic Policy* (Honolulu: East-West Center Press).

Stowe, Judith A. (1990) *Siam becomes Thailand: A Story of Intrigue* (London: Hurst).

Swan, William L. (1996) 'Japan's Intentions for its Greater East Asia Co-Prosperity Sphere as Indicated by its Policy Plans for Thailand' *Journal of Southeast Asian Studies*, Vol. 27, no. 1.

Tarling, Nicholas (1978) *Rice and Reconciliation: The Anglo-Thai Peace Negotiations of 1945* (Bangkok: Siam Society).

Thak Chaloemtiariana (1979) *Thailand: The Politics of Despotic Paternalism* (Bangkok: Social Science Association of Thailand).

Thamsook Nummonda (1977) *Thailand and the Japanese Presence 1941–1945* (Singapore: ISEAS).

Vichitr Vadakarn (1941) *Thailand's Case* (against France) (Bangkok: Thai Commercial Press).

Wilson, David A. (1966) *Politics in Thailand* (Ithaca, NY: Cornell University Press).

Wilson, David A. (1970) *The United States and the Future of Thailand* (New York: Praeger).

Vietnam

Vietnam in the nationalist era up to 1940

Cady, J. F. (1967) *The Roots of French Imperialism in Eastern Asia* (Ithaca, NY: Cornell University Press).

Duiker, William J. (1976) *The Rise of Nationalism in Vietnam 1900–1941* (Ithaca, NY: Cornell University Press).

— (1983) *Vietnam: Nation in Revolution* (Boulder, CO: Westview Press).

— (1989) *Historical Dictionary of Vietnam* (Metuchen: NJ, Scarecrow Press).

Ennis, Thomas E. (1936) *French Policy and Developments in Indochina* (Chicago, Ill: University of Chicago Press).

Fall, Bernard B. (ed.) (1968) *Ho Chi Minh on Revolution: Selected Writings 1920–1966* (New York: New American Library).

Ho Chi Minh (1960–) *Selected Works*, 4 vols (Hanoi: Foreign Languages Publishing House).

Hue-Tam Ho Tai (1992) *Radicalism and the Origins of the Vietnamese Revolution* (Cambridge, MA: Harvard University Press).

Huynh Kim Khanh (1982) *Vietnamese Communism 1925–1945* (Ithaca, NY: Cornell University Press).

Karnow, Stanley (1984) *Vietnam: A History* (Harmondsworth: Penguin Books).

Lacouture, Jean (1969) *Ho Chi Minh* (London: Pelican Books).

Marr, David G. (1971) *Vietnamese Anticolonialism* (Berkeley, CA: University of California Press).

Marr, David G. (1981) *Vietnamese Tradition on Trial 1920–1945* (Berkeley, CA: University of California Press).

Marr, David G. (compiler) (1992) *Vietnam* (Oxford: Clio).

Ngo Vinh Long (1973) *Before the Revolution: the Vietnamese Peasants under the French* (Cambridge, MA: MIT Press).

— (1978) 'The Indochina Communist Party and Peasant Rebellion in Central Vietnam 1930–1931', *Bulletin of Concerned Asian Scholars*, Vol. 10, no. 3: 15–35.

Popkin, Samuel L. (1979) *The Rational Peasant: The Political Economy of Rural Society in Vietnam* (Berkeley, CA: University of California Press).

Post, Ken (1989) *Revolution, Nationalism and Socialism in Vietnam*, 4 vols (Aldershot: Dartmouth).

Robequain, Charles (1935) *L'Indochine française* (Paris: Libraire Armand Colin).

Robequain, Charles (1944) *The Economic Development of French Indochina* (London: Oxford University Press).

Sacks, I. Milton (1960) 'Marxism in Vietnam', in Frank Trager (ed.), *Marxism in Southeast Asia: A Study of Four Countries* (Stanford, CA: Stanford University Press).

Sampson, C. A. (1975) *Nationalism and Communism in Vietnam 1925–1931* (Los Angeles, University of California Press).

Scott, James C. (1976) *The Moral Economy of the Peasant: Rebellion and Subsistence in Southeast Asia* (New Haven, CT: Yale University Press).

Smith, R. B. (1968) *Vietnam and the West* (London: Heinemann).

Truong Buu Lam (1967) *Patterns of Vietnamese Response to Foreign Intervention 1858–1900* (New Haven, CT: Southeast Asia Studies, Monograph series, No. 11, Yale University).

Truong Chinh and Vo Nguyen Giap (1974) *The Peasant Question 1937–1938* (Ithaca, NY: Cornell University).

Vinh Sinh (ed.) (1988) *Phan Boi Chau and the Dong-du Movement* (New Haven, CT, Yale Center for International and Area Studies).

Woodside, Alexander (1976) *Community and Revolution in Modern Vietnam* (Boston, MA, Houghton Mifflin).

— (1988) *Vietnam and the Chinese Model: A Comparative Study of Vietnamese and Chinese Government in the First Half of the Nineteenth Century* (Cambridge, MA: Harvard University Press).

Literature and nationalism in Vietnam

Durand, Maurice M. and Nguyen Tran Huan (1985) *An Introduction to Vietnamese Literature* (New York: Columbia University Press).

Nguyen Du (1983) *The Tale of Kieu* (translated by Huynh Sanh Thong) (New Haven, CT: Yale University Press). A translation of the poem *Truyen Kieu*, written by Nguyen Du [1765–1820], which has the status of the 'national epic' of Vietnam.

Vietnam 1940–1954: the Vietnamese Revolution and the First Indochina War

Bodard, Lucien (1967) *The Quicksand War: Prelude to Vietnam* (London: Faber and Faber). A shortened English version of his *La guerre d'Indochine*, published in five volumes by Editions Gallimard, 1963–67.

Dalloz, Jacques (1990) *The War in Indochina 1945–1954* (Maryland: Barnes and Noble).

Devillers, Philippe (1952) *Histoire du Viet-Nam: de 1940 á 1952* (Paris: Editions du Seuil).

Devillers, Philippe and Jean Lacouture (1969) *End of a War: Indochina 1954* (London: Pall Mall Press).

Drachman, E. R. (1970) *United States Policy towards Vietnam 1940–1945* (Cranbury, NJ: Associated University Presses)

Dunn, Peter M. (1985) *The First Vietnam War* (London: Hurst).

Fall, Bernard B. (1963) *Street without Joy: Insurgency in Indochina 1946–1963* (Harrisburg, PA: Stackpole Company).

Gurtov, Melvin (1968) *The First Vietnam Crisis: Chinese Communist Strategy and United States Involvement 1953–1954* (New York: Columbia University Press).

Hammer, Ellen Joy (1966) *The Struggle for Indochina 1940–1954* (Stanford, CA: Stanford University Press).

Irving, R. E. M. (1975) *The First Indochina War: French and American Policy 1945–1954* (London: Croom Helm).

Kaplan, Lawrence S., Denise Artaud and Mark R. Rubin (eds.) (1990) *Dien Bien Phu and the Crisis of Franco-American Relations 1954–1955* (Wilmington, DE: SR Books).

Lockhart, Greg (1989) *Nation in Arms: The Origins of the People's Army in Vietnam* (Wellington, Allen and Unwin).

McAllister, John T. (1969) *Vietnam: The Origins of Revolution* (London: Allen Lane).

MacDonald, Peter (1993) *Giap: The Victor in Vietnam* (London: Fourth Estate).

Mus, Paul (1952) *Vietnam: sociologie d'une guerre* (Paris: Editions du Seuil).

Randle, Robert F. (1969) *Geneva 1954: The Settlement of the Indochina War* (Princeton, NJ: Princeton University Press).

Rosie, George (1970) *The British in Vietnam: How the Twenty-five Year War Began* (London: Panther).

Sainteny, Jean (1972) *Ho Chi Minh and his Vietnam: A Personal Memoir* (Chicago, IL: Cowles).

Tonnesson, Stein (1991) *The Vietnamese Revolution of 1945: Roosevelt, Ho Chi Minh and De Gaulle in a world at war* (Oslo: International Peace Research Institute).

Tran My-Van (1996) 'Japan and Vietnam's Caodaists: A Wartime Relationship 1939–1945', *Journal of Southeast Asian Studies*, Vol. 27, no. 1.

Truong Chinh (1963) *Primer for Revolt: The Communist Takeover in Vietnam* (New York: Praeger).

Vella, W. F. (ed.) (1973) *Aspects of Vietnamese History* (Honolulu: University of Hawaii Press).

Vo Nguyen Giap (1965) *People's War, People's Army* (New York: Praeger).

Vietnam 1954–1965

Anderson, David L. (1991) *Trapped by Success: the Eisenhower Administration and Vietnam 1953–1961* (New York: Columbia University Press).

Blair, Ann (1992) *Special Consideration: The First Embassy of Henry Cabot Lodge in Vietnam* (Clayton, Victoria: Monash University Press).

Bouscaren, A. T. (1965) *The Last of the Mandarins: Diem of Vietnam* (Pittsburgh, PA: Duquesne University Press).

Browne, Malcolm W. (1965) *The New Face of War: A Report on a Communist Guerilla Campaign* (London: Cassell).

Buttinger, Joseph (1967) *Vietnam: A Dragon Embattled*, 2 vols (New York, Praeger).

Cable, James (1986) *The Geneva Conference of 1954 on Indochina* (Basingstoke: Macmillan).

Dooley, Thomas A. (1956) *Deliver us from Evil: The Story of Viet Nam's Flight to Freedom* (New York: Farrer, Strauss).

Duncanson, Dennis (1968) *Government and Revolution in Vietnam* (London: Oxford University Press).

Fall, Bernard B. (1960) *Le Viet-Minh: la République du Viet-Nam 1945–1960* (Paris: Librairie Armand Colin).

— (1966) *Vietnam Witness 1953–1966* (London: Pall Mall Press).

— (1968) *The Two Vietnams: A Political and Military Analysis* (New York: Praeger).

Fishel, W. R. (1968) *Vietnam: Anatomy of a Conflict* (Itasca IL: Peacock).

— (ed.), (1961) *Problems of Freedom: South Vietnam Since Independence* (New York: Glencoe).

Fitzgerald, Frances (1973) *Fire in the Lake: The Vietnamese and the Americans in Vietnam* (New York: Vintage Books).

Halberstam, David (1965) *The Making of a Quagmire* (London: Bodley Head).

— (1972) *The Best and the Brightest* (New York: Random House).

Higgins, Marguerite (1965) *Our Vietnam Nightmare* (New York: Harper and Row).

Lacouture, Jean (1966) *Vietnam: Between Two Truces* (London: Secker and Warburg).

Nolting, Frederick (1988) *From Truth to Tragedy: The Political Memoirs of Frederick Nolting* (New York: Praeger).

Pike, Douglas (1968) *Viet-Cong: The Organization and Techniques of the National Liberation Front of South Vietnam* (Cambridge, MA: MIT Press).

Race, Jeffrey (1972) *War Comes to Long An: Revolutionary Conflict in a Vietnamese Province* (Berkeley, CA: University of California Press).

Scigliano, Robert (1964) *South Vietnam: Nation under Stress* (Boston, MA: Houghton Mifflin).

Sheehan, Neil et al. (eds) (1971) *The Pentagon Papers as Published by the New York Times* (New York: Bantam Books).

Smith, Ralph (1983) *An International History of the Vietnam War*, Vol. 1: *Revolution versus Containment 1955–1961* (Basingstoke: Macmillan).

— (1985) *An International History of the Vietnam War* Volume 2: *The Struggle for Southeast Asia 1961–1965*, (Basingstoke: Macmillan).

Spector, Ronald H. (1985) *Advice and Support: The Early Years* (New York: Free Press). (A history of the United States army in Vietnam.)

Thayer, Carlyle A. (1989) *War by Other Means: National Liberation and Revolution in Viet-Nam 1954–1960* (Sydney: Allen and Unwin).

Warner, Denis (1964) *The Last Confucian: Vietnam, Southeast Asia and the West* (Harmondsworth: Penguin Books).

Vietnam 1965–75

Barrett, David M. (1994) *Uncertain Warriors: Lyndon Johnson and his Vietnam Advisors* (Lawrence, KS: University of Kansas Press).

Braestrup, Peter (1977) *Big Story: How the American Press and Television Reported and Interpreted the Crisis of Tet 1968 in Vietnam and Washington* (Boulder, CO: Westview Press).

Cao Van Vien (1983) *The Final Collapse* (Washington, DC: Center of Military History, United States Army).

Clarke, Jeffrey J. (1988) *Advice and Support: The Final Years* (Washington, DC: Center of Military History, United States Army).

Ellsberg, Daniel (1972) *Papers on the War* (New York: Pocket Books).

Ford, Ronnie E. (1995) *Tet: Understanding the Surprise* (London: Frank Cass).

Hatcher, Patrick Lloyd (1990) *The Suicide of an Elite: American Internationalists and Vietnam* (Stanford, CA: Stanford University Press).

Isaacs, Arnold R. (1984) *Without Honor: Defeat in Vietnam and Cambodia* (New York: Vintage Books).

Kahin, George McT. (1986) *Intervention: How America Became Involved in Vietnam* (New York: Knopf).

Kattenburg, Paul M. (1980) *The Vietnam Trauma in American Foreign Policy 1945–1975* (New Brunswick, NJ: Transaction Books).

Kelly, Francis J. (1991) *The Green Berets in Vietnam 1961–1971* (Virginia: Brassey's).

Kissinger, Henry A. (1969) *American Foreign Policy: Three Essays* (New York: Norton).

— (1979) *The White House Years* (London: Weidenfeld and Nicolson).

— (1982) *Years of Upheaval* (London: Weidenfeld and Nicolson).

Kolko, Gabriel (1986) *Vietnam: Anatomy of a War 1940–1975* (London: Allen and Unwin).

McNamara, Robert S. and Brian van de Marx (1995) *In Retrospect: The Tragedy and Lessons of Vietnam* (New York: NYT/Random House).

Moore, Lt.-Gen. Harold G. and Joseph L. Galloway (1993) *We Were Soldiers Once ... and Young: Ia Drang, the Battle that Changed the war in Vietnam* (New York: HarperCollins).

Olson, James Stuart (ed.) (1993) *The Vietnam War: Handbook of the Literature and Research* (Westport, CT: Greenwood Press).

O'Neill, Robert J. (1969) *General Giap: Politician and Strategist* (Melbourne: Cassell).

— (1969) *The Strategy of General Giap since 1964* (Canberra: Australian National University).

Palmer, Bruce (1990) *The 25-Year War: America's Military Role in Vietnam* (New York: Da Capo Press).

Pike, Douglas (1986) *PAVN: People's Army of Vietnam* (Novato: Presidio Press).

Prados, John (1995) *The Hidden History of the Vietnam War* (Chicago: Dee).

Shaplen, Robert (1971) *The Road from War: Vietnam 1965–1971* (New York: Harper and Row).

Sharp, Ulysses S. G. (1969) *Report on the War in Vietnam, as of 30 June 1968* (Washington, DC: US Government Printing Office).

Sheehan, Neil (1989) *A Bright Shining Lie: John Paul Vann and America in Vietnam* (London: Jonathan Cape).

Snepp, Frank (1977) *Decent Interval: An Insider's View of Saigon's Indecent End* (New York: Random House).

Turner, Robert F. (1975) *Vietnamese Communism: Its Origins and Development* (Stanford, CA: Hoover Institution Press).

Wirtz, James J. (1991) *The Tet Offensive: Intelligence Failure in War* (Ithaca, NY: Cornell University Press).

Index